THE RAILWAY MOON

PETER BRAINE

pmb publishing

Richard Moon, from a family gathering at Crewe probably
taken at time of the 1887 Jubilee when he was 72. LNWRS

THE RAILWAY MOON

Some Aspects of the Life of Richard Moon 1814-1899
Chairman of the London & North Western Railway 1861-91

PETER BRAINE

pmb publishing

First published in 2010 by
pmb publishing
PO Box 892
Taunton
TA1 9HY

pmbbrain@aol.com

A CIP Catalogue of this book is available from
the British Library

ISBN: 978-0-9565290-0-8

Cover designed by AB Design Group
Front cover image: *Locomotives at Stafford, by Gerald Broom*
Back cover image: *Bust of Moon, NRM*

Typeset in Sabon 10½ by
www.chandlerbookdesign.co.uk

Printed in Great Britain by the
MPG Books Group, Bodmin and King's Lynn

CONTENTS

LIST OF ILLUSTRATIONS AND MAPS

MAPS

ACKNOWLEDGEMENTS

As my search for details on the London & North Western Railway and Richard Moon began as far back as 1984 many people have responded to my enquiries. The number of librarians and archivists contacted over the years is so great that it is not practical to list them all individually. Nevertheless I must acknowledge their support with grateful thanks for without their help and advice this book could not have been written. Doing justice to the information they provided however proved difficult as being in full time employment I lacked the time needed to collate this into book form. And when in retirement I did complete a draft I shelved it for many years, uncertain as to whether I had written a railway history, a biography or something unsatisfactory in between. It was members of both the LNWR Society and the Railway & Canal Historical Society, in particular Harry Jack who eventually persuaded me that that I should publish regardless.

In addition to Harry Jack I am also indebted to Malcolm Reed, John Gough and David Hodgkins. All were kind enough to read and comment helpfully on a first draft. While working on his masterly history of the L&NW Malcolm Reed had generously sent me drafts of his own chapters on Moon. David Hodgkins not only gave me similar assistance by copying relevant extracts from his work on Watkin, but let me press him further into painstakingly undertaking a more editorial type review which proved both insightful and challenging. His own research into Edward Watkin had initially paralleled mine into Moon, but the result in his case was to prove far more definitive. For general readability I persuaded Liz Grant to plough through a revised draft and thank her for her corrections and suggestions. I must also thank Jim Allan, Louise Atkins, Sheila Braine, Martin Smith, John Stuckey and Sheila Stuckey for their assistance in proof reading sections of the final text. I should add however, that in making changes to correct or improve as a result of any of these reviews, all errors or opinions expressed remain entirely my responsibility.

All the family descendants I contacted were enthusiastic in their support. Mary Moon kindly let me photograph the portrait of Moon as a young man and to copy Jasper Moon's scrap book of family press cuttings (Jasper was her father, a grandson of Moon). Her brother Edward (the 5th baronet) let me take extracts from the Crewe Jubilee booklet presented to Moon. Mrs Christine Watson surprised by producing an oil painting of her great-grandfather which proved to be an earlier family version of the later infamous one of Moon in the National Railway Museum. And Mrs Dilly Gloag kindly lent me the family photographs of Moon at Copsewood Grange in 1893 which included her grandfather Arthur and his brother Basil as boys with their grandfather, Moon. Uncovering Erminois, a booklet of family records compiled by Canon Charles Moor, the husband of Moon's niece Constance, saved much research time and for which I thank the Society of Genealogists for bringing to my attention.

Robert Smart, Keeper of the Muniments at St Andrews University answered patiently my many queries on Moon's education in Scotland and Anne Dick went beyond her duties as local studies librarian in Whitehaven in providing background on the Brocklebanks. Many other individuals have assisted with information and advice. Apologising to any I may have missed through an aging filing system, I list these alphabetically as follows:

David Alcock, Ivor Brown, John Brown, B.Cluett, Hugh Compton, David Deakin, Neil Frazer, H.W.Gwilliam, G.Hardy, Martine Hollins, Michael Keef, John Marshall, John Norris, Mrs.D.M.Owen, Harry Paar, David Patrick, David Pennington, David Power, Paul Reynolds, Peter Sperring, Rev.R.C.Toogood, Rodney Weaver, G.D.Whitworth, Marjorie Whitby and Mike Williams.

For illustrations I have acknowledged where possible original sources in the captions. LNWRS refers to the London & North Western Railway Society, NRM the National Railway Museum and ILN to the Illustrated London News. Norman Lee and Ted Talbot of the LNWRS were particularly helpful and John McGoldrick of the NRM kindly arranged to have the Moon bust photographed. All efforts have been made to identify copyright owners and I apologise for any inadvertent infringement and ask that any such owners contact me. I thank Gerald Broom for permission to reproduce his painting of the locomotives at Stafford, Gwyn Briwant Jones for his painting of the locomotives at Pontypool Road, Dorothea Worsley-Taylor for the portrait of Edward Watkin and Robert Hasell-McCosh for the one of E.W.Hasell. For the print of Jack Hill's painting of the Caledonian racer of 1888 I have not been able to trace the owner of the original. I thank E.T.White for the postcard of Bank House and Nicola Coverdale for her hospitality in showing me over her family's part of Bevere and for the photograph of the house.

Harry Jack kindly agreed to review the historic data on which I based my maps although I take full responsiblity for the details given and layouts drawn.

Peter Braine   *February 2010*

INTRODUCTION

This book is about a man and his railway. The man became a pillar of the Victorian establishment and his railway at one time was the largest public company of any type in the world. Yet today, outside the realm of railway historians and enthusiasts, he is largely unknown.

Many railwaymen are well remembered. Memorials to the work of engineers such as the Stephensons, Locke and Brunel, remain in the bridges and cuttings that transformed the landscape of nineteenth century Britain. As important as these men were to the history of railways, their work could not have taken place without the vision and finance of others. And once built the railways needed yet another breed of men to run them effectively. Until he was thirty-seven Richard Moon fitted into none of these categories.

Too young to have participated personally in the financing and promotion of the first lines, Moon's early career was spent in a family cotton trading business in Liverpool. However while still only in his early thirties he 'retired' from the commercial world and retreated to rural Worcestershire, apparently content to live on an inheritance which included income from railway investments. Then many Liverpool merchants seeking a profitable outlet for their wealth had been attracted by the high dividends paid by the early railway companies. However when competition and escalating costs reduced earnings such investors were quick to demand remedial action.

Significantly part of his family's investment portfolio was in a group of companies which amalgamated in 1846 to form the London & North Western Railway, today's West Coast main line from Euston. Though born a giant this company was soon struggling to keep up the dividend rate of its former constituents and contain a seeming insatiable need for new capital, a struggle all too familiar with railways today. With his income being eroded, Moon began probing and questioning the company's policies and actions, so much so that when the board was reconstructed in 1851 the company elected him as one of their new directors.

Without railway experience but skilled commercially, the energetic young Moon soon made his mark in accounting and purchasing matters, delving into such unfashionable items as supplies of water, coal and gas, stationery, clothing, even the maintenance of watches and clocks to ensure punctuality. He undertook a detailed investigation into the management of horses, little could move to or from the railway without them. Showing a remarkable grasp of detail, his eagle eye missed nothing. To quote *The Times* he had that 'infinite capacity for taking pains which Carlyle identified with genius'.

Taking pains led him in ten years to the chairmanship of the company, a position he held unrivalled for thirty years during which the railway's route miles nearly doubled and capital almost trebled, with profitability (in terms of percentage dividends paid) eventually exceeding those of any other comparable company.

His life spanned the conception, birth, development and consolidation of the railway system in the UK. As a boy he probably witnessed the opening of the first properly organised passenger carrying company in the world, the Liverpool & Manchester Railway, and in old age he was the first to be awarded a baronetcy for services to railways.

Throughout the whole of his chairmanship years Moon's grip on the company never slackened. Leading by example in long hours of work and travel, he sought only to secure for his shareholders a sound investment and for the public an efficient service. He let no other company or interest, rare among his contemporaries, distract him. He retired when, in his own words, he felt no longer able to do his duty. Inevitably over such a long period in office the reforming zeal of youth shifted to one more conservative, even reactionary in his last years, but his concern for the company never wavered.

So unusually dedicated was he that any account of his railway career must inevitably overlap that of the London & North Western railway and its competitors. This book therefore straddles the twin paths of biography and railway history. The risk that it may fall between the two is made worse by Moon's intensively secretive nature and the lack of details on his personal life, particularly during his formative years in Liverpool and the retreat to Worcestershire. So many myths and anecdotes abound concerning his steely aloofness, his frugality and obsession with detail, that it became an intriguing task to uncover just what were the facts. A press quote after his death perhaps best sums up the difficulty. The *Liverpool Courier* referred to his 'almost morbid objection to anything concerning himself', resisting 'all efforts made to allow the public to become acquainted with anything of a personal nature'. The article continued: 'we know that always he maintained the same reserve and that everything in the way of biographical facts was steadily and firmly refused to inquirers. Again, he was gravely offended if any subscription he gave was mentioned in public'. Enough evidence abounds to show he contributed generously to his church and to charities.

Dismissive of politicians, 'dilettanti gentlemen of Parliament' he once called them, Moon was seen as the archetypal hard man of Victorian business. He was near the end of his career when he apparently only reluctantly accepted his baronetcy. Born in 1814, he died in 1899. Sir Richard he may have become, but for generations of railwaymen he was uniquely Mr Moon.

Much of the personal anecdotal information published after his death has so far proved impossible to verify. No family papers have been traced and most of the correspondence found is railway related. One of the assumptions that unfortunately has coloured descriptions of his character stems from his analytical style of management. The word usually used is 'autocratic'. Carried to extremes are descriptions by railway historians Hamilton Ellis and O.S.Nock. The former has written that he was 'one of the most terrifying personages in Victorian private business', his appearance in keeping with his character. Ellis the artist described the company's official portrait of him as 'a face severe to the point of caricature with its cold, hard eyes below rocky brows, its knife thin mouth below a deep upper lip, its steeply angular lines under the cheeks'.

Nock wrote in 1960 that 'the picture most usually drawn of him today is that of a cold, austere, even ruthless "skinflint", one who kept down the speed of trains in order to save money and so on'. To be fair to Nock, a prolific writer of popular railway history, he did add 'so he may have been, but he was one of the ablest, clear thinking of administrators, and he had a rare gift of getting the right man into key positions'. Harold Perkin, writing in 1971, continued in the same vein, seeing him as 'cold, steely, aloof and incorruptible' but preferring 'to rule by fear rather than persuasion'.

On Moon's retirement the acidic *Railway Herald* reported that he 'was no doubt a friend of the shareholders, but the railway servant has seldom seen such a bitter opponent of the rights of labour to recognition in the hands of the capitalist'. In promoting the interests of his company Moon was never ashamed to call himself a capitalist. The more financially orientated *Railway New* recalled in its obituary that Moon 'was very unselfish, scrupulously just and considerate to employees', although it did add that he was 'very severe with servants of the company who did not do their duty to the public'. John Pendleton, a contemporary source of many of the anecdotes repeated by later commentators, was more balanced when he wrote in 1896 of Moon being 'imperious, a strict disciplinarian, severely just and indefatigable worker', but who 'sometimes broke through his stern mask to do a kindly deed'.

David Stevenson, who worked closely under Moon as a goods manager, even more warmly described him as 'a man of grave aspect, with a pleasant smile enhanced by its rarity; always approachable to those of his officers in whom he believed'. In his musings published in the year Moon retired, Stevenson wrote that 'he had a single eye for the company's interest, an insatiable capacity for details ... alike indifferent to good or evil repute, and tenaciously pursued the even tenor of his way'. Another long serving manager, J.Slinger of the Lancaster Canal, remembered 'with affectionate gratitude ... the long and uniform confidence and kindness' which Moon showed to him.

Among modern commentators, Brian Reed has written 'his photographs show a grave and unemotional man, but he had a happy family life'. Malcolm Reed has written that 'Moon's devotion to L&NWR affairs, coupled with his intensely reserved personality, set him apart from most of his contemporaries, and this has perhaps affected his subsequent reputation'. He commented that 'many of the anecdotes that have survived about him relate his frugality, while the fact that most British railway history has been written from the perspective of competing companies has reinforced the general portrayal of Moon as a stern and unsympathetic individual'.

Trying to sift through contemporary accounts for the facts has been an interesting challenge. However so much remains unknown, the lack of family papers proving a major restraint, that this book cannot be taken as definitive. Nevertheless it is hoped that enough has been presented, if not to form judgements, at least to provide a better understanding of a unique individual.

ABBREVIATIONS in Text *(Railway companies unless otherwise noted)*

B&B	Bristol & Birmingham
BCN	(Canal) Birmingham Canal Navigations
BL&CJ	Birkenhead Lancashire & Cheshire Junction
B&LJ	(Canal) Birmingham & Liverpool Junction
B&OJ	Birmingham & Oxford Junction
BW&D	Birmingham Wolverhampton & Dudley
C of DSP	(Ship owner) City of Dublin Steam Packet
C&H	Chester & Holyhead
C&W	Cockermouth & Workington
CLC	Cheshire Lines Committee (Midland, GN & MS&L)
D&D	Dublin & Drogheda
GC	Great Central
GJ	Grand Junction
GN	Great Northern
G&SW	Glasgow & South Western
GS&W	Great Southern & Western
GW	Great Western
L&B	London & Birmingham
LB&SC	London Brighton & South Coast
L&C	Lancaster & Carlisle
L&M	Liverpool & Manchester
L&NW	London & North Western
L&PJ	Lancaster & Preston Junction
LMS	London Midland & Scottish
LW&SS	London Worcester & South Staffs
L&Y	Lancashire & Yorkshire
M&B	Manchester & Birmingham
MGW	Midland Great Western
MSJ&A	Manchester South Junction & Altrincham
MS&L	Manchester Sheffield & Lincolnshire
MT&A	Merthyr Tredegar & Abergavenny
NA&H	Newport Abergavenny & Hereford
NE	North Eastern
NL	North London
NS	North Staffordshire
OW&W	Oxford Worcester & Wolverhampton
RCA	(an association) Railway Companies Association
S&B	Shrewsbury & Birmingham
S&GJ	Shrewsbury & Grand Junction
S&H	Shrewsbury & Hereford
SE&C	South Eastern & Chatham
SSR	South Staffordshire
SU	(Canal with a railway) Shropshire Union
SV	Birmingham Wolverhampton & Stour Valley
TV	Trent Valley
W&FJ	Whitehaven & Furness Junction
W&S	Warrington & Stockport
WJR	Whitehaven Junction
W&H	Worcester & Hereford
WJSC	Wolverhampton Joint Station Committee
WMR	West Midland

CHAPTER 1

ANCESTRY & YOUTH

Sir Richard Moon took the title Copsewood Grange for his baronetcy. It was the name of his house near Coventry where he lived with his wife and unmarried daughter for the last ten years of his railway work and for almost another decade in retirement until his death in 1899. The vast, multi bed-roomed mansion, so out of character with the man, only adds to the many unsolved enigmas surrounding the man. It was even alleged that if it had not been for his wife opening the letter announcing the honour, he would have refused it.

He had no previous family connections with the area, being born and brought up in Liverpool and then for over twenty years living in Worcester.

The ancestry of the Liverpool Moons has been traced back to the scattered rural communities lying between Preston, Kirkham and Lancaster. As was typical at that time most of the local employment was based on agriculture and the pattern of settlements in the area has changed little over the centuries. The early Moons or Moones appear to have prospered mainly as yeoman farmers and local traders. However by the end of the eighteenth century, as one local historian put it, 'many families of Lancaster merchants, seamen and others migrated from the county town and transferred business experience, talent and energy to Liverpool, which soon outstripped the elder seaport in importance'.

It seems that the earliest ancestor who can be proved was Robert Moone of Newsham who was buried at Woodplumpton around 1615. Woodplumpton is listed in the Domesday Book. The present parish church of St Anne's dates from the first half of the sixteenth century. The early Moons or Moones appear to have prospered mainly as yeomen farmers and local traders. Apparently, as with many English families at the time, they ceased to use the

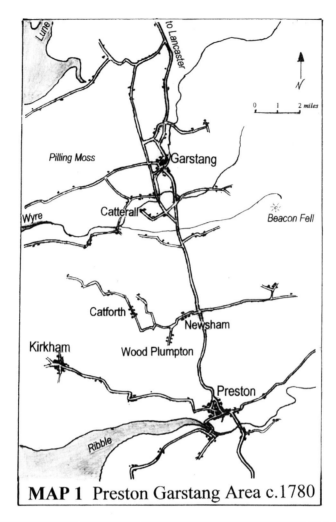

MAP 1 Preston Garstang Area c.1780

1. Woodplumpton Church

St Anne's Church, Woodplumpton, probably early sixteenth century but restored
c.1748 with Georgian exterior and bell cupola.

final 'e' in their name around the beginning of the eighteenth century. Many Roberts, as well as Edward and Richard appear to have been traditional family names making it difficult at times to identify without reference to a location. For example Robert Moone of Catforth, who had been married three times, was buried at Woodplumpton in 1691. He was sufficiently well off to leave legacies to three servants and money to poor parish householders.

Jonathan Slinger, writing on the occasion of Moon's funeral in November 1899, reminded the family of their association with the area. He recalled their ancestors having the freedom of Lancaster, referring to a Robert Moon living at Woodplumpton where property still bears his name.

Slinger's Robert appears to have been the first member of the family to trade in the county between Lancaster, Liverpool and the West Indies with a number of slaves on sugar plantations in Kingston, Jamaica. He died in 1778. A year later one of his sons Edward made a will as 'late of Kingston Jamaica, but now of Catterall, Co. Lancaster, merchant'. It seems as if this son Edward was the first of the family to have been a full time merchant. His grandson was Moon's grandfather, another Robert (of Catterall).

Robert of Catterall was baptized at Garstang in 1759 and as a yeoman married in 1781 the twenty one year old Ann, daughter of James Fisher the rector of Garstang. It appears that the rectors of Garstang from the eighteenth to the nineteenth century had traditionally been the Pedder family. Fisher was fifty six, and for ten years had not risen above a parish curate when he succeeded James Pedder on his death in 1772.

Robert and Ann had seven children, all sons except the youngest. A history of the parish suggests a modest family background with limited resources to bring up six venturesome sons all of whom were destined to become prosperous merchants. When Robert died in 1819 his will was proved at almost £600. By 1821 Ann was living with one of her sons, Edward, in Liverpool and by 1827 they were listed in Liverpool Gores Directory as 'Gentlewoman' and 'Merchant' respectively at 75 Islington. The six sons in order were James, Richard, Edward, John, William and Henry. The second son, Richard, Moon's father, was baptised in Garstang on 1 October 1783 and by 1807 was listed in Gores as a merchant at 25 Mount Pleasant,

Liverpool. Still only in his mid twenties it seemed he was the first of the brothers to have succeeded in being listed as an independent Liverpool merchant.

No details have been found regarding the early progression of the five other brothers from boyhood in Garstang to mercantile prosperity in Liverpool and the Americas. What is known is that by 1830 the partnership of Moon Brothers was estimated to be the sixth largest Liverpool importer of cotton.

Liverpool's cotton trade originated in the eighteenth century, expanding rapidly after 1780. The normal way to progress in this business would have been from dependence on the slave trade. In spite of mounting agitation against the trade in London throughout the 1780s, with support from Manchester and Bristol, Liverpool generally remained firmly opposed to abolition. The city's merchants dominated the trade and those with plantation interests in the West Indies and South America were economically dependent upon it.

Though the brothers' partnership was formed after abolition had been enacted, family connections with Jamaica and Brazil suggest the Moons' trading background would have been no different from most other leading Liverpool merchants. The success of Wilberforce's campaign that led to the 1807 Act meant that from the 1 May of that year it had become illegal for a British subject to trade in slaves (the trade itself was to carry on for many decades after this, in Brazil for example slavery was not abolished until 1888).

The first reference to the Moon Brothers partnership was to Richard and Edward in 1816; a local directory showing Richard Moon, Merchant, at 1 Stafford Street with his 'Counting House' at 7 Manesty's Lane. Their ties with Brazil were important enough for younger brothers, John and Henry, to take up residence there.

Richard senior had married in 1808 the twenty-three year old Elizabeth, daughter of fellow Liverpool merchant William Frodsham, by license in St Anne's church, Richmond, Liverpool. They had nine children, the first, a daughter was born in 1810 when their address was 26 Brownlow Street. Another daughter followed and then Richard, the first of their two sons.

Young Richard was registered as being born on the 23 September 1814. Unlike his older sisters he was not baptised until he was almost two years old when his parents had moved to Islington.

As further children were born, at regular intervals until 1823, the Holy Trinity parish registers in Liverpool record the baptisms of all but the last two. By then they had moved to Irvine Street, Edge Hill. Strangely none of the local parish records shows these last baptisms, particularly as Elizabeth died in 1825 and her burial is recorded in the Holy Trinity register.

The missing baptism records could be interpreted as a period when the parents' commitment to the Church of England may possibly have wavered. This could be an explanation of the unusual decision to send the two boys to St Andrews, though it seems unlikely. The boys' later commitment to the established church is not in doubt as evidenced by Richard's election as a parish churchwarden and Robert's career at Cambridge.

Richard was eleven years old when his mother died. The timing of her death suggests a tenth confinement being the cause. Nothing has been found to show how this affected the family at the time. In his early forties his father was left with a young family of two boys and five girls ranging from fifteen to two years old (two girls died in infancy). Ann the children's grandmother was living nearby and it could be assumed that in her mid sixties she would have been able to provide some support, although she does not appear to have moved into the household. Although the eldest child, Eliza Ann, was fifteen she would not have had to act as housewife and mother. Care of the children would have been left in the hands of trusted servants.

Richard senior never remarried. No evidence of any strong political views has been found, nor any involvement in Liverpool public affairs, although in later life he was listed in 1839 as one of twenty-three members of the Charitable Institution, Infirmary, Brownlow Street (this list included some of the leading citizens of Liverpool).

It is assumed that Richard's early schooling was at a local 'academy' or possibly by a visiting tutor. The quote given below suggests a school but, as is the case with so many anecdotes told of Moon in later life, it has not been possible to verify it. There were many establishments in Liverpool catering for wealthy families though no records have been traced of their pupils. What is known however is that when he and his younger brother Robert reached the age of fourteen they were sent to St Andrews University;

2. Ann Moon
Ann Moon (1760-1845), Moon's grandmother. Canon Moor

3. Richard Moon senior
Richard Moon (1783-1842), Moon's father, the first of the family to be listed
(1807) as a Liverpool merchant. Canon Moor

and two years later, when Richard left St Andrews in 1830, he joined the family business. Robert never did so, going on to Queens' College Cambridge as a pensioner (no scholarship or bursary) to pursue an academic and legal career. Whether there was any conflict between father and son over Richard joining the family business is not known. Many obituaries following Moon's death repeated the story that he wanted to join the church. In this respect *Berrow's Worcester Journal* for 25 November 1899 is worth quoting as it touches on another aspect of his character. It wrote that when 'quite a little boy' he:

> Trudged along Liverpool streets to school, and in a bookseller's shop which he passed his eyes looked long and oft on some gaudy coloured book. The woman inside at last noticed his evident interest in her wares, and offered him the coveted volume on credit. Eagerly availing himself of the offer, he carried the prize home, to get a lecture from his maid and to be threatened with a debtors' prison. He was much distressed in mind, and at last sought out his grandmother, to whom he told his trouble. But, he said, to the end of his days that incident gave him such a horror of debt that it never left him, and he would not go on credit for anything. ... It was at this time that he wished to take orders in the Church: but his father did not favour the plan, and the young man returned to Liverpool, to enter upon a mercantile profession.

At St Andrews the boys spent two annual October to May sessions at United College. Richard was not yet sixteen when he left and had not followed a course that suggested he intended to graduate there. The Scottish universities at that time were very much local universities for the arts students. They were attractive to students from the north of England, but usually if they came from dissenting church backgrounds or had local family or business connections. It was not unusual for boys of fourteen to attend especially if they came from better off backgrounds, but the normal age was fifteen or sixteen. Entrance standards would have been kept low to give boys from country schools in Scotland the same chance as the privately educated to enter a university.

4. St Salvator's College c.1767

St Salvator's College, St Andrews, from a pen and wash sketch (c.1767)
showing building before reconstruction in the 1830s. The college formed
part of the United College of St Salvator and St. Leonard.

Courtesy University of St Andrews Library, OL1-10.

5. Liverpool mail coach 1830s

Liverpool mail coach for London in the 1830s. Similar stage coaches left
Liverpool's Golden Lion daily for Glasgow and Edinburgh. Author

English boys could take advantage of the 'secondary schooling' level of first year studies as the Scottish degree took four years not three (the normal age for graduation in Scotland then being nineteen or twenty). It does seem therefore that the Moons were sent to St Andrews only to finish schooling.

Contemporary comments on the poor state of the college buildings in the late 1820s are confirmed by the Royal Commission on the Scottish Universities. Visiting United in the summer of 1827 the commissioners observed that 'the most pitiable desolation was found to prevail': the Common Hall and School was 'entirely ruinous and incapable of repair'; the classrooms 'extremely mean, small, confined, and insufficient'; and the north building 'in a most dilapidated state'. It was not until October 1828 that the commissioners approved plans for rebuilding. A new wing was started in 1829 but not completed until 1831. A professor is quoted as saying they 'should not only have a complete suite of classrooms, but a fabric of somewhat creditable aspect that would announce itself to be a college, and not be mistaken for a cotton mill'.

Richard's subjects in his first year were advanced Latin, maths and chemistry; in his second year, advanced Latin, physics and maths. Taking early classes in physics and chemistry was normally for those not intending to graduate. Such students frequently went on to follow careers in medicine, the army or engineering.

It is to be wondered how the brothers remembered their two long terms at St Andrews. Two six month sessions of 'pitiable desolation' may have been conducive to character forming but hardly to learning. It is tempting to surmise that the impact of such an environment on Moon explains the apparent lack of warmth in his character. By all accounts it must have been a harsh environment for a young teenager to have been thrust, although probably no worse than many of the English public schools at the time. And there was also the added rigour of the journey from Liverpool to Scotland in the pre-railway age. Opinions differ as to how the two boys would have travelled: possibilities include sea and canal as well as stage or post coach. In Richard's case it is again tempting to speculate whether the travelling experience was seminal. Cary's Roads for 1828 showed a daily stage coach leaving the Golden Lion in Liverpool's Dale Street at four thirty in the morning for Glasgow, followed by one half an hour later for Edinburgh, both journeys shown as lasting thirty hours. And, as shown in the British Almanac for 1829, a steam packet also left daily for Glasgow.

Referring to possible family or business contacts to explain the choice of St Andrews, there were Moons in Dundee (Moon, Langlands & Co were textiles wholesalers with retail premises, and a William Moon was listed as a merchant), but no direct family link with the Liverpool Moons has been established. However Moon's father was trading at the time with Scotland in linen and calico. There was a flax spinning industry in Fife and Russel Mill in Springfield was then owned by a George Moon. The name may have been a coincidence, but if trade had brought the Liverpool Moons in close contact with him then his residence at Springfield could well have provided a refuge for the young Moons during the sparse holidays. It was customary for the continuous six months session to be broken by only three short breaks: Christmas Day, New Year's Day and 'Handsel' Monday (the first Monday in the New Year when traditionally gifts were given). However accounts of the Fife linen industry suggest that trade with Liverpool, using the Forth Clyde canal and coastal shipping, became uncompetitive as cotton prices fell and the wet-spinning linen industry in Ireland grew. Indeed George Moon was bankrupt in 1844 and he had been a leading figure in the industry, giving evidence to a House of Commons Select Committee on the 1823 changes to linen regulations.

When Richard came home from St Andrews the opening of the Liverpool & Manchester railway was imminent. This company was the first steam locomotive and passenger-carrying railway, built and organised specifically for that purpose. The project for a railway between the two cities was first promoted in the early 1820s. Despite the family's later interest there is no evidence that any of the Moons were prepared to invest in what was, after all, a highly speculative venture at the time: neither the original subscription list nor the first shareholding in the company contained a Moon.

Construction work on the railway began in 1826 and the tunnel between Edge Hill and Wapping was dug through by June 1828. The tunnel was gas lit and opened to the public by July 1829. Both events could have been witnessed by the Moon boys whose home in Irvine Street was within easy walking distance of the Edge Hill tunnel mouth. Living so close the family would have been unusual if they had not joined the crowd witnessing the opening ceremony. When the first train left Liverpool for Manchester young Richard would have been eight days short of his sixteenth birthday. He could hardly have been unaware of the progress made on the local tunnel during his two six month absences and it must have been with some interest that he looked forward to the actual opening on the 15 September. If as a teenager he did take the opportunity to walk the gas-lit tunnel down to the dock at Wapping, it is interesting to speculate what his thoughts may have been decades later when he was a company director responsible for reviewing the tunnel's safety.

CHAPTER 2

LIVERPOOL MERCHANT

Joining a prosperous family business would have been a natural step for a young man to take. If Moon had seriously contemplated joining the church there is no evidence that he was in conflict with his father over the matter. Indeed as the older son he may well have considered it his duty to support his father and in doing so may have made it easier for his brother Robert to pursue an academic and legal career.

When Richard joined Moon Brothers the firm had become the sixth largest cotton importer in Liverpool and the leading one specialising in supplies from Brazil. However of the thirty major Liverpool merchants listed in 1830 only three others were importing South American cotton.

In the 1790s the bulk of cotton imports had come from the West Indies with the US being insignificant. The first cotton from Brazil was imported from Maranham in 1781. By 1820 Brazilian cotton peaked at 16% of total imports but the US had come from nowhere to almost 50%, as similarly had the surge through the East India company to over 25%. Cotton from the West Indies halved and soon was to fall away to under 1%. The decade 1820 to 1830 then saw a rapid expansion in the cotton trade generally, with increasingly more of the imports being concentrated in the hands of a small group of Liverpool merchants. The growth had come from a doubling of imports from the United States. In contrast imports from Brazil remained static. Over the next twenty years Brazil, as a source, continued at the same level, whilst the US doubled again. During the 1846-50 period the US supplied over 80% of total bales imported whilst Brazil represented less than 4%. The effect on Moon Brothers was that, although they took more Brazilian cotton than any other importer, they were not growing as those merchants taking cotton from North America.

Much Brazilian trade in the earlier days would have been through Lisbon and the Moons must have had a presence there. After 1822 when Brazil proclaimed independence some direct representatation could have been considered. However it is not known when the Brazilian end of the partnership was established as John & Henry Moon of Maranham.

Maranham was the region in the north-east of the country where the cotton was grown. The older brother John was based there with Henry down in Rio de Janeiro, probably to be nearer the export market for Lancashire textiles. Henry's death in 1826 was bizarrely noted in a family history as killed in Lisbon 'because, being short-sighted, he did not remove his hat when the King passed'. Portugal was at the time close to civil war over the succession, the king being challenged by his brother. By coincidence, sixteen years later John was also to die in Lisbon. He was coming home with his wife and family and was presumably taken ill en route.

San Luiz was the region's main port for exports and Alcantara (across the bay from the port) the commercial centre. In the second half of the nineteenth century cotton growing and both towns went into serious decline, the decay of former fine merchants' houses in Alcantara only being arrested by attempts at restoration a century later.

According to a B.G.Orchard, a Liverpool commentator, writing at the end of the nineteenth century, the region was not 'conducive to English settlement'. He complained of the 'unhealthy climate, the billions of insects, the limited society, the distance from English social, political and religious activity' and added that 'Tennyson rightly declares that one year of European life is worth a cycle of Cathay' and 'no Englishman with a soul above dollars would wish to end his days in Brazil'.

The Moons' partnership lasted for about thirty years. As no record has been found for their Brazilian company it is not known whether they had plantations or simply commercial and residential premises. In either event it seems likely that John would have been resident in Alcantara. Of the two other brothers who initially remained outside the partnership, James subsequently joined in 1840, and William the youngest, who though continuing to trade independently, also had interests in Brazil.

No record has been found of Moon's early years of commercial life in the business. That he gained for himself a solid reputation is however evident. As partner 'Richard the Younger', he was named in 1840 in John's will as one of the co-executors of his estate in Brazil. That he was familiar with the property inheritance problem there was evident when many years later he referred to the problem in one of his addresses to L&NW shareholders. Acting as a go-between for the two ends of the trading partnership would have been logical for a young man joining the business. This would have involved many weeks at sea, most probably in ships owned by the Brocklebanks. It can be no coincidence that one of the earliest Brocklebank ships was named *Maranham* and it would be surprising if it had not brought in cotton for the Moons. There was another reason why such links were likely.

Moon was in his early twenties when in October 1836 his eldest sister Eliza Ann married Ralph Brocklebank. And the family association was to become even closer when within four years Moon himself married Ralph's young half-sister, Eleanor Brocklebank [see Moon and Brocklebank family trees shown as appendices]. The Brocklebanks were from Cumberland where John, Eleanor's father, lived at Hazel Holme in the parish of St Bees with his business in Whitehaven, which before the rise of Liverpool, was a leading port with shipbuilding as well as trading interests.

Ship's captain Daniel Brocklebank, on his retirement in 1800, passed his shipping business to his two sons Thomas and John (a cousin of John of Hazel Holme). Thomas managed the shipyard and John the ropery. Thomas soon moved to Liverpool and became the senior partner of the business, which had become the firm of T & J Brocklebank which at its peak in the nineteenth century owned over fifty sailing ships.

The partners Thomas and John remained bachelors, John died in 1831, but their sister Anne married Captain Wilson Fisher. Their only son, Thomas Fisher was to be the chosen successor to control the business when senior partner Thomas died in 1845. But in the meantime Moon's future brother-in-law Ralph had moved in 1827 from the ropery in Whitehaven to assist in the Liverpool office. Four years later Ralph's second cousin, the young seventeen-year old Thomas Fisher joined him. J.F.Gibson in writing of the Brocklebanks pictures them at that time working in Liverpool from 'a small dark

6. T&J Brocklebank's *Perserverance* built 1819

T&J.Brocklebank's 512 tons burden *Perseverance* built 1819, latest of fourteen sailing vessels then comprising the partners' fleet. By 1845 fifty ships were owned, one of the largest fleets in the country. Chandler

7. John Moon

John Moon (1787-1842) one of the Moon Brothers partners based in Maranham in Brazil. Canon Moor

room in which Thomas planned and from which Ralph or Thomas Fisher went forth to the docks to talk with masters, inspect cargoes and to see to the requirements of passengers'.

At a similar age to Thomas Fisher, the young Richard Moon would by then have been in his father's office in Tithebarn Street. It is not difficult to visualise the young men, possibly together, checking bales of cotton, shipments of hides and beginning to learn the first principles of commerce which were to stand both of them in such good stead in later years. Brocklebank ships were sailing regularly to South America and it is likely that it was the trading association with the Moons that first brought the families together. In 1830 the Brocklebank's *Mary* was making the round trip between Liverpool and Maranham in five months and in 1845 the *Crown* in three and half months. It was not unusual then for merchants to take part ownership in the ships and for the shipping concerns to have an interest in their cargoes. Although by 1839 Moon Brothers had dropped to the sixteenth largest Liverpool cotton importer, they were still the dominant importer from Brazil and listed as being both ship owners and agents.

Richard Moon and Eleanor Brocklebank were married by the Rev Thomas Tattershall at St Augustines Church, Walton, Liverpool on the 27 August 1840; Richard was twenty six and Eleanor twenty. Richard's occupation was shown as Merchant. Amongst the witnesses listed at the wedding were Richard's younger sisters, Thomas Fisher and his sister Jane, and Ralph Brocklebank.

On his marriage Richard was admitted as a partner. He was publicly listed for the first time as Richard Moon Junior, Merchant, in the 1841 Liverpool Gore's directory. He then had his own house in Shaw Street. Previously he had lived with his father at 48 Shaw Street. His Uncle Edward was listed at 9 Shaw Street. The 1841 census listed Richard Moon aged 25, merchant, his wife Eleanor aged 20, Edward aged one month and four house servants.

Looking at Liverpool's Shaw Street as it appeared at the end of the twentieth century it is just possible to visualise it as the new fashionable address for Liverpool's wealthy merchants and traders of the 1830s. According to Pevsner the street was laid out between 1826 and 1829. It comprised several groups of three-storey terraced houses along one side with stable blocks behind and facing open fields where a new church, St Augustines, was consecrated in 1830. The university's conservation of Abercrombie Square gives a good indication of comparable housing.

Richard and Eleanor had moved into 4 Shaw Street, the house previously listed as the Rev Tattershall's (he moved to number 71). It is possible that Moon's religious outlook was strengthened by close contact with Tattershall who in 1839 was energetically promulgating the Trinitarian case against the Unitarians in the public debate then raging in Liverpool. The Unitarians had a strong influence in Liverpool with many leading members active in public affairs.

In view of Moon's later interest in railways it is worth considering if at that time he ever met the railway engineer Edmund Bury who was another early resident of Shaw Street. He was listed in the 1841 census as a forty-year old Engineer with two servants. With a foundry and works in Liverpool he had a contract to build the locomotives for the London & Birmingham Railway, one of the constituents of the L&NW. Another local resident was George Crosfield. The Crosfields had developed a profitable soap works in Warrington and George was to become a large shareholder in the L&NW, becoming a director in 1869. Another Crosfield, Henry, established a successful food importing and wholesale grocery business in Liverpool and invested substantial sums in railways. As an auditer to the L&NW more will be said of him later, especially as he was to become a trusted confidant when Moon became chairman of the company.

Liverpool in the eighteen thirties and early forties was growing at an impressive rate. Business life in the city was driven by the growth in shipping and the docks to support Lancashire's manufacturing development. It should have been an exciting prospect for any young businessman with capital, initiative and energy. On the other hand the flood of unskilled labour that poured in to build the docks, man the ships and handle the cargoes, was to create the worst housing and health problems of any city in Britain.

To take advantage of Liverpool's trading opportunities and yet remain immune from the surrounding squalor was not something Moon seems to have come to terms with in the sixteen or so years he spent in business there. What is remarkable is that the ties with the Brocklebanks did not encourage him to continue to devote his career to merchanting and shipping.

This was in marked contrast, for example, to Ralph Brocklebank. Ralph remained active in Liverpool shipping and insurance, chairing for a period in the 1860s the then newly formed Mersey Docks & Harbour Board, amassing a fortune and dispensing liberally to charities. When he died in 1892 his net estate was valued at over £790,000. A fellow Brazilian trader, Yorkshireman John Moore also became active in shipping circles. He rose from an early career in Rio to establish in Liverpool his Brazilian trading house John Bramley Moore and Co, becoming chairman of the Brazilian Chamber of Commerce and also the Dock board.

What may first have influenced Moon in turning aside from following similar paths was the family position in 1842. Early in that year the Moon Brothers partnership received a double blow: the death, in February at the age of 59, of Richard Moon senior and in May, at the age of 55, of John, the remaining family member in Brazil. The local company in Brazil must then have been dissolved. The remaining senior partners in Liverpool, James and Edward, were then faced with the problem of how to continue the business; James was over sixty and Edward in his late fifties. A lot must have depended on how much the twenty-seven year old junior partner Richard, the only one listed as representing the next generation, wished to commit to the business.

As has been noted John had made his will, during a visit to Liverpool in September 1840, and named his nephew Moon as one of his executors (the others were James and Edward). It is not clear why John appointed Richard junior in preference to Richard senior unless it was in recognition of his closer knowledge of the Maranham business, or the recognition of the need for a younger active family representative to handle affairs in Brazil. John left his land and property to his children and, after settlement on his wife, left the residue to the executors. Although resident in Brazil, John still hoped he would be subject to the laws of England in passing on his property, but from comments in his will he seemed realistic enough to accept that disposal of his estate would have to be determined by local law.

Moon had complained at one time in his later years (reporting to L&NW shareholders) over the 'repudiation of American states' of his family's property rights. At first sight 'American' suggested the United

8. Moon as young man
The young Richard Moon, probably at the time of his father's death in 1842
when contemplating his future with Moon Brothers. M.Moon

States but in the context of the family background it is clear he was referring to Brazil, the repudiation being a direct reference to John's fears over the penal effect of Brazilian law. The problem over the retention of expatriates' property there would have stemmed from the varying interpretations of that part of the 1827 Anglo-Brazilian commercial treaty which covered the rights to administer property. Although the treaty allowed for inheritances by Briish expatriates to be administered by British representatives, this appeared to be not so if one of the heirs was Brazilian. John's wife was Brazilian. Whatever the case, his death may have required attendance by the executors to resolve and also effective legal representation in Brazil; and they may not have agreed on how the problem was to be handled. Moon himself eventually renounced his executorship.

Richard senior's personal estate was significant for the period, being valued at £88,000. The terms of his will placed considerable responsibility on his two sons Richard and Robert. Although Richard was one of his father's three executors, his brother Robert and their uncle Edward being the others, it is likely that as the eldest son he would have taken the leading role in settling the estate.

Under his father's will the seven surviving children were to receive the sum of £10,000 each, Richard and Robert to receive theirs absolutely, but their sisters to have the sum invested in trust for their income and administered by the executors. After legacies the residue of the estate passed to Richard and Robert absolutely. The will was quite specific in detailing the trustees' responsibilities for investing and controlling the legacies. Their father left instructions that the trustees should invest:

> In any of the public stocks or funds of Great Britain, or on mortgage of real or leasehold securities in England or Wales, or on the funds of the Corporation of Liverpool or of the Liverpool Dock Trustees, or in the purchase of any shares in the Liverpool & Manchester Railway Company, in the Grand Junction Railway Company or in the London & Birmingham Railway Company, or in the Bank of Liverpool or on the bonds or mortgages of any of the aforesaid Railway Companies with power to change such stock, funds, securities or investments from time to

time as occasion shall require and upon further trust that the said trustees or trustee do and shall pay the interest dividends and income of each daughters respective legacy … into the hands of each daughter during her life on her receipt for her sole and separate use free from the debts or controls of any husband she may marry.

Although all five surviving daughters eventually married well, under the will the trustees remained responsible for ensuring their independent income. When Moon referred to his family, he clearly meant more than his own immediate dependants. However of most significance is the fact that the specific railways mentioned formed the major part of the amalgamation in 1846 that gave birth to the London & North Western Railway.

As the 1840s progressed the nation's speculation in all railways had grown apace culminating in the peak years of 1845 and 1846. It is unlikely that Moon or his wider family would have been immune from the railway investment "mania" that so affected the country during this period. For example Moon himself subscribed £400 to the speculative London Worcester & South Staffordshire (a line projected to counter the proposed broad gauge Oxford Worcester & Wolverhampton) and further sums of £400 to branches and extension to Dudley; and also £350 to the Shrewsbury & Grand Junction. His brother and James also subscribed £1,000 and £2,000 respectively to each of the LW&SS lines and £150 and £550 to the S&GJ. Additionally James subscribed £4,500 to the Sheffield Ashton-under-Lyne & Manchester. All would not have been lost as shares would not have been paid up. Moon had already been subscribing to other companies, for example the Birkenhead, Lancashire & Cheshire Junction.

The general financial crisis that hit all businesses by the second half of 1847 is well illustrated by Herapath, who writing in his *Railway Journal* for 1 May, commented under 'Liverpool Affairs' that:

The market is almost stagnant, the few transactions which take place being between the jobbers for the settlement of the account. Any large quantity of stock would, at the present time, be perfectly unsaleable, so severe is the monetary pressure. The bills of the most wealthy house here were, it is said, this week, refused to be taken in payment for goods in Manchester, in consequence of the extreme difficulty experienced in getting them cashed! Is the Bank to be relieved, or are our merchants to stop payment?

Moon would have been approaching twenty-eight when his father's will was proved in August 1842. As an executor for his uncle he could well have been away in Brazil for part of the year. He renounced his executorship in his uncle's estate in March 1843. In the meantime he must have already been considering his day to day involvement in the commercial heart of Liverpool for when his second son Richard was born in July, he had moved out to the surrounding countryside at West Derby.

This did not apparently end his association with the business as both he and his uncles were still shown as the partners in 1845; and Moon was still listed as such in the 1846-47 West Derby electoral roll. However in the 1847 local Liverpool trade directories the Moon Brothers partnership was no longer shown.

For Moon to have moved out of the city at that time is understandable. Fears of an epidemic of typhus and typhoid fever spreading to the more wealthy areas were beginning to be realised. The medical officer of health for Liverpool, Dr W.H.Duncan later estimated that during 1847 nearly 60,000 suffered from fever, and 40,000 from diarrhoea and dysentery. Liverpool was in the throes of suffering the most fatal year in its history. Duncan paints a picture of a city in 1847 where by the end of June no less than 300,000 Irish had landed in Liverpool:

> Of these it was ... estimated that from 60,000 to 80,000 had located themselves amongst us, occupying every nook and cranny of the already overcrowded lodging houses, and forcing their way into the cellars ... In different parts of Liverpool 50 or 60 of these destitute people were found in a house containing three or four small rooms ... and upwards of 40 were found sleeping in a cellar.

Moon's residence in West Derby, 'Claremont' along Sandforth Road, was newly built, probably by Willliam Imrie in 1840. Although designed to give the appearance of one large house, it was in fact two houses. Imrie (the senior partner of the shipbroking firm Imrie & Tomlinson) at one time occupied one half and let the other. Moon for a short period was his tenant. Many years later when chairman of his railway, Moon must have recalled his days there when the route of the competitive Cheshire Lines Committee railway cut deeply through the edge of the property. Coincidentally Thomas Ismay, the founder of the White Star shipping line and mooted at one time as Moon's successor as chairman of the L&NW, had also lived there. In the 1980s Claremont was owned and restored by Carla Lane, the TV writer of *Liver Birds* fame.

By moving out of Liverpool only to West Derby, Moon could still have intended to remain in business locally. However as far as the partnership was concerned it seems that his uncles, influenced by the loss of their Brazilian connection, the lack of a stake in the dominant American market and a doubt over the commitment of their young partner, had already decided to dissolve the business. This does not explain why Moon did not continue on his own. Twenty years were to pass before any further reference to a Moon trading in cotton in Liverpool was listed (in 1867 a V.B.Corrie withdrew from the firm of Corrie & Co and with Edward Moon Junior started Corrie Moon & Co). By then of course Richard Moon had long been fully committed to his railway. However his uncles, Edward and James, remained in the Liverpool area presumably to enjoy their retirement years. In the meantime it seemed that younger uncle, William, remained active as an independent.

With so many members of the Moon family relying on income from holdings in railway companies, in particular the L&NW, it is conceivable that the young Moon had already begun to take on the role of family representative in protecting these interests. He remained in West Derby until his third child, a daughter Eleanor, was born in 1847. By this time he could well have been looking for a more suitable home to bring up his growing family. What is remarkable is that his choice was nowhere near his L&NW railway. Aged only thirty-three he had effectively retired from the commercial world of Liverpool. The electoral roll for

1847-48 year shows him living over a hundred miles away at Kempsey in Worcestershire.

Before following Moon to Worcestershire it is worth visiting Liverpool at the end of the twentieth century. The streets and houses where the Moons lived were still in existence (other than Brownlow Street which was built over by the hospital). In spite of the urban desolation that parts of Liverpool became in the second half of the century, it is still possible to realise how attractive the merchants' town houses in Shaw Street would have been in viewing restoration projects such as the university's Abercrombie Square area.

Although truncated by modern road development, sufficient of Stafford Street remained to appreciate that in an earlier age the well-proportioned terraced houses would once have been desirable residences. The attraction of housing in Islington is more difficult to appreciate. The street became part of a soulless inner city highway. However from the terrace of housing on Irvine Street, high above the city on Mount Vernon, it is easy to see how early in the nineteenth century this would have been a desirable place to live away from the tentacles of Liverpool's inner city sprawl. Little evidence remains though of the churches. Not only was the original St Anne's soon demolished but the new church built a century later in 1871 is also gone. St Augustine's in Shaw Street was destroyed in the Second World War. Holy Trinity too was bombed and although restored in 1950, it was damaged by fire in 1969, then vandalised and finally demolished in 1970.

CHAPTER 3

RETREAT TO WORCESTER

Moon's choice of a small village on the east bank of the river Severn four miles south of Worcester, seems as surprising a decision as the retirement itself. No evidence has been found of relatives there, nor that he was attracted to, or ever engaged in, any business or industry in the area. Though the local glove trade or the retirement of a Lancashire cotton manufacturer to the village could have provided contacts, it is more likely that he was familiar with the locality as a result of holidays in nearby Malvern: the spa was popular with wealthy families from the north.

When Moon first arrived in Kempsey there was no station there, nor indeed in the city of Worcester itself. The local station was Spetchley on the line from Birmingham to Bristol, part of the original Birmingham & Gloucester Railway, which had been leased (together with the Bristol & Gloucester) to the Midland Railway. The railway-owned free omnibus from Spetchley served as the only 'rail' link to the city until a branch from Abbots Wood opened in 1850. From Spetchley it would have taken five hours by train via Birmingham to either London or Liverpool.

Although the line to Gloucester was one of the earliest trunk routes radiating from Birmingham, it never formed part of Moon's L&NW railway. Kempsey had tried to establish its own station by obtaining platforms and shelter at an isolated level crossing two and half miles away at Pirton, but it was little used and was already closed before Moon came to the area. It would not have been easy, even allowing for servant help, for the family to have moved with their furniture and effects from West Derby to the village. For his wife, with two boys under six and a baby daughter only a few months old, the journey must have been particularly stressful.

A local history of the village refers to Moon living there in 1849, at Bank House, when 'he entered into negotiations to buy the property, but the sale was not completed'. One of several imposing residences, Bank House stood in twelve acres of grounds with a three-stall stable and coach house. It had been available for purchase or rent for some time, becoming vacant following the death in November 1845 of its owner Thomas Ingledew.

The estate had been auctioned in early 1846, but not found a buyer. 'A more delightful retreat is not to be met within the county,' the local paper asserted, 'the situation being everything that the most fastidious could desire' and 'for a family wishing retirement it is a very desirable residence'. The location is described as having pleasing views, in particular of the 'noble' Malvern Hills and being 'bounded on the west by the turnpike road leading from Worcester to Cheltenham, from which latter place it is distant about two hours drive. There are two pews in the parish church belonging exclusively to this estate'.

Despite these attractions the house remained unsold until auctioned again, with vacant possession, in 1851. How seriously Moon as the sitting tenant negotiated to purchase is not known. Though his fourth child, John Arthur, was christened there in July 1849, by the following April he had moved to the northern outskirts of Worcester, to an even larger house forming part of the church-owned Bevere Manor estate in the parish of Claines.

The arrangements at Bevere (pronounced as "reverie" not "severe") suggest at first another temporary stay. As was the case with many old church estates Bevere Manor was subject to lease and tenancy renewals. A twenty-one year lease, dated November 1846, from the Dean of Worcester (subsequently the Ecclesiastical Commissioners) was held by Sir Henry Broughton with a seven-year renewal of tenancies. However by 1855 this lease was transferred to a wealthy Worcester contractor, John Hughes.

Francis Jenkinson held the tenancy. Already a long term resident (the census for 1841 listed her with three adult children and nine servants, together with another family, the Hon Charles Dundas, clerk, with five children and two servants), Francis was possibly the elderly widow of Jenkinson, the Dean of Worcester between 1817 and 1825.

In the summer of 1849, Mrs Jenkinson announced that she was moving to Malvern. She held a number of public sales to dispose of

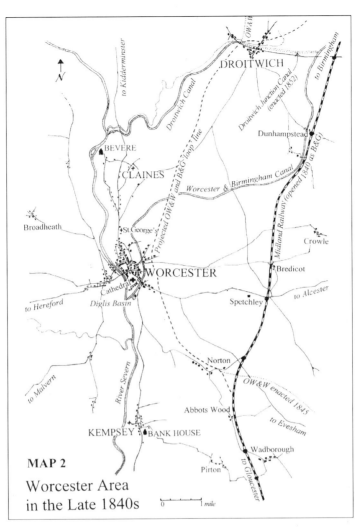

MAP 2

Worcester Area
in the Late 1840s

0   1 mile

9. Bank House, Kempsey
Bank House, Kempsey, near Worcester, rented by Moon when he 'retired' from
commercial life of Liverpool in 1847. E.T. White

an impressive list of effects, including her 'valuable library of books', which included volumes on the bible and Worcester cathedral. Possibly alerted by these sales notices, the Moons met Jenkinson, or her representative, and clearly satisfied her that that they were a suitable family to sub-let to for the remainder of her tenancy.

In 1851 the census return, misleadingly showing the property as Bevere Lodge, listed Moon, 'former merchant', as the occupier with his family and seven servants. 'Lodge' could have been a hangover from the days when the house was shared (strikingly similar to Moon's position at Claremont).

Moon was never to own the freehold at Bevere. He never used the word 'manor', always giving his address as simply 'Bevere'. Not until 1854 does his name actually appear in the property records when he was shown only as 'occupier'.

It was of course not unusual at the time for men of means and standing, not to own their home. However the annual rental of £215 was a significant outgoing.

A late nineteenth century sale notice described the mansion as being approached through 'prettily disposed pleasure grounds by a well timbered carriage drive with entrance lodge', and occupying a 'charming position, commanding beautiful views of the fertile valley of the Severn and the surrounding district'. Fifty-nine acres in total, the estate included a forty acre 'homestead' and Bevere Island in the Severn, with extensive stabling and a coach-house for five carriages.

When Broughton gave up the lease Moon ought to have been well placed to take over instead of Hughes. He may have been deterred by the conditions, in particular the length of the lease, yet he was to remain living there for the duration of the twenty-one year term. And during his tenancy he could have had the opportunity to take outright ownership for Hughes took title to Bevere Manor in June 1863.

Moon's agreement with Jenkinson would have ended with her tenancy in 1854 and he had to decide whether to commit to the renewal. Subsequent correspondence with Hughes found in Martin Curtler's letter files indicates that his negotiation with Hughes was difficult. His threat to move out would not have been an idle one, as by then he was deeply involved in his railway. That he chose to negotiate at all suggests either the influence of his wife, or, despite his almost full time railway work, he still did not see his long term future as being so committed to the L&NW: a letter to his railway chairman at the time suggests this.

Moon's tenancy renewal negotiation came to a head when he was away from home on railway business. He left the matter to his wife to settle, together with their powerful neighbour, T.G.Curtler (a leading local magistrate and vice-chairman of the county's Quarter Sessions). Acting on behalf of his son Martin (Moon's solicitor), Curtler wrote to Hughes's solicitor on 7 September 1854 that he had gone over the latest draft with Mrs Moon:

> And she knows Mr Moon's mind respecting it, he having left instructions with her. He is gone from home and will not return until Friday evening and this he does purposely to conclude this business on Saturday [missing a L&NW board meeting to return]. Mrs Moon desires me to say expressly that if the business is not settled Mr Moon will give up the whole affair and will go to a house near Stafford which he has actually taken subject to the right to declare on or before Monday. The alterations I have made are few but Mrs Moon says it is useless to attempt to alter any one [there followed a list of points including repairs]. And Mrs Moon says they will on no account extend the period for landlord's repairs beyond the 1st May. I am writing this in Mrs Moon's presence who desires me to add that any further discussion will be useless and that the lease as now settled must be ready for Mr Moon's signature on Saturday morning next or they will be at an end

Hughes's demands appeared unreasonable: for example, maintaining the right to enter the property at any time, to fell the timber, to forbid the letting of the grass, restricting the frequency when the lawns were mown and not accepting responsibility for repairing fixtures and such items as stable drains.

As the Moons remained at Bevere for another fourteen years, presumably Hughes conceded to Moon's requirements. Incidentally Stafford would have been ideally located for his railway work and, when he eventually did leave, it was to Tamworth in Staffordshire.

The house at Bevere still exists, well preserved but divided into an impressive terrace of three. The hamlet of Bevere Green remains very much as it was in Moon's time, a collection of large houses near the river dominated by Bevere House (tastefully converted into flats) and in Moon's time the imposing residence of T.G Curtler. All of which is in stark contrast to Bank House, which degenerated into a transport cafe before being demolished completely and developed into an estate of bungalows.

The parish of Claines stretches from the outskirts of Worcester northwards and to the east of the Severn. There is no traditional village centre, the church and its setting forming a quiet backwater despite a nearby dual-carriageway. A guide to the parish refers to the 'much-loved 15th century church' and with 'all its trees, grass, roses and other flowers, the churchyard is a very pleasant place'. Elgar's grandparents are buried there and the guide tells of the composer, as a young man working in Worcester, often walking out to Claines to sit in the churchyard to read his music scores in quiet and lovely surroundings.

Also buried in the churchyard, though no local record now seems to exist, were the parents of Moon's great railway contemporary Sir Daniel Gooch, chairman of the Great Western Railway. Gooch's father, John, was buried there in 1833. He was travelling between his home in Bedlington in the north-east and his job in Tredegar in south Wales when, staying with his sister in Worcester, he became fatally ill and was buried locally. Gooch later refers in his diary to bringing his mother, who died in 1863, to Claines to be buried in the same vault as his father. Moon was still living in Claines at the time, by then he was chairman of the L&NW and would have known Gooch personally. It is a remarkable coincidence that the chairmen of the two greatest nineteenth century British railway companies had such close associations with Claines.

Within around twelve months of moving to Bevere, Moon was elected, at the vestry meeting of 24 April 1851, the vicar's churchwarden for the parish, an astonishing appointment for a thirty-six year old relative newcomer. Perhaps as was the case in his later life, he had already generously donated funds to the church. What is also remarkable is that he took on this duty after being elected a director of the London & North Western Railway.

*   *   *

The L&NW had been formed for less than five years when Moon became a director. The first meeting of its shareholders had been held in the Euston hotel on 7 August 1846 when the chairman reported that the act to consolidate the London & Birmingham Railway, Grand Junction Railway and Manchester & Birmingham Railway had received the royal assent on 16 July. Malcolm Reed in his history of the company has written that the Act of Parliament incorporating the L&NW was:

> A product of the parliamentary session which saw the greatest volume of railway legislation ever brought forward in the United Kingdom, resulting in the approval of over 4,500 miles of route and more than £131m in new capital. But whereas the majority of the railway companies which gained statutory authorisation in 1846 were new undertakings, floated in the enthusiasm of the railway mania, the L&NW Act sanctioned the amalgamation of three existing railways, two of them the earliest trunk lines in Britain. The company thus created had almost 400 miles of route already in operation and a share capital of over £1.7m, dwarfing even the Midland Railway, which had been formed by a similar tripartite merger two years earlier.

The Grand Junction (which the year before had absorbed the pioneering Liverpool & Manchester Railway) together with the London & Birmingham had been paying annually the maximum dividend allowed of 10%. When fully opened in September 1838 the L&B provided the only rail route from London to, not only the west midlands, but also the east midlands and Yorkshire. This monopolistic position had enabled the company to pay regularly 10% since 1842.

Directors representing the London & Birmingham and Grand Junction had met as a preliminary amalgamated board on 13 December 1845, when they elected as their chairman George Carr Glyn and as his deputy Charles Lawrence (chairmen of the L&B and GJ respectively). This board then continued to meet regularly even though the company was not authorised for another six months. The geographical extent of the railway was so great that among the items they first discussed was the problem of the 'different time for almost every place on the railway and the great advantage that could be almost universally felt if London Time could be adopted throughout the whole line'. They introduced standard time on the opening of through services via the Trent Valley line two years later. The design for a common seal of the new company was agreed which 'should represent the figure of Britannia, encircled by the Inscription "London & North Western Railway Company"'.

The two main constituents had obtained their own Acts of incorporation on the same day: 6 May 1833. The Liverpool & Manchester had already opened in 1830, proving an instant success, consistently generating dividends up to the capped 10%. The GJ matched their success. It is not surprising that Moon's father had listed these two predominantly Liverpool owned companies together with their trunk link to London, the London & Birmingham in his will.

Links to Bolton, Preston and Lancaster had contributed to the growth of the Grand Junction which also absorbed the Chester & Crewe Railway providing the link for the Holyhead route to Ireland. However initially it was not the GJ that supported the incorporation in 1844 of the Chester & Holyhead Railway, but the ambitious L&B. The GJ had taken exception to the Holyhead company's support for an independent line to Birkenhead as a more direct route to Merseyside. In fact such disagreements between the GJ and the L&B had grown to the extent that neither trusted the other. The L&B never saw the GJ as their *only* link to the north-west and the GJ resented their dependence on the L&B for access to the south. Negotiations to resolve these differences took place only after posturing by both sides. The L&B threatened to amalgamate directly with the Manchester & Birmingham Railway for access to the north; the GJ proposing retaliatory action by using a projected Great Western Railway line to Birmingham for the south.

The Manchester & Birmingham Railway, the third constituent of the L&NW was a Manchester promoted company for a more direct line to the south. Their link to the GJ at Crewe was originally seen as no more than a branch from a projected main line via Macclesfield and the Potteries. However faced with opposition from the GJ, who naturally saw the route as a competitor, and their own escalating costs of construction (in particular the massive viaduct at Stockport), the M&B were forced to compromise. When their Manchester to Crewe line opened in 1842 it was in agreement with the GJ who routed their Manchester service over the new direct line and allowed M&B trains to use their line to Birmingham. The M&B however continued to use the threat of competitive links to the south to force their way to the negotiating table and join the logical amalgamation of the two squabbling main companies. They strongly supported a line through the valley of the Trent to shorten the route by nine miles between Stafford on the GJ and Rugby on the L&B.

Five 'gentlemen' had met on the 11 April 1844 in Manchester to promote the Trent Valley company, Though Robert Gardner was in the chair the prime mover was Edward Tootal. Both men were associated in the Manchester textile business. Five directors of the M&B became members of the provisional board of what became the Trent Valley Railway which was authorised on 21 July 1845. But it was Tootal who led the TV delegations to both the L&B and the GJ, skilfully playing one off against the other. He initially reached agreement with the L&B for that company to lease the TV as part of their 'arrangements' for a 'direct communication between London and Manchester'. Strong objections from the GJ led to further discussions and the final resolution of the issue was a major factor in bringing about the formation of the L&NW. Two years and three days after their 'gentleman's meeting'in Manchester, Tootal was in the chair when the TV agreed to sell out, without a line yet built, to the three companies for £583,324! Tootal was subsequently to become an influential L&NW director.

Although the L&NW was a formidable railway from birth, with its main trunk lines from London to Birmingham, Liverpool and Manchester, the heady days of the 10% dividend were already over. Inevitably other railways sought their share of the traffic potential. Faced with the broad gauge Great Western Railway for the west midlands and Merseyside traffic and the Great Northern Railway for Yorkshire and across the Pennines to Manchester, the new company fought to maintain its position. Policies used were both expansionist and defensive, from building new lines to securing protective traffic pooling agreements and even crude blocking tactics.

Capital expenditure had doubled between the last year of the constituent companies in 1845 and when Moon became a director in 1851, but revenue increased by little more than a quarter and the dividend rate almost halved. It was not surprising that shareholders like Moon were dissatisfied and that emotional demands for closing the capital account were rampant.

The L&NW's 1846 act of incorporation had resulted in a complicated structure of main and subsidiary boards of directors. The main board comprised eight directors from the L&B, six from the GJ, three from the M&B and one from the Duke of Sutherland (a seat carried forward from the Liverpool & Manchester Railway days for his support in overcoming canal opposition to that company's authorisation). However subsidiary boards had to remain in place for five years in order to provide continuity with local committees based in London, Birmingham, Liverpool and Manchester. At the end of five years this multi-level structure was to be replaced by one central board of directors.

The chairman, George Carr Glyn, was a London banker who had early appreciated the importance of railways. At a time when many still saw railways as only isolated speculative ventures that could not compete nationally with canals, he took the lead amongst financiers in backing railway development. Born in 1797, the fourth son of Sir Richard Carr Glyn Bt, he became a partner in the family bank in 1819. He joined the promoters of the L&B in October 1830 and became its chairman in April 1837. To quote a 1960 bank review, when Glyn joined the railway world 'everything was strange and untried. But whereas others tried to devise new principles for the new power, he applied the ordinary rules of business combined with his own practical wisdom. With his experience of banking he insisted from the first on careful accounting, accurate returns and systematic costing'.

The L&B and subsequently the L&NW were not the only railway companies using the services of Glyn's bank. The bank backed the GW in 1833 and within ten years twenty two railway accounts were held. The rapid expansion of the 'railway mania' period gave them over a hundred railway company accounts in 1845 when almost one third of their total deposits were railway accounts. Glyn himself had also chaired the North Midland

Railway until the infamous Hudson took control in 1842.

The first general manager of the L&NW was Captain Mark Huish. A former Indian army officer he had begun his railway career in Scotland. Born in Nottingham in 1808 he entered the East India company in 1823. He served in India until 1834 when he returned to England for a three year leave, but decided not to return and sought employment at home. He became secretary to the Glasgow Paisley & Greenock Railway in November 1837 until he resigned in 1841 to become secretary and general manager of the Grand Junction Railway. After that company amalgamated with the Liverpool & Manchester he was appointed manager of the combined operations with Henry Booth of the L&M becoming the secretary. When the GJ in turn became part of the L&NW, Huish was given the overall general management with Booth continuing as northern secretary in Liverpool and the former L&B secretary, Creed, covering the south in London. Creed retired from his secretarial duties in 1848 and these were taken over by Charles Stewart.

Huish in his early railway career had proved an able administrator. He was to need all his skills and his dominant personality in the unprecedented task of managing such a large organisation as the L&NW.

CHAPTER 4

JOINING THE RAILWAY

When the L&NW directors met their shareholders at the company's February 1848 meeting they reported results 'after perhaps the most disastrous period upon record in our commercial history; a period of enterprise, speculation, and excitement having been followed by its natural consequence, a season of extreme stagnation and unprecedented difficulties'. Such was the legacy of the "railway mania".

Whilst accepting some reduction in times of difficulty, investors were soon demanding that returns be quickly brought back to previous levels. In an attempt to improve performance the company instigated in 1848 an internal investigation into their affairs under one of their directors, Captain C.R.Moorsom (rear admiral in 1851). Moon at the time had already begun probing the company for details on a number of matters, for example writing on the proposed merger of the company with the Great Western and the London & South Western. The following year he was urging the company to combine with others to obtain exemption from the Government's passenger tax. The 5% duty on all fares (except the 1d a mile 3rd. class on the "Parliamentary" stopping-at-all-station trains) was an issue, which Moon was to become personally involved with when chairman of the company.

Throughout 1849 there had been demands for closer scrutiny of railway accounts, from both the government and dissatisfied shareholders. However the attempt by the former to impose direct control was naturally opposed by the companies. A Shareholders' Audit Bill was promoted as an alternative to the Government's bill requiring each company to send one delegate to a permanent central board charged with continuously auditing all companies. The Shareholders' alternative was to have each company elect a committee of five shareholders to audit their own accounts.

10. Euston Station

The imposing railway Moon had joined: frontage of Euston completed in 1838, showing the Propylaeum (the 'Doric Arch') with its four lodges. NRM

11. G.C.Glyn

George Carr Glyn, chairman L&NW 1846-52,
created Lord Wolverton 1869. NRM

Though members had to be qualified as directors they had not to be on the board or an official of the company. This committee would elect two persons annually to act as the company's auditors for the ensuing year.

By the end of the year there had been a series of public regional meetings of shareholders on this matter. Possibly Moon may have attended one of these.

At the L&NW's 22 February 1850 shareholders'meeting a committee was urged to liaise with other companies to present the shareholders' version of auditing as 'the more effectual protection of the interests of the shareholders, but free from all Government interference or control'. Moon obviously attended this meeting for he'd asked for a private meeting afterwards with the company secretary, Charles Stewart to discuss *how he might proceed to become more directly involved in company affairs* [author's italics]'. What transpired is not known but subsequently, on 9 April, Moon wrote asking for a list of directors and the committees on which they served. Stewart obliged and a week later Moon returned the list. 'Requiring it only for the object which I have already explained, you may rely on no improper use being made of nor will it be shown to anyone.'

Moon may have considered the auditor route to join the company but it seems that the uncertainty caused by the rival bills may have decided him to pursue the director option. In the event both bills collapsed and a single compromise bill proposed but by then Moon was clearly seting his sights on becoming a director. On the 19 July he wrote a long private letter to Stewart advising him that he had:

> Not taken any steps beyond speaking to Friends for their votes as opportunity offered to place me on the Board of Direction of the London & Northwestern: in the uncertainty as to the effect of the Audit Bill (if passed) on this subject deeming it useless to give any formal notice of my intention to become a candidate for an early vacancy. Should the Shareholders Audit Bill have passed there would of necessity be such vacancy in February 1851, but as this is for the present hung-up I do not see my way so clearly; more especially as the number etc of the direction

will be undetermined until some definitive arrangements for the future be settled by the proprietors. With this view Mr Glyn told me [presumably in correspondence - see below] the directors (as I understand) intend to propose a Committee of Proprietors to aid the present direction in drawing out a plan for the future constitution of the board etc.

Now with a view to my ulterior purpose I think it would give me some more intimate acquaintance with the whole subject if I can become a member of this committee and therefore I shall be much obliged by your informing me with whom the selection of the parties to be proposed as members will originate, whether with the board of directors themselves or to be left by them to the proprietors. In the former case, having several friends amongst the directors, I would ask one of them to propose me or perhaps ask Mr Glyn as I am not acquainted with him and so would not be elected by favour. If the proprietors at the general meeting next month (which I shall attend) will be expected to propose this committee themselves perhaps you will indicate with what section it will originate as I shall be in Liverpool next week [and] I will attend to it there. I have no other reason for marking this communication private than the wish to be more careful on this occasion not to let my name be proposed to a general meeting without being tolerably secure beforehand of an election.

The reference to not wanting to be elected 'by favour' appears typical of the man, less so his sensitivity over possible rejection. This latter comment is significant as it highlights an aspect of his character not generally associated with him. It will be seen again in a later chapter when, as a senior director, he resigned over being rebuffed publicly by a colleague. His reference to "speaking to friends" is most likely to have meant former associates in the Liverpool cotton business, several of which were influential L&NW directors. No record has been found of the previous occasion he refers to, which possibly may have been over an auditor appointment.

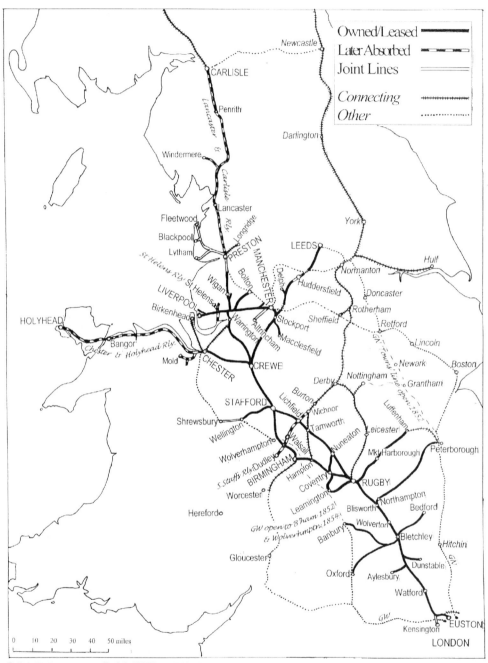

MAP 3   L&NWR : LINES OPEN BY END 1851

& connecting lines from original L&B (at Rugby and Hampton) plus GN and GW threats

Whatever further contacts Moon made they were clearly timely. By the time the L&NW's monthly board met on 15 August the decision to form a committee of shareholders to consider the question had been taken. At the following days's half- yearly shareholders' meeting it was reported 'that such Committee do consist of the following gentlemen, viz., Henry Crosfield, J.C.Ewart, George Hadfield, James James, J.M.McLeod, Richard Moon, the Hon P.S.Pierrepont, Thomas Porter and William Rutson'.

How the committee was appointed is not clear. Moon does not appear to have attended this meeting nor received prior notification, although he must have approved his name being put forward. He wrote the following to Stewart on the 3 September 1850. 'Having been some time from home [a long weekened] I have only this morning received yours of the 29th ult. It will be agreeable to me to act on the Committee to which you allude and I shall be glad if we are able to tender any service to the Company.' Whether all appointees served is not recorded. Those subsequently minuted as accepting were Moon, Rutson, McLeod, Hadfield and Crosfield; with Rutson appointed chairman and Crosfield secretary.

On the 9 September Moon formally notified Stewart 'that it is *my intention to become a Candidate when a vacancy may occur in the Board of Directors of the London & Northwestern Railway Company* [author's italics]'.

And so the die was cast. He was two weeks short of his 36th birthday.

In the meantime, though Moon had been appointed to the Shareholders' Committee and presumably waiting to be briefed on where and how to proceed, he did not relent in his criticism. Accompanying his notification of the 9th was another typical letter:

> What or if any provision is made in our accounts against the risk of fire to the stations, houses, warehouses, etc., of the company. It seems a very important circumstance and no doubt has had the attention of the Directors but as I do not see in the accounts any notice of it I shall be obliged by your informing me what is our position in regard to it. I should also wish to know to what parties the right of free passes over the line is at present conceded. Finally I would

ask whether the receipts of the Coventry & Nuneaton line are included in the general receipts of the company?

It is also evident from this letter that he had discussed with Stewart the effect on the company of the connection to Worcester being opened, saying he had also written to Captain Huish. He told Stewart:

> We ought specially to watch the new arrangements of the Bristol & Birmingham [B&B] on the opening of their loopline from Worcester to Abbots Wood that it should not act against us as it naturally inclines to favour the Southern route via Cheltenham: very different would have been the case had this loop been opened through to Stoke on the north of Worcester. *But this I believe is not intended* [author's italics].

Unless Moon was singularly unaware of local developments this latter comment needs explaining. The 'loopline' was part of the GW sponsored Oxford Worcester & Wolverhampton Railway authorized in 1846. It offered an alternative line through Worcester and Droitwich to the deviation proposed by the existing Birmingham & Gloucester Railway from Abbots Wood to Stoke (Moon's B&B in the quote above was the company formed from the merger of the Birmingham & Gloucester with the Bristol & Gloucester prior to their takeover by the Midland Railway in 1846). The Midland was given running powers over the loop and provided the service when the first section was opened in 1850 from Abbots Wood into Worcester. With the OW&W struggling to finance construction and to break the shackles of the broad gauge, Moon must have assumed that the link from Droitwich to the Birmingham line, which was not vital for their own service, would finally be abandoned. Cuttings and embankments for the whole loop line from Abbots Wood to Stoke Works had been substantially in place as early as 1847, being reported in a 'forward state' by the local *Berrow's Journal* of 25 March. A year later the same paper reported that the 'line had been levelled and the ballast placed'. Within months of Moon's letter to Stewart work had recommenced on the Stoke link (although the line was not opened until February 1852).

No details have been found of the investigation carried out by Rutson's committee, nor Moon's role. He clearly would not have taken his duties lightly and he persisted with his other queries. A letter of 18 October insists that the fire risk information be sent to him and that the failure to open the Stour Valley line was 'an ugly item'. In December he was seeking an urgent interview with Stewart, but by then possibly to seek the views of senior officers on behalf of the committee.

Belatedly, at their 14 December meeting, the directors themselves agreed to form a committee to prepare a report for consideration. This committee, under Glyn himself, reported to a special meeting of the board on 9 January 1851. They agreed the principle that 'supervision by committees of directors with paid officers responsible for the conduct and management of their respective departments, reporting periodically through general committees to a central controlling authority, is very well suited to meet the general requirements of the service'. They thought that the 'system now in force ought not to be materially altered'. The question remained, however, as to the number of directors necessary to perform the central duties with 'regularity and efficiency'. The ending of the old structure meant that effectively the board was reduced to eighteen directors. Glyn's committee therefore concluded that 'in order to meet the requirements of the London & North Western line proper and represent the company at the boards of the sixteen undertakings in which the company are interested, the number of directors should be 30'. Two days later Rutson presented his committee's findings.

Having already had the directors' report the shareholder representatives agreed that the committee system with paid officers was 'well suited' and that the number of directors should be increased. Not surprisingly, considering some had a vested interest in the outcome, they also concluded that, 'after duly considering the detailed statement of the duties required from the directors laid before this committee by the officers of the company, it is the unanimous opinion of the committee that the number of directors should, as recommended in the report submitted by the board of directors, be increased to Thirty'. They did disagree though with Glyn's committee over the re-electing of directors. Six directors were to retire annually and seek re-election. The board wanted all six to be able to do so, the shareholders only four. The board formally dissented insisting that all six, if they wished to be, should be re-elected. The shareholders' insistence on the enforced annual resignation of two directors was to become a bone of contention that was to last well into Moon's chairmanship years.

In selecting the twelve new directors some lobbying would no doubt have taken place; but in many cases the choice would have been obvious, for example where senior local committee members or former directors of constituent companies were candidates, particularly if they were leading representatives of specific interest or trade groups. In Moon's case there would have been many factors that offset his lack of railway experience, not least of which must been have his willingness to become involved, his and his family's substantial shareholding and his Liverpool business experience. Also his probing of accounts and operating practice could well have marked him out as being less difficult inside the company than outside. A further factor may have been location in an area critical for expansion plans into south Wales.

Whatever the reason, Moon's application was successful. At the tenth half-yearly meeting of the company on 21 February 1851 he was elected one of the twelve new directors. He was exceptional in that he was the only one not currently active in any firm or business, and apart from James Heywood, a Manchester banker, all the others had already been railway directors. Half of them were already involved with the L&NW as former local directors: G.R.Chappell, Sir Charles Douglas, John Ellis, R.D.Mangles, T.W.Rathbone and Edward Tootal. Ellis in fact had become chairman in 1849 of the Midland Rly. Of the remaining, J.Brook had been associated with the L&NW's Yorkshire companies, The Hon P.S.Pierrepont and H.W.Blake were directors of local companies backed by the L&NW and J.C.Ewart was chairman of the Liverpool committee of shareholders. Interestingly only three had been on Rutson's committee: Pierrepont, Ewart and Moon.

Moon was one of the six new members present at the first meeting of the new board convened the same day as his election. It had taken him less than four years to progress from self-imposed retirement to a seat on the board of the country's leading company. Within a month he agreed to serve on the board's Audit Committee and within a year he was serving on seven other L&NW committees and chairing one of them.

From clues in his later correspondence with the railway it does seem that Moon did not initially intend to become so involved. Whatever work he undertook for the railway inevitably meant long hours of travel and time away from home. His family was growing, in June 1851 his wife gave birth to their second daughter Edith May, their fifth child under ten, and he had made commitments to his parish. From Easter 1851 he was the vicar's churchwarden for Claines and despite the growing intensity of his railway work he did not resign from this office until Easter 1858.

In the 1850s the patron of the living at Claines was Sir Offley Wakeman Bt. of nearby Perdiswell Hall. The parish was also responsible for St George's Chapel in Barbourne where the Claines vicar was the patron. St George's was built as a wooden mission chapel (the current church dates from around 1895) to serve the developing fringe of northern Worcester. Moon was quickly engaged with both churches, in particular the increasing expense of St George's.

Inheriting a loss brought forward in the vestry accounts, he immediately set to work to balance the books. He became closely involved in enforcing the church rate and serving as a member of the local 'Nuisance Removal Committee'. Compulsory Church rates had long been a source of conflict between dissenters and the established church and were not abolished until 1868. The last three of his seven vestry accounting years were with solicitor Martin Curtler who, as has been noted, was the son of Moon's neighbour T.G.Curtler.

Finding himself with such an influential neighbour, Moon could have had no better introduction to established local society. Both Curtler senior and church patron Wakeman were politically Conservative, actively supporting protectionism and strongly opposed to the introduction of the catholic hierarchy. Moon seems then to have been sympathetic to all three causes.

Although never apparently interested in aspiring to be a member of the land owning elite, he believed in maintaining the social order and had little time for the vagaries of indecisive management, whether it be in the vestry or national Government (in a letter to his L&NW chairman in 1858 he was particularly scathing about Lord John Russell's vacillations).

Agricultural agitation against free trade policy had found a ready voice in the local Worcester press. A leading article in *Berrow's Journal* in June 1848, on sugar duties and the 'West India Distress' had complained of the 'ruinous concession to the grasping and destructive spirit of free trade', that slave owners would be encouraged as there was no differentiation between 'Slave Free' and 'Slave' sugar. In May 1849 the paper had reported the 'Great Agricultural Meeting' for the county at which the depression in agriculture and commerce was reviewed. T.G.Curtler was a key speaker complaining of the partiality and unjustness of free trade. By January 1850 around a thousand local owners and occupiers of land petitioned for a further demonstration.

Moon had little in common with the tenant farmers who comprised the majority of those demanding the return of protectionism. However close contact with Curtler, actively campaigning in favour, could have been decisive in persuading Moon to support publicly the cause. In June 1850 Curtler attended the National Protection meeting in Liverpool and Moon may have accompanied him, using the opportunity to lobby for his railway cause.

Curtler chaired the county's Protectionist banquet the following May and with Moon present proposed the toast "Protection to British Industry and Capital". As a representative of rural England still smarting from the repeal of the Corn Laws, Curtler clearly thought little of politicians, a view to be echoed by Moon in later life. Curtler railed that:

> Ever since that fatal moment in 1846, when men in high places and great authority thought fit entirely to change their opinions and turn round their own policy - when they thought themselves justified in repudiating and throwing to the winds all their former speeches and opinions - when they thought themselves justified in breaking their solemn vows - when they felt no hesitation in handing over their best friends and supporters to their enemies.

These were early days in Moon's public career and he was soon to subjugate his private political views to the interests of his railway.

When chairman of the railway, he was at pains to adopt a more pragmatic approach, seeing it expedient to support the Government of the day, but only if necessary to safeguard the interests of his company. He certainly did not hesitate to berate the government if he thought the reverse was the case.

Also current at the time of his churchwardenship were fears roused by the attempted introduction of a Catholic hierarchy. Protests were held throughout the country. It was under the headline "Papal Aggression" that the local press for example reported the meeting of the established clergy of the archdeanery of Worcester which included Palmer, the vicar of Claines. This was followed by a petition, under the heading "Popery" in which over seven hundred leading inhabitants of the county sought a meeting 'to consider what steps it may be desirable to take with reference to the late measure of the Court of Rome in appointing Prelates having jurisdiction within this country'.

Moon was a signatory to this petition together with Curtler and Wakeman and all three were among those attending the subsequent meeting held in Worcester's Shire Hall. Significantly Curtler seconded an amendment to the proposed address to the bishop which further protested against 'the introduction into the services of our established church, by some of the clergy, of the principles and practices of the Church of Rome'. With Curtler, Wakeman and Palmer all active "no popists", and with Curtler's anti-tractarian views it is reasonable to suppose that Claines was a more evangelical parish and that its newly appointed churchwarden would have been similarly inclined.

At his first annual vestry as warden, April 1851, Moon was already a member of the committee approving the accounts. The accounts which the committee had passed for the previous year showed annual expenses to be £124.15s.1¾d. with a small 'out of pocket' balance of £1.16s.8½d. The committee also passed the charity accounts for the parish which showed a deficit of £11.13s.4½d. on a total of £31.10s.0d. At the end of Moon's tenure he handed over a favourable vestry balance of £28.16s.6d. With expenses of both churches to cover Moon had maintained a favourable balance in excess of £20 for each of his years in office.

Figures have not been found which showed the state of the charities' accounts although it would be out of character if Moon

12. Bevere, Claines
The west front of 'Bevere', the house at Claines, Worcester,
occupied by Moon 1851-68. N.Coverdale

13. Claines church
Claines Parish Church. Moon was the Vicar's
churchwarden 1851-58. Author

had not quickly also brought these into balance. Throughout Moon's period as warden it is clear that he took his fund raising duties seriously. As was to be frequently the case with the L&NW, Moon was not afraid to force through unpopular measures if he thought them necessary. At a Claines meeting held on the 3 September 1857 Moon's proposal, seconded by Wakeman, for a 1¼d. church rate to recover estimated costs of £102.5s.0d. was rejected by a show of hands of 35 to 28. Moon immediately reacted by enforcing a poll of all ratepayers.

The poll took three days 'owing to the state of the roads'. Eventually 320 were found for the rate and 265 against. Opposition to paying rates to the established church was of course not confined to parishes such as Claines. The amount of 1¼d. was not just the issue: an increase from 1d. had been accepted in previous years. At stake was whether the church should continue to exercise the right to obtain funds through a compulsory levy. It was the wardens' responibility to ensure payment was obtained.

Problems in obtaining payment were highlighted in April 1855 when the wardens were 'instructed to enforce payment of all rates for last year not hitherto paid except in cases where in their opinion the parties should be exempted from poverty'. This resolution was passed at a meeting chaired by Moon himself (the Rev Palmer had left and his replacement Crowther had not yet arrived).

Perhaps the most remarkable of all Moon's parish duties involved his membership of a sub-committee formed following a special meeting called 'for the purpose of considering what steps should be taken in this parish with reference to the Nuisance Removal Act of 14 August 1855'. Wakeman chaired this meeting (the new vicar was still not appointed) and Moon, then his fellow warden, and three others were appointed as the 'Nuisance Removal Committee'. Under the provisions of an Act 'to consolidate and amend the Nuisances Removal and Diseases Prevention Acts 1848 and 1849', if there were no health or highway authorities already in existence, such a local committee had to be formed. In 1850 the town council of Worcester had voted against appointing a 'Medical Officer of Health' suggesting as an alternative an 'Inspector of Nuisances'. The Act required each vestry to appoint up to twelve members chosen annually for this purpose. Their remit included investigating 'any pool, ditch, gutter, watercourse, privy, urinal, cesspool, drain, or ashpit so foul as to be a nuisance or injurious to health, any animal so kept as to be a nuisance or injurious to health', and any 'accumulation or deposit'. The latter could be excused if proven to be necessary for any business or manufacture providing it had 'not been kept longer than is necessary...and that the best available means have been taken for protecting the public from injury to health thereby'.

The committee was empowered to enter premises, examine drains, inspect food, etc., and to enforce remedial action through the courts with heavy penalties for default. It would be easy to caricature a grim-faced Moon intimidating likely offenders, That he was involved at all, even on the periphery of such matters as sanitation and drainage, is an indication of the extent to which he was prepared to undertake unglamorous work.

Other matters in which Moon found himself representing the parish were in negotiations with the local gas company and insuring against fire. Both churches were insured for the value of £500 each. The vestry agreed with Moon's proposal in 1852 to pay £30 to the gas company to liquidate the debt on the gas fittings at St George's chapel, and a year later to his proposal to pay off the balance of £20.13s.8d. Economy in the use of gas was to feature strongly in his early work for the L&NW.

When Martin Curtler and Moon were the joint wardens they dealt with many minor charity and legal matters. Typically some were simple bequests, for example George and Ann Wingfield's who invested £100 in Government securities for income to buy gowns for poor women with the 'minister and churchwardens to be the managers'. Curtler also represented both Wakeman and Moon in other issues.

Moon's name had begun to appear in the Worcester press for other matters, for example his contribution in 1850 for the erection of a chapel and other improvements at the infirmary, and as one of the subscribers for a new organ in the Corn Exchange. In February the following year he was listed, unaccompanied (his wife would have been pregnant with their fifth child), among the "elite" of the county attending the 'Masonic Ball'. It is not known if he was actually a mason. If he was, no evidence has been found that he was active.

He did not attend the anniversary celebration procession later that year when 'nothing like it had been seen in the city for fifty years'.

He and Curtler were each £5 subscribers for promoting the holding of the Royal Agricultural Society's meeting in Worcester in 1853. An 1851 list of those taking out game certificates included Wakeman and Curtler but not Moon. Also in his early years at Bevere he found himself the only "esquire" serving on a special jury in a county court action to recover £177 in a claim that faulty goods had been sold. The plaintiff was a chain maker and the defendant a manufacturer of nails and small chains, both from Cradley near Stourbridge. The case rested on whether or not the chain was of 'merchantable' quality: the testing of the chains being the issue. No doubt Moon fell back on his Liverpool trading background in making judgement. And this same background must have been one of the reasons he found himself, amongst his many other railway company duties, chosen to chair the board's Stores Committee.

CHAPTER 5

COMMITTEE MAN

With its new thirty strong membership, the L&NW board was able to consolidate its working through a more structured committee system. There were ten main committees ranging from line operations to overall staff functions. Eleven more committees covered associated companies and subsidiaries and another eleven the joint operations with independent companies. A central controlling committee, a form of cabinet headed by the chairman, comprised the senior directors and others representing the main committees.

The dominant operating committees, such as the 'Locomotive' and the 'Road & Traffic' met as three regional sub-committees based on the original constituent companies in London, Liverpool and Manchester.

In 1852 Moon was, in addition to the Audit and Stores Committees already mentioned, a member of Rates & Taxes, Capital Expenditure, the Southern section of the Works Construction & Estates, and the joint company committees for the Birmingham and Shropshire Union canal companies. He had also undertaken to devise a staff superannuation scheme. By 1853 he was additionally on the joint committees for the Wolverhampton Joint Station, Stour Valley and South Staffordshire railways. And by 1854 he had joined the Superannuation Committee.

Within months of joining the company, at the 12 April board meeting, he together with three of his colleagues were also delegated to join the 'board of the Newport Abergavenny & Hereford Railway if requested'. This resolution followed a letter fom Mr Hughes of Worcester 'in reference to the formation of a line of railway from Worcester to Pontypool'. It is not known whether this Hughes was Moon's Bevere landlord and it is not clear why such a letter appeared to prompt the minute. The project was already well known to at least the senior L&NW directors.

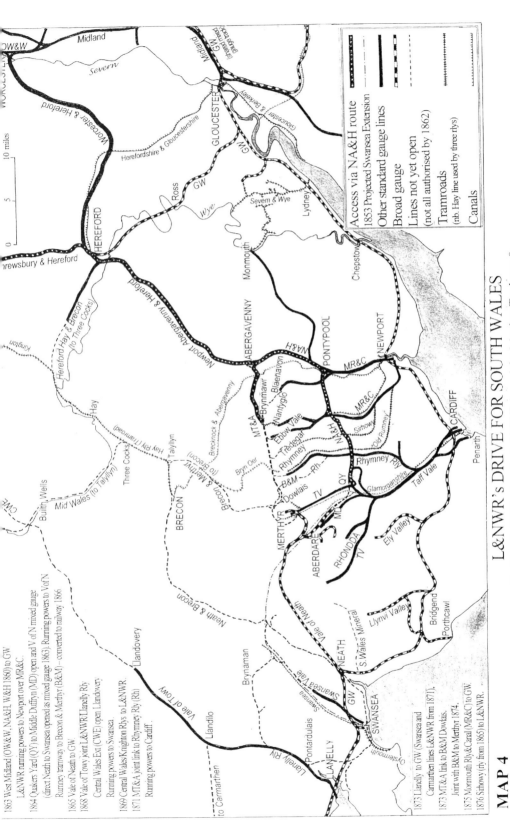

MAP 4

L&NWR's DRIVE FOR SOUTH WALES

Position in 1862 when the L&NWR leased the Merthyr Tredegar &
Abergavenny Rly at the heart of the Coal and Iron Districts

Legend:
- Access via NA&H route
- 1853 Projected Swansea Extension
- Other standard gauge lines
- Broad gauge
- Lines not yet open (not all authorised by 1862)
- Tramroads (nb. Hay line used by three rlys)
- Canals

1863 West Midland (OW&W, NA&H, W&H 1860) to GW
L&NWR running powers to Newport over MR&C.

1864 Quakers Yard (QY) to Middle Duffryn (MD) open and V of N mixed gauge
(direct. Neath to Swansea opened as mixed gauge 1863). Running powers to V of N
Rumney tramway to Brecon & Merthyr (B&M) — converted to railway 1866

1865 Vale of Neath to GW

1868 Vale of Towy joint L&NWR Llanelly Rly.
Central Wales Ext (CWE) open Llandovery.
Running powers to Swansea.

1869 Central Wales Knighton Rlys to L&NWR.

1871 MT&A joint link to Rhymney Rly (Rh)
Running powers to Cardiff.

1873 Llanelly to GW (Swansea and
Carmarthen lines L&NWR from 1871).

1873 MT&A link to B&M Dowlais.
Joint with B&M to Merthyr 1874.

1875 Monmouth Rly&Canal (MR&C) to GW

1876 Sirhowy (rly from 1865) to L&NWR.

A line from Worcester to south Wales had been one of many promoted at the time of the "mania", part of what later became the L&NW's drive for the south Wales mineral traffic. One of the two prongs of the L&NW's approach to secure a share of this trade was through Worcester (the other was via Shrewsbury). At the next L&NW half-yearly meeting (August 1851) the chairman was to report the progress being made.

Glyn told shareholders that he had ordered surveys to be made for a continuation of the Buckinghamshire lines to Worcester and Cheltenham, that a line from Worcester to Hereford was being 'actively promoted' and that 'from Hereford to Abergavenny there is a line on the narrow gauge already sanctioned'. By narrow, he meant standard as opposed to the GW's broad gauge.

The Buckinghamshire Railway, though nominally independent was leased to and controlled by the L&NW whose interest had always been motivated by the potential to expand westwards. However a route onwards from Worcester into south Wales had first been promoted by the Welsh Midland Railway in 1846, a product of the 'mania', which though never authorised had negotiated with two other companies from Hereford, one southwards to Pontypool and the other north to Shrewsbury. The line to Pontypool was the narrow gauge Glyn had said was already sanctioned (authorised in 1846), the Newport Abergavenny & Hereford referred to above.

On the failure of the Welsh Midland the NA&H had amended their Act to connect at Hereford directly with the line authorised to Shrewsbury, the Shrewsbury & Hereford Railway, and also obtain powers to extend beyond Pontypool to the Taff Vale railway at Quakers Yard. Such a company would thus be 'accommodating the most important mineral district lying between Pontypool and Merthyr, and forming the connecting link between Merthyr, Liverpool, Manchester and the northern districts of England'.

As with many companies at the time the NA&H had languished through lack of capital and their powers had not been exercised when Moon came into the picture in 1851. These would lapse if work was not commenced by August of that year. This had led the company to renew their attempts to secure the finance to start acquiring the land and various tramroad companies forming part of the route. The L&NW's initial response had been to encourage the 'landed proprietors and others interested in the district to proceed in the formation of the railway' and, as has been seen, approve their own directors joining the company's board. Many of the local subscriptions had not been taken up and moving quickly the L&NW secured some of the forfeited shares. And at a meeting of the NA&H on 20 May 1851 the number of directors was increased from five to fifteen. The additional ten were to comprise representatives of the 'Monmouthshire Mineral District', Hereford 'City and Council', and the L&NW in the persons of Moon, Blake and Carnegie.

However the link which Glyn reported as being 'actively promoted' between Worcester to Hereford was far from straightforward. Following the failure of the Welsh Midland a line had been unsuccessfully promoted in 1847 by the Midland Railway from their Birmingham & Gloucester line. During the depression that followed little further was done until stirred by the NA&H activity and a separate Worcester & Hereford Railway company promoted. Moon was not present at the 28 June 1851 meeting of Worcester townspeople convened for considering this project, as both the L&NW and the Midland Railway were represented by their shared solicitor Samuel Carter, who promised the railway companies' support.

Moon was present however at a further meeting of the W&H promoters on 16 July held at the Ledbury "Feathers Hotel" and reported in the *Worcester Herald* as being 'numerously and influentially attended', Earl Somers the Lord Lieutenant of Herefordshire presiding. As this was the first time Moon had spoken in public on behalf of his railway it is worth quoting the report of his remarks in full. Some of his comments also provide interesting background to the problems of overcoming the continuing opposition from some landowners to railways generally and the difficulties in raising finance in the aftermath of the 'mania':

> Mr. Moon, in acknowledging on the part of the London and North Western Company the vote of thanks to them and the Midland Company, said that although the directors were completely strangers to the landowners and inhabitants of that district, they were nevertheless most desirous of assisting them to a line of railway. The basis on which they

stood was to do all in their power to promote the good of the whole community, by bringing as many lines of railway into operation as could be usefully employed. (Hear.) He was certain that the present line would be for the mutual benefit of the company and all concerned, and he could only add that it was the object of the directors to promote the progress of human improvement, and the rendering of mankind a united community by means of a common centre of amity and civilisation. (Cheers.)

Following an eulogy on the benefits of railways by Thomas Heywood of Ledbury, who was to be the chairman of the W&H company, Moon then rose to state what the intentions of the L&NW were in regard to the proposed railway. He said that it was:

To aid the formation of the line in every way in their power and with the most perfect good faith, because they were satisfied that it was really required by the wants of the locality. (Hear.) Mr. Heywood had so well stated the reasons in favour of the line, and he (Mr. Moon) so entirely concurred in his views, that it was quite unnecessary for him to say more on that head; but he trusted that the landowners of the district, who had so great an interest in the matter, and all others concerned, would bestir themselves as so important an object deserved, and he believed that they would experience little or no difficulty. (Hear.)

He was sure that it must be evident to all that every aid in their power should be afforded by the landowners along the proposed line, and moreover he believed that it was their wish to support it. (Hear.) A branch to Ledbury, if that plan were determined upon, would give that town the advantage of railway communication and bring it in contact with the important districts on either side. (Hear.) Besides his connection with the London and North Western Company, which had under its management the whole *foci* of railways of the North and North West of England extending to Scotland, he was a director of the Newport and Abergavenny Company, whose line traversed a district of which the population was wholly manufacturing or mining; so that whether they looked to the north or south they would have the means of carrying their produce to the best description of market, and they would also be furnished with the means of enjoying those improvements in civilisation and the amenities of life, so appropriately referred to by Mr. Heywood. (Hear.)

Again he would say that he hoped they would not find any opposition as in old times, when to run a railway through a country was regarded as an evil, and its introduction steadfastly resisted, but on the contrary he hoped, and he had no doubt, but that all parties would be agreed as to the advantages to be derived from the line and anxious to promote its success. (Cheers.)

With a capital of £360,000 in 36,000 shares the first local advertisements seeking applicants for the W&H (deposit £1 per share) appeared locally in September. The support of the L&NW and Midland companies was indicated in the listing of the sixteen member board, only five were local directors. There were five representing L&NW interests made up of two from the L&NW (Moon and E.Tootal) and three from the Buckinghamshire Railway. The Midland had three members and the remaining three represented the NA&H.

With the backing of the L&NW the directors considered purchasing the Hereford & Gloucester Canal for part of the line of the railway. Heywood and Moon formed part of a committee that met at the "Foley Arms" Great Malvern on 12 August and reported favourably that the canal section between Ledbury and Hereford, which had been opened only from 1845, 'would be very advantageous to the projected railway'.

Meeting at the "Star & Garter" in Worcester on 22 August, the W&H directors resolved 'that the respective members of this board be requested to take such measures as may appear best to them, to promote applications for shares from parties in the towns and locality immediately interested as well as in more remote parts'. They were not successful. By November a local paper reported that the *Railway*

Gazette was 'amazed' that Worcester had not subscribed for more than a thousand shares. By March of the following year, Moon, in explaining the still unsatisfactory financial position to the L&NW board, 'urged upon members of the Board who had not already subscribed to take each 50 shares in that undertaking'.

In the meantime the L&NW had reviewed with the Midland their position with the NA&H, Moon being one of the directors involved. At their meeting on 18 October 1851 the L&NW board voted on a motion that it was 'inexpedient' for the company to 'pledge itself' to support a company 100 miles from its system. This was only narrowly lost. Moon then raised the question of the W&H, pointing out that, with local support falling so far short of expectations, it was likely the L&NW and Midland would have to give financial support. Directors then had further reservations, Glyn even suggested limiting the line, 'for the present', from Worcster to Malvern.

Clearly dissatisfied with progress in the area the L&NW delegated in January 1852 Thomas Smith (deputy chairman), Robert Benson and Carnegie to negotiate with the NA&H to 'best secure the influence of the L&NW Company in that undertaking'. A 'working agreement' was announced by the NA&H in February which included financial terms for the L&NW to work both their line and the W&H when they were opened. This was premature in the case of the W&H. Opposed in March by a wide coalition of interests (GW, Worcester canals, local turnpikes and the Severn shippers) their bill was thrown out in the Lords. An unanabashed NA&H however reported that 'the agreement between the L&NW and the NA&H continues in force and it is intended to apply in the next session for parliamentary powers to amalgamate this company with the L&NW'.

At the L&NW's September board Moon and Tootal were requested to join, as representatives of the company, the board of the proposed Swansea Junction Railway. This line had been projected as a continuation of the already approved Taff Vale Extension of the NA&H from Quakers Yard, up the Aberdare valley and across the head of the valleys into the Tawe valley for Swansea. Incidentally this was the L&NW board meeting at which Glyn's letter of resignation was tabled. For so long the driving force for routes into south Wales he felt he could no longer ignore medical advice and that the directors needed to replace him with 'a successor able to devote his whole time to and more capable of sustaining the increasing responsibilities of the position'.

It was Moon who submitted to the October board his and Tootal's joint report advising that the projected Swansea Junction should, 'with some assistance ' be ready for Parliament by the next session. The report highlighted the threat from the broad gauge GW and reported progress on N&AH and the need to support the Swansea Extension as the means of 'connecting the whole of the Narrow Gauge Lines, and to bring them by means of the Worcester & Hereford Lines into direct and continuous communication with the Midland and North Western Railways system'.

It was resolved that as it was of the 'utmost importance to the interests of this company and its Midland ally to promote a narrow gauge communication with south Wales, this board depute Mr Moon and Mr Tootal to assist the Midland Joint Committee … to determine the best mode of carrying out the Swansea Junction Railway'.

In the 1853 parliamentary session the L&NW and Midland again cooperated in supporting a resubmitted Worcester & Hereford Bill but now they were opposed by the GW specifically promoting their own line, the Worcester & Hereford Junction Railway. The GW only withdrew their Bill when securing parliament's refusal to grant L&NW and Midland any powers to lease or work the line. On that condition the original W&H Railway was authorised. Although Moon and Tootal were among the fifteen directors named, the L&NW's position was untenable without powers to use the line. And in view of parliamentary hostility to railway mergers in general, the Bill for the L&NW/NA&H amalgamation was withdrawn.

Plans for the L&NW entering south Wales through Worcester were thereafter never realised. The Swansea Junction Extension Bill was rejected, the Buckinghamshire was never extended and no agreement reached with the Oxford Worcester & Wolverhampton Railway which would have been necessary for the approach to Worcester. The OW&W had been authorised in 1845 to build from the GW's Oxford branch through Evesham and Worcster and from there via Dudley to join the Grand Junction at Wolverhampton; it was to stumble from one financial crisis to another before finally falling into the GW camp.

Nevertheless the L&NW attempted to honour their agreement to work the NA&H. The line from Hereford to Pontpool was opened on 2 January 1854, (the Shrewsbury & Hereford a few weeks earlier). At Shrewsbury a connection was made to another local company, the Shrewsbury & Chester (the L&NW's own branch from Crewe to Shrewsbury, authorised in 1853, was not opened until 1858). Disputes between the L&NW and the two Shrewsbury companies led to delays in the natural flow of traffic and must have been an embarrassment to Moon. He had remained a local director of the NA&H and was present at their meeting in August 1854 when the directors regretted 'their inability to give a satisfactory report of the working of the line by the L&NW' and complained that 'due provision has not been made by the L&NW for the development of your property'. Their report went further, stating that unless an impartial joint committee under an independent manager was set up then the arrangements with the L&NW should end. The arrangements did end.

Although the L&NW continued to loan carriages and wagons, the NA&H purchased locomotives from the contractor, Thomas Brassey, who was working the S&H. For a few months Brassey worked both lines before the NA&H took over themselves from the beginning of 1855 (the L&NW withdrew their stock in April and Brassey in May).

With the withdrawal of L&NW support the W&H was unable to complete their line, all work stopping in early 1856. The NA&H extension to Quakers Yard was also suspended. But by then Moon was preoccupied with other aspects of L&NW affairs.

* * *

Though Moon's home near Worcester made it convenient for the L&NW to use him to represent their interests in the west Midlands, his immediate benefit to the company was to be in administrative matters. As has been seen at the first meeting possible following his election as a director, he had joined the Audit Committee. He served that committee until March 1855, missing only three of the monthly meetings held. It was this committee that uncovered in early 1854 'the serious losses which the company had sustained through various acts of embezzlement committed by Mr Goalen, the chief accountant and superintendent of this [Audit] office'. Glyn attended the committee and suggested changes which included 'an improved method of remitting monies to Euston'. It was resolved that the board approve 'the officers of Account and Audit be separated and rendered as distinct as the nature of the business permits'.

Although the two offices were separated and made independent of each they remained under the overall control of the Euston based Southern Division secretary Charles Stewart. Hoy was appointed chief accountant at £400 p.a. and Stephen Reay given responsibility for the audit office at £350 p.a. Later Moon was to take this one step further when subsequently he recommended the separation of the financial and secretarial affairs of the company. The auditor Reay rose to become the company secretary during Moon's chairmanship of the company and one of his closest confidants.

Some of the other Audit Committee issues covered included the returns made to the Railway Clearing House and the need for more meaningful cost accounts from Pickfords and Chaplin & Horne. As carrying agents for the company their costs were thought in November 1854 to be too high and the committee called attention to 'the mode in which these accounts are rendered and that a more extensive examination should be made'. The future role of these agents was to exercise Moon greatly as his responsibilities widened.

Moon was a member of the Rates & Taxes committee from 1852. From a letter he wrote in October 1855, over a change in the meeting date, he regretted he could not attend as it would be 'first meeting of that committee which I haven't attended since my appointment'. It seems the date was changed for the minutes of the October meeting showed he was present. He maintained his hundred percent attendance record until he retired from the committee following a reorganisation in 1858. Almost as consistent was his colleague Joseph Brook who with E.Tootal formed a sub-committee for the many reviews held with solicitors on rating assessments, appeals and payments.

Railways generally had been challenging the principle of how they were assessed for local rates since their early days. It was probably too late when Moon became involved to change this. The basis used was 'train mileage', i.e., the miles of railway in the parish and the frequency of the trains run over them. Substantial sums were at stake: for example it was accepted as a compromise when the St Pancras vestry reduced the assessment on the company from £34,331 to £21,000 (this large sum presumably covered Euston and its approaches).

With many parishes looking upon their local railways as fruitful sources of income there were many more references to negotiations to effect reductions. At a 1855 meeting it had been reported that the Audit department's returns to Birmingham parish had shown 'Train Miles' higher than that based on the company's "Time Bills". The Executive Committee's attention was drawn to the need for a more careful preparation of the Train Mileage Return 'having reference to the effect of such returns upon rating'. Part of the problem stemmed from the days when railways were first opened and assessed no differently from canals whose property was not burdened by carrying costs, it being thought that railways would follow the same principle and not necessarily have the cost of running the trains! Unfair valuations of railway property became even more of an issue towards the end of Moon's chairmanship when local government reforms were introduced.

The train miles discrepancy could have been an issue when Moon reported in 1856 the unsuccessful result of his negotiations with the Board of Guardians of Birmingham 'as to settlements of Poor Rates in dispute'. At the same meeting the company's solicitor reported that he had been asked to prepare clauses giving amended powers of appeal against these rates as the Government were introducing a bill for the amendment of the Poor Law. The committee resolved that 'every exertion' be made with other companies to get the clauses inserted. [Railways failed to obtain their 'relief of railways' clause in the Poor Law Amendment Act.] The dispute with Birmingham eventually went to arbitration and the report on the settlement, read at Moon's last Rating meeting on 12 March 1858, reduced by half the assessment on the company's stations and lines in the area.

In the settlement of water rates the committee's negotiations frequently overlapped agreements made by the company's Stores Committee. As a member of both committees Moon became personally involved in many water company negotiations, which will be covered in later chapters.

Another example of Moon's commitment was when in April 1852 he agreed, in consultation with the leading managers, to decide 'on the precise objects to be secured by any plan for providing a superannuation and casualty fund' for the staff. This was also to be 'combined with a provision for the widows of servants of the company and to ascertain whether such objects may not be obtained on reasonable terms through any association or through the medium of some established insurance company'.

As ideas for a scheme had not been forthcoming Moon found himself at the end of the year writing, on Christmas day, determinedly to Stewart the company secretary as follows:

> Beyond your own I have not received so far any suggestions on the subject….With regard to the different principle on which we start, viz., one mutual insurance, the other by a company, I will consider it, but meanwhile it occurs to me to point out that this must be for the determination of the board….I propose that we should have the next meeting with officers on Wednesday to arrive at some idea of the wishes of the general body of officers; without this I shall still be very much in the dark, but I will not despair of satisfying the majority.

He did reach agreement with the managers and presented a scheme to the board which, after minor amendments, was agreed. At the February 1853 shareholders' meeting the company adopted the 'Mutual Assurance & Superannuation Fund for the salaried servants of the company' with the 'concurrence of the company's officers'. And the directors 'have considered it right to aid by a liberal contribution the fund in question'.

As if all this was not enough Moon undertook yet another task that demonstrated his willingness to apply himself to what he later referred to as 'hard labour', this was the Stores Committee, the committee he was to dominate for nine years from April 1852 to March 1861. During this period the committee met on one hundred and seventy three occasions, an average of once every two and half to three weeks. Moon missed only two of them and not until he was elected deputy chairman of the company did he relinquish his duties.

"Stores" is too prosaic a word to describe the committee's scope. The committee had been first established in 1848 as a result of the Moorsom enquiry into the 'state of the establishment, as to salaries and wages, stores and current expenditure of all kinds, and the alternatives and changes which may be required'. The enquiry's recommendation on stores had read:

> Another subject which has occupied our attention is that of stores required for the several departments and looking to the large amount expended annually and to the evils inseparable from the practice now in force of allowing a variety of authorities, committees, heads of departments and storekeepers to enter into contracts and make purchases, we strongly recommend that for the future, all stores of whatever description be obtained by contract founded on public tender and that they be placed under the management of a General Storekeeper. We would suggest also that a Special Committee be appointed to whom the details should be referred for arrangement.

On the 13 May 1848 the board 'approved the principle of obtaining stores by contract founded on public tenders' and appointed a committee to arrange the necessary details. Subsequently a committee met on 9 June when it was agreed that Captain Carnegie RN be appointed chairman, Boothby deputy and a twenty-seven year old assistant, Edward Watkin secretary. A second meeeting on 14 July, under Boothby, proposed 'that a General Stores Committee, who shall have charge of the purchase of all stores and the general business connected therewith and with the distribution and use thereof, shall be appointed'. Estimates of usage were to be submitted by departmental heads and that 'General Conditions' be issued to tenderers. Accounts were to be kept of receipt and issue of stores. The committee proper met under Carnegie on 7 September when they agreed a procedure for asking for tenders and the placing of subsequent contracts. At the second meeting the first contract was agreed, stationery. Annual returns had shown the company was spending over £3,970 and a contract was given to McCorquodale, the lowest bidder at under £1,762. They agreed that coke, used by locomotives at the time, be reviewed at the next meeting. By November the committee was preening itself over contracts for stationery, printing, coke and clothing where savings of £14,253 were estimated.

However early optimism was soon tempered by unreliable usage estimates and slack accounting control. Carnegie had continued as chairman, although not always present, until being re-called to active service. He did not seek re-election at the February 1852 shareholders' meeting (he was re-elected a director in 1856 and although appointed to the Stores Committee never again became an active member).

No record has been found of the board's deliberations in early 1852 over finding a replacement for Carnegie. Richard Barrow had stood in temporarily, chairing two meeting in February, the last one comprising only himself with the Southern superintendent Capt. Bruyeres in attendance. They recorded a decision on uniforms 'that the whole issue in May of great coats, police and other coats, porters jackets, trousers be waterproofed in the cloth; that the Euston and Southern issue be waterproofed by Reynold's process and the Northern and North Eastern issue be waterproofed by Labron's process; that the Cloth used on the Southern division be sent direct to the tailor for the process'.

No meeting was held in March, but at the next meeting, 8 April, Moon had not only taken Carnegie's place as a committee member but was appointed chairman. Eight other directors were present, an unusually high attendance. Barrow himself was present and could have offered himself as an alternative for a ballot took place. 'Mr. Ellis MP who acted as Teller declared Mr. Moon to have the majority of votes and he was thereupon chosen as chairman'. Ellis, one of the newly elected directors with Moon in 1851, was not actually listed as attending (though a committee member) so presumably he was called in to provide impartial adjudication.

It seems apt that Moon's 'storekeeper' career should start by approving Barrow's minute on textiles. As will be seen in the next chapter the report of his own first meeting was hardly more exciting, yet within months the subjects he began enquiring into were requiring pages to minute the details covered. It was the work of this committee that laid the foundation for his future unrivalled knowledge of the company.

CHAPTER 6

STORES

Moon's first meeting as chairman of the L&NW's Stores Committee was recorded as follows:

> Read complaint as to quality of tube supplied by the Tube Co. which had been dealt with by the Crewe Committee. Read letter from Mr. Trevithick complaining of bad quality of boiler plates supplied by Rushton & Eckersley. The defects had been remedied. Mr. Wordsell was authorised to make a small experiment as to the practical value of Oxichloride of lead (Pattinson's) as compared with white lead. Read letter from Shaw & Sons offering to supply hardware. Read letter from Imperial Gas Company stating their intention voluntarily to reduce the contract price for gas for Euston and Camden from 4s/6d to 4s/- per 1000 feet for the remaining period of the contract, viz. to April 1852. The charge for carriage of brushes (Marsden & Sons) was referred to Capt. Huish to arrange. Read letter from Thornton & Sons offering a cheap description of oil, Mr. Watkin to have a small quantity tried. A serious complaint of the bad quality of the ropes supplied by Briggs was referred to Messrs. Lyon and Brooke, Mr. Watkin to have samples of rope tested for the information of those gentlemen. Mr. Watkin was authorised to have the patent paint included in [the] contract supplied direct from the inventor Mr. Williams of Liverpool.

Though brief these minutes typified what was to follow, in both the detail and range of materials covered. Moon questioned not only costs, usage and general issues such as methods of stock control, but sought reports on improvements to even traffic and departmental management. Responsibilities for implementing decisions were allocated and, in many cases, Moon himself undertook to investigate and report. Nothing seemed too small to matter. To refer to all the items eventually covered would fill a book in itself. However, examples of this work needs to be given if only to provide some understanding of his character and what motivated him.

One of the first matters referred to him personally was a dispute over a payment of £208 to printers McCorquodale & Co. for clerks at Euston. He settled by agreeing half the claim. There were to be many further references to McCorquodale, for example, printing the "Time Table Books" and other official company forms. The hand of Moon can be seen in a minute covering the renewal of the 1853 stationery contract at existing prices and for the stock at head office in Euston to be removed to McCorquodale's works: 'the company to be at no further expense for the salary of clerks to be employed in the distribution of stores ... a sum in commutation of the freight and carriage of the stores on the railway to be agreed upon and to be paid by ... McCorquodale'.

Attempts to control the escalating costs of stationery, however, proved difficult. The committee found themselves having to react to criticism that costs had doubled between 1849 and 1854 to over £18,000. Apparently irritated at the company's inability to control these costs, Moon eventually issued one of the longest single minute then recorded by the committee. It is quoted verbatim as an example of the extent to which he was prepared to intervene personally.

It was ordered that the Goods Superintendents be instructed to meet the chairman [Moon] and Mr. Brook at Mr. Morgan's office Birmingham on Tuesday the 26th instant, and that Mr. Stewart and Mr. Reay be requested to attend. That Mr. Reay assimilate all the forms now in use in the coaching department and that the contractor be prohibited from making any alteration in any forms or books for the use of any department without the sanction of the committee. Supplies of stationery to be furnished quarterly on estimates carefully prepared, and that any intermediate application be vigorously enquired into, and that in both cases the respective superintendents, who shall forward them to the Audit to order from the contractor, first striking out all requirements not on the contract. The Audit not to pass for payment any bills for stationery otherwise than under the above regulations and to submit half-yearly a report on the use and cost of printing and stationery for each department and station. That a circular be sent to each station agent signed by Mr. Stewart requesting them to use every endeavour to economise the use of all descriptions of stores, and to carry out the views of the committee generally on this subject. Mr. Reay to lay before the committee on 26th instant samples of the paper suitable for books, forms, etc., in use. That the attention of the agents Messrs. Pickfords & Co. and Chaplin & Horne be called to the cost of stationery purchased by them at prices which it is believed are from 10 to 15% higher than the company's contract: and that as regards the standing forms and books in ordinary use by the company, that these be in future obtained from the company contractor. The consideration of the company's Time Tables and Books was deferred till next month.

Clothing was another subject which seemed to occupy the committee unduly in early years. The Labron waterproofing complaint and the 'question of future mode of supply of clothing' were both referred to Moon personally. On the expiry of Labron's contract the committee agreed that Moon's fellow director Brook would purchase cloth directly and a Mr Compton's offer to make up the clothing was accepted with the 'coats and greatcoats of the policemen and pointsmen on the open road and greatcoats of the guards being waterproofed by Mr. Sharp'.

Joseph Brook was to become the most closely associated member with Moon during his early years of Stores work. Old enough to be Moon's father, Brook could almost be said to be his mentor. Born near Huddersfield in 1786, he was one of the additional directors elected with Moon in 1851. His early career was with the family bank, but he eventually established himself as a leading wool merchant before taking up his interest in railways. Strongly Conservative and supporter of the established church, he took a leading role in the public life of Huddersfield. He was one of the first directors of the Leeds Dewsbury & Manchester Railway in 1845 that amalgamated with the Huddersfield & Manchester Railway to form the basis of the North Eastern division of the L&NW. Brook was to serve as the company's Huddersfield director until his death in 1858.

It was agreed that Brook would report on the future supply of clothing after visiting the Lancashire & Yorkshire Railway's 'establishment'. Although expedient to use Brook's textile experience his direct involvement in purchasing could have been open to the criticism of conflict of interest. And that view should have been even more the case with Barrow when it came to coal contracts, for he was a significant midland coal producer, yet jointly with Moon he evaluated coal tenders. Some background on Barrow is perhaps relevant as he was also associated with Moon in the only known investment Moon made outside the railway during his time with the L&NW, Wolverhampton Water Works (examined later).

Born in 1787, Barrow had been, with his younger brother, a successful London merchant trading with Spain and Portugal and pioneering business with China. Apparently amassing a fortune he 'retired' while still only in his early fifties. Whether he actively sought a fresh challenge is not known but by 1840 he had taken over from his older brother a family coal and iron business at Staveley near Chesterfield, where he succeeded in developing it into one of the biggest of its kind in the country, creating a virtual new town in the process to house and provide facilities for his expanding workforce. In the meantime he had clearly invested heavily in railways, being elected a director of the L&NW soon after its formation (oddly also in the Shropshire Union canal company where he presumably was attracted by plans to convert its waterways to a railway). How he then found the time, and motivation, to dabble in such relatively mundane matters as railway company uniforms appears even more remarkable.

Clothing costs were important enough to be raised by the main board which in 1855 brought the committee's attention to the cost 'of clothing for the breaksmen [sic] of the goods trains, viz. (exclusive of rug, macintosh and great coat) £2.17s.5d., whilst that of the porters is only £1.0s.6d. per man and the latter clothing probably better adapted to the rough work of these men'. Moon's response was typical: he 'ordered that a return be made of the total cost of clothing supplied during 1854, where supplied, and distinguishing the number of each class, and the cost per suit per man'.

Some success was achieved in reducing clothing costs when comparing half years in 1855, but Moon was not satisfied. His committee made the following recommendation to the board in October 1856:

> To discontinue the supply of mackintoshes and great coats to agents, foremen and coaching gangmen who are not exposed to the weather, and that caps be supplied to these parties and ticket collectors instead of hats, that cord instead of cloth trowsers [sic], and worsted embroidery instead of silver be supplied to gangmen, that bankriders be dressed as porters, that no mackintoshes be supplied to messengers, and that no rugs be supplied to any parties; that Locomotive Superintendents be required to state in their orders for great coats the names of the drivers for whom they are intended, as in other departments, that the requisition for clothing for Camden be sent for the consideration of the Goods committee, and Mr. Perrin to draw attention to the 3 foremen being supplied with 2 body coats each in the year contrary to general practice. Mr. Perrin was instructed to apply to the committee before furnishing any clothing to the heads of the police.

Despite their own earlier suggestions for economy the board did not accept lowering standards and rejected caps for hats and the use of cord and worsted embroidery. However Moon continued to scrutinise clothing expenditure, for example his committee noting a Goods Committee minute a year later on supplying overcoats to horse drivers in Liverpool. He pointed out that such an issue would be equivalent to a permanent increase in wages, which were considered adequate for drivers to provide their own clothing.

The Mr. Perrin referred to was the secretary of the committee who had replaced Watkin. Though occasionally suffering from ill-health Watkin had proved an energetic young officer acting as secretary to many committees, including the Worcester & Hereford Railway and was privy, when assistant to the general manager

Capt. Huish, to many aspects of L&NW policy. This was to prove of benefit to him after he resigned in 1853 to become the general manager of the Manchester Sheffield & Lincolnshire Railway and subsequently their chairman. Ambitious and hard working Watkin became probably the nearest of contemporaries to match Moon in his knowledge of railway minutae. But that was where the comparison ended. A wily negotiator with fingers in many pies he was never trusted by Moon as will be seen when their two companies clashed competitively for the London Manchester traffic.

Estimating quantities in calling for tenders remained an area of difficulty for the Stores Committee. A minute complained that the information 'supplied by the heads of departments had, in many cases, been loosely made up: for instance 90,000 lbs. of brass tubes had been specified as required on the Southern division whereas 237,000 lbs. had already been supplied and used'. Departmental heads were 'requested to give more careful attention to this important matter'. At the end of each year 'a statement be laid before this committee showing the amounts in money of each contract as let and the actual total amount of goods invoiced under it, with a statement of the various reasons, if any, justifying any marked differences'.

The tenders received and contracts placed, usually in November for the following year, were all reviewed and recorded by the committee with the prices quoted and accepted. Generally the lowest bids were accepted but not in all cases. Main items were supplied on annual contracts, but smaller articles were frequently fixed for two years. In a list of thirty five contracts placed for example at the end of 1852, over forty main items were covered. These included 'coals' (separate contracts were let for each main type of coal and for specific delivery points), iron ('Yorkshire' and 'Staffordshire' were shown separately as was 'pig iron', 'iron castings' and 'iron work') and heavy manufactured goods such as axles, wheels and 'steel springs'.

Other materials listed included items ranging from 'brass tubes for locomotives' to 'carpets and rugs' and a miscellany of items including cotton waste, 'coach trimmings', hats, caps, varnishes, oil ('burning' and 'various tallow and turpentine'), copper, lead, leather and so on. It was agreed that 'palm oil and tallow be not contracted for and that Mr. Earle arrange with some respectable broker in Liverpool to purchase these articles on commission sending the goods in quantities required by the various departments'. After reviewing market prices in considering reserve stocks for these materials at Crewe, Moon wrote to the company chairman that 'after consulting some of my colleagues I have concluded that it is better to go as heretofore taking the chance of markets and buying for current wants only'.

Coke had been the normal fuel for locomotives in the early days of railways and there were numerous references to negotiations and disputes over supply contracts. The first reference to Moon's involvement was in 1854 when he reported negotiations in a dispute over quantities and the supplier complaining that he was not being paid on time.

The L&NW had its own coke ovens at Camden and Peterborough. Coke supplies were important enough to be administered by a full time superintendent who in 1856 was personally appointed by Moon and Brook. As the use of coal for locomotives became more significant Moon also began to take a personal interest in the handling of coal tenders. A contract at the end of 1853 'was referred to the chairman [Moon] and Mr. Barrow to make arrangements for 6 months supply'.

The continuing involvement by Barrow is interesting. For example at the end of 1854, Moon reported they had accepted tenders from six companies for 'coals' comprising thirteen separate quantities for different grades to various delivery points.

Although the results of experiments with locomotives burning coal were regularly monitored the supply and distribution of coke remained a key issue. It seems clear from correspondence that the individual locomotive superintendents, especially McConnell, objected to having the availability of coke subject to central control. Typically Moon examined the problem personally and in detail, visiting suppliers and reviwing the deployment of wagons to secure distribution. Clearly reinforced in his view that central control was vital if economic levels of stocks and supplies were to be achieved, Moon wrote, on 20 December 1856, a long letter to Chandos justifying his policy against criticism that supplies were being too restricted and complaining that the locomotive superintendents were going over his head to the Executive for authority to change arrangements. It becomes clear that this was only one of many issues where Moon considered he was not getting the support he deserved. He ended his letter saying:

> I trust that not only on Coke questions but on all questions referring to Stores, their consumption, stock, quality, etc., you will be good enough to refer to us the monthly Reports of the Superintendents ..... Such information would be very useful to the Stores Committee. The Superintendents are not amenable to us and will only defer to what they consider their own committee (the Executive). Believing you sincerely desirious for the good of the Company and that you give me credit for being anxious to do the best with the important though troublesome department under my charge, I shall be very glad if you will give us support to extend our usefulness.

At this time Moon was already seriously disillusioned by the board's seeming inability to ensure that his other recommendations for cost control were not being implemented. It needs to be noted at this point that in the summer of 1854 Moon had been appointed to head an ad hoc board committee to investigate costs of all departments and make recommendations for improvement. His work in this area is reviewed in the next chapter but his obvious frustration over the failure to implement many of his proposals obviously spilled over into the coke issue.

By the end of 1856 he was clearly questioning the whole value of his work for the company. He concluded a long diatribe to Chandos in October by wishing 'that you may be enabled to obtain from the Board at its meeting tomorrow such an expression of opinion as will enable me to shape my future course'. It does seem that he really was reconsidering his whole role with the L&NW. On the coke question he pressed again just before Christmas and finally on the 31 December wrote that as 'there was no imprudence in the course pursued by the Stores Committee', he could not agree with the opinion that he was in "error". He went on:

> That whilst a reference of Mr McConnell's appreciation and the strong recommendation of the Executive Committee

is one thing, the overruling of the action of the Stores Committee contrary to the openly expressed strong opinion of myself as chairman is very different. I think it is right to place in your hands my resignation of the position of Chairman of the Stores Committee and will not attend the next meeting ... in order that you may make the necessary arrangemenst for filling my place.

Unfortunately no record has been found of Chandos's response. As will be seen, Moon was to resign again in three years time, again during a Christmas break and over a very simiar issue: his committee being overuled by another, and also involving McConnell.

That Chandos succeeded in smoothing things over is apparent as Moon's chairing of the Stores Committee continued unabated in the New Year. Comparative figures showing engine miles run and fuel consumed were being reviewed by the end of 1857. Figures for November showed that for the Northern and North-Eastern divisions combined, 5.58 million miles were run on 220,586 tons of coke (no coal) and for the Southern, 3.4 million miles on 131,390 tons of which 22,798 was coal. Interestingly around 2.5 miles per ton were averaged in both cases.

As chairman Moon was frequently involved in settling price disputes. One of the earliest recorded was in 1853 when he had minuted: 'some deductions for excess prices charged on extra quantities of iron supplied by the Patent Shaft Co. were referred to the chairman to give such orders for their payment or otherwise as he might deem desirable'. Moon was always careful to ensure his committee formally authorised him before he negotiated contracts personally. Anyone in his position was vulnerable to accusations of bias from suppliers failing to obtain contracts, or worse of accepting 'inducements'. It says something for Moon's integrity that throughout the whole of his time directly responsible for purchasing only once was it ever publicly questioned (this is covered in a later chapter).

The first contract reported as being specifically handled by Moon was in 1854 for the additional supplies of 'iron, springs, wheels and axles' required for building the new cattle, coke and brake wagons. In reporting on contracts for iron it is interesting that "Yorkshire" was not considered as suitable, nor as cheap as "Staffordshire".

As well as placing supply contracts Moon's committee began to impinge on traffic management matters. In using his committee to raise issues not strictly within his orbit Moon, where he came into conflict with other directors and managers, did not hesitate to call upon the board's senior Executive Committee, the 'cabinet' chaired by the chairman of the company, to support his recommendations. For example in 1855 he complained of material being bought outside contract. He reported that apparently 'further purchases have been made including spun yarn for 56s/- cwt which under contract was 40s/- and the committee refer the whole matter to the Executive Committee considering that such proceedings are most irregular and must be at once put a stop to'. The purchases had been authorised by the Liverpool goods manager, Braithwaite Poole.

Poole had been senior goods manager for the Grand Junction Railway and became the L&NW's representative and permanent chairman of the Railway Clearing House's conference of Goods Managers. He was to be dramatically dismissed the following year for not exercising sufficient control over his staff.

Moon did not refer to the board only for their support. He was quick to criticise if he thought other directors were interfering with his own authority. For example when the Executive made proposals for disposing by sale or barter unserviceable stores, a prickly Moon pointed out 'that matters of this kind have always been dealt with by them [his Stores Committee] and that they object on principle to the sale of stores by barter'.

So many examples of meticulously recorded items were covered that keeping up with the minutes and reports must have been a major preoccupation in itself. That Moon read every one is evident from the tone of his meeting minutes. No item escaped his attention, no lapses in reporting or recording were allowed to pass without comment or even censure, no item too small to escape his notice. Individual accounts were formally presented and recorded as authorised, such as £310.5s.4d. to Christy & Co. for hats, £3.15s.7d. for travelling expenses and even 13s.6d. for buttons!

A ticket contract was given to J.Edmondson in December 1854 (Edmondson's printed card tickets had by then been in use for over ten years on the Liverpool & Manchester Railway). Wire rope for the Waterloo tunnel in Liverpool (the tunnel of his boyhood), which was authorised in 1856 for replacement, was subject to approval by Moon. It was to be 'at the same price and on the same terms, if better cannot be done, returning the old rope as then agreed subject to a guarantee for 2½ years if possible'.

A tender was accepted for 'watch clocks'. References to watches and clocks began regularly to occur in the minutes which culminated with the committee calling for a return of all 'clocks on the line and the system and cost of winding and repairs'. What is astonishing is that Moon himself undertook this task, submitting to the 9 July 1857 meeting a detailed report on "Winding and Repair of Clocks".

Moon also reported in 1857 that he was considering the best method of purchasing timber and subsequently recommended using J.Fazakerley in Liverpool to buy on 1½% commission. However some directors objected to his choice of Fazakerley on the grounds that as he was a timber dealer he should not be employed as an agent to buy timber. This appears to be one of the rare occasions where Moon's judgement in such matters could be said to be questionable. At first it seemed he did not accept the board ruling that it was 'not expedient to employ dealers in the purchase of stores' for he reported a further meeting with Fazakerley and it was agreed that three months forward requirements be given so that timber could be bought in larger lots. However the committee, on reading a letter from Fazakerley to Moon, eventually agreed to end the agency and accepted an offer from Duncan Easing & Co. to buy in Liverpool at 1%.

An interesting glimpse into the problems of handling cash is given by a minute 'on the insufficiencies of the iron safes in use on the Stour Valley line and it was referred to Mr. Stewart to consider if the cash cannot be made up each evening including the last train but one, and forwarded to the care of Mr. Robinson, Birmingham by the last train'. The committee considered 'that any ordinary safe would be no protection where there is no policemen on duty, or any inhabitants living near'. This was later very evident when the board, in seeking shareholder approval in August 1857 for new capital, asked for £6,000 for long postponed housing on the line which had:

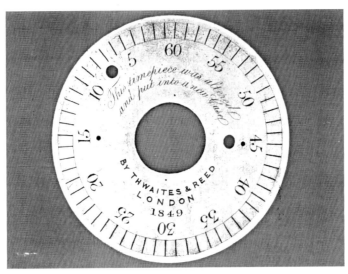

14. Clock plate Euston station

Maker's plate of an original London & Birmingham clock in the Great Hall at Euston. Thwaites & Reed had continued as main suppliers to the L&NW before losing out to lower cost makers. NRM

15. L&NW office wall clock

John Walker began supplying and servicing L&NW clocks in the 1850's when similar contracts were given to Hurt & Wray and Richard Heslop. This fine mahogany cased example of an office clock dates from around 1850. NRM

Become absolutely necessary to provide against the demoralisation amongst your servants which has taken place from the wretched and inferior class of lodgings in those districts and which has brought them into contact with bad characters. This had already tainted the character of some, and unless removed, may taint the characters of all.

Incidentally in entrusting the cash to Robinson, the committee seemed to have overlooked a rather obvious point, he apparently did not have a safe in Birmingham. On reading a letter from him, it was 'ordered that a safe be provided'.

In 1855 Moon's Stores Committee was given a wider remit when taking over responsibility for purchasing and control of materials in the company's various locomotive, carriage and wagon works. This was to be but a first step that was eventually (in 1858) to give an enlarged committee overall control of manufacturing. These increased responsibilities were brought about by changes to the board's committee structure. Mention has already been made of the Executive Committee and some background to how this came about is relevant to Moon's other activities.

The advent of the thirty-man board in 1851 had changed little the committees of directors. However, exercising overall control through such a large body clearly was proving difficult. By June 1852 Glyn raised the 'expediency of appointing an executive committee of directors'. And the following month it was agreed that the Special Affairs Committee should appoint three of their members to consider the matter with the chairman and deputy chairman. It hadn't helped that Glyn was not a fit man and his deputy Thomas Smith was under 'pressure of renewed affliction' in his family.

Though Smith had chaired the 18 September board that had tabled Glyn's eventual letter of resignation, he announced that he too needed to stand down. Glyn's letter referred to the 'necessity of some organic change in the distribution of the functions of the Executive body'. Smith's resignation was not accepted until November (Ledsam acting as temporary chairman) when the Hon George Anson and Robert Benson were elected chair and deputy chair respectively. With Anson, a major-general still on the active army list, the board presumably hoped for a renewal of vigour in directing the company's affairs. Benson too was only thirty eight. His father, also Robert, a Liverpool merchant specializing in the financing of trade had been a director of the Liverpool & Manchester Railway. When he died in 1846 his son had taken his place as L&NW director (the young Benson married Capt. Moorsom's daughter Eleanor the following year). Robert junior had been set up by his father with a cotton manufacturing business in Manchester, but by 1852 he had wound that up to establish his main interest, his own banking firm in London, Robert Benson & Co.

Anson's reign did not last long. In June 1853 he gave notice of his resignation on being re-called to active service. Unfortunately Benson had only accepted the deputy role 'for a time only'. In addition to his new bank Benson also had an interest in Liverpool merchanting with J.W.Cropper and David Hodgson and was clearly preoccupied with affairs of his own. So the direction of the company again drifted until the election in October of the Marquis of Chandos as chairman (Benson in fact remained deputy until February 1858 when Moorsom, then a vice-admiral, was appointed). The background to Chandos and his subsequent relationship with Moon will be examined in more detail later. For the purposes of this Stores review, it should be noted that it was Chandos who introduced, in March 1855, the first significant changes in the L&NW's committee system.

Matters dealt with by the several Traffic and Locomotive committees were to be dealt with by one oversall committee, comprising the chairman and twelve senior directors meeting at least twice a month in London and Birmingham alternatively. The first meeting of this new special Executive was in Birmingham on 22 March 1855. However the chairman continued to run a separate Special Affairs Committee which was responsible for external relationships and this overlapped the new committee when handling inter-company agreements. Centralised control by committee therefore continued to prove difficult and further change necessary. Moon was to be largely instrumental in recommending combining these two committees in 1858.

Part of the original Locomotive Committee's work had been to review stores for the various works including calls for tenders and agreeing contracts. The new committee at first continued this practice and it was the general manager Huish who raised the obvious clash with the Stores Committee. He drew the Executive's attention 'to the large stock of stores and recommended that some arrangements should be come to between the Executive and Stores Committees to define the duties of the latter committee'. Whilst the Executive's response to this is not recorded it does seem that Moon's committee then began to take over more of the work of controlling all stores.

So at the end of 1855 Moon's work with stores entered a new phase when he was unanimously re-elected chairman of a reconstitued Stores Committee. Most of the board members re-appointed with him were by then regularly present at his meetings with the relevant departmental officers, representing all the main spending departments of the company, in attendance. These included the three locomotive superintendents (Ramsbottom from Longsight, Trevithick from Crewe and McConnell from Wolverton) and the managers of the other works (Owens from Newton wagon works, Slater from Saltley and Worsdell from Crewe carriage works). Although Moon personally had already become more closely involved with all departments of the company in his other investigation work, he was now able as part of his new responsibility to exercise direct control, undertaking with Brook 'to inspect the mode of conducting the business of the Stores departments at the various establishments'.

This two-man sub-committee wasted little time in getting down to business. Moon was quickly calling Trevithick's attention in January 1856 'to the heavy stocks of various kinds of stores at Crewe and outstations and the committee were of the opinion that some portion of scrap steel should be sold'. At the same meeting Moon and Brook also presented a report recommending changes in Wolverton's locomotive stores department. But it was Trevithick in particular who came under increasing scrutiny. A letter was read from him 'on the subject of errors committed in calculation of cost of stores issued, and it was resolved that the explanation of Mr. Davis is not satisfactory and that greater care must be exercised in future'. This was but only the beginning of a purge on Trevithick.

Moon and Brook completed their works' visits in April 1856. A summary of their findings, using Crewe as an example, was outlined in a long minute for board approval, which not only highlighted Moon's fervour for cost control and understanding of modern accounting principles, but was scathingly critical of Trevithick:

The system there [Crewe locomotive department] is nominally the same as that generally adopted, but there is an entire want of responsibility and connection between the different parts, resulting in disorganisation and confusion. Stocks and accounts at the outstations unnoticed and unknown, so that at Vauxhall, Birmingham, Walsall and Preston, if not at others, there is every reason to believe great inaccuracies and deficiencies exist, nor is there any hope or remedy for these evils so long as the head of the establishment does not take that responsibility and supervision, which it is his duty to exercise. Without some change being made indeed the sub-committee are quite unable to recommend any course for your adoption with the least probability of its being successful, at the same time they are justified that some great change is absolutely needed.

Moon's committee had already begun to demand more information, calling for the accountant to provide half-yearly 'tabular statements showing consumption of stationery, oil, grease, gas, coal, clothing and general stores at each station', and for departmental heads' attention 'be called to the stock and consumption of stores and especially to see that provision is made for keeping the grease covered from dust and in a cool place'. A postscript to these demands raised the question of managing the company's horses.

The Stores Committee had first referred to horse management in April 1856 when considering the purchase of provender and asking for a return on all horses used, in particular the number hired. In September it was reported that 223 were owned and 1,164 hired. In London a total of 824 were in use of which only 34 were owned. Concern over this and the high cost of 'horse keep' in the goods departments at Camden, Liverpool and Birmingham, led Moon and Brook in February 1857 to review further. They reported within two months and recommended the appointment of Edward Livock as Inspector of Horses at £150 p.a. plus travelling expenses. Given a list of all stations and departments using horses, Livock was instructed to report on conditions, stabling, management, provender and costs 'with a view to introduce if practicable, a more economical mode than the present system combined with greater efficiency'.

16. Railway cartage horse
L&NW cartage horse *Sunbeam*. Though taken in 1907, when around 6,000 horses
were in use by the company, the 4 year old was probably typical of the 1,387
reviewed by Moon in 1856. NRM

17. Gas lamps at New Street
Gas lamps at New Street station in the 1880s. Moon's obsession with gas use had
led to his own Gas Report in 1858. LNWRS

The brief concluded 'without wishing you to report until you have made yourself thoroughly master of the subject we rely upon your best efforts to let your arrangements be made without unnecessary delay'.

Livock took six months to complete his review and the committee approved his report on 'Horse Management' and the 'form of Horse Register Book'. In the meantime the original credit given to Livock with Glyn's bank for expenses was increased from £100 to £250 as 'the number of horses to be replaced had so much increased'.

Initially the committee attempted to control directly the buying of all horses with a register kept in the accountant's office at Euston. 'All payments and purchases be passed through the committee monthly' and 'that, except in emergency to replace horses unable to work, Mr Livock must not purchase horses without a minute of this committee'.

It seems that the Executive's Traffic members took exception to the Stores Committee exercising sole control over Livock, as the authority to purchase was later amended to include the Traffic Committee. However by April 1860 it was apparent that even this was too rigid a control when it was agreed that 'the superintendents apply direct to Mr Livock for any replacement of horses that may be required'. Also it had become clear that the general manager, by then William Cawkwell, could also be referred to for approval. In all cases however the authority for approving additional horses had to be detailed individually and carefully recorded in the Stores Committee minutes.

As Moon's Stores Committee probed more into the works' stocks of stores and methods of control it seems that some of the superintendents questioned the committee's authority. At the Executive meeting on 11 April 1856, a director, Matthew Lyon, sought clarification of the extent of the 'supervision of the stock of stores in the various departments by the Stores Committee, and stated that that committee were in some doubt how far that supervision was meant to extend'. The Executive resolved 'that the Stores Committee should exercise such supervision over the stores in stock as to prevent unnecessary accumulation and to check, from time to time, the stocks in store in the several departments'.

An attempt to play down any over-stocking problem was made when senior director Hardman Earle questioned 'the several superintendents present what proportion of their stocks of stores were obsolete and of unserviceable kind and patterns, and it did not appear that they had any great amount of such obsolete stores'.

Moon does not seem to have been present when these particular exchanges took place although he was recorded as being so. Meetings of the Executive and Stores Committees at Euston overlapped at times so directors who could be members of both, or whose specialist input was required, would switch between meetings depending on the subjects discussed. Moon, not then an official member of the Executive, generally gave priority to continuing to chair his own committee unless his presence was necessary to discuss a specific issue. He generally continued this policy even after he was appointed to the senior committee. Lyon was a member of both the Stores and the Executive.

One of the results of looking at the methods of controlling stores in the various departments was a growing awareness of the need for more consistency in accounting methods. Moon and Brook joined Benson, who chaired the board's Finance Committee, and the auditors in a 'committee with power to review the accounts of the several departments with a view to the establishment of uniformity of system and arrangement generally'.

No review of this period of Moon's Stores work would be complete without highlighting his obsession over economising in gas usage. It was in the May of 1856 that he first questioned gas supplies in detail, calling attention 'to the cost of gas for the Dudley Port station for the quarter ending 30 December last which was £49.4s.1d. and it was ordered that Mr. Norris be requested to enquire and report'. It turned out that there had been a leakage caused by ground settlement. Later in the year he 'brought under consideration consumption of gas in the tunnels at Birmingham and Mr. Ledsam who attended the committee was requested to give such instructions to the stationmaster as he may consider necessary to economise the consumption'.

In April the following year Moon was demanding a comprehensive return 'of the number of feet of gas consumed at each station during the year ending 31st. Dec. 1856, the number of lights and hours of burning, and the number of people employed attending to gas and fittings, with their names and wages'. Using the returns and backed by personal verification at many of the stations, Moon later submitted his own detailed report to the committee. He called for more accurate records of consumption, criticising widespread variations in usage and demanding greater control over expenditure. He made comparisons between specific stations including numbers of lights and the costs of supplies including the company's own gas making plants. He recommended that each station kept a daily log to enter the 'number of lights, hours burning, and feet of gas consumed, so as to be able to detect any leakage or waste and forward it periodically to the party recommended to be appointed to attend to the gas, so that he may be able to draw comparisons and call attention to any waste'.

This 'Chairman's Report on Gas' which Moon presented on 7 January 1858 is not only remarkable for its detailed analysis, but his motivation for doing so. He had by then progressed to a position on the board where he was giving confidential advice to his chairman on the broader management of the whole company.

CHAPTER 7

INVESTIGATOR

As the 1850s progressed the dividend rate of the L&NW declined steadily. To despairing shareholders and directors alike hopes of reversing the trend seemed as far away as ever. More was needed to improve the situation than counting the cost of such items as gas, grease and a guard's coat. That Moon stuck so conscientiously to such details should not be seen as perverse. He saw no need to differentiate between costs, all had to be justified; none was sacred.

He had been less than three years with the company when he first began to raise wider issues, giving notice at the August 1853 board:

> That in order to secure the fullest information as to the necessity and policy of all extensions of the company's system of railway, no project for a line be submitted for adoption by the board unless in the first instance a report in writing thereupon, detailing the reasons which render the project expedient and desirable, be presented to the board by a sub committee consisting of the directors residing in or best acquainted with the district affected.

Although he agreed to withdraw the motion at the following month's meeting the principle was an approach he never deviated from when responsible for any item of expenditure. His resulting frustration could well have led to the outburst that followed when he 'brought under the notice of the board the costly nature for the reception of Her Majesty on the occasion [summer 1853] of her journey over this company's line'. He did at least succeed in having a return ordered of the costs incurred and the amount 'paid by the crown' for the year and similar returns for the previous three years. It was subsequently shown that some of these expenses had not been approved by the board and 'in no way' had contributed 'to Her Majesty's comfort or convenience'.

It was at the November 1853 board that a former Manchester & Birmingham director recently elected to the L&NW board, William Rawson, first gave notice of his intention to propose a special investigation 'to examine the establishment and current expenditure'. Though many directors, such as Moon, must have welcomed this, it was not until the following summer that a decision was taken when Rawson together with Moon, Tinne and Heywood were appointed 'to investigate the state of the several departments as to salaries & wages, stores and current expenditure of all kinds and to report such alterations and modifications as may be required'. Such a brief was almost identical to the one given to Moorsom in 1848.

Though Rawson had quickly joined the influential Locomotive Committee both he and Tinne were relatively inexperienced in comparison with Moon. Tinne had been with the company for less than six months. Although Heywood had been elected with Moon he had not devoted much time to the company. It seems the committee themselves agreed on Moon being their spokesman.

Added urgency was given to the investigation when soon after the committee started work the general economic climate and performance of the company deteriorated further. The board had decreed that capital expenditure should be limited 'to works absolutely and immediately necessary for the accommodation of the traffic'. In early 1855 the company reported that 'the sudden contraction of business since the commencement of the present year, in nearly every branch of trade has rendered necessary a revision of the working arrangements generally...with a view to retrenchment'.

Before examining the work of this committee it is timely to note in more detail the young aristocrat who had been elected as the new chairman of the company. The deferment of Rawson's original proposal could well have been as a result of the Marquis of Chandos wanting to review the position for himself first.

Chandos had been elected a director and chairman of the L&NW at the 15 October 1853 board meeting. With Benson ruling himself out, the senior board members had spent a summer searching for a new chairman. Born in 1823, educated at Eton and Oxford, MP for his family seat of Buckingham, a 'High Tory', protectionist and anti-Catholic, the Marquis of Chandos, only son of the Duke of

Buckingham, was a true establishment candidate. Nevertheless his selection seemed a surprising choice for a company needing more than just a figurehead. Without railway or company experience he had been appointed to the chair of Britain's largest company when just thirty years old. But there was more to Chandos than at first appeared.

In 1845 the twenty-two year old Chandos had seen his father (the second Duke) spectacularly accumulate debts of over £1million (which included lavishly entertaining the Queen at Stowe, the largest and grandest of his many houses). The son was faced, if he waited passively for his inheritance, with having no income and an undischarged bankrupt on his hands. The alternative was to attempt to control the estate himself, disentail the property and sell what he could to eliminate the debt.

By 1847 the young Chandos had taken action to enforce the transfer of the estates into his name and taken responsibility for his father's debts. Still only twenty-four, he then began a process of ruthlessly selling what he could to pay off creditors. The estates were vast, but then so were the debts; great country houses such as Stowe, Wotton, Avington and Gosfield Hall, Buckingham House in London, land in Ireland, house contents, they were all considered for disposal. Stowe was reduced to an empty shell, its 'Capability Brown' grounds abandoned. It has been estimated by historian F.M.L.Thompson that Chandos realised £1.5 million on disposals.

By the early 1850s Chandos appears to have largely resolved his financial affairs. His father, without an income and increasingly embittered, ended his days at his son's expense, ironically, in the Great Western's hotel in Paddington which, newly opened at the time, was regarded as one of the finest in London. Living off credit he continued to accumulate debts, £125,000 in less than two years!

Chandos married a commoner in 1851 and settled with the not inconsiderable remnants of his estates at Wotton, near Aylesbury. After a period in the Treasury of Lord Derby's brief administration in 1852, he was ready for a new challenge in 1853. His only previous contact with railways was as a landowner in negotiation with the Buckinghamshire Railway. It was then that he would have met Glyn as that company was largely financed by the L&NW and leased to them from 1851. Chandos would also have known the Hon. P.S. Pierrepont, a director of the Buckinghamshire Railway, who had

18. Marquis of Chandos

The Marquis of Chandos, Chairman of the L&NW 1853-61. Succeeded to dukedom (3rd Duke of Buckingham & Chandos) in 1861. NRM

19. C.E.Stewart

Charles Stewart, L&NW secretary 1846-65. LNWRS

joined the L&NW with Moon. Pierrepont's seat at Evenley Hall near Brackley was not too distant from Wotton. It was Glyn who proposed Chandos as director and chairman with Pierrepont seconding him.

The L&NW had acquired a young chairman whose experience in estate negotiations, litigation and finance belied his years. It did not take him long to become immersed in L&NW affairs, working closely with senior directors and the general manager Huish.

Moon's investigating team spent six months before reporting their preliminary findings. Amongst their more fundamental and controversial recommendations was a reduction in the number of locomotive, carriage and wagon works. On its formation in 1846 the company had inherited a miscellany of works and establishments all of which were still in existence ten years later. The Grand Junction had concentrated both locomotive and carriage building at Crewe, but still maintained original works at Edge Hill in Liverpool and Ordsall Lane for making and repairing wagons. Though the London & Birmingham Railway's works at Wolverton, centrally placed for their line, were initially built only to maintain locomotives supplied by contractors, they had begun manufacturing by the 1850s. The L&B had also leased premises at Saltley in Birmingham for carriage and wagon manufacture with additional repair facilities at Euston for carriages, and at Camden and Watford for wagons. The Manchester & Birmingham Railway had concentrated locomotive and wagon works at Longsight, Manchester. The amalgamated company had added to these works when setting up rolling mills at Crewe and leasing premises at Newton for wagon work. There was little objection in principle to the need for reducing the number of facilities, the problem, exacerbated by vested interests, was where, when and how.

Moon's committee recommended quite sweeping changes: put simply they proposed the consolidation of the locomotive establishments into one, centralizing the control of the carriage works and the concentration of all wagon making at Newton. This last change would have meant the closure of not only the outlying wagon works but also Saltley. But it was the locomotive proposal that caused most controversy; still jealously guarding old company loyalties a divided board immediately referred this to a special committee comprising Chandos, Benson, Earle, Lyon and Moorsom.

Under pressure from Earle and others defending the status quo, Moon found himself having to justify the carriage and wagon proposals and must have been frustrated when these in turn were also referred to the same ad hoc committee looking at the locomotive arrangements. The latter eventually reported, inconclusively, on the locomotive works: it agreed that the 'consolidation of the several locomotive departments is very desirable', but that the proposal needed to be 'referred to a sub-committee of the Executive'. Earle even dissented from this, but lost his motion that the existing divisional system be fairly tried under the new committee arrangements. The carriage proposal was unanimously rejected, as was the concentration of all wagon building at Newton. However the closure of the works at Longsight, Edge Hill and Ordsall Lane was agreed.

The committee reported further on the locomotive issue in July when they agreed that:

> The three divisions should be consolidated under one general superintendent whose personal services should especially be directed to the working of the engines in concert and cooperation with the general manager. That the workshops at Wolverton, Crewe and Longsight be under the control of the general superintendent with an assistant at each who shall have charge of the repair and building of the engines. ... They were not prepared to recommend an immediate change but that in all future arrangements regard should be had to an ultimate consolidation.

Thus Moon for the time being had to be content with this. Despite the nature and importance of his investigation work he was not then a member of the Executive. Though he had given up his place on the Audit Committee he remained a member of the Rates & Taxes and of course had been confirmed as chairman of an enlarged Stores Committee. With the locomotive arrangements shelved and only part of his wagon and carriage rationalisation agreed, Moon could well have then fallen back on devoting his energies to his additional stores responsibilities. However throughout the summer of 1855 he continued to probe many other aspects of the company's operations and it seems clear that some directors became concerned over the extent to which he was interpreting his investigation brief. Though many matters still remained outstanding a special board convened in August recorded their appreciation of his work as if it was completed. A unanimous vote of thanks was passed to the members of the committee and:

> Especially to their chairman Mr. Moon for the zeal and very great labour they have bestowed for many months in carrying their investigations into the various departments of the line, bringing before the directors in their reports a mass of information which, if rightly improved [sic], the directors trust will be of permanent benefit to the concern.

But if the board then expected Moon to rein back they were mistaken. He persisted for many more months in meetings with both directors and officers in reviewing and re-considering findings. In the meantime the continuing unsatisfactory results from the company provoked the shareholders to form their own committee 'to confer with the board on the general policy of the company, the rate of expenditure and the best mode of increasing the present dividend to a more reasonable remuneration for the vast capital expended on the undertaking'. Discussions with board members followed and at the shareholders' meeting in February 1856 the directors accepted that no addition to capital would be made 'without the work having been approved of and an estimate previously sanctioned by a vote of the general meeting'. At that meeting the shareholders' spokesman, J Parker, commented:

> It was but justice to the directors that he should inform the meeting that when he first proposed the appointment of a shareholders' committee he had no idea that the subjects with which he proposed to deal had already engaged the serious attention, and had been to a considerable extent worked out in detail, by the directors. Expenses of management, extensions and the augmentation of capital, were the great bugbears which he was anxious to attack; and when the committee met he found, somewhat to his

surprise he must say, that the detail of all those questions had been very carefully and elaborately carried out by a sub-committee of the board itself, which had been most ably presided over by Mr. Moon, one of the directors - (cheers).

This was probably the first appreciation publicly accorded Moon for his L&NW work. The value of Chandos to the company was also acknowledged. Impressed by his efficiency as chairman 'and being of opinion that the interests of the company would be greatly promoted by his continuance in that office, [the shareholders] respectfully request that the board will take into its early consideration the arrangement by which his valuable services may be permanently secured to the undertaking'. At a previous board in June 1853, the former chairman Glyn had noted that as the chairman's job was so time consuming it should be paid. It seems that Chandos had reminded colleagues of this minute for the meeting agreed that he should be paid £2,000 per annum

Moon's further report on his investigation work at the end of 1855 included twenty-one revised recommendations ranging from minor salary issues to reorganising divisions. The first recommendation was an attack on directors' patronage, proposing that apprentices and junior officers be appointed only by examination and merit through departmental heads and committees. The board disagreed, confirming the principle of nomination by directors in rotation, but they did concede the necessity for examinations. Moon, Moorsom and Ledsam were to form a sub-committee to report on how the nomination system could be 'extended and also on the system of examination to be adopted'.

Proposals for officers' salaries and job grades were agreed. These included the principle that a rate for the post was to be established and the holder's salary not increased unless promoted. Reorganisations agreed included the engineering of the line, which was to be placed under one head; the coaching [passenger] traffic was to be controlled through only two divisions (Northern and Southern) and the Manchester office abolished. The attention of Pickfords and Chaplin & Horne was drawn to their high charges as agents for outside terminals. The Executive subsequently proposed that the border between the two passenger divisions should be just south of Stafford with the Trent Valley line forming part of the Southern division, which made Stafford and Birmingham the 'points of junction'.

Pickfords and Chaplin & Horne worked the London goods stations under contract to the company and were also the collection and delivery agents in the area. For the latter services the L&NW paid allowances per ton to them so they could provide a free service to customers within town areas, the allowance being subject to periodic revision on reviewing actual costs. In the 1840s Pickfords had been carriers for the London & Birmingham taking complete responsibility for collecting and delivering, paying the railway a 'toll' for the carriage as they had with the canals. The Grand Junction on the other hand had always carted and carried their own goods, using Chaplin & Horne as their agents on the L&B line. On amalgamation the GJ practice of the railway company being their own carrier was generally adopted using 'agents' for collection and delivery services only. In London, however, the internal running of the major goods stations themselves had remained with the agents. Moon was to become increasingly concerned over the company's dependence on private carters for handling goods and merchandise traffic. The recommendation that the company take into their own hands the internal working and arrangements of Camden, Haydon Square (east London) and Poplar warehouses, was part of his policy of reducing this dependence.

Proposals which were adjourned for further review included the amalgamation of the Northern and North-Eastern committees, the abolition of the Liverpool office, and the setting up of a new permanent committee comprising the chairman of the various committees and those directors attending the goods conference 'to watch over the earnings and expenses of the railways, etc., of the company and their management generally'. This was the first reference to a stronger chairman's committee which eventually replaced the Executive and Special Affairs committees.

The board agreed the union of the two northern committees, but the Executive subsequently found difficulties in implementing this; Earle again protesting and eventually persuading the board to suspend the minute until the locomotive arrangements were decided. A frustrated Moon was to end a note to Chandos in the summer of 1857 by pleading for him to make 'an effort to have only one northern sub-committee meeting … I am sure it is the only fair course towards our officers'.

Moon's recommendation 'that the financial affairs of the company be committed to the charge of a distinct officer and that as two general secretaries are not required one of these officers be requested to undertake the whole of those duties' was not accepted. It appeared that the long serving Northern secretary, Henry Booth, at sixty-six had been half promised he could stay on in Liverpool until he was seventy. As will be seen Moon had little time for Booth who had been given to him to act as secretary for his investigation reports.

A number of other recommendations illustrate the scope of Moon's investigations: a new department for controlling goods, mineral and cattle traffic; a separate central division for goods; and responsibility for control of wagon movements to include carriages and horse boxes. All were deferred.

Given the extent to which Moon was probing these wider issues it became obvious to even his most die-hard opponents that he should, in his own right, be a member of the board's senior policy committee. His eventual appointment to the Executive, formally recorded at the board meeting of 10 November 1855, still left him in an anomalous position: the minute being qualified 'but that the number [of directors] be not permanently increased beyond the number of members originally appointed'.

Regarding the locomotive recommendations it was not until March 1856 that the directors considered again a report from Chandos's ad hoc committee. A stormy meeting ensued. The report repeated the background and concluded 'that the continuance of the present three divisions is not best calculated for the ultimate management. Although they do not advise any immediate or violent change, they recommend the board to take advantage of any opportunity which may present itself for attaining the result indicated'.

However Matthew Lyon, a member of the committee, dissented. Moon took the opportunity to force a vote on an amendment that 'the board reaffirm the principle that a consolidation of the several locomotive departments is very desirable, and as a first step in that direction resolve that the locomotive departments of the present

Northern and NE divisions be placed under one management and that Mr.Ramsbottom be appointed superintendent of the amalgamated division'.

John Ramsbottom, dubbed the 'father' of the modern locomotive as a result of his many inventions, had begun his career as a textile machinery engineer and had initially joined the Manchester & Birmingham Railway as a locomotive foreman before taking over the locomotive works at Longsight, Manchester. This became the North-East division of the L&NW when the Leeds line was opened. He had progressed rapidly and in 1856 been given additional responsibility for the rail rolling mill set up in Crewe. Moon clearly recognised Ramsbottom's potential to extend his responsibilities still further.

Chandos sat on the fence, reaffirming his view of the advantage of having one overall general superintendent but 'the several establishments continuing to be managed by superintendents of experience and ability'. Narrowly Moon's amendment was lost 11 to 8 and the report accepted 13 to 3. The locomotive problem was to simmer for another year before Chandos saw an opportunity to act. This is covered later. In the meantime this was not the only Moon recommendation that was not being implemented.

By the October of 1856, faced with a hostile, or at best an indifferent board meeting the following day, Moon wrote a long, at times angry, note for Chandos demanding action. He was in Euston for meetings of his Stores and the Executive Committees on Friday the 10th. and must have spent most of the evening compiling it. He felt 'induced' to write beforehand in the hope that Chandos could:

> Elicit from the Board at their meeting tomorrow some decisive expression of opinion such as shall, either on the one hand, by the adoption of a vigorous scheme of reform in our present system of management, save my late Colleagues [his investigation team] and myself the mortification of further defeats, or on the other hand relieve me from the responsibility of appearing to acquiesque without remonstrance in a system of which I strongly disapprove, and so closing, so far as I am personally concerned, the long and arduous struggle which I ... have hitherto maintained.

He then went on to say that when presenting 'our reports to you last year the extraordinary developments which they contained led yourself and others ... to regard them with some degree of doubt and we bore patiently the course you prescribed in allowing your officers to give their explanation of some of the points'. He said he had agreed not to counter the managers' statements 'from the perfect conviction which we entertained that the lapse of time would amply verify our assertions'. He claimed they had:

> Cause to complain of the statements which were at that time made to the Board by Capt. Huish, which merely had the effect of throwing a veil over defects and failures of whose reality he was well aware and I think it a circumstance calling for the strongest animadversion [sic] that by intimidation of our secretary Mr Long and by other means that Gentm. should have been a party to the withholding of information from your Committee and so preventing the truth arriving through our medium at your knowledge. The opposition thus raised against us however must have given way, even had subsequent events not proved the general truth of our declarations.

It is not clear what he meant by subsequent events but the Liverpool goods manager had been dismissed earlier in the year and the sacking of the Manchester goods manager, Salt, was about to be confirmed at the forthcoming board meeting. However Moon did concede that:

> Although the general management of Capt. Huish has forfeited my confidence, I am ready to admit that many of the defects which he took to himself a blame [sic] were naturally inherent to the system adopted, which led him and other chief officers ... to act as if the affairs of the Company were under their uncontrolled management to the exclusion of the action of the Board and its various Committees. ... So weakened had the powers of the Executive thus become ... and so lax its control that whatever orders might have been issued by the Board or Committee or Managers, it was

either unknown or uncertain whether they were ever carried out, nor did any responsibility attach to the neglect of them.

He went on to quote as an example the board minute that agreed the capping of officer salaries and that a list of reductions be presented for review. 'As to the first of these orders, so clear, so peremptory in its terms, it is notorious that little or no progress has been made in attempting to carry it out', and as to the second no such report 'has ever been presented to us'. He demanded that his committee's recommendation for a permanent "Committee of Enquiry" be implemented 'to watch over the earnings and expenses' and that the findings of his investigation committee be referred to them. It seems that his report had not been copied to all directors for he asked for it to be printed and circulated.

All of this was by implication strongly critical of the company chairman, but without a record of Chandos's response his reaction can only be surmised. Soothing the 'injurious effect', as Moon put it, 'of the local jealousies among ourselves' was no doubt a role Chandos thought he needed to play. However Moon was leaving little room for compromise when he continued, 'we have had our various Committees, Northern, Southern, Crewe, Manchester, each with their various prejudices and antagonism, nor need I remind you how Gentlemen from Liverpool and Manchester refuse to meet as one local Committee and so prevent the bringing about of a complete and general amalgamation'.

Though admitting that some improvements had been made (he mentioned the Liverpool and Manchester goods stations), Moon stressed that 'necessity has driven us to reorganize' and 'very much more might have been effected ... if a strenuous effort had been made to work upon commercial and economic principles'. He then went on to 'particularise' the issues that remained outstanding: the amalgamation of the locomotive departments, centralizing the engineering of the line under one head, control of coaching traffic through only two divisions, and additionally three more points on which decisions needed to be made. He listed the latter as, firstly the central control of goods, cattle and mineral traffic; secondly taking over immediately the working of the London goods stations, especially in view of the imminent review of Pickford and

Chaplin & Horne arrangements; and thirdly the management in Liverpool. In concluding he reminded Chandos there were also other recommendations that needed to be reviewed such as Wagon building and Finance, but 'I will not trespass upon your time with regards these at present'.

What effect this outburst had on Chandos in handling the next days's board is not apparent from the minutes other than that the critical one, the locomotive arrangements, remained shelved. However forced changes were in the wind. These concerned the locomotive arrangements for running the Lancaster & Carlisle Railway.

The Lancaster & Carlisle had been authorised in 1840 with £250,000 and £100,000 of its capital subscribed by the Grand Junction and London & Birmingham Railways respectively, giving the amalgamated L&NW a substantail holding. Their line extended from the existing Lancaster & Preston Junction Railway and, opening in 1846, completed the through route from Euston to Carlisle. At Carlisle connection to the Caledonian Railway gave access to Glasgow in 1847 and Edinburgh the following year, thus initiating the West Coast route from London to Scotland.

Though the L&C and the L&PJ remained independent companies, the L&C took over the management and the L&NW provided the trains until 1857 when the L&C purchased their own locomotives and rolling stock. In 1859 the L&C absorbed the L&PJ and from 1 August was permanently leased to the L&NW for a guaranteed 8%. Though Moon appears not to have taken any direct part in negotiating the lease, the steps that led to it will need to be examined later in looking at his role when chairman of the company in forcing the Midland Railway to open a competitive route to Scotland.

The change in 1857 suited both parties: the L&C wishing to reduce costs and the L&NW able to use resources for growing business elsewhere. In March of that year Chandos had reported that in the summer the contract for supplying the L&C would terminate. This meant that sixty engines and over a million train miles would not be required (the L&C bought forty of the engines). This was the circumstance that Chandos was looking for. Deprived of such a large part of its services the separate existence of the NE locomotive department could no longer be justified.

20. Hardman Earle
Hardman Earle (1792-1877), Liverpool cotton broker active in early
railway development, one of the promoters of the Grand Junction and a
director of the L&NW since formation. The township formed to serve
Newton works is named after him. LNWRS

21. Edward Tootal
Edward Tootal (1799-1873), the Manchester silk manufacturer and
L&NW director 1851-73 who played a key role in the formation of the company;
a 'behind the scenes' negotiator and friend of Robert Peel. Salford Library

The L&NW board agreed Chandos's recommendation for 'the immediate consolidation of Northern and NE Divisions' and formed another committee to decide how to implement (Chandos, Benson, Moorsom, Blake, Earle and Lyon). The controversial issue was, of course, who should be the new division's locomotive superintendent. It was finally resolved in May exactly as Moon's proposed amendment of over a year earlier. But it had not been without a fight.

Earle had again led the objectors. He had argued that there was no pressing need to amalgamate 'nor has the occasion arisen, namely, the retirement or removal of one or other of the superintendents'. Having failed to delay the change Earle then proposed, that if the divisions had to be combined, then the Crewe superintendent Trevithick should be appointed. He claimed that Trevithick had 'successfully conducted the department' for seventeeen years with mileage, expenditure and capital 'greatly exceeding the other two divisions put together ... without any corresponding increase of his salary and with a regular and systematic reduction in the expenses'.

But with a fuller board present Earle's faction was now outvoted, losing by over three to one and the report was approved with Ramsbottom's salary agreed at £1,000 and Trevithick to be paid £3,000 to retire.

Hardman Earle was one of the six GJ members of the inaugural L&NW board, being a veteran from the early days of the Liverpool & Manchester Railway. Born in 1792, he was reputed to be the oldest railway director in the country when he died in 1877. Although a generation apart from Moon, Earle had a somewhat comparable background in that he was a Liverpool man, a partner in a cotton broking business (Salisbury Turner & Earle) and at one time a churchwarden (in the Liverpool parish churches of St. Peters and St. Nicholas). He had been associated with the Liverpool Gas Light Co but, unlike Moon, was an active Liberal and, full of public good works was eventually honoured by Gladstone with a baronetcy in 1869 for political service. When the L&NW moved their wagon works from Edge Hill to Newton in 1853, Earle, who had been the director responsible for both the move and developing the housing required, had his name given to the township created: Earlestown.

To be fair to Earle part of his case for Trevithick was not necessarily only his Grand Junction bias. Ramsbottom's outside interests were a general concern and his demands for a higher salary were seen by some to be excessive. That Chandos had been undecided is evident from a note he sent to Moon. Unfortunately as with all Chandos's correspondence to Moon at this time no copies have been traced to detail his concerns. Moon's own letter in reponse, however, leaves no doubt where he (Moon) stands on not only Trevithick but his policy on paying for good management which he was to follow throughout his chairmanship. This letter, dated 5 May 1857, is therefore quoted virtually in full:

> I feel much obliged by your note of the 3rd inst. but greatly disturbed to notice the conclusion at which you seem to be arriving. I assure you it will never answer either for your own reputation as the successful head of a great company or for our interests as shareholders. It is not that Trevithick is not clever or honest but we want more than that. From all our experience of him I am sure both you and I are satisfied we shall never have any vigour or strength in his management, there will always be those rocks ahead, if he is opposed instead of bearing it down he will shut himself up, if a difficulty comes he will not take the responsibility, he will not speak to his foremen or order his accountant or give notice to his men but we shall extend wider the laxity and want of system on his division by adding the N.E. to it. We shall never know what our engines are doing, or what they might do if they were most scientifically disposed of and the least loss of profitable running to be made with them. However I should never have done if I were to put together all the disadvantages of this arrangement and you are well cognizant of them.
>
> On the other hand I do not see the difficulty about retaining Ramsbottom which is I understand from Mr. Lyon dependent on his getting £1,200 p.a.; he (Ramsbottom) mentioned to me in Liverpool that this would be his ultimatum, that he thought it only fair having in view

private business but that with this, and the position he would hold as one of two engineers for this great concern, he would <u>finally</u> [sic] cease to think of private business. Of course I said nothing. If such be the case I sincerely trust you will not let £200 p.a. stand in the way. Mr. Lyon spoke suggesting £1,000 p.a. to Ramsbottom and McConnell and £200 a year to the former for the rail works. I would give both £1,200 a year - a trifle in the salary is nothing to get the men you want and having two first rate we may by and bye be able to have one head of the Locomotive at a higher salary when we get the machinery into good working order but I look upon the labour for any one taking Crewe to put in order as herculean.

It is the man not the system on which we must depend - no system could work with Trevithick's weak command and I shall despair of any good to our concern if he is retained. I am also sure my Lord if we think of the flourishing state of the Trade of the country and of our beggarly 5% dividend when we know it may be improved, we should not hesitate to try more vigorous measures and an entirely new plan so that we may get direct control and a strong hand upon our work. Again I entreat you not to miss this opportunity, as you have written me I concluded you wished me so to do and I have therefore spoken very freely, sincerely hoping you will have courage to face all the disturbing elements before you.

Contrary to some commentators, Moon's only motive in forcing the retirement of Trevithick was in the interests of efficiency. Stores meeting minutes show Moon generally accepted without reservation Ramsbottom's views whereas Trevithick's were almost invariably questioned. Earle's support for Trevithick was backed by the celebrated civil engineer Locke under whom Trevithick had trained. Under pressure from Locke at the next shareholders' meeting Chandos tactfully responded that although it was unnecessary for him to say 'no man would be dismissed for honesty, integrity, or economy ... the directors must reserve to themselves the full right of employing such persons as they think best adapted to perform the duties required'.

The problem with Trevithick was that he appeared unable to perform as a manager and consequently had no base from which to stand up to Moon. The son of a famous father, born in Cornwall in 1812, Trevithick had joined the Grand Junction when only twenty-eight, becoming their locomotive superintendent at Edge Hill the following year. He retired to manage estates in his native Cornwall.

In contrast to his opinion of Trevithick, it is interesting to note Moon's rating at the time of McConnell, the Wolverton superintendent. David Stevenson described McConnell as 'a strong and determined man of the rough sort'. That McConnell could stand up to Moon was probably a point in his favour, but he was to overplay his hand when Moon sought further change (as will be seen later). The NE move had always been for Moon only a first step towards the goal of amalgamating the whole locomotive department.

In the meantime Moon did not relent in his pursuit of cost reductions. His Stores Committee work continued apace and his investigation work drew him into reviews of such matters as salaries and legal costs. However far greater problems than administrative were now facing the company. Traffic management and operating policies were coming under increasing pressure. His experience in these areas had been limited initially to the abortive Worcester & Hereford. His position as an active locally based west midlands director, however, soon found him co-opted into a number of other board committees covering the area. Such commitments marked his further progress to becoming a senior director of the company.

CHAPTER 8

WEST MIDLANDS

The choice of Moon to head the L&NW's investigation into its own costs had clearly marked him out as a young director willing and able to commit his time to the company. He was not yet forty when selected for this work. And when asked additionally to represent the board on local area committees, he would no doubt have seen that as no more than doing his duty; though he must have been aware of the wider railway experience such work gave him.

In 1852 he had joined the Southern section of the 'Works Construction & Estates' committee. In this case it may have been significant that its chairman was J.F.Ledsam. Ledsam could already have known Moon through T.G.Curtler, Ledsam also being a local Worcestershire county magistrate. Ledsam was one of the original London & Birmingham directors who had been deputy chairman of that company since incorporation and one of the founder members of the L&NW board. Also in 1852 Moon became a member of the joint committees with the Birmingham and Shropshire Union canal companies; and the following year, those with the Wolverhampton Station, Stour Valley and South Staffordshire Railway.

The Birmingham Canal Navigations (to give that group of canals its full title) was an amalgamation of local companies first authorised in 1768 for the coal, iron and merchandise traffic of Birmingham and the Black Country. Essentially locally owned, the group had been a flourishing concern, but with the advent of the railways had looked to protect their interests by considering a railway of their own (along the line of their main waterway between Wolverhampton and Birmingham). In this they had the support of the L&B and the Shrewsbury & Birmingham Railway, the former then looking for an alternative to the Grand Junction for a route to the north-west. Together with these companies, the canal company agreed to subscribe to what became the Birmingham Wolverhampton &

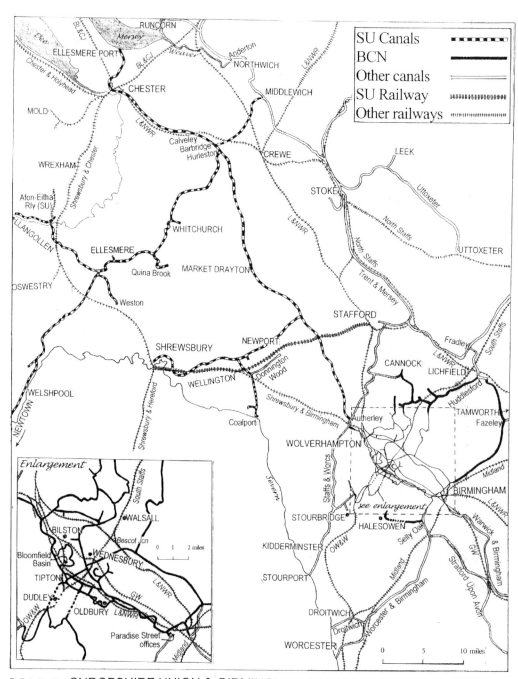

MAP 5 SHROPSHIRE UNION & BIRMINGHAM CANAL NAVIGATIONS

Position in 1854 when SU abandoned Railway projects

Stour Valley Railway (subsequently generally referred to as the Stour Valley). At the same time the L&B saw an opportunity to gain control of the canal by guaranteeing its 4% dividend. This was accepted by the canal and confirmed by the L&NW in 1846 (who had by then succeeded to the L&B powers). The L&NW later leased the Stour Valley, the delayed opening of which had so exercised Moon when writing as a shareholder.

Clearly it was not in the newly formed L&NW's interest to continue to support a competitive rail route beyond Shrewsbury to the Mersey. The dispute with the protesting Shrewsbury & Birmingham company which followed is touched on below in looking at Moon's involvement with the Wolverhampton Station Joint Committee. Before that a note on Moon's other main canal interest is relevant.

The Shropshire Union was formed in 1845 from a merger of two canals, the Birmingham & Liverpool Junction and the Ellesmere & Chester, with ambitious plans to convert their canals into a railway network. Changing their name to Shropshire Union these canals obtained powers in 1846 to expand their network further by merging with the Shrewsbury Canal, absorbing the Montgomeryshire and projecting four railways based on waterway routes. However they largely failed with their railway conversion plans. The Shrewsbury to Stafford line was the first and subsequently the only one of the proposed conversions to proceed; it included the stretch between Shrewsbury and Wellington authorised as a joint line with the S&B railway.

Faced with the alternative of either going it alone or developing their railways with a strong partner, the Shropshire Union (incorporated in 1846 as Shropshire Union Railways & Canal co.) took the obvious choice. They agreed terms, announced in December 1846, for the L&NW to guarantee a 'rent' equal to half the % dividend paid by the L&NW, 'such rent to commence when and as the several lines of railway shall be completed; all surplus profits up to 6% were to go to the Shropshire Union, thereafter to be shared with the L&NW'. In the meantime the SU proprietors were to receive 4% from their canal income. The works were to be executed and the undertaking managed by a committee comprising an equal number of directors of the two companies.

And there for the time being the matter rested, the L&NW not particularly interested in having the railways built and the canal company struggling to maintain canal traffic and unable to fund the other conversions. By early 1849 the canal board had taken powers to abandon their other railways, but nevertheless asked the L&NW for the lease terms to be effective as soon as the Stafford line was opened in the summer. Having been assured that the SU would not resurrect their other railway projects the L&NW agreed to implement the lease and guarantee the loan interest and dividend on the canal stock. The canal historian Charles Hadfield wrote: 'one cannot help thinking that the L&NW, in spite of the financial stringency of the time, lost great opportunity by not making use of the Shropshire Union's power to help its own expansions; later it was to lose others by its supine and negative attitude to other railway projects put up by the quite lively S.U. joint board'. Hadfield conceded though that 'on the canal side [i.e., as opposed to the railway projects] ... the directors were given a very free hand'.

Moon remained a member of the joint SU Committee (which had become the SU Amalgamated Board by 1859) into the early years of his L&NW chairmanship. In his initial attitude towards canals he demonstrated not only an awareness of their complementary role in serving an area as intensely industrialised as the west midlands, but also their advantages in carrying bulk loads. For example when access to the Cannock Chase coalfield was being considered Moon wrote in August 1853 'the Birmingham Canal extension is the true mode of supplying an outlet to the working of the minerals on the Chase'. In 1860 Moon reiterated the advantage of canals for bulk materials. Reacting to rate cutting competition from the Grand Junction Canal Company he wrote to his chairman warning that 'the canal will always beat the railway for bulk and can deliver in much better order and will always prevent our getting anything beyond small and odd lots ... and which need quick delivery'; an interesting viewpoint from a man about to become the chairman of Britian's largest railway.

Increasingly Moon came to be accepted as the L&NW director to whom west midland canal matters were referred. His view on the advantage of canals for bulk traffic was not peculiar to him. It was generally perceived at the time that canals could offer a greater threat than perhaps their means justified. The Grand Junction Canal was competing effectively with both the L&NW and the GW for traffic between the west midlands and London. A high proportion of this traffic originated on the Birmingham canals. It is worth noting that in the first twenty years of the L&NW lease, the tonnage over the BCN actually increased by nearly 50%. With over 150 miles of BCN canals and 200 miles of SU, the L&NW's interest in waterways was significant.

In addition to these canals the railway took a minority interest in the Rochdale Canal and owned the Huddersfield, Lancaster, St Helens and Coalport canals. Moon became a long-standing member of both the Birmingham Canal Navigations and Shropshire Union boards and, as the L&NW began to be called upon to meet guaranteed payments, so he tightened his control over their capital investments and the rates they charged. With the SU, the L&NW had to make up a deficit on the guarantee as early as 1851. In the case of the BCN, the canal was able to meet guaranteed levels of payments out of income until 1874 (with the exception of 1868). Both canals remained separate legal entities throughout Moon's time with the L&NW and he always listed his directorship of the BCN separately from his L&NW membership.

There were two other canals not related to the L&NW on Moon's doorstep at Bevere: the 'Droitwich' bordered his estate and the 'Worcester & Birmingham' his Claines parish. When in the twilight of his career he received the freedom of the borough of Crewe at their 1887 jubilee celebrations, he jokingly referred to when 'he made himself two votes by becoming a 40s. freeholder by a share in a canal which passed through Worcestershire'. It is not clear which one he meant, nor the significance of the vote.

When Moon first joined the Wolverhampton Station Joint Committee the war with the GW was not over. This committee brought him into direct contact with the 'ugly item' he had referred to before joining the L&NW. He had written in 1850 that he'd heard there was 'some hope of a settlement of our differences with the Shrewsbury & Birmingham and other parties in the same quarter under which we shall be able to open the Stour Valley line … and make amicable arrangements with the Great Western as to these districts'.

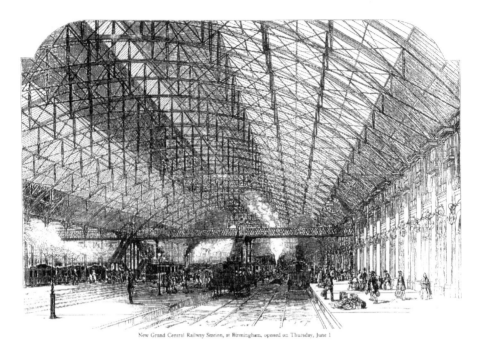

New Grand Central Railway Station, at Birmingham, opened on Thursday, June 1

22. Birmingham New Street 1854
Birminghams's new central station, New Street, when opened in June 1854. ILN

23. Birmingham Canal offices
The Paradise Street, Birmingham, head office of the Birmingham Canal
Navigations; opened in 1771, demolished 1928. LNWRS

Wolverhampton had been at the heart of the L&NW's battle to deny the GW a 7ft broad gauge route to the Mersey. Despite the 1846 findings of the Government's Gauge Commission that the narrow gauge of 4ft 8½ins should become the standard for any new line, it was then far from clear how this was to be applied to extensions of existing routes. The conflict in the west midlands had not only involved competition with the companies that eventually came under the control of the GW, but also stemmed from the pre-amalgamation feuding between the L&NW's own constituent companies.

Strenuous efforts had been made by the L&NW to take control of the key company, the Shrewsbury & Birmingham. The Stour Valley company, which the L&NW had supported and leased in 1847, had been incorporated in 1846 to build a line between Wolverhampton and Birmingham. However the Shrewsbury company had retained powers to extend through Wolverhampton for running powers over the Stour Valley into Birmingham. Critically these powers were conditional on the S&B remaining independent of the GW. The Stour Valley and the S&B then agreed to build a joint line and station at Wolverhampton to be managed by a committee of three directors from each company. At the end of 1851, when the SV gave notice that their line was to be opened, the S&B announced a service over it to connect to the L&NW's proposed new central station in Birmingham (subsequently New Street). The extension to New Street however was a directly owned L&NW line and not part of the Stour Valley, therefore the L&NW claimed the S&B's running powers into the station were invalid, and furthermore that the S&B had then become part of the GW and so forfeited such rights.

The S&B maintained they were still independent: a fine point made on the basis that their agreement to join the GW had not yet been implemented. Brooking no further argument, the L&NW physically blocked the track at Wolverhampton and the police had to be called to prevent public disorder. The L&NW then further responded by closing the SV line on "safety" grounds, not opening it until the summer of 1852, but by then the S&B had signed a formal traffic agreement with the GW. When Moon came into the picture at Wolverhampton, problems still remained over controlling the goods stations and access to the Birmingham canal. A compromise was reached in June 1853: the L&NW taking the joint goods station

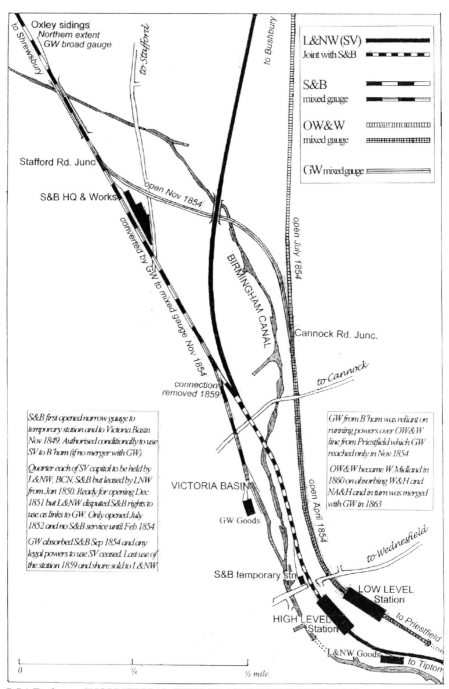

Oxley sidings
Northern extent
GW broad gauge

to Shrewsbury

to Stafford

to Bushbury

L&NW (SV)
Joint with S&B

S&B
mixed gauge

OW&W
mixed gauge

GW mixed gauge

Stafford Rd. Junc.

S&B HQ & Works

open Nov 1854

converted by GW to mixed gauge Nov 1854

open July 1854

BIRMINGHAM CANAL

Cannock Rd. Junc.

to Cannock

connection
removed 1859

S&B first opened narrow gauge to
temporary station and to Victoria Basin
Nov 1849. Authorised conditionally to use
SV to B'ham (if no merger with GW).

Quarter each of SV capital to be held by
L&NW, BCN, S&B but leased by LNW
from Jan 1850. Ready for opening Dec
1851 but L&NW disputed S&B rights to
use as links to GW. Only opened July
1852 and no S&B service until Feb 1854.

GW absorbed S&B Sep 1854 and any
legal powers to use SV ceased. Last use of
the station 1859 and share sold to L&NW

GW from B'ham was reliant on
running powers over OW&W
line from Priestfield which GW
reached only in Nov 1854

OW&W became W. Midland in
1860 on absorbing W&H and
NA&H and in turn was merged
with GW in 1863

VICTORIA BASIN

open April 1854

GW Goods

to Wednesfield

S&B temporary stn

LOW LEVEL
Station

HIGH LEVEL
Station

to Priestfield

L&NW Goods

to Tipton

0   ¼   ½ mile

MAP 6   WOLVERHAMPTON RAILWAYS IN THE 1850s
Battleground between L&NW and GW: Moon joined Station Jt Committee 1852

south of the passenger station, and the S&B at Cannock Road to the north.

In the meantime the Oxford Worcester & Wolverhampton was still struggling to complete its line. This was the company serving Worcester, which was to provide Moon with his most direct route to London. The delays in opening the line had been the subject of much agitation in the local Worcester press. No evidence has been found of any involvement by Moon in this or of any interest by him in the company. The OW&W was eventually to provide the link that enabled the broad gauge Birmingham Wolverhampton & Dudley Railway to reach Wolverhampton. This company had been effectively projected as an extension of the Birmingham & Oxford Railway and both these companies became part of the GW. Neither the OW&W nor the GW's Birmingham companies had opened their lines to Wolverhampton when the S&B was in conflict with the L&NW.

Though by the end of 1852 the OW&W had opened to Dudley, a year later they still had not proceeded beyond Tipton, being content to use the connection there with the SV line for access to their Wolverhampton station. (The SV's station was subsequently called the high level station.) At the other end of their route the OW&W finally reached Oxford in 1853: their line opening throughout from Dudley to the junction with the GW at Wolvercot in June. This led to an agreement for the L&NW to open a service from Wolverhampton to Dudley and over the OW&W line for a connection north of Oxford via the Buckinghamshire Railway for Bletchley and Euston.

As a Worcester resident Moon was to become very familiar with this service to London as it provided a shorter alternative to using the Midland Railway's line to Birmingham. Through carriages to Euston were facilitated in April 1854 when the Buckinghamshire was extended to join the OW&W at Yarnton, which enabled the L&NW to run direct to Bletchley and connect to main line trains for Euston. By October a west to south curve at Bletchley completed a route for full through running.

Once they became better organised, the OW&W ran the service themselves over their portion of the route with the L&NW taking over at Handborough. There are numerous references in L&NW meeting minutes to complaints over the OW&W service, no doubt many stemming from Moon himself.

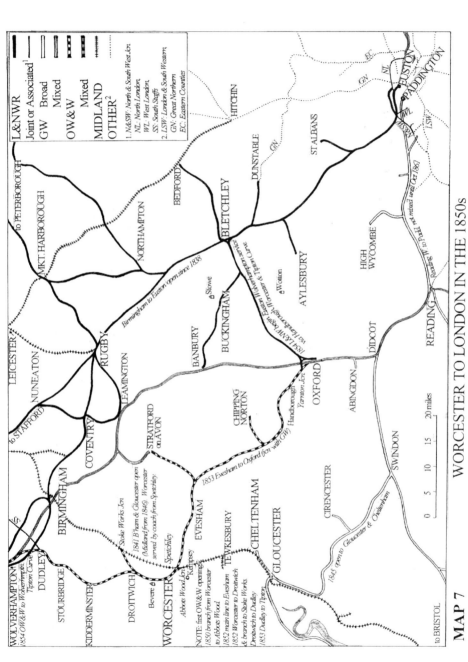

MAP 7 WORCESTER TO LONDON IN THE 1850s

Showing railways open by c.1860

Note when Moon moved to Kempsey only Spetchley was open for Worcester

The L&NW's Worcester line trains to Euston were to last until September 1861. In October the GW improved their alternative service from Oxford by adding the standard gauge rail to their main line from Reading to Paddington. However already in the spring of 1861 the railway politics in the area had changed dramatically. In July of the previous year the OW&W had absorbed the companies that had witnessed Moon's first foray into railway politics, the Newport Abergavenny & Hereford and the Worcester & Hereford, and renamed itself the West Midland Railway. The newly amalgamated company then attempted to negotiate with the L&NW for a new route via Banbury to London. Moon was to object strongly to any such negotiation but events soon made any protests irrelevant. After an attempt by the West Midland to support a bill independent of both the L&NW and the GW for access to London, the railway world was suddenly shocked by the withdrawal of this scheme in April 1861 and a merger of the West Midland and GW announced.

As he was to remain in Worcester for many more years, the opening of an exclusive GW route from Worcester to Paddingon would still have been the most direct service for Moon to use for his many meetings in London, but it is not known if he regularly used this service.

The Wolverhampton Station Joint Committee continued in being after the GW controlled low level station was opened at the end of 1854. As relations between the GW and the L&NW improved, some Shrewsbury to Birmingham services continued to use the high level station and the Stour Valley line. Negotiations for the eventual purchase by the L&NW of the original S&B share of the high level station were not completed until 1858, Moon being one of the three L&NW directors empowered to settle with the GW. The SV line, although leased to the L&NW, remained a separate company until absorbed in 1867 with a group of other companies including the South Staffordshire Railway.

Moon had been deputed to represent his company in negotiations with the South Staffordshire to secure control over what had been an independently promoted line. Incorporated in 1846, from a merger of two earlier companies centred on Walsall, the company provided a south-west to north-east link from the OW&W at Dudley to the Midland Railway at Wichnor, south of Burton-on-Trent.

Its main route cut across the lines of the L&NW and those of the GW (BW&D) between Birmingham and Wolverhampton. The route was open by the end of 1850 and agreement reached with a private individual, J.R.McClean, to operate the line. This was despite the interests held by the L&NW and the Midland in subscribing to the capital of the company and being represented on the board (both large companies had been anxious to keep out the GW).

In August 1850 the line had been leased to McClean for a guarantee based on 4% of the capital, rising to 4½% after eight years and 5% after fourteen years, the lessee depositing £10,000 as security for fulfilling the contract. Having initially declined to work the line, the L&NW had offered as early as February 1852 to take over from McClean guaranteeing a payment based on 80% of their own dividends. Although not taken up by McClean, he did contract for the L&NW to supply motive power. However with his increasing interest in other activities, such as the local water works and coal mines on Cannock Chase, he may well have begun to reconsider his railway lease. The L&NW had partly financed his branches to the coalfield at Cannock and Norton by paying £40,000 in shares and £96,000 in loans. McClean agreed to rent the branches for 4% on the capital expended.

Moon first attended a SSR board in February 1853. Surprisingly he had little knowledge of the company beforehand, writing to Stewart the L&NW secretary asking for 'an idea of the policy of our company if there be any matter requiring attention'.

Exploitation of the coalfield on Cannock Chase had led for demands for improved rail and canal access. The SSR was promoting an extension to the coalfield. Unable to attend the local company's meeting in August, when the extension was to be considered, Moon was still uncertain over the stance he should be adopting and wrote again for guidance. He admitted that he 'did not know exactly how the matter with reference to the Cannock branch was left over at our board last week'. In saying he preferred the canal extension, he commented that 'the proposed railway line is out of the direction ... being too near the cropping out of the district and that moreover there is not sufficient trade on the SSR lines for the minerals which will be used naturally for the supply of the Birmingham district'. He added that 'there is further to be considered how far such a project will prevent other parties being able to get a footing in the district and the determination of the coal owners to have such additional mode of egress'. From this tentative introduction Moon was soon to move centre stage in the negotiations that led to the SSR being absorbed into the L&NW system. As the only main board member among the L&NW representatives on their board, he had by the end of 1857 taken the lead in dealing with McClean and reviewing possibilities for taking over the lease. Difficulties had been experienced in getting McClean to settle locomotive accounts, and tolls of £7,500 for running over the L&NW were unpaid. Moon found an ally on the SSR board in Philip Williams (L&NW director in 1861). Neele in his *Reminiscences* noted that on the opening of the Cannock branch Moon and Williams 'had a special engine to take them along the line'. A revealing aside on Williams, and conditions in the area at the time, was a press report (*Wolverhampton Chronicle* 13 October 1858) of his chairmanship of a meeting of 'coal masters' when rejecting a claim from striking colliers in Oldbury and West Bromwich. Men in all other areas of the local coal field had apparently accepted a cut in wages from 5s.0d. to 4s.0d. as a result of depressed trade, where 'at this reduced rate an ordinary Collier may readily earn 28s.0d a week with the usual allowance of two quarts of beer and his fire coal in addition'.

Negotiations with McClean became protracted. Moon had written to Chandos on 4 January 1858 saying agreement with McClean seemed 'impossible at any reasonable price' and hoped that Stewart had not led McClean 'to expect we shall buy him out'. Moon had offered to guarantee 4%. However he told Chandos they should be prepared to go to the 80% of the L&NW dividend if necessary though adding 'not a whisper of it ought to be heard'. Moon seemed to have been unnecessarily secretive, the 80% would hardly have been any more attractive than a straight 4% (even less on the poor L&NW dividends for 1858 and 1859).

Negotations were further protracted by McClean's frequent absences through either illness or such projects as reporting on the Suez Canal. It was not until Moon became L&NW deputy chairman that a final settlement was agreed. After a decisive SSR board meeting on 18 March 1861, Moon wrote to Stewart 'we have passed everything today as agreed except ... substituted Charles Forster's name for Mr Glyn as one of our representatives'. He then informed

Stewart that the board 'have elected myself chairman and Chawner deputy chairman and yourself secretary'. The L&NW directors reported to their August 1861 half-yearly meeting that 'all questions, the subject of arbitration, were withdrawn, on payment of the sum of £110.098.16s.7d., including the lessee's interest in the unexpired term of eleven years in the agreement known as the "Four Towns" agreement" [traffic pooling between Birmingham, Wolverhampton, Walsall and Dudley]'.

It was during his earlier disputes with McClean, in the summer of 1857, that Moon, as a L&NW director, made his only known venture outside the railway. He invested privately with some fellow L&NW directors in the Wolverhampton New Waterworks Company. That he should have done so in an industry which could give rise to a conflict of interest suggests, despite his increasing commitment to the L&NW, that he still regarded his involvement as somewhat detached. This attitude was to be confirmed in a long letter he wrote the following year to Chandos on the problems of management and direction, which will be examined later. What seems so out of character, given the dedication he subsequently gave to the L&NW, was to land himself in a dispute over financing the growth of a water company at a time when he was actively engaged in administering water supply contracts. This dispute led him to write to an unwell Chandos on 7 April 1858 apologising for giving so much trouble 'with this Wolverhampton squabble, and shall be thankful when it is set at rest as far as its introduction into L&NW affairs is concerned, but fear it will interfere with my usefulness to the railway for some considerable time to come'.

The problem came to a head at the end of 1858 when Moon was summoned to the then Court of Common Pleas, albeit as a witness, on behalf of the water company. The case involved disputed calls for payment of company shares. The publicity generated did little to enhance the reputation of either the water company or its subscribers. The background to water supplies in Wolverhampton was far from straightforward. A company had been authorised in 1845, but had struggled to meet even a third of the demand estimated and found it necessary in 1850 to obtain further powers to tap new sources. The latter proved even less productive and lacking capital for further development, the company considered selling its works to the town.

Terms however could not be agreed and the town sought powers to secure its own water supply. In the meantime a new company was promoted, all three bodies seeking parliamentary powers in 1855. After a costly nine day parliamentary hearing the new company defeated the town's bill.

The Wolverhampton New Waterworks Company was enacted with a capital of £100,000. However with the old company still in existence, no new works were started until the new company eventually negotiated to purchase the old facilities; the transfer being enacted in 1856. The principal promoter and chairman of the new company was George Holyoake, a local banker who appeared to have been motivated by the opportunity to sell his land for a new reservoir. When this seemed impractical, he lost his keen interest in the project and subscriptions failed to meet the capital authorised. Matters languished until the summer of 1857 when pressure to proceed with new work led to resumed activity to secure finance.

The company succeeded in allocating 5,000 of the £5 shares, a quarter of the original capital, to 'Messrs T.Ashton of Manchester and R.Moon of Bevere, Worcester'. In his court evidence Moon stated he was allotted 1,500 shares on 15 July 1857. Up until then only about 3,000 shares had been taken, but neither T.Ashton nor Moon was aware of that at the time. With the work at last started Holyoake, whose bank had lent the company money, was aware of the need (under the Act) to complete the share subscription contract before the borrowing powers of £33,000 could be exercised. In spite of strenuous promotional efforts and the allocation of shares in part payment to three contractors, there remained a shortfall of 1,356 shares. To complete the subscription contract Holyoake and fellow director, banking partner Sir Francis Goodwicke, considered allocating shares nominally to their company secretary. In the end they allocated the 1,356 shares to themselves as bankers, but with no intention of meeting any calls for payment. The company then offered debentures for the loan capital.

Another Ashton, J.H., assuming the subscription had been legally met, advanced £5,000 in October. As other calls on shares were made, dissatisfaction grew over Holyoake's refusal to meet his on the 1,356, as did general criticism over the way the company was run. By the end of 1857 Moon, together with a Mr Tootal had become directors, and other non-local investors, mainly from Manchester, began to influence affairs. During early 1858 further board changes were made with local members being displaced by J.Bancroft, J.Brook, T.Ashton, J.H.Ashton and M.Lyon. Holyoake resigned and Bancroft became chairman. All these new members had presumably discussed the investment whilst meeting as shareholders of the L&NW. The Tootal was probably Henry (brother of Edward) who with Holyoake and Goodwicke were also directors of the Shropshire Union canal company. Thomas Ashton was the younger brother of Samuel, a L&NW director, and later succeeded him in building the family cotton manufacturing business into one of the leading ones in Manchester.

Bancroft, Brook and Lyon were all L&NW directors as was the main contractor who had taken 5,000 shares in part payment for materials, the iron pipe supplier Richard Barrow. Bancroft had also been earlier associated with Holyoake in an adjudicating role as his representative in valuing the land for the potential reservoir.

A note here on James Bancroft is relevant. A self made man he was to become a trusted associate of Moon after Moon became chairman of the L&NW. He had pursued an early career as a Manchester merchant and, as Alderman Bancroft, an active member of the city corporation, chairing its Improvement Committee which oversaw the redevelopment of large areas of the city. At the same time he established a formidable reputation as a private arbitrator settling land and other disputes involving, for example, both public bodies such as the corporations of Liverpool and Manchester, and private companies including water and railways at home and abroad. It was as an energetic sixty-year old that he had been elected to the L&NW board in February 1858. His direct railway experience had been varied. An early shareholder (as Moon, E.Tootal and Ashton had been) in the Birkenhead Lancashire & Cheshire Junction Railway, he was not only elected to that company's board in early 1848, but also appointed chairman. As such he had flirted with both the L&NW and GW in attempts to sell or have that company leased by them, eventually resigning as chairman in frustration over lack of board support. He had also been on the board of the Blackburn Railway and taken part in that small company's unsuccessful fight in 1857 to resist being taken over jointly by the Lancashire & Yorkshire and East Lancashire companies.

The new Wolverhampton Water board set about securing the finance and completing their works. But when overdue calls on shares were chased, Holyoake still refused to pay on his, claiming they were in part discharge of the company's debt to his bank and similar in principle to issuing paid-up shares to contractors. The company pressed the claim and took him to court, Moon and Ashton giving evidence on their behalf.

The company's case was dismissed on the grounds that Holyoake was never officially registered as a shareholder for the 1,356 shares in dispute. The company abandoned the case, probably on the grounds that even if he were proved to be a shareholder Holyoake would still claim the shares were paid-up as security for his bank's loan. Incidentally in suing another alleged defaulter, J.Hawkesford (one of the original subscribers and director), the case led to one of the judgements which confirmed the principle that a subscriber for shares could not be held liable for payment until legally registered as a shareholder.

When the Holyoake hearing was held at the end of 1858, Moon still had shares in the company (though he had divested himself of a third). In October he had been listed by the local paper in the 'highly influential company' of guests at the opening of South Staffordshire Waterworks at Lichfield and Walsall, which incidentally were engineered by McClean. It could not have helped local relationships that Holyoake was a director of the Shropshire Union. Matters between the L&NW and the canal company were strained at the time by a number of disputes. These though were but side shows to the troubles brewing elsewhere in the L&NW. Grappling with problems of overall direction and management, the company was faced with yet further demands for economy and how to respond to growing competition.

CHAPTER 9

OUSTING OF HUISH

Although Moon's progession to senior director had been recognised by his appointment to the L&NW's Executive Committee, it seems that he was not convinced that such a forum should take priority over his own committee work. He was not able to attend the regular meetings of the Executive without disrupting the work of his own. Convinced that the committee structure was ineffective, particularly its lack of control over the principal officers, a frustrated Moon gave notice at the 9 January 1858 board meeting 'that at the next ordinary board he should make a statement of his views as to the future management of the undertaking, and propose a motion with reference thereto'.

It becomes clear that Moon meant more by 'management' than criticism of Huish and other officers. When the matter was discussed at the 12 February board it is evident that some disagreement took place. The board minute covering Moon's motion read that:

> It would conduce to the more efficient administration of the affairs of the company if they could be brought under the more continuous control and direction of the board or of a portion of its members specially deputed for that purpose, and that the mode of carrying out this view be specially considered at the next meeting of the board. An amendment was moved that further consideration of the important question raised be postponed, was lost, the numbers being 7 for, 14 against, as was also a further amendment to substitute "practicability" for "mode", the numbers being 9 for, 11 against. The original question was carried, the numbers being 15 for and 4 against.

When the matter was considered at the next board the chairman and deputy chairman were requested to 'devise a programme' and a 'selection of members' for the proposed strengthened executive. This was to be 'on the understanding that the chairmen of each committee form, with the chairman and deputy chairman, a special or central committee to supersede the existing Special Affairs and Parliamentary Committees'. Guidance was given that there should be four or five main committees, the number of members of each committee should be not less than three or more than five, and if possible, no director should be a member of more than one committee.

Though Moon's forthright views on the need for reforms may not have endeared him to some of the older established directors, it is clear that by then he did have the confidential ear of his young chairman. A note from him to Chandos dated 1 March 1858 is remarkable for the frankness with which they reviewed the suitability of fellow directors for membership of these new committees. Moon thought that a list of directors he mentioned (Chandos, Moorsom, Lyon, Bancroft, Benson, Tootal, Ashton, Moon, Brook, Thompson, Clements) 'is almost too much to call it a working list but it is the best I can pick' ... 'nor could I give you my estimate of them in writing'. Having said that he then went on to do so:

> Of whom likely to act, Chandos Lyon Moorsom Bancroft Moon Brook Tootal (at least he wrote me to say "If I remain a director I shall not wish to be out of all your committees as you may suppose"). He is a good man if he would work but will not be here before June or July [Tootal was abroad]. If you don't put him for chairman [of a committee] he will be a good committee man for any requiring strength. Ascertain from Ashton what he would do. My own scheme was for [committee] chairmen: Moorsom Lyon Bancroft Moon, perhaps Thompson for Finance if he would undertake to do it well, though he was unsuccessful as a banker in the management of Heywood's firm. You see the materials are deplorable between those who would not accept and those who are not equal to the posts proposed, yet once appointed difficult to displace. None of the Liverpool men will do at all. ... It has been suggested to me that we should put the mayor of Liverpool James Holme, who has done the Lancashire & Yorkshire

such good service in the Dock Committee, on our board
and that he would be willing to come. He is rather a vulgar
man but hard-headed and we want some one in Liverpool
of that sort.

At the next special board meeting following the above exchange
the chairman reported that his new structure would require five
standing committees besides the Special Affairs or 'Chairman's
Committee'. These were to cover: Finance (including capital
expenditure), Traffic (including goods and the Chester & Holyhead),
Permanent Way (also combining branch lines and estate), Audit
(including rating and superannuation), and Stores. A proposal
to combine Stores with Traffic was considered. Moon not only
argued strongly against this, but also wanted all manufacturing and
production material to be controlled by his committee. Moon won
the day when it was agreed that 'the control of the large expenditure
for materials can <u>not</u> [sic] be efficiently performed by the Traffic
Committee in addition to the other duties, and recommended the
continuance of a Stores Committee ... and that the charge of the
expenditure in the manufacturing establishments be also vested in
them'. The later was to include, for example, the authorisation for
laying down a complete locomotive building programme.

Reference to the Chester & Holyhead Railway was to cover the
L&NW's responsibilities for running services over this line and the
Irish mail contract. Moon's involvement in negotiations that led to
the absorbtion of this company is covered below. In the meantime
the reformed Chairman's Committee was to meet weekly in London
(the day before the board in the week that it met) to review the points
arising from all the various committees and other subsidiary boards.
The principal members and the committees they headed were as
follows: Smith (finance), Moorsom (traffic), Lyon (permanent way
& estate), Ledsam (audit & rating) and Moon (stores & locomotive
expenditure). This new committee however was still not what
Moon had envisaged for within months he was complaining over
its inadequacy. At least the problem of overlapping was avoided, no
director was appointed to more than one of these main committees.

Moon's new Stores & Locomotive Expenditure Committee
comprised Blake, Brook, Grant and the Marquis of Stafford (son

of Duke of Sutherland). Local area committees were to continue consisting of directors resident in the different divisions 'to pass accounts ... and deal generally with any matter referred to them by the Board or Committees'. Grant was to be the representative on the Lancaster & Carlisle company board; Tootal on the Manchester South Junction & Altrincham, Rochdale Canal, North Union and Preston station; and Mangles the North London. The only directors not listed in any of the new committees were Benson, Ellis and Glyn. At the 13 March board Chandos was re-elected chairman and Moorsom elected deputy.

Older statesman Moorsom shared Moon's scepticism and clearly had doubts over his own role in the new structure. Moorsom had written earlier to Chandos as follows:

> The board has dealt so fairly with the question of reform that I feel they have a right to look to me for such aid as I can give in the attempt to carry it out, though I was not prominent in raising or discussing the proposed plan. I am willing as an old member of the board to give my help. On the other hand I have considerable doubt whether, with so numerous a board, a small number charged with administrative function on the principle of individual responsibility will be able to hold their own for long. The administrations of William and Anne were continually upset by the Privy Council (more than the House of Commons) till the cabinet system grew up, and then the privy council went to sleep. Will our board follow their example? I have also another doubt, whether the men can be found to give a fair chance to the plan. I must however take such part as the board may select me for, or make room for someone else, and at present it would not be right to take the latter course, though I have expressed the opinion that the greatest benefit that could be conferred on the company would be the retirement of some half dozen of us old directors.

Both Moorsom and Earle were sixty-five in March 1858 and together with Cropper, Glyn, Grant, Ledsam and Smith were the only remaining members of the original L&NW board; Moon was then forty three, Chandos only thirty four. As a ship's captain Moorsom had enjoyed a distinguished career at sea before rising to Rear-Admiral in 1851 and Vice-Admiral 1857. He joined the London & Birmingham in 1833, as Birmingham secretary, being elected to the board in 1839. His experience in administering its contruction led to his chairing the Birmingham & Gloucester railway 1842-3, and then resident director of the Chester & Holyhead in 1844. From 1849 he chaired the C&H until giving way to Peto when negotiations for the L&NW to lease the company fell through in 1851. As has been noted he headed the L&NW's 1848 internal investigation but his later work for the company mainly concerned locomotive and traffic affairs.

Although Moon had taken no direct part in the earlier talks leading to the Chester & Holyhead purchase, he did become a member of the team appointed to agree final amalgamation terms. His disagreement with Chandos over the settlement makes interesting reading, not only for the insight it gives into his attitude to bargaining, but also with reference to his later defence of the deal.

Authorised in 1844 with a share capital of £2.1 million, the Chester & Holyhead had been backed by the London & Birmingham who subscribed £1 million and appointed half the directors. In September of that year Moorsom accepted the position as resident director to facilitate development and subsequently moved to Chester, being paid the appreciable sum of £1,000 p.a. In 1847 the company reached agreement for the L&NW to operate the line and the following year, when the Conway bridge was ready, the first through Irish mail service was run (by using the road bridge across to Anglesey). Not until the first tube of the Menai Bridge was opened in March 1850 was this a satisfactory service and the L&NW had been reluctant until then to develop traffic.

Impatient local C&H shareholders, led by W.Jackson (one of the directors appointed originally by the connecting Chester & Birkenhead railway), then threatened to give a lease to contractors Peto, Betts & Brassey which forced the L&NW to seek parliamentary authorisation to take over the debt and lease the line. However the Bill was abandoned and with Peto elected to the C&H board a new working agreement with the L&NW was negotiated. When Peto took personal responsibility for meeting overdue debt interest,

24. C.R.Moorsom

Vice Admiral C.R. Moorsom (1792-1861): resident director
Chester & Holyhead from 1844 (chairman 1849-51) and
L&NW vice-chairman 1858 and chairman Jan. to May 1861. NRM

25. Chester Station c.1860

Opened in 1848 the joint station at Chester in c.1860. Built by the
C&H and Shrewsbury & Chester, it subsequently became jointly owned
by the L&NW and the GW. Chester History & Heritage

Moorsom, who had been chairman since 1849, resigned leaving Peto and Jackson effectively in control of the local interests.

A new working agreement between the C&H and the L&NW was reached in 1854 and in the summer of 1855 the L&NW, C&H and the City of Dublin Steam Packet companies were authorised (under the Act for the "Improved Postal & Passenger Communications with Ireland") to set up a joint committee to operate steamers for mails and passengers. Yet another new agreement was then reached whereby the L&NW undertook to work the line by providing the plant and rolling stock with the local company maintaining the track. By early 1856 the L&NW had taken over all the working stock and equipment and in July a joint committee was formed to control the line. Within twelve months it was agreed that all staff would become employees of the L&NW. However the C&H maintained its separate existence as a company with Peto still representing the independent shareholders.

By the end of 1857 the companies did agree to amalgamate, but the L&NW balked at taking over the loss making steamers as the new mail contract starting in 1859 specified the Dublin company's boats. The C&H then refused to sign the mail contract until favourable merger terms with the L&NW were agreed. And to strengthen their position they sought powers to raise more capital and give other railway companies access to their line. The L&NW rejected such arrangements and the C&H then threatened to seek an alternative agreeement and prepared a Bill for running powers over the L&NW Chester and Crewe line to connect with other railways. It was following this last threat that Moon joined the L&NW team to help conclude a satisfactory settlement.

Earlier, in September 1858, Moon had complained to Chandos 'with regard to the C&H, I hardly know what to say …we have done enough for the sake of getting no dividend on our million invested'. He went on to criticise the arrangements, the costs and the capital in relation to income, contrasting Peto's statement of the traffic at £200,000 p.a. with their own figures where the total traffic exchanged in 1857 was only £117,246. It had been when the L&NW's Special Committee reviewed the report on the situation given by Chandos and Smith that it was agreed that Moon and Tootal should join the negotiating team (the exclusion of Moorsom seems surprising).

Chandos and Smith, however, appeared to have continued discussions without involving their colleagues. Moon wrote on 18 October asking Chandos not to agree to the 2½% guarantee on the C&H agreement and suggesting ½% every half year. He also warned Chandos from taking Stewart, 'I would advise you to prohibit Stewart from talking to Peto or any of the party because every wavering tone and look tells against us in price'. And, he added, always take with you Tootal 'who is certainly a practised hand at that kind of thing. …It is all a question of management in bargaining'.

For reasons that are not clear Chandos and Smith still continued to negotiate on their own, Moon complaining in a 4 December letter that the four of them had been appointed by the board to consider the arrangements. A week later, after agreement had been reached, he again wrote to Chandos strongly criticising him over the unsatisfactory settlement. Accusing him of not having the power to agree and not consulting himself and Tootal, Moon wrote 'I do trust another time you will treat your Cabinet Council more openly. … However it is no use crying over spilt milk but this I do feel, that it is no light matter to saddle our concern with a settled permanent burden of £3,500,000 (beyond our own million) … that we might have bought it on very much better terms if the cards had been well played'. He went on to say that Stewart, and also Smith, were afraid of Peto and his board.

To his credit Chandos appears not to have taken offence in attempting to justify the agreement, leaving Moon to respond that 'we must agree to differ'. The £3.5 million burden referred to by Moon comprised the balance of the £1.1 million ordinary shares, issues of preference shares totalling nearly £1.2 million (plus a commitment for a new issue of £0.2 million) and loans of nearly £1.1 million. Moon's suggestion of phasing ½% does appear to have had some effect as the dividend guaranteed on the £1.1 million stock held by the independent shareholders was nil for 1859 and 1860, 1% in 1861, 2% in 1862 and 2½% in 1863 and thereafter. The agreement was ratified by shareholders of both companies. Peto did well to obtain the 2½% guarantee, but both sides were criticised by their shareholders: the C&H for selling out just as the company was moving into a position to make a return and the L&NW for paying too much. The market agreed with the latter viewpoint and the C&H shares jumped in value. The take-over was effective from the 1 January 1859. When later as chairman Moon was faced with a shareholder complaining over the favourable terms given he was to retort: 'what did the latter get? 2½ per cent for their £100. It surely was not a bad bargain to have such a line with Ireland at the end of it for 2½ per cent'.

Returning to Chandos's new committee of chairmen, or 'Special' Committee as it came to be called, it met for the first time on 18 March 1858 and the new enhanced Stores Committee a week later (appropriately at the main manufacturing works in Crewe). In the meantime dissatisfaction over the management, following the poor trading results, led Moon to write to Chandos in April: 'how are we to make both ends meet with present prospects of traffic? I shall be obliged to press my resolution as to our manager [Huish] in order to get a chance of economy in our working'. And Moorsom wrote at the end of May that 'the whole of our executive detail is in a most unsatisfactory state'. Moon renewed his criticism in June when following a difficulty over the availability of wagon sheets he wrote:

> It is much easier to get over a difficulty by increasing the quantity by a large outlay of money than properly using what we have got ... Capt. Huish will resist the application of the knife to our expenses as far as he can. The present system is an imperfect attempt to carry out our recommendations of 1855 and you know I have always been of opinion it did not half do what is wanted beside being unnecessarily expensive ... One way or other we must stop the capital expenditure and reduce our expenses.

Moon also took the opportunity to criticise Huish for running extra excursion trains for the Queen's visit in competition with the GW (between London and Birmingham) as 'pure folly'. And Moorsom wrote again to Chandos on the 2 August complaining that:

> The company's affairs are such as to require the regular administration of persons above the position of executive officers. Much of the unsatisfactory results we experience

is from circumstances which no administration could possibly avert, but much also arises from there being no responsible administrative body, knowing everything and acting continuously, and yet so as to leave the officers responsible for the execution of orders. ... The present arrangements are satisfactory to no one.

Reiterating this view on 6 September, Moorsom added: 'these functions are not provided for in our system and are necessarily carried on by the executive officers, except as they are fitfully interfered with by individual directors. It is this which has spoilt our chief officers, destroyed their responsibility, and made them a sort of hybrid, and will continue to do so whoever may replace them'.

These comments had followed discussions between Chandos and his senior colleagues. Chandos had earlier suggested removing Huish by appointing him to the board, but Glyn had written on 5 September saying he did not agree. Moorsom however, in his 6 September letter, had continued:

Your main question is how to deal with our present manager. I have always considered that the inevitable course would be to offer him a seat at the board, and have so expressed my opinion. If he declines I would on no consideration agree to a pension or its equivalent, as in Trevithick's case. I think it is for the chairman to decide a fitting time for this. If you say now, I concur. As to a successor, it has often occurred to me that Stewart is more fit for manager than secretary, and I should be disposed to offer it to him, but without an increase of salary, as I should not think of giving any manager more than £1500 a year, and I think £1200 sufficient. ... If Stewart were to decline I should prefer looking out for a person not tainted with railway management to begin with, which he whom you name must very deeply be. I should desire an intelligent executive officer - not an intriguing, web-weaving protocoller [sic], and I confess I do not know such a one.

Moorsom's criticism must already have been well known to Chandos. In November 1854 he had already complained strongly of Huish interfering in locomotive affairs. 'If we had a manager,' Moorsom had written:

> Who instead of sitting all day on a tripod, like a Delphian Oracle of old - fulminating prophesies - were to occupy himself out of doors on the line ... and learn by his own knowledge the real facts, instead of taking for granted every scrap of paper that anybody writes against the locomotive, the directors would be spared much trouble that it is not their place to take, and our affairs would be more satisfactorily managed.

This view was echoed by David Stevenson who, in his memoirs, wrote that Huish 'managed the line from his office, seldom visiting the stations, but left the details almost wholly in the hands of his responsible officers'.

It was not until the annual dividend reached the nadir of 4% in 1858 that the ineffectiveness of continuing a policy of aggressively relying on protective agreements forced directors like Moon to demand change. It is not clear when he first began to have doubts over Huish. A letter he wrote to Chandos in October 1855 suggests that he was already dissatisfied. 'I have not much hope of agreeing with Capt. Huish on many points, since having looked over our evidence, but we shall see what can be done'. However Moon could then have been referring to some aspects of his investigation work when it would have been surprising if there had been complete agreement. But by the autumn of 1856, as has been seen in his 10 October letter to Chandos, there can be no doubt of his criticism of Huish's management. And by 1858 he considered the situation had reached crisis proportions and that the arrogance and lavish management style of Huish were significant contributory factors in the company's poor performance.

To understand the L&NW crisis that came to a head in 1858, it is too simplistic to lay the blame only on the lack of control over costs and the shortcomings of management. Railway companies generally had underestimated the costs of replacing track and infrastucture and the increasing requirements for additional locomotives, rolling stock and new equipment. Added to this had been a steep rise from the mid-fifties in material prices generally. Fruitless arguments over whether some costs should be allocated to capital or revenue simply detracted from the problem. Calls for closing the capital account were totally unrealistic even if no new lines or extensions were built. And, of most significance, had been the advent of greater competition. Additional railways were promoted and authorised without any regard to a centrally planned network, being attracted by existing traffic patterns, which inevitably led to duplication of facilities and services.

As the largest company with originally a near monopoly of services from London to the midlands and the north-west, as well as being the dominant company in the west coast route to Scotland, the L&NW had the most to lose. The GW wanted a share of their west-midlands traffic; and a new company, the Great Northern, projected as the London & York, as well as fringing into the east-midlands, wanted a share of the Manchester traffic as well as the Scottish. It was the strategies and tactics used to mitigate against these threats that had so brought the L&NW into disrepute, none more so than those used to contain the Great Northern (see Map 3).

The GN had first run a through service from London to Yorkshire, albeit via their 'loop' Boston and Lincoln line, in 1850 when their main line from London to Peterborough opened. They posed a more competitive threat when their direct 'towns' line from Peterborough to Retford opened in 1852. This established a competitive east-coast service to Edinburgh via York that was independent of the L&NW and Midland route via Rugby and Normanton. The lines of eight separate companies were then involved in services between London and Scotland. An "Octuple Agreement" was signed to pool receipts between London and Edinburgh with proportions allocated based on a given traffic flow, fixed for five years. The young GN accepted a lower share than could have been expected for their new direct route, but accepted this as preferable to uncontrolled competition.

A separate agreement between the six Euston route companies for traffic north of York allocated proportions and routes between themselves: the so-called "Euston Confederacy". For traffic up to York, the GN sought a similar agreement with the L&NW and its Midland and MSL partners for traffic between London and the six towns of York, Leeds, Wakefield, Doncaster, Sheffield and Lincoln. Failing to agree on the apportionment all parties accepted arbitration by W.E.Gladstone (then President of the Board of Trade). A "Six Towns" agreement was signed taking effect (also for five years) from 1 January 1851. Four additional towns (Nottingham, Newark, Stamford and Peterborough) were included in 1853. By these agreements the L&NW had undoubtedly held on to a share of traffic to places more directly served by the GN, and also of traffic from Euston on the Normanton route to York, which never justified their allocation under the Octuple Agreement.

The weak financial position of the MS&L led them in 1854 to agree to work even closer with the L&NW, in return for a guaranteed minimum level of traffic receipts, by denying the GN access to their line at Retford for a route to Manchester. The L&NW and the Midland had also drawn closer, the two companies proposing amalgamation in 1853 but eventually signing in 1854 a "common purse" agreement (pooling receipts under a joint managing committee on the basis of existing traffic flows).

With the Octuple due for renewal in 1856 a stronger GN demanded a fairer share and refused to concede that they should be kept out of the east midlands and Manchester. Both parties flexed their muscles with fares cut initially between London and Peterborough (which both the L&NW and the Midland reached only through long branches) and the West Riding before arbitration was agreed. A shareholder at the L&NW's February 1856 meeting hoped 'that in future disputes in respect to traffic, the directors would employ men with diplomatic minds, and not traffic managers'. However by the time arbitration judgement was given in May 1857 the matter had become academic. The L&NW's pooling agreement with the Midland was declared illegal and in June the MS&L, in a complete reversal of policy, announced they were breaking their 1854 agreement with the L&NW and would cooperate fully in developing through traffic with the GN at Retford and compete aggressively with them for the London Manchester traffic.

In the recriminations that followed both the MS&L and the L&NW blamed the other, the former claiming that the L&NW had not honoured their side of the agreement and that Huish had gone behind their back to negotiate a separate agreement with the GN for a division of territory. Both Chandos and Huish publicly denied these allegations countering that the MS&L had been unable to provide evidence and ignored the terms of the agreement to give notice or go to arbitration. The L&NW appeared justified in exposing the fickleness of the MS&L in breaking what they considered a legally binding agreement. The irony of the situation was that the 1854 agreement had been largely negotiated on behalf of the MS&L by their newly appointed manager Edward Watkin, who had then only recently resigned from the L&NW as Huish's assistant.

Many commentators have pointed the finger at Huish for the breakdown in relations and it would have been in character for him to overplay his hand in negotiations. No one, however, would have been more aware than Watkin of the value of the Retford link as a competitive route from the south to Manchester. It would have equally been in character for him to use expediency in 1854 and opportunism three years later to switch so abruptly to support the GN.

At a meeting of the L&NW Executive on 1 July 1857, Huish was mandated 'to take such steps under the sanction of the chairman as may be necessary to neutralise the efforts of the competing companies by running additional fast trains and otherwise'. Confined to Bevere by his doctor Moon wrote to Chandos on 21 July 1857 that he had heard of proposals to run trains from Manchester to London in 4½ hours 'during the approaching competition'. He could 'scarcely credit it and trust you will not assent to any such arrangement except in the last resort of our opponents doing almost the same'. His solution typified an approach he was to adopt when running the railway (though not always finding it convenient to put into practice):

My own view would be to aim first at exact punctuality in any speed attempted and governed by that to fix only a few minutes quicker than the other route. It seems to me that the Sheffield [MS&L] are bound to try to get some of the traffic at all risks if we try to shut them out entirely and we shall only force them to quicker to reduce the rate, whereas I think our object should be rather to let them have a little traffic making that the least amount that will stop their mouths - we cannot keep it all from them without

a ruinous competition in prices under which we shall
suffer most and the Sheffield next, the Great Northern not
suffering in any case.

He went on to add that he was 'not going to enter into a general
discussion but merely will repeat my hope that no attempt will be
made to run in less than 5 hours except on compulsion and that
Liverpool will not be included', otherwise 'we shall never get them
back again to the old times'. He added that he would stop only at
Stafford and Rugby with the Manchester trains. However on 24 July
the L&NW Executive (Moon was not listed as present) agreed Huish's
proposals for the August timetable to have at least three fast trains
from London to Manchester in 4 hours 40 minutes. Discontinuing
express fares to Liverpool and Manchester was also considered.

At the August shareholders' meeting full support was given to
the directors in pursuing whatever measures 'may be necessary to
protect the traffic of this company from unjustifiable aggression'. As
one shareholder put it 'if there were to be competition he hoped it
would be no sham competition' and quoting the Duke of Wellington,
'if there is to be war let it be a good one'. C.H.Grinling, the historian
of the Great Northern, wrote: 'armed with the fullest sanction of
warfare from an enraged half-yearly meeting, the Euston authorities
proceeded to arrange their September time-table in the spirit of
fiercest competition'.

Chandos though had confidently assured his shareholders that
'the traffic of your line, properly developed and economically
worked, will maintain for you your position, and that you are quite
able to protect yourselves against any attacks that may be made
upon you'. He said that their profits 'must rest, not on agreements
which are liable to be broken and disturbed in this manner, but upon
the accommodation afforded to the public, upon the efficiency and
certainty with which the business of your line is conducted'. He
also explained that although the Midland agreement had been, 'in
consequence of certain legal proceedings, cancelled', they need not
fear that 'relations of friendship which have subsisted between the
two companies' would in any way be affected. He cited the presence
of Ellis as an L&NW director who was also the Midland's chairman
as evidence of their mutual interests.

26. Mark Huish
Captain Mark Huish, general manager of the L&NW 1846-58. NRM

27. Edward Watkin
Edward Watkin (1819-1901). An 1858 portrait when General Manager of the MS&L during the dispute with L&NW. Formerly Huish's assistant before resigning from the L&NW, he subsequently became chairman of the MS&L.
Dorothea Worsley-Taylor

Chandos's confidence in continuing Midland loyalty was misplaced. The Midland extension to Hitchin was open and Ellis would have known that discussions were already under way for his company to operate over the GN into London. Within a year the Midland was running to Kings Cross in direct competition with the L&NW.

One of the critical aspects of the fight for the Manchester passenger traffic was the control of London Road station in Manchester, which although jointly owned by the MS&L and the L&NW was worked by the latter. The two companies originally had their own facilities in the station but under their 1854 agreement the MS&L had agreed to lease their part to the L&NW. They now claimed their share back. The L&NW refused saying their agreement should stand and obviously were not going to hand over facilities if used against them. The L&NW did not refuse to provide a service, but 'difficulties' arose. In September 1857 the L&NW Executive were reviewing reports of 'the probability of the Sheffield company attempting to take forcible possession' of part of the station and introducing their own staff to take over a booking office. At the end of the month the secretary of the MS&L/GN Joint Committee wrote to the L&NW complaining that their passengers 'are impeded and misled, and the trains are detained and every possible obstruction is offered'. He alleged that when they attempted 'to book their own passengers in their own office, their clerk was summarily ejected from their premises by the servants of the L&NW'.

The MS&L were forced to take out an injunction to obtain possession of their part of the station. The matter however remained unresolved for most of 1858. In the meantime both sides made further rate and fare reductions. As the dispute hardened neither side seemed capable of compromise. Neither Watkin nor Clarke, the GN manager, now trusted Huish. Chandos was forced to concede that 'the day is gone when we can rely on complicated arrangements built up and dependent on the supposition of the interests of every company remaining the same from year to year'. There were then too many roads open which would render it 'almost a hopeless task to attempt to keep the interests of all these companies in the same direction through a long series of years'. Although this was a realistic assessment and one used by Moon himself when becoming chairman, it is doubtful if such remarks comforted those investors complaining of the 'frightful' competition. One letter to Chandos thought many shareholders 'with nearly their whole means at stake may well begin to tremble for the ultimate fate of their property, their stock below par, with money superabundant in the market'.

Neighbouring companies became alarmed over a possible knock-on effect. Led by the North Eastern Railway a number of senior directors from other railways first met in March 1858 in an attempt to offer mediation. Further meetings were held and various proposals were sent to the warring parties. Chandos grudgingly agreed to restore the Peterborough rates as 'evidence of this company's desire to meet the wishes of the mediating companies'. And although prepared to submit accounting matters to mediation he would not agree to submit the broken 1854 agreement, claiming there was nothing on which to arbitrate.

At the GN board's insistence, not surprising in view of Watkin's volatility, the new traffic arrangement between their company and the MS&L was to be formalised by a Parliamentary Act. The Bill was strongly contested by the L&NW, giving rise to scenes of bitter conflict in Committee and extracts of revealing inter-company correspondence were published. On 15 April Moon wrote to Chandos saying 'we should issue a concise and clear statement of our wrongs and position and I have an intimation if we did so, we should have *The Times* on our side'. He thought it clear that the 'the public view is lost in the confusion of what has hitherto been written ... and I would strongly recommend to you without loss of time to try your own hand at a short lucid statement steering clear of the intermediate discussions and shewing the real facts and only the facts of the case'.

Although the L&NW succeeded in discrediting some of the evidence against them, the Parliamentary Committee unanimously approved the MS&L/GN traffic Bill, commenting that the 1854 agreement had never been enforceable.

Although faced with the seeming inevitability of having the GN permanently in Manchester, Chandos still maintained the legality of the 1854 agreement with the MS&L and that the L&NW's stance at London Road was justified. The GN made a conciliatory offer to increase their London Manchester fares but only if the

L&NW would follow. Warily in June 1858 the two sides adopted a comparable fares schedule from London to Manchester and Liverpool, but competition remained rife. The GN/MS&L Bill was enacted the following month.

The L&NW did in fact get *The Times* on their side but not the weekly *Railway Times* which remained consistently hostile to both Chandos and Huish. An extract from the issue of 26 June was typical: 'no man of honour, no company of repute, can deal with such parties. They must drag down all who cling to them. As a man is known by his associates, so must the L&NW proprietors be regarded as participating in the criminality of their undismissed executive'.

Further attempts were made by outsiders to mediate, one was Moon's 'rather vulgar' Holme. Holme wrote to Chandos on 17 July saying that the unfortunate competition begun by the MS&L 'will, if persevered in, lead to sad mischief'. He suggested the possibility of the L&NW, Midland and GN companies uniting in purchasing the MS&L. Chandos's reaction at the time to this far-reaching solution is not known, but opposing the idea later was, as will be seen, to have fateful consequences for his future with the L&NW.

In the meantime another deputation of directors, representing seven companies, met in the Euston Hotel on 29 July. That such a group had found it necessary to gather was not just an indication of how bad the industry saw the situation, but how important it was to have some objective body to settle railway disputes in general. They could only ineffectually conclude however, that rates and fares should be 'so fixed to realise the largest amount of net profit to companies entitled to them'.

The dispute was to drag on for another four months. In August Chandos was forced to detail publicly the history of the conflict, admitting the company had 'suffered a very heavy loss' and attempting to justify the company's position. He told his shareholders that they had been accused of wanting to maintain 'exorbitant rates' and restore 'fares which were out of date'. He told them 'that is a convenient argument to use, when the object is to induce people to believe that one company is liberal and another illiberal', pointing out that his company's fare for the 189 miles from Euston to Manchester had been 42s.0d., yet the GN's for the comparable 191 miles from Kings Cross to York was 50s.0d.

Ahead of another meeting with the mediating companies on 9 September an increasingly beleaguered Chandos had clearly discussed tactics with Moon. Writing on the 3 September Moon wrote: 'I don't think you will find any one at the board equal to Tootal in weight and ability combined for your purpose next Thursday if he will give his mind - his great fault seems to be skirting a difficulty until his blood is up. Bancroft is a better man in some respects but I doubt his being a good second and also weight [sic], though he is cool'. On the 6th Moon wrote again dismissively critical of many of his colleagues, which went far beyond just the need to resolve the GN conflict.

This 6 September letter of 1858, though one of the longest found, is another worth quoting in full. Although he repeats some of his earlier criticism of colleagues, Moon outlines a management philosophy that within three years was to take him to the chairmanship of the company, yet at the same time he protests that it would not be fair to expect him to commit himself further other than temporarily. He wrote:

> I look upon this week to be the turning point in the fortunes of our railway - if you are strong and courageous I believe we may revive its prosperity but if you are slack it will assuredly go from bad to worse - at this moment it depends on you as to the course you adopt. I trust therefore you will receive as I intend the few remarks I am induced to make to you this morning. First at the meeting of the Railway Companies let me entreat you to probe every case ... as far as our own individual company is concerned I do trust you will carry out your resolution as to Huish and compel the board also to come to some final determination as to the future management. The only mode I am sure is a small committee of directors constantly sitting and consulting each other, acting in unity on one defined plan - the concern is too big for anything less than this and its details too voluminous to be kept in sight at all so as to make a judgement worth having without some such close attention. I know your materials are poor for this purpose but try it. I believe there is no other hope for the concern than resolutely shutting the capital account as nearly as

possible and rebuilding the traffic of the company on the more sure foundation of locality than heretofore. We have two things to do - to earn money and to spend money - the first as much as possible, the second as little as possible. The first embraces policy and traffic - the second all the other affairs of the concern. I put them into these four heads:

-Policy
-Traffic and Locomotive expenditure
-Works - [permanent] way - estate
-Finance - rates - accounts

Now if you will take the bull by the horns, yourself and Admiral Moorsom may work out the first, Lyon the works, Bancroft finance or traffic. Moon - either of the above two, and the stores and locomotive expenditure as at present. You are already paid, the Admiral says he will work if he is paid and I understand his friends talk of £500 pa. I know that would secure Bancroft and Lyon. *I am content without because I could only take those duties temporarily to aid in starting you or until such time as you can find some good man able and <u>willing</u> [sic] to take part off me. To give so much time as I do at present is not fair to me and would alter the whole course of my life. I could not do it continuously for a term* [authors italics].

You know the traffic is not worked now, or at all events either the Admiral or Mr Ashton will satisfy you it is not - nor are the other points and if I took the finance etc. I would consider the chief business of it would be to bring before those managing the different departments every point requiring looking into, which we shall never know at all except by one man passing his eye over <u>all</u> the receipts and payments of the company. With some such small committee we might hope for success.

You remember the career of the Duke in the Peninsula - when he went there first he checked everything himself.

If the army had to be moved he sent for the quartermaster, went over his list of stock of provisions, cattle, sheep, etc. (comparing them with his own list which he had procured himself) and satisfied himself. He got rid of every fellow that was idle or wicked or thoughtless and by the time they had got to the battle of Salamanca he went to bed and going said to the aid-de-camp, tell Lord - I shall move the army in the morning. Everything was prepared, he had no occasion to do it himself and the army did move. This is what we must do. You must not be content with Huish (and in getting rid of him don't say much about his good qualities for as to management he has known none, everything in our concern is done by the weight of money and not by skilful management). Don't be content with Huish. I don't know much of human nature's infirmities [but] bring back Stewart to his true position and make a good secretary of him. Booth who is worse than useless and positively obstructive must go - Mills Hare Norris Cooper Bruyeres etc. by degrees we must weed them all and have good tools to work with, giving every soul in the establishment to understand the interests of the company must not be trifled with, that merit will be promoted and rewarded but that all neglect indolence or want of ability and knowledge must go. I sincerely trust you will have courage to go through with it.

Do not be afraid of Mr Glyn - you will have the proprietors at your back and many of your colleagues are ready to help you - and for yourself I believe you have to determine this week whether you will work this out to a successful issue or let your character as a public man and leader rank with Lord John Russell's - there is no via media - it must be a radical change or none. What has to be done is to be done only by a long course of perseverance and watchfulness. The concern's prosperity can't be brought back in any way in six months. As our opponent Watkin would not be Commissary General in the Crimea [D.Hodgkins, biographer of Watkin, has found no evidence that he was actually offered the position] because they would not give him the whole command and he would not subject himself to failure by having some fellow in a corner he did not know of, pull a thing and open a valve which leaked out all the steam and spoiled his course. So you must take special care that no one shall be in a position quietly and unseen to thwart all your measures without you knowing how it happens. I trust you will be resolute and your success will be in proportion - I will do all I can for my own and family's interest in the concern to aid you.

Unfortunately no clue has been found regarding what other interests were making claims on Moon's time other than commitments to his wife and children and the wider family investments. Wolverhampton Water could not have been significantly demanding.

Chandos did eventually force the resignation of Huish, which whether justified, had become almost inevitable. Huish's letter of resignation, dated 11 September 1858, was read at the board meeting of the same day. The directors resolved unanimously 'that in accepting Capt. Huish's resignation this board desire to record their sense of his great ability, integrity, unwearied industry, and steady devotion to the interests of this company during the lengthened period of 18 years, as well as the expression of their personal regard and esteem'. "Resolved unaminously" sounds a shade hypocritical given the views of such directors as Moorsom and Moon. It does not seem that a board appointment was formally considered.

Despite Moorsom's objection, a payment of £3,000 or eighteen month's salary was agreed. This was not a generous settlement considering the nature of the service Huish had given and for taking the blame for so aggressively implementing a policy set by the board. A committee comprising Chandos, Moon, Earle, Grant, Lyon, Tootal, Bancroft and Ashton were appointed to select his successor. As deputy chairman, Moorsom should have been on this committee, but he seems to have disassociated himself from the selection. Moorsom wrote to Chandos three days later that 'the salaries you name are absurdly excessive for the duties and the qualifications of the men who receive them. They grow out of peculiar circumstances, which have changed. Such men, at such salaries, are lifted out of their sphere, and soon learn to think themselves necessities'.

Moon however was already aggressively probing further. A week after Huish resigned he was pressing Chandos on not only his replacement but a number of operational fronts: to continue excursion trains into GN territory, to discourage Midland specials from Rugby, not to carry Lincolnshire grain at rates 'already fearfully low' and that not attacking the Grand Junction (the canal from the midlands to London) over low coal rates to Leighton 'will not do'. And he raised the locomotive shedding problems at Crewe. 'You had better let the sheds at Crewe and Wolverton be built. The latter is not so essential but the former is. I think we ought not to let it stand over - charge it to Revenue or anything you like but when you think that there are 40 engines working from Crewe every day you will see it is impossible to do the work properly. McConnell's is a mere store.' He continued, 'no one can pretend to say it is possible to get men to clean them or wash out or get underneath them out of doors in the winter - it is not a question of mere storage, though that would be bad enough'.

He ended this diatribe with a footnote. 'Everyone seems to rejoice in our having got rid of Huish. I have a letter this morning from a Friend who winds up as follows and it is the general view of the Commerial Community.' His friend's extract concluded that the "L&NW has been too long managed in a magnificent style, I mean more particularly as regards the accommodation to passengers, in special carriages and frequency of trains on parts of the system where the return is not adequate". Moon ended his own letter by saying that he had no doubt that this was true and that 'holding traffic and connections for some ulterior and permanent division which has never come yet, and never can come, [is] only a day dream. ... We must do what we do well, do less, get more and reduce our trains, accommodation and expenses especially the speeds. We must rebuild the concern quietly as the Midland did theirs on the surer foundation for better paying local Traffic'.

On 1 October Moon was writing again to Chandos complaining over the working out of Birmingham of a Liverpool express, quoting McConnell saying 'he would be hanged if he could not make better arrangements'. He advises Chandos to review the situation 'because it needs a strong hand ... for old Bruyeres and Norris are not the men to rely on in such an emergency'. Commenting further, he urges

Chandos to 'bring on a scheme for the future direction of the concern as it ought to be finally decided without loss of time. At present we are nowhere'.

Surprisingly Huish appeared to have shown no outward bitterness in giving way to the pressure on him. He was to continue to act for many years as a consultant to the company in helping settle a number of issues. In his letter he wrote that he felt that he was 'acting in accordance with a duty which I owe to the board and to the interests entrusted to your care, by resigning my charge, in the hope that, by a change of management, some progress may be made towards a settlement of the present embarrassments'.

Moorsom was not the only senior director who thought Huish should have been found another role in the company where his knowledge could be used. After the board meeting, Ashton wrote a revealing note to Thomas Smith saying, 'I cannot contemplate on our proceedings ... with all the satisfaction I could desire. We have made Huish the scapegoat for the difficulties we are under and why? Because he has too pertinaciously stood up for our interests'. Smith had supported Huish in recommending the company match the Great Northern's service, for example one of the issues raised had been whether or not to provide cushions and lamps in second class carriages. In his Stores Committee, Moon had considered this extravagant, but Smith had insisted the company maintained 'the natural superiority of their route in all classes of passenger accommodation'. Writing to Chandos after the resignation Smith still defended Huish commenting that although he had his faults he had a lot of knowledge which they should be able to use.

It seems that candidates to succeed Huish were considered from both inside and outside the company. Moorsom's reference to a possible 'tainted' alternative could have been to any one of a number of experienced railway managers. For example Glyn had commented on the manager of the Lancashire & Yorkshire, William Cawkwell, as 'a plain small man and generally respected' with a 'thorough knowledge of our northern business', but adding others were well thought of, for example Sheriff was a 'good man'. Glyn's judgement on the latter seemed to have been borne out when A.C.Sheriff, who had been traffic manager for the North Eastern and then general manager of the OW&W, subsequently became a director of the

Metropolitan and other railways and MP for Worcester.

Moon, in a letter to Chandos written after returning home from the board meeting which accepted Huish's resignation, made a further reference to using Bancroft as 'a right hand man'. He suggested Chandos sought Tootal's 'views as to future paid employment [as] Ashton and himself brought Mr. Bancroft on to the board'. Moon then added that before committing yourself to him 'you should also know (I tell you in strict confidence) that the qualification he holds is Ashton's to whom the shares in his name belong. Lyon is under the impression that he [Bancroft] would have been a candidate for the managership if opportunity had offered but I can hardly think that'. As has been noted Bancroft had been a director since February 1858 and talk of paying him for his services had already been raised.

In the event the choice fell on an outsider, Glyn's 'plain small man', William Cawkwell. Chandos announced at the 23 September 1858 Special Committee that he had arranged with the Lancashire & Yorkshire chairman for Cawkwell to 'undertake the duty of general manager at a salary of £1,800 for the first year, £1,900 for the second year and £2,000 for the third year, subject to twelve months notice'. That the L&Y had attempted to retain Cawkwell 'by an offer of "a few hundred" is suggested by a note from Earle to Chandos on 15 September [L&NWR archives] who thought that 'they [L&Y] will endeavour to get us to take Mr Smithells'. Smithells was Traffic Manager for the East Lancashire, but Earle 'did not think he would be up to our work'. Charles Mason, manager of the Birkenhead & Cheshire Junction was also mentioned by Earle who agreed with Bancroft that 'he is clever and quick but rather showy than solid and I doubt whether he has sufficient calibre for so responsible a position'. This view of Mason was to be substantially at odds with Bancroft's recommendation in 1861 for Mason to become the L&NW's general goods manager and the subsequent high opinion of the man held by Moon.

Cawkwell's start to his railway career had been a humble one. In 1840 he had joined the unopened Manchester & Leeds as the first station clerk at Brighouse. Working his way up the hierarchy of the company that became the Lancashire & Yorkshire, he was appointed their goods manager in 1849, then traffic manager and effectively general manager in 1853. On joining the L&NW in 1858 his colleagues in the railway world paid handsome tribute to him in the form of a public dinner. It was alleged he had turned down a similar offer from the Midland. His manner was in marked contrast to his predecessor Huish. Cawkwell was eventually to be elected a director of the L&NW and become a long serving member of the board, holding the position of deputy chairman from 1881 until his death in 1897. His long and loyal service almost matched Moon's in nearly forty years with the company.

To return to the conflict of the summer of 1858, the war of words between Watkin and the L&NW had continued unabated. *The Railway Times* of 4 September had published Watkin's correspondence alleging the L&NW were charging 7s.6d., when their costs were 15s.6d. of which the Midland's toll was 9s.2d. The outcome of the September meeting of the mediating companies had been to propose arbitration on all matters, which meant not just fares and rates but issues subject to litigation. On the latter point Chandos still refused to budge: the outstanding legal matter being the rights at London Road station. The MS&L case was about to be heard in the high court. Various individual members of other companies tried to mediate and the companies themselves again met collectively to form a semi-official body, which met for the first time as the Railway Companies Association on 4 November. It was only then that Chandos bowed to pressure and accepted the need to reach a settlement out of court and for arbitration over the use of London Road.

An agreement between the three parties, L&NW, MS&L and GN was signed on 26 November. It seems that both Tootal and the newly influential Bancroft had played significant parts in persuading Chandos to accept what was in effect a significant climb down. *The Railway Times* for 4 December gloated that the whole affair 'ends by the complete subjugation of London and North Western pretension. The right of the allied companies [MSL GN] to convey traffic to every place to which the L&NW considered it had a monopoly is acknowledged; and Manchester, Liverpool, Warrington, and Huddersfield, with all the intermediate and surrounding towns, are admitted to be as much the property of the one system as of the other'.

C H A P T E R   1 0

A FOOL FOR MY PAINS

The net result of the turmoil of 1858 was that L&NW's ordinary dividend for the year proved to be the worst in the company's history. In fact the dividend rate was to remain at under 5% (marginally above in 1860) for the next four years; a far cry from the 10% of 1846. Yet hopes remained that given effective management and tighter control of costs a return to the old levels was possible.

Within the company the inaugural meeting of the new combined Stores and Locomotive Expenditure committee had been, fittingly, held at Crewe on 24 March 1858. Moon and Brook were the only directors present. It was explained, 'as the intention of the Board, that this committee will in future take charge of the locomotive departments and that all matters affecting these establishments and the stock of vehicles must be brought before it'.

The Crewe superintendent, John Ramsbottom, was left in no doubt what to expect under the new regime. He was told to report on a whole string of issues: the general condition of the stock, the locations including total number of people employed at each, vehicles standing and cover for how many, wages expended in 1857, materials, production schedules met and proposed, including replacements, renewals and heavy repairs; and finally 'capabilities for building, repairs and renewals, and generally on the working of the departments and the points requiring attention as affecting the increase of efficiency and reduction of expenditure'. At the next meeting held at Euston on 8 April all the other works' superintendents were asked to report in similar detail.

As the year progressed the Committee's meetings began to take a new shape with their agendas being increasingly set by the results of reviewing these reports and the minutes of other committees touching on stores matters, which included the five other main board committees and the three area sub-committees, in particular the Traffic and local area committees. Moon must have passed many a train journey or evening in his hotel keeping up with the mass of minutes circulated (the Special met weekly and the Traffic and Permanent Way every fortnight). Of the main committees only the board itself and the Finance and Audit met monthly.

Moon and Brook seemed set to continue their partnership as the core of the new Stores Committee. But they met together for the last time at Euston on Friday 9 July 1858. For over two days they had ploughed through such details as the value of each locomotive as 'it stands at present in capital account and for each of the last eight half years of the number of miles run by each engine, amounts spent upon it in repairs, and the like in renewals and rebuilding'. But when, on the Saturday, Brook returned home to Huddersfield, he was an ill man. At the age of seventy-one he developed bronchitis and did not recover, dying at home six days later.

It was Moon who moved at the next L&NW board, seconded by Glyn, the company's appreciation of the 'zeal and unremitting attention with which for many years Mr. Brook devoted himself to the service of this company'. Regarded as the "father of Huddersfield", Brook was given a public funeral at which eight thousand people attended the procession through the town. The appreciation published by the *Huddersfield Chronicle* made reference to his railway interest:

> In the discharge of his duties as a railway director Mr Brook has been most indefatigable. To him, to a great extent, this town is indebted for that beautiful station front and square, the construction of which led to the formation of John William Street, and what may be well called "new Huddersfield" ... and to his exertions we are largely indebted for the railway accommodation now so amply afforded to the town. In fact the last few years of his life have been spent in promoting the welfare of the railway company of which he was a director, and to the institutions of the town, to the entire disregard of his own personal comfort; indeed personal neglect may be shortly given as the cause of his death.

Brook seems a typical example of wealthy, public-spirited men of the age, who saw service to the community as a duty. That they should also carry this attitude into the administration of a railway, however, appears at first sight to be surprising. But then being a director of a powerful and influential company like the L&NW would be seen by many as being on a par with any public works. Moon did not attend the funeral. Although in Crewe the day before, he chose to return to London to attend a meeting of the L&NW Special Committee. Brook's replacement on the L&NW board, recommended by Tootal, was W.E.Hirst, also of Huddersfield.

The calling for tenders and the placing of contracts for materials continued to be an important part of the Stores Committee's work but increasingly a widening range of other matters came under scrutiny. Moon was of course already familiar with the various manufacturing works as a result of reviewing their methods of controlling stores and from his cost and accounts investigations.

The officers attending his meeting frequently outnumbered the directors forming the committee. The term 'officer' was used generally at the time to refer to the managers of the company, from such senior positions as the general manager and locomotive superintendents (already over a thousand men were employed at Crewe) to the specialist departmental heads. Cawkwell did not at first regularly attend as Huish had done, being called in to report or advise as required. Engineering materials and costs now also came under the committee's scrutiny. Responsibility for new civil engineering projects had remained divided between outside consulting engineers for the northern divisions and the company's own engineer William Baker for the southern. Henry Woodhouse was the permanent way engineer for both divisions until the end of 1859 when the engineering departments were reorganised following the death of consulting engineer Robert Stephenson. Other specialist activities were reviewed and their officials brought before the committee.

Although the overriding issue during this latter stage of Moon's stores responsibilities became the rationalsiing of the locomotive departments with ongoing reviews of expenditure and engine building programmes, there was no let-up in the control over more mundane activities. Many of these continued to be referred to Moon personally, for example: the changes necessary in the staff of the coke department following the increasing use of coal. With the declining need for the lighter weight coke wagons, Moon questioned the apparently excessive number of such wagons still working and urged their transference for goods use. They were soon reviewing a 'plan and specification of a type of coal wagon for locomotive coal (to carry not less than 6 tons)'. Obviously critical of the way wagons were being used and controlled, Moon then proposed that his committee took over direct responsibility for regulating 'the supply and movement of wagons'. The Traffic Committee agreed to consider and Moon undertook personally to report on the subject.

Dated 20 December 1858, Moon's report on wagon stock was written from his home at Bevere and presented to the 22 December meeting of his committee at Crewe (almost to himself, only Moon and new Huddersfield director Hirst were present with officer Worsdell in attendance). Unsurprisingly the report's recommendations were approved and passed to the Special Committee who in turn referred them to the Traffic Committee for adoption. Basically Moon proposed the abolition of the existing local arrangements with the audit office taking over the statistical and accounting returns and a new office set up centrally in Birmingham for 'the home working of the L&NW sheets and wagon stock' where daily returns from all principal stations were to be made for the control of empty stock and spare sheets.

For many years Moon had been advocating the consolidation of all wagon manufacturing at Earlestown. His frustration at the continued manufacturing in the leased works at Saltley is evident from one of his comments in his 4 December 1858 letter to Chandos. He asked for replacement wagons at Saltley to be stopped and ordered on Earlestown instead. Complaints over hot axles were attributed to an increasing use of brass castings and the 'bad quality and non-lubricating qualities of the grease now in use'. Typically Moon was later to take a close personal interest in the composition of grease.

The committee also became closely involved in the design and production of carriages. As has been noted, Moon objected to the cost of improvements in 2nd class accomodation demanded to match the GN service to Manchester. He also feared that the improvement would take business away from the profitable 1st class. The additional cost was estimated at £10 per carriage and instructions were sought

28. Wagons at Oldham

A panorama of wagons and sheeting taken in 1876 at Clegg Street, Oldham,
showing both L&NW and privately owned, mainly collieries. Gallery Oldham

29. Luggage roof racks

Carriages at New Street showing roof racks with ropes and sheets for luggage
taken in early 1860s. LNWRS

from the board 'as to the mode in which this expenditure should be proceeded with if finally determined upon, as they have ascertained that the Great Northern are removing them from theirs except those running to Manchester'. When later the committee met at Saltley to inspect the works and the question of 'stuffing 2$^{nd.}$ class carriages was again considered ... it was resolved that special instructions be given that these carriages be carefully kept to London and Manchester trains'. Cawkwell reported in January 1859 on his meetings with the GN, Midland and GW when it was agreed that no more 2$^{nd.}$ class carriages were to be stuffed and those already done were requested not to be used on competitive lines.

The common practice at the time of carrying luggage on the roof of carriages led to many complaints of damage by fire from engine sparks and it was agreed to build three replacement 2$^{nd.}$ class carriages each with three passenger and one luggage compartment. It is not known whether this was one of the first examples of what later became such obvious standard practice. In the meantime the problem continued and Moon's committee resolved 'to request the Traffic Committee to issue instructions that the luggage be more carefully covered over with sheets at stations so as to lessen the chance of cinders getting under the sheets' and the 'carriage superintendents were instructed to report what better arrangements can be made for improving the fastening of the sheets'.

The problem of burning luggage had been made worse by the increasing use of coal. In June 1859 Ramsbottom was ordered to discontinue burning coal on his passenger engines ('except those adapted for its own consumption') 'until luggage compartments are made in second class carriages which will remove the luggage from the roofs and at the same time the objection to coal burning'. McConnell on the Southern division had not the same problem as his engines were better adapted to avoid the problem. Somewhat unreasonably the Traffic Committee suggested that Stores find some way of making sheeting 'incombustible'.

The need for special carriages for the Post Office was noted when the Traffic Committee minute was read asking for the shells of five additional sorting offices and five mail tenders to be put in hand for the 'accelerated Irish Mail traffic service'. It appeared that Moon was not happy over the additional expenditure being incurred. He questioned the carriage superintendent's authority under which he was building six Post Office carriages and demanded a copy of the clause in the contract under which the company had to provide the stock. He personally reported on the insurance of the Saltley works. It appeared that no cover had been provided and he undertook to resolve the matter himself. His proposal to insure the buildings and machinery for £20,000 for one year at a cost of £105, including duty, was agreed subject to the solicitor's confirmation.

The committee took on further additional responsibilities when the Chester & Holyhead was absorbed. The C&H had been worked by the L&NW since 1847 but the actual company was not taken over until 1 January 1859. In the previous October Moon had ordered a 'comparative return' showing the consumption of stores at the stations along the line, but it was not until early 1859 that the committee recorded that 'the rule of the company on this subject be now extended to Holyhead and the steam boat service'.

When Moon's Stores Committee first met at Holyhead, in May 1859, the only director present was Moon himself. The "committee" visited the stores, shops and vessels at Holyhead, Bangor, Rhyl, Mold Junction and Chester. The insurance and depreciation funds for the steamboats were reviewed and Captain Hirste, the Holyhead marine superintendent, was instructed to report when the *Telegraph* and *Sea Nymph* were laid up 'with a view to recover the premium'. At the following month's meeting the Special Committee's attention was drawn to the question of insuring the vessels (they had not been covered since 31 March), 'recommending that some amount of insurance be immediately effected upon them'. The insurance of the landing stage sheds, etc., at Holyhead and of the stores, buildings and goods at North Wall, Dublin was also reviewed.

A far cry from Holyhead was the control of machinery at a goods depot in east London. A dispute had arisen over the responsibility between McConnell as Southern locomotive superintendent and Baker as divisional engineer for the control of the depot machinery at Haydon Square. This seemingly minor matter was to have wide repercussions. McConnell's report had been referred in November 1858 to Moon who instructed Baker, McConnell and David Stevenson, the goods manager concerned, to meet him at the depot. Two weeks later Moon reported on the meeting which agreed that the staff working the machinery be transferred to the southern division locomotive department, but conditional on McConnell reporting at the next meeting if any changes were required. Objecting to McConnell's proposed changes to the buildings and machinery, Baker had written directly to Chandos and the subject was deferred for further consideration. Baker had also wanted clarification of his responsibilities and a salary review.

Moon wrote to Chandos on 4 December complaining that he hardly knew 'how you can arrange a minute to meet the case'. It was in this letter that he wrote that Baker 'is no match for McConnell and not fit for maintenance of works which to be economical requires the repairs to be ordered and done under the master's eye whereas he has no genius for details'. However he went on to suggest that Chandos accept Baker's letter and 'alter the whole system of engineering [and] put all new works under one engineer for the whole line and make [Francis] Stevenson, Baker's assistant, clerk of the works to attend to repairs and maintain all existing works'. Having one engineer was a recommendation Moon, in his investigation work, had made four years earlier. Moon clearly saw in Stevenson a temperament more suitable for routine of maintenance. His apparent condemnation of Baker needs to be seen in this context, or else it is a rare example of misjudgement, which he later significantly revised. Following the death of Robert Stephenson, Baker was appointed the company's engineer and was to give long and distinguished service to the L&NW.

Faced with the growth in traffic throughout 1859, the increase in locomotive power and rolling stock requirements meant higher maintenance costs and more renewal of the the permanent way. Changes in the organisation to handle this were brought forward by the Chester & Holyhead takeover. And, from the 1 August 1859, the situation with the Lancaster & Carlisle had also changed when an agreement to lease the company outright to the L&NW took effect. No evidence has been found that Moon took any key part in the latter negotiations which led to the guaranteed 8% lease, but as the L&C was to continue as an independent body well into Moon's chairmanship years before being dissolved it will be necessary to return to this later.

With the lines of both the C&H and the L&C now under the control of the L&NW, the Special Committee approved in November

1859 four engineering districts for the maintenance of the line with all new civil engineering works centralised under Baker. Moon's committee was quick to demand a report on the 'future arrangements of stores for the permanent way and engineering departments' and 'what may be most advisable bearing in mind the cost of carriage'.

With gas supplies and installations being part of the locomotive superintendents' responsibilities, Moon continued to insist on details, for example in early 1859 he demanded that they report:

> The quantity of gas consumed at each station and works in the years 1857 and 1858 respectively, together with the particulars of the charges to be made in each case to other parties, and also submit balance sheets for the same periods in every case where it is manufactured by the company charging interest at the rate of 7½% on the amount expended in buildings and fixtures for the gas works, also the cost of new works, meters and fittings at each station continuing same returns each year.

Ramsbottom was not present at this meeting and it is not difficult to imagine his reaction when reading he had to make yet another gas report. Moon's strictures on gas supplies led to conflict with the Traffic Committee who wanted better lighting at stations, Moon demanding less, despite such complaints that on the arrival sides at Euston and Birmingham it was impossible to read the luggage labels! Ramsbottom was soon openly complaining to the committee that 'water and gas business occupied a very large portion of his time'. A minute dryly recorded that it was 'referred to Mr Moon for consideration'. However Moon did not relent: both superintendents continued to submit monthly reports on both gas and water. An example of what Ramsbottom was probably trying to avoid was laying gas pipes which were to be extended in the streets of Crewe. In July 1858 the two locomotive superintendents were ordered to make 'a return of all watering places for engines giving the name of the party supplying the water, from what source obtained, the annual quantity consumed and the price paid'. Moon followed this up in October by instructing them to 'take charge of the water arrangements on both divisions'. And Moon himself continued to be involved in negotiating water supply contracts, presumably seeing no conflict with his ongoing involvement with the Wolverhampton company.

With the enhanced responsibilities of the Stores Committee it is remarkable that Moon felt fit to record so many items of trifling expenditure. Perhaps the most extreme example was a request from the Telegraph office at Watford for a chair and coal scuttle! The committee's secretary, Perrin, was asked 'to ascertain if the company is bound by the contract to supply furniture'. They were not, it being so minuted at the next meeting when the Telegraph company's request was declined.

Of more momentous significance was when Ramsbottom raised in July 1859 the problem of the 'short accommodation of shop room and tools at the Crewe works', which had resulted in working excessive overtime and preventing the making of many articles which had to be bought out at higher prices. This led Moon to resurrect the whole issue of rationalising the works. He had his committee minute that 'the most natural mode of giving the additional accommodation appears to be by removing the carriage department from Crewe and absorbing the shops into the locomotive establishment [which] would enable the board to carry out the recommendation of a former committee to concentrate the carriage and wagon establishments'. At the next meeting he went further in highlighting the lack of space at Crewe when compared to Wolverton and the need for rationalising the carriage and wagon works.

Crewe then comprised 20,209 square yards of shops to maintain a stock of 464 engines; Wolverton had 28,450 to maintain 316. 'It is quite clear the room at Crewe is inadequate for the business', and that absorbing the 8,240 square yards occupied by the adjoining carriage department 'naturally suggests itself'. (Moon's earlier letter to Chandos regarding the forty engines at Crewe, referred to the local running shed.) The committee reminded the board that they had for a long time considered reducing the number of carriage and wagon works, and were satisfied that Saltley and Earlestown had ample space for the maintenance of the company's stock: the area of Saltley being 34,400 square yards, and of Earlestown 24,219.

Probably at Moon's prompting, Ramsbottom was recorded as commenting 'he may have been misunderstood' if the committee at the previous meeting thought he was proposing to make additional items which had not previously been made at Crewe. He pointed out that the 'tyres, axles, merchants iron etc.', which he was having to buy from outside owing to the pressure of other work, particularly on his furnaces and steam hammers 'are subject of course to the drawbacks of inferior quality, higher prices, and irregularity in delivery'. The manufacture of components within the company's facilities, in particular at Crewe, was to become a key part of Moon's policy when he became chairman of the company.

Although the board agreed in principle to the proposed changes a further report was required 'looking forward to the probable increase of traffic and the best mode of making the carriage shops and yards gradually available for this purpose'. At the Stores meeting in October 1859 Ramsbottom presented his plans and estimates for the proposed alterations and enlargements 'which were minutely examined by the committee'. After inspecting the area Ramsbottom was directed to send some further information to Moon who then was to 'frame a minute' for the board.

These Crewe expansion proposals opened up the old debate on the need for two locomotive works. McConnell was now coming under increasing criticism from Moon, not only over the large increase in stores, but also, in October 1859, for an explanation of the preparation necessary for the 'large number of engines now building'. It is interesting to note, in view of Moon's later loss of confidence in McConnell, that this building programme was reviewed in detail and agreed by his committee. As Ramsbottom had at Crewe, McConnell was making the case for additional accommodation at Wolverton following the increase in engine stock. Faced with demands for expenditure at both Crewe and Wolverton, the board in November asked for 'a fair comparison of the relative advantages of retaining the present limits of the two locomotive divisions or of making Stafford or Crewe the limit', and for each superintendent to report to the board their divisions's requirements:

> That such reports be accompanied by the following returns: the daily mileage of engines of each division from 1 Jan to 31 Oct, the number of engines in work and the spare engines in stock; the outlay required at Wolverton and Crewe respectively to keep up the present working; an

estimate of the outlay that would be required at Wolverton to make the most of the present area of the works; the additional mileage that the engines could then work with the most useful effect; an estimate of the outlay beyond the present requirements, assumed at about £20,000, if the Lancaster & Carlisle and the Lancashire & Cheshire Junction [BL&CJ] lines be added to the Crewe division.

When the reports were reviewed at the December board it appears that the superintendents had not consulted each other. McConnell recommended Crewe as the boundary, Ramsbottom had not changed the existing arrangements whereby the Northern Division not only worked the line between Crewe and Stafford but also the Trent Valley line to Rugby. Moorsom who chaired the Traffic Committee, proposed a 'select' committee to consider the proposals. Moon protested seeing little point in discussing such arrangements, being convinced of the eventual need for one locomotive establishment based on Crewe and so proposed no change in the limits. However 'after a full discussion' Moorsom's motion was carried, by 16 to 9.

A committee comprising Chandos, Moorsom, Smith, Cropper, Earle, Moon, Clements, Bancroft and Blake were appointed to report 'whether any and what alteration it may be expedient to make in the respective divisions'. This committee met at Euston on 15 December with officers Cawkwell, Stewart, Ramsbottom and McConnell in attendance. McConnell estimated that by extending to Crewe his division could run 1,500 more passenger miles daily without increasing the number of engines or making men's hours 'unduly long'. Ramsbottom commented that he had not seen McConnell's estimates or statements, but 'even if Crewe were made his southern limit he should still have to light 47 or 48 engine fires there daily out of the present 57 [and] 16 of his goods engines would lose 800 miles of their daily work'. And he was 'so short of shed room at Crewe that he could not spare cover for any southern engines, which would require an additional outlay for a shed'.

The committee adjourned after accepting Ramsbottom's current need for thirty additional heavy goods engines. However, they noted that 'the Southern Division had a margin of unemployed power which Mr McConnell estimated could take the additional duty and

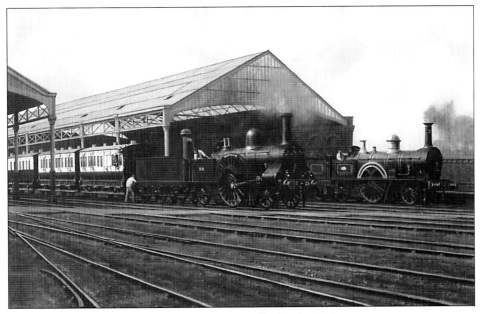

30. Locomotives at Stafford early 1860s
Changing 2-2-2 engines at Stafford in early 1860s, Wolverton 'small Bloomer' on
right waiting for Crewe loco to be uncoupled. Painting by Gerald Broom.

31. J.Ramsbottom
John Ramsbottom, locomotive superintendent whose L&NW career
progressed from Longsight in 1842, to Crewe in 1857 and finally
overall L&NW 1862-71. NRM

meet the gradual increase of traffic without requiring any addition to be made to it for at least two years'. Nevertheless Ramsbottom was asked to examine McConnell's details and the two superintendents were to consider, instead of an arbitrary division, both working over certain portions of the line 'so as to get from each engine in steam the longest daily mileage with the least amount of waiting for load'. (Significantly the L&NW were already recording detailed locomotive running costs, for example a two page statement comparing divisions had been reviewed at a meeting of the Executive in May 1857 which showed costs per train mile.)

They all reconvened at Euston on 22 December. It was a fateful meeting for Moon. The joint report from Ramsbottom and McConnell now recommended 'that Stafford be the limit of the two divisions and that the length between Stafford and Bushbury be worked jointly as may be found best to meet the "Time Bills"'. The meeting minutes record agreeing the boundary at Stafford and approving the views of McConnell that 'of the 73 northern division engines running trains south of Stafford he [McConnell] would require 44 as the proportionate number to be transferred to his division'. He further promised that 'he could undertake the work with 34 if he was allowed to build 10 additional ones to make up the number during the ensuing twelve months and had the necessary accommodation at Wolverton at once to order'. Moon, as subsequently will be shown, did not believe him.

It is perhaps worth noting at this point that Moorsom probably did genuinely accept McConnell's claims. He had known McConnell since their days on the Bristol & Gloucester Railway when, as the newly appointed chairman of the company in 1842, he had given a young McConnell his head in running the locomotive department.

Moon's protests were in vain. It was agreed that Wolverton, in view of the increased southern division working be enlarged at a cost of £18,000 (instead of the previously proposed £8,000) so as to be able to turn out 35 engines per annum. Ramsbottom was left to protest that although the release of 39 engines would give him 'immediate relief' the engines were not goods engines. He needed thirty more goods engines and unless '10 more of this class were commenced at once he should, if the traffic continued to grow, be greatly pressed for power next autumn'.

Although the committee did not give Ramsbottom his additional engines, they did agree, 'notwithstanding the relief afforded by the transfer of the Trent Valley lines from Birmingham to Stafford to the Southern division', that the 'enlargement of the Crewe shops be proceeded with forthwith'. The cost was estimated at £20,000.

Without approval for his thirty engines the agreement to expand Crewe facilities was a hollow victory for Ramsbottom, especially so when he was also asked to enquire and report if there were any new engines for sale which could be recommended for purchase. For Moon it was worse. Having accepted in effect that McConnell's utilisation of locomotives was better than Ramsbottom's, the decision to increase investment at Wolverton had been the last straw. The approval of his carriage and wagon changes was academic. The recommendations were put to the board and agreed at their meeting on 14 January 1860.

Disagreeing fundamentally with the decision on both locomotive building and operating arrangements, Moon, before he left Euston on that Thursday before Christmas, immediately wrote to Chandos and resigned his chairmanship of the Stores Committee. His letter of 22 December 1859 reads:

> I can not hope to carry the board with me against the opinion of the committee over which your lordship presided today although I believe that opinion to be based on unsound data and certain to result in a large duplicate expenditure on capital account whilst the advantage proposed is entirely problematical. It only remains for me therefore to resign the chairmanship of the Stores Committee and with it of course the seat on the Special Committee to which I was nominated in virtue of that office.

Although no record has been found of Chandos's reply, he obviously reacted sympathetically. After what must have been a Christmas of much heart searching Moon was writing from Bevere on 31 December thanking Chandos for his 'kind note' and agreeing to a meeting. But he stuck to his resignation. He criticised Moorsom for backing McConnell over himself, saying that the issue was not whether there should be one or two locomotive works, although he quoted the previous board minutes agreeing that this would be desirable. His main reason was the lack of support and confidence in his management of the Stores Committee:

> I was defeated not by force of argument but by the necessities of the northern division, that is virtually, because, you yourself quietly [sic] defeated me by refusing in October 1858, when they could have been built at Crewe in quiet times ... by postponing the enlargement of the shops there. ... That having no confidence in McConnell's upright truthfulness and disbelieving his statements and report which I am certain are misleading, it should come almost to a personal issue in which one of our colleagues, Admiral Moorsom, could use in McConnell's presence as an argument that he would take his opinion against mine ... that I could therefore no more hope to have any control over him, and that the committee last week absolutely superseded the Stores Committee in its own proper functions giving the superintendents carte blanche to do almost as they like. ... Whereas nothing previously could be had for northern division, money was ordered to be spent like water for the south, that you yourself suggested the money at Wolverton should be treated as capital whilst that at Crewe is to be revenue. ... And finally, that in any point where the Traffic and Stores Committees meet, the latter must go to the wall because being only trouble and hard work none of the stronger members of the board care to not [serve] upon it. ...As it is whoever takes charge will have to begin again with both divisions, McConnell's ambition to go to Crewe still keeping up the old irritation, having before him the absurd idea of Admiral Moorsom that, if northern were worked as southern or rather by McConnell, a great saving would ensue. ... In conclusion I would ask you, how, after my plans have been spoiled, my chance of control over the officers destroyed, my own committee superseded ... I can feel otherwise than humiliated and unwilling to have anything more to do with a concern where there is no

consideration for any labour or care or time to work out
a plan, but the whole is overthrown without hesitation
and the triumphant party allowed to trample on the other.

Even if this outburst is dismissed as no more than pique, there
can be no doubt that Moon was genuinely hurt. Though pride,
even arrogance, could be levied against him, this is not the man of
steel, lacking in feeling, so frequently depicted. And he had a case.
He had put more energy into his work and strived harder on behalf
of the company than probably any other member of the board.
At forty-five, a time when most men could have expected to be
reaching the peak of their career, he had put himself back where he
started a decade earlier when pondering how he might best protect
his family's investments.

Although Chandos persuaded him to attend the next Special
Committee on 6 January and had a private discussion with him
beforehand, Moon did not change his mind. He wrote the following
note to Chandos before he left Euston:

> Upon a careful consideration of all the circumstances and
> referring to our conversation last night I feel that after
> the severe rebuff I have sustained I can only adhere to
> the resignation contained in my note of 22 ult. You must
> therefore provide some one else to take over the Stores
> Committee next Thursday but I will attend the board on
> Saturday to answer for myself. The decision of the Special
> Committee has satisfied me only on one point which will
> serve as a warning to others who may serve the London &
> North Western Co. faithfully in the vain imagination that
> it will be thought for the interest of the company to reward
> such service with success and honour, viz., the result to
> myself of nine years uninterrupted labour that I was a fool
> for my pains. Having awoke to the consciousness of this
> disagreeable fact I ask myself *cui bono*?
>
> PS I must not conclude without expressing my sense of
> your very kind consideration towards me.

CHAPTER 11

RETURN TO THE FOLD

It was clearly an embittered and disillusioned Moon who returned to his Bevere retreat that December night in 1859. Looking back over his nine years of 'uninterrupted labour', he may well also have reflected with his wife on how fatefully he had begun the last of them. Their twelve-year old elder daughter, Eleanor, had died on 26 January 1859, the death certificate recording, 'cerebral congestion'. The shock had caused him to miss a board meeting a week later, an event unusual enough in itself, only the third missed since becoming a director. Even more remarkable was that throughout the whole of his thirty years in the chair, he missed only two meetings and one of those again being the result of a family death

Now in early 1860 he was faced with a round of both Stores and Special meetings as well as the monhly board. Sticking to his resignation, he did not attend the first scheduled Stores Committee on 12 January, which was chaired by Blake, nor the board's Special Committee the following day. In his resignation letter he had, of course, ruled himself out of the latter. But, as he had intimated, he did attend the board meeting on the 14th·, when a summary of the December findings was read. This meeting also agreed to split the traffic superintendence of the line into six districts. Moon was minuted as only raising an insurance matter and seconding a request for a report on a trial length of track.

Contemplating his future with the company, he no doubt would have discussed his options with his wife. There are few clues to his relationship with Eleanor. What little there are suggest that she not only supported him, but provided comfort and security in his home life. Moon's letters to Chandos made more than one reference to the importance of his family to him. That the family remained so long in Worcester, when it must have been very inconvenient for him in his railway work, also suggests that his wife was well settled there, and that was what mattered to him. She was coming up for her fortieth birthday. They had been married for over nineteen years.

What seems reasonable to presume is that, at this time of crisis in his lfe, she would have promised him support in whatever he chose to do. Whether she actually advised him to continue his work can only be speculated upon. Given the evidence of the letter over the Bevere tenancy, she can certainly be said to have known his mind.

The other person who could be said to have known Moon's mind was his chairman Chandos. Neither he nor Chandos could possibly have dreamt that within twelve months their roles were to be reversed, with Moon trying to persuade Chandos not to resign. And that, eighteen months to the day from his resignation letter, Moon would become chairman of the company. It was to be a remarkable twist in a career for one who had complained about giving too much time to the company. Despite their differences Moon did seem to have had respect for his young chairman. Chandos, in turn, was clearly well aware of the value of men such as Moon to the company.

That Moon had considered alternative business investments is evident from subsequent correspondence. It is likely, however, that he would have divested himself of shares in the Wolverhampton water company, particularly by the time he agreed a quote from them to supply the railway at Wolverhampton and Bushbury.

It is not known who or what persuaded Moon to change his mind over chairing the Stores Committee, for he missed only the Blake meeting. With an interim one cancelled, he resumed his chairmanship with the meetings held in Earlestown and Crewe on 24 and 25 January respectively. Chandos would no doubt have persisted, and Moorsom may well have made some effort to conciliate Moon's feelings, recognising that the resignation was more than just pique.

When he did return to the fold, however, it is evident that he was far from certain that he was doing the right thing. He wrote to Chandos on 25 February that he had:

> Now got the lease of that Madeley property for perusal. It certainly is very tempting and I have been more that half inclined to join in the undertaking which almost certainly [sic] promises £3 or 4,000 a year with little liability or requirement of capital and the probability of a much

greater return. I know I should have to give up the L&NW but feeling that I have been badly used in the locomotive arrangements and other points I have lost the affection for it which our long holding (since 1829) had given me. On the whole however, seeing the chance came to me through the L&NW position I won't avail of it individually, but we ought not to lose the opportunity of so <u>greatly</u> furthering L&NW interests.

Madeley was a Staffordshire coal property, which lay on the route of a proposed link from the L&NW into the Potteries joining the private Silverdale railways built by R.Sneyd for his coal and ironworks. Although a Bill had been tabled in early 1859 the link was subsequently dropped when agreement with the North Staffordshire Railway was reached.

To return to his committee work, no record of his resignation was noted. He was promptly into his stride at Earlestown by drawing the secretary's attention 'to the delay in sending out the minutes of this committee'. And if the locomotive superintendents Ramsbottom and McConnell thought they could offload responsibilities for such irksome items as gas and water they were soon instructed otherwise. Moon reported that he had read McConnell's gas reports for November and December and, among the many items arising, it was ordered 'that the proposed improvement of light at the clock on down side of Watford Station be carried out by removal of lamp from St Albans platform'.

Regarding the controversial locomotive affair, Moon had written ahead of the meetings to both superintendents asking for progress reports on implementing the new divisional arrangements. He had clearly accepted that, notwithstanding his personal views, his duty lay in carrying out the wishes of his board as efficiently as possible. However it was not until the following day's meeting at Crewe that the Stores Committee formally noted the findings of the board's committee on the changes.

The transfer of the carriage building shops at Crewe to Saltley was largely completed by the end of March with superintendents having been instructed 'to effect the transfer with as little displacement as possible by the working people'. Worsdell, the carriage superintendent at Crewe, was retained by the company in recognition of his thirty-one years satisfactory service and given responsibility for grease, lamps and distribution of station stores including sheets and some purchasing. The men transferred from Crewe to Saltley were found to be on a lower wage rate than comparable Saltley workers and Moon subsequently agreed to raise some of the transferred men's rates (apparently at Crewe the low rates had been supplemented by guaranteed opportunities for additional piece work).

During 1860 the additional miles opened and the increased train miles run were imposing a considerable strain on the company's locomotive resources. Moon's committee was faced with having to revise upwards their estimates for additional engines and rolling stock. Ramsbottom in particular came under increasing pressure, as he demanded more engines and with greater power. The Great Northern competition had made both Ramsbottom and McConnell aware of that company's improved locomotive performance and comparisons were made with the GN's newly introduced 2-2-2 design with 7ft driving-wheels. Ramsbottom had reported in May that he did not think the engine would be as powerful as some on the L&NW's southern division.

Though McConnell thought the weight of 'engines working the southern division need not be exceeded', he was looking at increasing capacity. The issue became critical and required the presence of both Chandos and Moorsom at the Stores Committee meeting to agree weights for the 'present standard classes' of engines being built. However in view of probable future traffic requirements it was agreed to let McConnell experiment with five passenger engines of a higher capacity, and Ramsbottom was asked to consider 'what corresponding alteration should be made in the engines of the northern division'.

Increased size and higher speeds were mixed blessings as far as Moon was concerned: having to compete for traffic was one thing, the resulting increased track wear and fuel costs another. It probably took the presence of Chandos and Moorsom at his meeting to approve the increased weights. The following month Moon's committee delayed a decision to increase to ten the number of larger express engines being built by McConnell until the results of the

32. Crewe North Junction mid 1860s

Crewe North Junction in mid 1860s with Trevithick and Ramsbottom engines,
all with typical tall Ramsbottom chimneys. NRM

33. Early 4 wheel carriage

An ex-L&NW four wheel tri composite class passenger carriage dating from late
1850s (found in a slate quarry in 1900). Such carriages would have been among
the standard for the time. LNWRS

'experiment' were seen. The five experimental were special large 2-2-2 Bloomers which were not a success (at 1¾ tons over specified weight only three were built).

Moon sought a joint meeting with the Traffic Committee to consider in what way provision should be made for the present tendency to increase the weights and speed of certain trains. Despite Moon's caution, McConnell was ordered at the October meeting in Wolverton to lay down an additional ten ordinary Bloomers.

Moorsom also attended the Stores Committee when the salaries of the two locomotive superintendents were discussed. Both were advanced to £1,200 per annum. Despite the responsibilities and authority that these high salaries reflected, Moon continued to plague both superintendents over matters of routine detail. For example he became personally involved in the costs of shunting. The superintendents were asked to review how shunting hours were recorded. When it became apparent that these came from the drivers' own records, Moon undertook to examine the matter personally. When he presented his report on shunting it was 'resolved to recommend that no allowance for shunting be authorised unless the statement of the drivers be certified by the station masters'.

Another aspect concerning drivers which had received considerable attention at that time was the best method of communicating with the guard. Moon's committee had noted the Special Committee's order that the rope and bell system be implemented and Moon himself reported that he had authorised 'the fitting of the Irish & Scotch Mails with a communication by whistle between guard and driver'. The superintendents were ordered 'to make necessary provisions for the whistle on the engines immediately', which they did.

Moon's apparent obsession with gas continued uanabated although Ramsbottom eventually persuaded him that control over his division's gas arrangements should be given to a specialist superintendent, who would report directly to the Stores Committee. His similar attempt to divest himself of water responsibilities was not so successful and although he succeeded in having station plumbing and closets, etc., passed to the engineering department, he was told to remain responsible for locomotive supplies and the water companies. With the need to increase timings on the Irish Mail contract this was to lead to an interesting development that was to revolutionise how locomotives could replenish their water tanks.

It was at the 30 June 1860 Stores meeting that Moon reported, 'after consulting with Lord Chandos' that 'he had authorised Mr Ramsbottom to patent his invention for picking up water for engines'. On 12 July he further reported he had 'authorised the trial of the plan for picking up water on the Holyhead line between Colwyn and Conway,' and in August the Works Committee were requested 'to re-lay half mile of the road for the experiment'. At the 8 November meeting Ramsbottom reported that the 'watering troughs for supplying his engines had been completed on the down line … and found to answer extremely well and recommended that a similar trough be put down on the up line'. It was agreed to recommend the latter at a cost of £350 and the track engineer Lee was to report the best way of supplying water to the troughs. Lee's note on the subject was read at the 13 December meeting when his plan for feeding the troughs with water at Mochdre Marsh was agreed with the cost of the reservoir being £120 and the pipes £170. It seems this was the first example on any railway of water being fed to the engine tender while the train was in motion.

Whilst materials such as coal, coke, clothing, and stationery were still regularly monitored, the responsibility for manufacturing inevitably focussed the Stores Committee on wider issues. Involvement in locomotive design was soon followed by wagons and carriages. The growth in goods traffic demanded not only additional wagons but also increased siding capacity. The board were requested to authorise a further 1,000 wagons to be built at once on capital account. What must have been one of the first references to the modern concept of containerisation arose from a Traffic Committee reference in April 1860. A sketch was submitted of 'a luggage van made in two portions and capable of being detached from its truck for the purpose of sending Irish luggage through without breaking bulk and requesting that one might be built for trial. Mr Watson [City of Dublin Steam Packet Co] to be advised of its dimensions that he may prepare the mail boats to receive it'. It was agreed that such a 'luggage van' be built. Also that month the Stores Committee agreed to recommend to the Board the building of a 'Commercial Inn' at Crewe.

When the previous month the resignation of Slater, the Wolverton carriage superintendent, was confirmed, the Stores Committee with the [company] chairman and deputy chairman were delegated to select and recommend a suitable replacement. What is not evident from the meeting minute was yet another disagreement involving Earle who considered that the redundant Worsdell, with his long serving Crewe carriage building background, should be given the job. Moon on the other hand was looking for a younger more vigorous manager capable of coordinating all the company's growing carriage building requirements. It was only 'after considerable discussion' that it was subsequently agreed, with Chandos and Moorsom present, that the superintendent of the Euston carriage shop, R.Bore, be recommended for the position.

When this was put to the board two days later Earle again objected and proposed that as the Stores Committee had questioned the competence of Worsdell, a committee be appointed to examine the carriages built by Worsdell and compare them with Slater's. It seems that the Grand Junction loyalties were a long time dying with Hardman Earle. His proposal was put to the vote but rejected by a two to one majority. Bore was appointed but, probably as a face saver for Earle, only 'provisionally'. Moon was clearly satisfied with Bore. He was to remain the L&NW's carriage superintendent for over twenty-five years.

Another area in which Moon's committee widened their authority was in the moving and distribution of carriages. They agreed to transfer responsibility from the manufacturing department, as was the case with wagons, to the outside inspection department under the wagon inspector, Hargreaves, at Stafford. Control was to be arranged through four divisions 'that in addition to looking after wagons, sheets, ropes, etc., ... each inspector in his district look after the carriage stock generally with their couplings, shackles, lamps, sheets, horse box partition, etc.'. The hand of Moon is clearly discernible in the policy laid down for Hargreaves to:

> Report within what districts carriages should be worked to certain large stations, the station agents at those and junction stations reporting to him daily the stock at hand, and that in future all applications for carriage stock be

made to him direct and that he also report how many empty vehicles small stations are entitled to keep for emergency, that in the whole arrangement he consult with the general manager who is instructed to issue a general order that all foreign [other companies] carriages be immediately forwarded home direct from the station at which they arrive ... and to report on the advantage of loading them home.

At Holyhead the company had inherited a significant number of vessels for the passenger and goods traffic across the Irish Sea. Moon found himself rationalisng the cost and size of the fleet as well as administering the stores requirements. It seems that he never forgot this introduction to shipping as throughout his chairmanship years he frequently spoke with warmth and pride of his vessels. He appeared to show no such feelings for locomotives.

Although the shipping contract for the Irish Mail service to Kingstown was lost to the City of Dublin Company, the L&NW had agreed to continue to run the Chester & Holyhead 'steamboats' on the Dublin North Wall service. Marine superintendent Hirste had previously been dealing directly with the L&NW Special Committee on the deployment of vessels, including the decision to build another new iron goods vessel 'specially adapted for the Dublin traffic'. Two other vessels were retained for the 'passenger service not accommodated by the mail boats'.

Moon initially appeared to have had some difficulty in getting Hirste to accept his committee's authority on matters of detail. He found it necessary to remind him that 'he reports monthly to this committee stock and consumption of stores sold during the month, purchases ex-contract, and complaints of stores, verification of stock, and statements of excess and deficiencies to be submitted half-yearly before being written off'. In April 1860 a tender for the new goods vessel, from Randolph Elder & Co, was accepted by the board subject to the quality of the iron being approved by the Stores Committee. This was to take Moon, in effect, into shipbuilding.

Of the eight C&H vessels taken over four, were reported as satisfactory, two under repair or being extended, and two wooden ones to be considered for disposal. Hirste reported 'that the extra

34. Paddle steamer *Cambria*
Painting of the *Cambria*, one of the early Chester & Holyhead's paddle steamers
first reviewed by Moon's L&NW Stores Committee in 1860. LNWRS

35. Original Euston Hotel
The separate identical west and east blocks flanking the approach to the station
which comprised the Euston Hotel before the new frontage linking them opened in
1881. The 'dormitory' west side, when opened in 1839, was called the 'Victoria'
and was probably the first railway owned hotel. L&NW public timetable.

cargo vessels although perhaps profitable to the whole system are not so *per se* as they are not constantly employed and when so have cargoes only one way as a rule'. He added though that the Goods and Traffic departments considered them as 'essentially necessary to the successful working of the trade'.

Although Hirste's recommendation to call the new boat "Admiral" was approved, the board changed this to "Admiral Moorsom". Hirste later reported difficulties in fitting out this vessel which had to be completed after receipt in Holyhead. The *Admiral Moorsom* was finally launched at the end of 1860. In the meantime one of the vessels reported as being extended, the *Cambria*, had been made ready for sea.

The accounts of the 'Steam Boat' department at Holyhead had initially been referred to Moon personally. He quickly raised the question of the boats' insurance and proposed creating a fund in lieu of paying premiums to an insurance company. He had proposed this generally to the board in January 1860.

By the end of 1860 it had become obvious that the company had too many vessels. Only two were kept constantly running and one in reserve was used only two or three times a week. The Traffic Committee agreed that the two old wooden boats should be sold, but buyers proved difficult to find with bids at auction being reported as 'extremely' low.

The other new responsibility for Moon's committee was supplies for the Lancaster & Carlisle line. Moon reported in August 1860 that he had inspected with Col Maclean (a long standing director of the local company and elected to the L&NW board in February 1860) the 'works' on the line. They recommended plans and estimates for necessary locomotive accommodation to cover twelve engines at Tebay Junction including coke and water.

As to be expected Moon had wasted little time in becoming involved so personally in his committee's wider brief, but what continues to astonish is that he still found time for relatively minor matters. Even when critical company issues were at stake he continued to preside meticulously, with the heads of all the relevant departments in attendance, over reviews of items ranging from the composition of grease to the working of brake trucks in Liverpool's Wapping and Lime Street tunnels. When it appeared that nobody could tell him whether the brakes in the Wapping and Waterloo tunnels turned different ways, Bore was instructed angrily to get the facts and report to the next meeting. It turned out that there were several different types of brake carriages and another meeting had to be called to resolve the matter.

Lists showing the number and description of the various vehicles belonging to the company used for conveyance of goods to and from the railway were prepared and subsequently referred to Moon. Tenders for 'weighing machines' were agreed, another for 'an illuminated and striking clock' to be erected outside the new goods warehouse at Birmingham. 'Mr Jones of Chester' was to 'report the cost of regulating this and the other clocks of the company in Birmingham by the Magnetic Current'.

Two dealers, Austin and Cowie had attended the committee in March 1860 and were recommended to the board 'to be employed for a time going over the line' to report on old machinery, equipment, warehousing and sidings 'not made full use of' and also 'where mechanical appliances might be used to save manual labour'. It appears that Austin, covering the lines north of Crewe, satisfied Moon in the details provided: his fourth and final report being reviewed in February the following year. Cowie's services were 'discontinued' in July.

When a report on the 'Repairs and Renewal of Cranes' at each station was reviewed, the locomotive superintendents were asked 'how far it may be worth while to purchase patterns from the original makers and what course they advise the committee to pursue so as to obtain uniformity'. This drive for uniformity and manufacture in house was to typify Moon's approach to cost reduction through standardisation. Samples were to be sent to the pattern room at Euston of 'every description of chair, tree nails, spikes, keys, fishing [sic] plates, and bolts & nuts for which contracts will be required in future'. Within weeks of moving up to deputy chairman of the board Moon was involving himself in both the design and supply of foot warmers!

Before leaving Moon's last year with his Stores Committee mention should be made of an incident where he found himself having publicly to defend his purchasing policy. At first sight this could have been potentially damaging to his career but it says much for his standing and integrity with suppliers that it was his accuser who was denigrated. The extraordinary outburst against him took place at the company's half-yearly meeting on 17 August 1860. His response is the first occasion he was recorded as speaking publicly to shareholders.

In the absence of Chandos (in Canada with the young Prince of Wales) Moorsom was in the chair. When he moved for the adoption of the accounts, an objection was raised by a Mr Puncher who, referring to the accounts as 'unskilfully cooked', asked for the name of gentleman who presided over the Stores Committee. Moon responded from the platform that he was the chairman of that committee. Moorsom then told Puncher that the directors were collectively responsible and 'he could not permit him to catechise particular members of the board'. Puncher countered that 'that being the case I will put my question through the chair; the first is - Do you know a gentleman of the name of Blakemore?'.

Moon confirmed that he knew Blakemore and agreed, in answer to Puncher's further questioning, that Blakemore supplied stores to the company as a contractor and as an agent receiving commission. Then Puncher asked if Moon remembered Blakemore being called before the committee and questioned on price and quality of stores supplied. Moon said he didn't. The report of proceedings then continued with Puncher saying that he believed Blakemore was 'closely related' to Moon. Moon denied this. Unabashed Puncher continued by asserting that the bulk of stores was bought on commission without the slightest check on price, and that shareholders were victimised through a system of 'scandalous jobbery'. However when challenged by Moorsom to substantiate his accusation Puncher could only hand over his own unsigned extract of a letter sent to him by post. When asked if the original document was signed, Puncher replied that 'the paper shall be forthcoming. I will go no farther. I will give up my authority. I have stated what I believe to be true, and it is only for Mr Moon to say or gainsay what I have stated'.

Moorsom however refused to accept that the accusation was anything other than anonymous and demanded that Puncher sign the charge for it to be 'properly authenticated', which Puncher did.

Moon's initial response that he did not remember Blakemore being called before his committee was perhaps a touch evasive. His

Stores Committee minutes contain numerous references to Blakemore including attendance in person. Given his obsession with detail, he surely would have remembered that in 1857 he had summoned the agent, with whom he had personally negotiated commissions, to explain a supply problem.

As a small shareholder in many companies, Puncher was notorious for criticising their policies and performance. In persisting with his charge, he moved and was seconded that a committee of investigation be appointed. However Moorsom refused to take the motion as Puncher withheld the name of the party making the charge. Former chairman Glyn now intervened to calm matters, saying Moon 'is naturally anxious to refute the charges made, and has been standing here some time for that purpose. But who is to substantiate those charges and how are they to be answered?'.

Puncher could only fall back on believing the statements were correct, admitting he could not prove them but that he would 'bring the document I took it from, if you like'. Moorsom then suggested that Moon had the option as a shareholder to address the meeting. Moon clearly considered that his own position and the company's purchasing policy needed affirming. The report of the meeting read:

> I differ from Mr Puncher in this respect - instead of being the proprietor of units of stock, I represent for myself and family a very large share in the capital of this company. I hold a name in the commercial world which had been untainted by any act which can discredit it. Surely no assembly of Englishmen will receive such an insinuation without the smallest proof. Mr Puncher might have ascertained who was the chairman of the committee and seen me: he has not adopted that course. He had the option of ascertaining the truth without making these slanderous statements in a public meeting. I might treat the insinuation with the contempt it merits but I will not do that. Gentlemen, there is no truth in the statement (hear, hear). I have seen Mr Blakemore, but I do not know him personally, nor his connections, nor is he connected with me in any degree. I do not mean to prosecute Mr Puncher, for I believe Mr Puncher has been imposed upon. I know

the system is not agreeable to the contractors [suppliers]. When I explain to you the position of these men, when I show you how the whole thing is worked, you will see the matter in its true light.

It had been the practice to contract for all manner of articles, and that course is still adopted for those required in large bulk. But there are thousands of small things for which a contractor is paid, and upon which there is no check of any kind; and any gentleman in business in the Birmingham district will know, if he wants to purchase little eyelet holes, small screws, rims for lamps, and such things, it is the universal practice to employ a factor or commission agent. From a consultation with a gentleman who was thirty years a director, Mr Ledsam, we were recommended to employ Blakemore & Sons and those gentlemen have worthily fulfilled their trust, not only to the satisfaction of the directors, but of the officers, who were at first opposed to the system, because they thought there would be a disadvantage and difficulty in persons who did not use them purchasing these small articles. On some articles we pay the factors 2½%, on some very minute articles 5%, on some 1%; it depends on the trouble they have in gathering them together. These accounts are passed by your storekeeper, then by your superintendent; they are paid only when audited and passed in the regular manner. I do not know anything personally of those gentlemen; and you will see there is not the smallest ground for what I can only call a most unwarrantable and contemptible proceeding.

Moorsom made the point that if the charges were true they would involve the whole board. However he thought 'most emphatically, that such things as have been described could not happen under the system established. If there be a committee more careful in investigating and recording the minutest acts, it is that over which Mr Moon presides ... and the most vigilant scrutiny is exercised over every act of every committee'. When, stubbornly, Puncher suggested that the press publish his document, a shareholder erupted to say that he had 'never heard so many cock-and-bull stories as I have from Mr Puncher. He has taken up an hour and a half in discussing an anonymous paper; it seems to me a most ridiculous thing. I think you did not do your duty, sir, or you would have stopped him at first'.

The episode was concluded by R.W.Hand (recently appointed as one of the auditors) moving that 'in the opinion of this meeting the statement of Mr Puncher is a gross and scandalous libel upon Mr Moon, and that this meeting has the greatest confidence in the honour and integrity of that gentleman, and place the greatest reliance upon him'. The motion was seconded and carried.

This incident, if it did nothing else, certainly brought Moon into the public eye. *The Railway Times*, although praising Moon and commenting scathingly on Puncher, felt that there should be an enquiry. Though saying that 'no person in the least degree acquainted' with Moon would give the 'slightest credence to the accusations made against him', they nevertheless felt that some shareholders 'may believe there is something wrong in the matter of stores. And those are not likely to have their doubts removed by any denial, however indignant, of the charges so improperly adduced at a public meeting'. The periodical was satisfied that Moon would not 'permit the matter to rest in its present unsatisfactory state', and that there would doubtless be 'a thoroughly probing inquiry; and, if no other advantage results therefrom than the compulsory silence of Mr Puncher at future public meetings ... the benefit will be sufficiently large to justify the proceeding'.

In fact the board did not formally take the matter further and Moon seems to have taken no action against Puncher. Blakemore continued as a purchasing agent. At Moon's last Stores meeting a new storekeeper in Birmingham was ordered to 'take the engineering and other stores wholly from Messrs Blakemore & Son as at present'. However the Blakemore affair did not quite end there.

Moon had become deputy chairman of the company when the Stores Committee (under his successor Richard Birley) uncovered a discrepancy: suppliers' reductions in price in return for prompt payments had not been passed on by Blakemore to the L&NW. At his 24 April 1861 Stores Committee meeting, Birley reported an interview with Blakemore's son who it appeared 'had made an error in the interpretation of the terms of the Contract [L&NW's], which he regretted, though in accordance with the custom of the Trade in the District'. It was agreed that the premiums received for prompt payments since the start of the business in 1856 should be paid over to the company and that in future 'Messrs Blakemore rigidly adhere to the understanding of the directors, that all allowances made by the sellers of goods be credited to the company, without any abatement of premium or otherwise'. This agreement was jointly signed by Moon, Birley and Blakemore.

No further public reference has been found to the affair. It does seem that Moon was right: the gullible Puncher was probably set up by a disgruntled supplier. Blakemore continued in business for many years, enjoying the L&NW's custom. Moon's standing in the company not only remained undiminished, but within six months his colleagues elected him deputy chairman of the company. The events that so rapidly led to this and subsequently to the chair itself, now need to be followed.

CHAPTER 12

STEPS TO THE CHAIRMANSHIP

As has been seen, by the end of 1860 Moon's detailed knowledge of L&NW administration was probably unrivalled and recognised even by those he had antagonised by his forthright views and drive for reform. He clearly had the ear of his chairman, had shown himself to be active and energetic and, despite the hiccup of his Stores resignation, proved his commitment to the company.

His involvement in west midland affairs has been followed, as has his secondment to the Chester & Holyhead negotiation. In addition, he was offering advice privately to Chandos on a number of threats and opportunities in the north-west. One such threat was the Lancashire & Yorkshire's proposed amalgamation with the East Lancashire Railway. Though a Bill in 1858 had failed in the House of Lords it had been passed in the 1859 session. The East Lancashire's line from Preston to Liverpool was a direct competitor to the L&NW for traffic between the two towns. Moon had urged his chairman to take an aggressive stance in protecting the L&NW's position.

In one of his many letters to Chandos at the time he advocated a competing Manchester to Preston line, reminding him of the agreement previously reached that 'gave Preston and Manchester traffic wholly to Lancashire & Yorkshire and Preston and Liverpool wholly to us'. He thought they should either have this understanding confirmed, or 'get such share of Preston and Manchester as the L&Y may get of Preston & Liverpool' by having an independent company build a line from Preston to Manchester with scope to amalgamate it with the L&NW. In February 1859 Moon was part of the L&NW deputation with Chandos, Moorsom, Smith Grant, Earle, Tootal and Bancroft to negotiate 'a new and comprehensive agreement' with the L&Y.

But satisfactory terms could not be agreed. Some indication of the problems between the two companies is given in a series of letters

Edward Tootal wrote at the time to George Wilson (of Anti-Corn Law League fame). Wilson was an Electric Telegraph company colleague and a director, later chairman, of the Lancashire & Yorkshire. Tootal wrote in August 1859 that 'it is evidently the interest of managers to get us by the ears - we can not increase the traffic from Preston - we can only direct or redirect at same or lower rates, or by giving facilities amounting to the same thing'. The following month Tootal wrote that 'if I know anything in this world I believe I know that Mr Smithells will be to you what Capt. Huish was to us - a very costly ... representative'. James Smithells, the former East Lancashire manager, had replaced Cawkwell as manager of the L&Y.

Tootal's efforts at peace making failed. The L&NW promoted their own line from Eccles to Wigan, tapping both the local traffic and shortening their route from Manchester to Preston. Also independent lines were promoted from the east Lancashire towns to the Wigan coalfield and Liverpool, with powers for the L&NW to subscribe (these lines subsequently became the Lancashire Union Railways and will be referred to later).

The position over the Birkenhead Lancashire & Cheshire Junction (renamed Birkenhead from 1 August 1859), the company its chairman Bancroft had tried to sell to either the L&NW or the GW, had become critical again. Its two main lines from Chester to Birkenhead and to Warrington were seen by the GW as natural extensions to Merseyside and Manchester respectively. Resistance from the L&NW had led to protracted negotiations, which finally resulted in the company being taken over jointly by the two main companies. Moon joined Bancroft (by then a L&NW director) and Earle as the L&NW members of the Birkenhead Joint Committee. For both Moon and Bancroft it was a renewal of even earlier days when both had invested in the company originally promoted as a route from Manchester to Chester.

Although these developments provide evidence of Moon's increasing involvement in wider areas of traffic management, he had not participated directly in the main area of conflict: the battle with the MS&L and Great Northern for the London to Manchester traffic. However after the agreement to end that war was signed on 26 November 1858, he was appointed with Chandos, Moorsom and Tootal (later also Bancroft) as the L&NW representatives on the Joint Committee to manage the traffic sharing arrangements between London and Lancashire. In the early months of 1859 the resolution of their discussions was the major issue on the agenda of the L&NW's Special Committee, the latter in fact being convened the same day to follow the meetings of the Joint Committee. In order to avoid the misunderstandings of the past, all three companies agreed that the new traffic arrangements should be sanctioned by Parliament and a Bill was prepared for the 1859 session. In the meantime disputes between them continued, for example over proportions to be allocated for the Liverpool traffic and the competition generally west of Manchester. More serious was the growing alienation of the Midland Company over their exclusion from the arrangements.

Chandos had attempted to reach a personal understanding with the newly appointed Midland chairman, G.B.Paget, but following Paget's early death and the temporary resumption of the chair by Ellis, relationships between the two companies worsened and it was mainly owing to Midland objections that the three companies' Bill was thrown out in the Lords.

Chandos, more than any other figure except perhaps Watkin, had been seen as the leading protagonist in the prolonged 1858 crisis. Whatever the merits of his case he had stood his ground firmly. But after the settlement he seemed to lose some of the grip he had on his company and early in 1859 became distracted by the serious illness of his father. At short notice he had to postpone chairing the February shareholders' meeting, leaving an obviously unprepared Moorsom to handle the usual criticism from certain shareholders. In fact Moorsom, when faced by a vote rejecting modest new capital requests, had to be 'rescued' by Smith, Glyn and a particularly forceful Bancroft.

In the early summer of 1859 Chandos also uncharacteristically missed several Special Committee meetings. Although an understanding was eventually reached with the Midland, another attempt to obtain parliamentary approval for the three companies' arrangements was rejected in 1860, this time on objections from the North Staffordshire. In the meantime the three new partners, L&NW, MS&L and GN, had proceeded warily to work together.

The GN were in a somewhat anomalous position as far as the Midland was concerned: on the one hand competing fiercely against them for the London coal trade, east midlands and Yorkshire traffic, yet at the same time supporting the Midland's growing use of its Hitchin to Kings Cross line. To complicate the position still further the Midland, although still reliant on the L&NW connection at Rugby for a large proportion of their London traffic, were no longer content to accept their small share of the pooled traffic to Scotland under the Octuple agreement. With running powers over the GN to Kings Cross formally secured in 1858, the Midland began looking for a fairer pooling apportionment based on a new central route. Until this could be agreed the Midland went against the spirit of the agreement by trying to keep the receipts from this route outwith the pooling arrangement, sharing only with those companies directly concerned. And to gain access to Lancashire they found a new partner in the Lancashire & Yorkshire Railway.

Alliances then shifted dramatically with the L&NW, MS&L and Great Northern now lined up against a Midland and L&Y combination. With the failure of their Bill to confirm traffic sharing arrangements, the three new allies had begun to resort to the sort of protective tactics that had so miserably failed under the old 'confederacy' orchestrated by Huish. Chandos appeared not only to have underestimated the ambitions of the Midland but also the difficulties of working with Watkin. Furthermore he was preoccupied with affairs of a different kind, for on 11 July 1860 he sailed from Plymouth for Canada accompanying the eighteen year old Prince of Wales as Keeper of his Privy Seal. The royal entourage toured Canada and America, not returning until October when Chandos found his L&NW Joint Committee with the MS&L and GN still trying to thrash out their difficulties. However, behind the scenes moves had been made to find a more permanent solution to their problem.

It is not clear who took the first steps in the far reaching proposal for the L&NW and GN to lease permanently the MS&L for a guaranteed dividend. What is though, was that the outcome ended the L&NW career of Chandos. It has been suggested that Tootal set the scene for Watkin to raise the idea at a meeting of the general managers convened under the Joint Committee of the three companies. Apparently Watkin, appreciating that his company could not hope to compete as a major player without further costly finance for expansion, saw that the natural links with the L&NW (their joint interests at London Road and in the Manchester South Junction & Altrincham) and the GN at Retford, offered prospects for a logical union of the three companies.

The deal, as later reported in *The Times*, would have been for the two larger companies to provide a guarantee to ordinary MS&L shareholders of '1½% per annum, increasing ½% per annum up to 3½% in perpetuity and the privilege of exchanging every £100 Sheffield [MS&L] stock into £65 (or £70) London and North Western stock'. Considering the MS&L had never paid more than 1% during the previous ten years this would have been attractive to their long suffering shareholders.

At the L&NW board meeting of 15 December 1860 it was Tootal who suggested he could make 'satisfactory arrangements' with the MS&L in conjunction with the GN. A board sub committee of Chandos, Moorsom, Tootal, Bancroft, Lyon, Mangles, Earle and Moon was appointed to carry out the arrangements. It seems typical that the L&NW's initiative should have come from Tootal. A Manchester man, he sat on all the joint committees in the area involving contact with the MS&L and had known Watkin since their Trent Valley days. He must also have thought he had reached an understanding with Denison the formidable GN chairman.

The threat of a competing Midland and L&Y traffic agreement was the deciding factor that brought the issue to a head. It was this threat that convinced Moon to support such a deal, as is evident from the letter he wrote to Chandos quoted below. The formal L&NW board minute for that December meeting gave no indication of the furore that followed Chandos's astonishing admission that, ahead of any discussion with his own L&NW directors who all agreed the lease, he had written to Denison saying that the L&NW would not support a guarantee to the MS&L.

Chandos's letter was all that a wavering Denison needed to persuade his own board not to back the guarantee either. The GN had just had their traffic agreement with the MS&L approved and saw no urgency for an even closer association.

The lease would not only have been the most effective way of both countering an awkward competitor and strengthening the new grouping's stance against outside threats, but changed the future railway map of Britain. There would have been no Cheshire Lines and the later dreams of Watkin, when chairman of the MS&L, for a new route to London would never have been realised. Although he retired through ill health in 1894, the extension he inspired to London opened in 1898, his company grandly renamed the Great Central Railway.

It is difficult to understand what prompted Chandos, prior to his board meeting, to write to Denison as he did. Moon however appeared to have been aware of Chandos's reservations and sought an opportunity to allay his fears. He wrote to Chandos on the Monday following the Saturday board meeting:

> I have greatly regretted being unable to have the interview with you which I asked last week as I think I could have satisfied your judgement and have prevented the contretemps which happened on Saturday and which I fear must have been very disagreeable to you. I trust however you will allow me to use the freedom which our having acted together so long gives me in expressing my hope that it will not induce you to think the decision places you in the greater difficulty to which you alluded at the board or to leave you discouraged and disheartened, but that you will after all unite with the others in seeing the best possible agreement made, ... Last Spring you spoiled my labour of several years in a moment yet I consented to carry on ... and do now carry out honestly a policy which I disapprove and I believe to be wrong. In the summer your casting vote alone gave us the Birkenhead and I am one of those carrying out that policy believing it my duty to pick up the pieces.
>
> This decision of the board is not on a general line of policy but on a case entirely exceptional brought on by the changed circumstances of the Lancashire & Yorkshire. I have all along warned our negotiators never to complete the agreement with that company unless the south traffic was secured to us as before and the board should not have sanctioned it without some such security being the only object of an agreement with them. They seem to have

been under the impression that our general powers of injury were sufficient to do so but the combination with the Midland has turned our flank. The former course of traffic is to be altered and our east-west traffic would be altogether in danger so that *however unpleasant it may be to have to deal with a man like Watkin, whom I think utterly unscrupulous and should be sorry to allow again to be on the footing of gentleman with me, I must for the general good put this in my pocket and re-adopt that policy which we affirmed years ago as to the Sheffield position* [author's italics]. And which would have been successful had Huish passed the traffic over, so as to give the Sheffield a dividend instead of paying only to the strict letter of the agreement and for the temporary profit of the moment to the L&NW and at sometime had behaved with less hauteur and acrimony than was his wont to people not so strong as himself. I won't go further into it. I trust you will think better of it and exert the powers of your mind to pick up the pieces - then again thinking over the policy which it is in our interest for the future to pursue.

Mrs Moon who is sitting by me in my study this cold morning desires to be kindly remembered to Lady Chandos and yourself.

Despite Moon's plea Chandos did not change his mind. The greater difficulty Chandos had alluded to was probably the question of his integrity: he clearly considered he could not go back on his word. Chandos took the L&NW chair for the last time at a special board meeting called for 5 January 1861 when it was recorded:

Lord Chandos submitted a statement explanatory of the circumstances connected with the letter which he had recently addressed to Mr Denison, chairman of the Great Northern. Mr Tootal and Mr Bancroft also gave explanations on the same subject. The question having been fully considered and Lord Chandos having tendered the resignation of his seat at the board retired. Whereupon the deputy chairman took the chair and the minutes of the Special Committee appointed on the 15th December and the report of the sub committee having been read, it was resolved that the resignation of the Marquis of Chandos be ... accepted.

In accepting his resignation, the board recorded tersely 'the zeal, ability and energy' of Chandos and allowed him to retain his free pass. The shareholders were a little more appreciative the following month when the respectful thanks of the meeting were unanimously voted 'for the able, faithful, and courteous manner in which he had filled the office of chairman of the company'. However the *Railway Times* considered that the loss of Chandos to the railway world would:

Not be seriously felt or even long regretted. Whatever his attainments, and his aptitude to learn is generally admitted, his Lordship had the misfortune to be more than ordinarily obstinate in his antipathies, if not implacable in his resentments. His temper, it had been remarked, might not be very bad for a nobleman, but was somewhat unbearable in an ordinary individual.

Herapath, a L&NW shareholder, regarded Chandos in rather a different light and probably reflected more accurately general opinion. He wrote in his *Railway Journal* for the 12 January that:

Men of Lord Chandos's stamp are highly valuable to railway proprietors, since he combined excellent business habits, and great ability in mastering railway questions, with high principles and sterling integrity. With one such man at a board proprietors may feel competent that their affairs, as far as the board are concerned, are faithfully administered. ... [He had become chairman of the L&NW] at a time when it was most difficult to satisfy the proprietors as to the business done or to preserve order at the meetings. The dividends were descending or, in the face of an increasing revenue, not enlarging as the proprietors expected.

Chandos's resignation as both director and chairman threw the L&NW board into disarray. Several directors appeared to have used the occasion to bring forward their own resignation and the remaining senior directors found themselves needing to regroup. The election of Moorsom to replace Chandos would have been almost a formality given his seniority and position as deputy chairman, the only question presumably being his own willingness to serve and for how long. He was elected unanimously a week later, moved by Glyn and seconded by Tootal. The board, appreciating the short term nature of his appointment (he was in his sixty-ninth year), then cast around more critically to select a deputy chairman. It was Earle who gave notice of a motion for the deputy chairman at the next board meeting.

Chandos was to play no further part in the direction of L&NW affairs although he remained a local director of the Buckinghamshire Railway. The *Railway Times* assumed Moorsom's appointment to be only temporary and commented on the possibility of Tootal or Westhead taking over although it felt that Tootal's Trent Valley antecedents 'are likely to militate against his prospects', and that Westhead 'has secluded himself'. Moon was not one of the names publicly considered. In terms of other directors the choice was not as wide as a thirty strong board would suggest. Herapath incidentally had commented wryly on Moorsom's appointment in his journal of 19 January. 'We are somewhat interested in this election, for whatever gifts the gallant gentleman may have, he has not that of the gab, and therefore the reporters will probably not have so much to do in future.'

Grant, one of the two surviving members of the Grand Junction contingent (the other being Earle), resigned. The 12 January board accepted his resignation with 'great regret' and recorded their appreciation of his 'high personal character and qualifications [and influence] very beneficial to this company'. Glyn, although he was to continue to serve on the board for many years, was by then taking little part in day to day affairs and Benson had clearly not been fully committed to the company for some time. Smith, with Glyn, one of the original London & Birmingham members, also resigned and in contrast to the brief tribute accorded Chandos, the board recorded their 'great regret' and 'personal esteem and respect of every member' as a result of 'the serious loss which they feel that the company sustains by being deprived of Mr Smith's services, and of [his] knowledge, ability and sound judgement'.

At the same meeting the resignations of Barrow and Pierrepont were accepted without recorded comment. Barrow was then over seventy and Pierrepont had already given notice the previous October that he was going to resign in view of his health.

Of the remaining longest serving directors, Earle, Cropper and Rathbone, the most active was Earle. However he appears to have ruled himself out as a candidate being in his late sixties. It is likely that Tootal also declined to be considered, not necessarily on age, although he was over sixty. His style suggests he preferred to operate behind the scenes, which was probably also the case with Earle; both were to remain active directors of the company well into their seventies. By virtue of their membership of the Special Committee, the other senior directors who could have been possible candidates for the deputy position were Bancroft, Lyon, Mangles and Moon. Lyon was the longest serving and most experienced, his railway career going back to the early days of the Manchester & Birmingham. Bancroft too could be said to have a background in railway direction and was a skilled negotiator. However neither Lyon nor Bancroft were young, both were over sixty. Mangles would not have had age on his side either, but his other interests may also have precluded him from being considered.

With the departure of Chandos, Moon, at forty six, was now the youngest of the active directors but on record as being unwilling to give more time to the company. Outside candidates must have been considered. That the directors were having difficulties in the selection was evident when Earle deferred his promised proposal at the February board and instead seconded Tootal in the election of J.P.Brown-Westhead to fill Chandos's director vacancy. H.C.E.Childers replaced 'city' man Smith. Proposed by Glyn, seconded by Mangles, Childers was to distinguish himself in later years becoming Chancellor of the Exchequer in Gladstone's 1880 administration (his tenure as a L&NW director was short: briefly a member of the Finance committee, he resigned in May 1864). The board replaced Barrow by another midland industrialist, Philip Williams, who was proposed by Moon and seconded by Benson. Replacements for Grant and Pierrepont were left for the forthcoming shareholders' meeting when Bramley Moore (of Liverpool docks fame) and Melville were elected.

The return of Joshua Proctor Brown-Westhead could have been significant. As a thirty-year old Manchester textile manufacturer in 1837, J.P.Westhead had been elected a director of the Manchester & Birmingham Railway at their inaugural meeting. In later years he had also been active in the Shropshire Union and the Trent Valley, but it was as a director of the London & Birmingham that he had been a founder member of the L&NW. But elected a Liberal MP, his initial interest in railways seems to have waned and he resigned from the L&NW in 1850 and was replaced by Lyon. In the same year, in compliance with the will of his uncle (J.Brown of Lea Castle near Kidderminster), he took the name Brown-Westhead and in 1852 became a Deputy Lieutenant of Worcestershire. It is possible that he was persuaded to rejoin the company with the prospect of eventually succeeding to the chair.

However two days after the board elected Childers and Brown-Westhead they met again, on the 9 February, and 'Mr Earle brought forward the motion of which he had given notice ... [and] after discussion it was on the motion of Mr Earle, seconded by Mr Glyn, that Mr Richard Moon be elected to the office of Deputy Chairman'.

Unfortunately no indication has been found as to the tenor of the 'discussion', nor whether alternative candidates were openly considered. That it was Earle who proposed him must have been one of the most significant factors in Moon's favour. As was the case following his Stores resignation, who or what convinced Moon to commit himself further to the company can only be surmised. What probably influenced Earle and his senior colleagues was that they needed someone active with a proven safe pair of hands to support an aging Moorsom, giving them perhaps time to make a final long term choice for chairman. Moon had presumably concluded he could not complete his work of reforming the L&NW by remaining an "amateur". It could even be suspected that by locking him into the administrative role of deputy, Earle and his colleagues gave themselves a wider option in seeking a more amenable and publicly known figurehead.

Although his Stores chairmanship and the consequential membership of the Special Committee were Moon's principal committee activities, he had been appointed to a number of signicant operational committees, for example the Birkenhead Joint Committee in August 1860. Earlier, in March, he had joined the Law, Hotels, Birmingham Canal, South Staffordshire and the Shropshire Union Amalgamated Board. It is not clear whether, on his appointemnt to the deputy chair, he continued this work. In his three and half months as deputy chairman Moon had hardly the time to work out where his priorities should lie, although the duties of the position had been clarified by Chandos, including an annual 'retaining fee' of £100, as recently as February 1860. 'He should be freed from the obligation to attend any of the ordinary committees and thus be enabled to devote the time formerly occupied in those duties to the assistance of the chairman in attending to the general policy of the company, and to the preparation of the business to be brought before the Special Committee and that committee before the board.'

From his last Stores meeting Moon had only about two and half months effectively as deputy chairman and would have had little time, for example, to contribute to the reports for the half-yearly shareholders' meeting in February. Nevertheless during his short time in the position he ominously raised at board level the question of further expenditure proposed by McConnell at Wolverton. The cost of developing in parallel two locomotive departments was not an issue he was to let lie. He succeeded in forming another special committee to enquire 'into the facts reporting how far the results bear out Mr McConnell's statements [justifying the need for expenditure] and how far they have been affected by other circumstances'.

Moon's disagreement with Moorsom in other matters had also become more evident. Relations between them had continued to be strained over some aspects of Birmingham Canal policy. However what brought matters to a head between them was Moorsom's negotiations with the West Midland Railway. This company, as has been noted in an earlier chapter, had been formed from the amalgamation of the OW&W, NA&H and W&H and was flexing its muscles for a a new route from Worcester to London by suggesting they jointly with the L&NW extended their respective lines (the L&NW from the Buckinghamshire's Banbury branch). However without any control over such a service, the benefits to the L&NW were marginal. So strongly did Moon object to even considering the idea that he walked out of Moorsom's meeting with the WMR delegation. He later wrote to Moorsom explaining his many objections: the unsatisfactory working arrangements and the waste of capital on a line over which the L&NW would have no guaranteed traffic. He ended his letter, dated 21 September 1860, 'having these views I shall do all that I can legitimately to prevent confirmation of the proposals'.

Although Moon actually lost a vote on the subject at the following month's board, subsequent events justified his stand. The sudden announcement of the WMR merger with the GW scotched all further thought of such ideas. When forced to justify (when he became chairman of the company) the L&NW's policy of extensions, Moon admitted the 'Buckinghamshire line was a failure' but only 'because the line went nowhere. Had it been carried through as originally proposed to Cheltenham or Worcester it would have paid'.

Whether the elderly Moorsom and his vigorous deputy would ever have satisfactorily worked together is, of course, academic. Moorsom attended his last board meeting on the 18 May 1861. He died suddenly at home just eight days later on the 26th.

The Times reported that his death followed an operation on an old wound received in the arm at the siege of Copenhagen, but commented that at the recent company meeting he had appeared in excellent health. He was sixty-eight and had been associated with the railway for thirty years. Herapath commented that little was publicly known of the 'gallant Admiral'; at meetings he 'sat generally quiet and unobtrusive, seldom taking part in the discussions, but when he did it was always to uphold the plans of the board, with a little too much of the quarter deck, many thought, in his manner'. The board's own tribute to Moorsom was generous. Moon, as deputy, was in the chair on 1 June when they recorded:

> With deep regret the death of their chairman Vice Admiral Constantine Richard Moorsom. Admiral Moorsom, having taken an active part in the affairs and management of the company for nearly thirty years, his colleagues had full cognizance of his qualifications when by their unanimous vote they elected him to preside over this board, a resolution to which they were led not more by their confidence in his

zeal, experience and tried ability than by their appreciation of the uniform courtesy and impartiality of his conduct, and the high sense of honour which formed so marked a feature in his character.

It was resolved to elect a new chairman at the next monthly board which was held on the 22 June. The senior directors had given themselves three weeks in which to decide the succession. It seems that the choice finally lay between the reforming, uncompromising Moon and a less disruptive, more establishment type figure represented by the re-emergent Westhead. Moon's own decision to offer himself would by then probably have been a formality, his decision to commit to such office already made when he accepted the deputy position. In the event his election was unanimous, significantly he was proposed by Glyn and seconded by Earle. Brown-Westhead was voted, also unanimously, his deputy, proposed by Benson and again seconded by Earle.

Typically the *Railway Times* writing after Moon was appointed could not resist taking a final swipe at the old regime, referring on 17 August 1861 to 'secret treaties and illegal division of receipts' and saying what was now needed was a 'thorough change of system' but:

> Our expectations in this matter were not great so long as Admiral Moorsom remained at the head of affairs. That gentleman, with all his good qualities and many worthy services, was too deeply schooled in the exploded policy of former years to enter, at his time of life, into a new arena. But these expectations took a firmer hold on our mind when Mr Moon was appointed to the chair; and we accept, almost without investigation, the crisis which has come upon the undertaking as a pledge that a security hitherto unknown over all the departments of management ... has been vigorously undertaken.

Given the circumstances and the state of the company, the board knew they needed above all a strong hand at the helm. Moon had been preaching reform, economy and cost control for so long that they had little to lose in letting him, finally, have his head.

CHAPTER 13

QUESTION OF CONFIDENCE

Moon chaired his first half-yearly shareholders' meeting on 23 August 1861. It was the 31st such meeting since the company was incorporated. Virtually unknown to the investing public and unproven in running any company let alone the largest in the country, Moon was given the chair at a time of uncertainty and a further decline in the dividend rate.

It was not that the company's trading profitability had fallen so markedly but 'interest and other fixed charges' had risen. As has been seen, Moon complained bitterly to Chandos over the company being burdened, for example, by the Chester & Holyhead debt and commitments to meet the high lease charge for the Lancaster & Carlisle. As a result fixed charges, which had been held throughout most of the 1850s to not much more than around £600,000, had increased dramatically, rising to nearly a million in 1859 and over that figure by the end of 1860.

The first item taken by Moon as chairman at the board on 22 June 1861 was 'the General Manager's monthly report including verdict of "Accidental Death" in the case of two enginemen killed by the fall of the Leek Wooton bridge near Kenilworth'. It was agreed to issue a notice 'under the solicitor's advice' for the 'examination of the bridges generally as shall reassure the public', but no minute recorded any regret or compensation to the drivers' families.

Controversially, at his second board in July, the directors split evenly over the proposal by the Duke of Sutherland, seconded surprisingly by Bancroft, for the election of the Earl of Caithness to fill Moorsom's director vacancy. At this early stage in the position Moon appears to have uncharacteristically trodden carefully in exerting his authority. Instead of using a casting vote he held a ballot and the proposal was rejected by one vote. Moorsom's vacancy was not filled until the shareholders meeting the following February.

Three years later Caithness was elected, proposed by Moon!

The first half-year results for 1861 were reviewed at the August board ahead of the shareholders' meeting. The new chairman was faced with having to propose a dividend rate which equalled the nadir reached in the disastrous year of 1858. After paying tribute to Moorsom, he opened his shareholders' meeting by referring to Brown-Westhead and himself having to come before them, 'not as my late friend and colleague Admiral Moorsom had the pleasure of doing, to propose to you a dividend such as you desire to receive', but to 'perform the disagreeable task' of proposing a dividend rate of 3¾%.

After admitting that they had accepted this position 'under a state of things worse than we looked forward to this time last year' he said that they had 'gone into a close consideration of all the circumstances connected with the concern'. He believed that the shareholders had an 'excellent' and 'thoroughly maintained' property, that the accounts were true 'in every point,' but that 'exceptional circumstances' had depreciated the dividend. He thought that 'with exertion, perseverance, and steady labour, although we do not promise you anything that may be in dreamland, we do hope that we shall be able to redeem the position'. He hoped to show that 'we can bring this concern into as flourishing a state as any of our neighbours; or, if we cannot do that, to make it at least acceptable to ourselves and those who are co-partners with us'. However having said that, he admitted that the position was so essentially unsatisfactory and difficult to explain that he intended to take some trouble to show them, 'as far as I can, the permanent causes which have brought about the difficulties in which this concern stands, as well as the future policy we propose, and the expectations we have for the future'.

It is worth reviewing in some detail this first address of Moon to his shareholders. Many of the points he made not only illustrate his grasp of the situation, but also provide an early pointer to the strategies he was to follow throughout his chairmanship. Reminding shareholders of the 'distressed state of the country' he referred to the district, 'which may be considered the centre of our system - south and north Staffordshire' as being 'almost shut up'. He quoted the superintendent at Wolverhampton recently telling him that they had only two days work a week there. Although Liverpool traffic had increased, it was 'one which is expensively worked, it comes one way only and while it ordinarily requires 250 empty wagons to be sent every day, it now requires a much larger number to be sent owing to the stagnation of trade inland'. And although the coal trade had also increased the Wigan traffic was decreased and competition between the Midland district and the districts of the Great Northern and South Yorkshire districts had lead to 'the rates being very much reduced'.

Explaining the difficulties in bringing down the expenses in proportion to the 'money earned' he admitted that 'there is an amount of backbone in these expenses that is not so easily reduced'. He attributed some of the large increase in locomotive expenses to the requirements of the Post Office in speeding up both the Scottish and Irish mails, the latter requiring two special trains per day each way. He considered the increased locomotive mileage to be 'so far unproductive', but added that when he was chairman of the committee managing locomotive expenditure 'we compared the expenses of our working with those of other companies ... and we could find no perceptible advantage that any of them possessed over the locomotive department of this company'.

Clearly Moon did not want to expose publicly the board's dissension over having two locomotive departments. He told them that they had 'also been able, in the competition that has existed, owing to the invention [the water troughs] of Mr Ramsbottom to run trains 80 or 100 miles, or more, without carrying what was previously considered necessary, viz. - a heavy tender full of water, of 20 or 24 tons. We are now running those trains with the ordinary tender between Chester and Holyhead'. Commenting on the added expense of running at high speeds, he claimed that 'cost increases with the square of the speed', but that they were not their 'own masters in that matter'. He said competition and the requirements of the public were pressing on all the companies and efforts should be made 'with the concurrence of our neighbours and the Post Office (who are able to put the screw on us with so many competitors) to consent, in the winter time more especially, to a reduction of the speed of the trains'. For sound cost reasons, running at high speeds had been an anathema to Moon and would continue to be so throughout his chairmanship; for him punctuality and service were always more critical.

In continuing to explain the causes of the company's problems he referred to the adverse effect on costs of two months exceptional frosts 'during which time it was almost impossible to get the trains along; the axle-boxes were frozen up every morning'. The increased cost of maintenance of carriages 'was almost wholly in the issue of new wheels'. Moving on to the increased maintenance of the track, he explained the need to set aside additional reserves to upgrade the line, referring particularly to the lease of the Lancaster & Carlisle, the 'quick trains to Ireland' and the increased cost of labour.

As part of his explanation for the increase in coaching [passenger] and merchandise expenses, he referred to the 'movement which has taken place in the country to advance wages ... especially in Manchester and Liverpool'. He lamented 'what is called the early closing movement' when extra expense was incurred by being 'obliged, by arrangement with the carriers of the larger towns, to shut our doors at two o'clock on Saturdays'. He then went on to 'the most disagreeable of all the items we have to deal with', compensation for accidents, 'because we feel we are working under a most unjust and unfair law'. Moon's objection was not to 'proper' compensation but to claimants 'mulcting companies to an enormous extent. I cannot see why the rich man who pays his three-halfpence per mile should receive more than the poor man who pays his three-halfpence'. The increase in law costs generally was seen by Moon as 'most disagreeable' for although parliamentary expenses were necessary, they had 'been much increased by the cost of defending compensation claims'.

Moon concluded his analysis of the overall company's problems by perhaps unwisely blaming the weather again: referring to the Shropshire Union being frozen for 'the best part of two months' and incurring heavy losses over the half year. 'We do not make these remarks by way of excuse, but to bring the subjects fairly before you. We say every exertion is used to reduce the expenses, to cultivate fresh traffic, so as to fill up the deficiencies, and endeavour to regain our position as a good dividend-paying line.'

In the discussion which followed, Thomas Wrigley, a shareholder who was to prove particularly persistent in his criticism, expressed the fears of a number present when he considered the crisis could lead to the condition in which the Great Western found themselves: for the first half of 1858 they had paid no dividend at all. Though admitting the correctness of Moon's explanations, Wrigley contended that they were unsatisfactory 'for the purpose of giving confidence to the shareholders. If the success of the concern was dependent upon such circumstances as a frost, or the falling off of £10,000 here, and an additional cost of £5,000 there, he should have no faith in the stability of the company'. He reminded shareholders that since the formation of the L&NW the dividend had declined from 10 to 3¾ per cent and he saw no prospect of an improvement. He had no complaint over receipts but 'if the expenses had been kept down as they ought to have been, the shareholders would have had the benefit. But the expenses had gone on increasing far in excess of the increase in traffic'.

Commenting further on major items of expense Wrigley then returned to a theme he had raised at previous meetings: that a company as large as the L&NW could not be 'properly governed and controlled from one centre'. Other speakers agreed. Others thought the less management the better. Closing the capital account was demanded, unprofitable coal traffic condemned, branch lines denounced. A motion was proposed that a policy of 'forming of branch lines ... ought on no account be persisted in'. In short the meeting degenerated into a critical harangue of policies and the bemoaning of competition, but with very few constructive ideas for improvement other than simply raising rates.

Moon had let the meeting have its head before dryly commenting that the 'differences of opinion ... evidence the difficulties which the board has laboured in arriving at any policy except as from time to time appeared to be the proper one'.

Before continuing, Moon noted that the 'great point with most speakers has been the changed position of the company. I can say, with regard to that, no one can feel it more than does my own family, who purchased the shares at a very high price'. Then after countering some of the more uninformed comments from the floor, he then went on to deal with Wrigley by reading from a prepared statement. It appeared that Wrigley had not only given notice of his criticism, but released 'his speech' in advance.

A Bury paper manufacturer, Wrigley was posthumously described as 'a public controversialist of the first order'. A critic of his own industry, he was an early promoter of railways through Bury,

36. T. Wrigley
Portrait of Bury papermaker Thomas Wrigley by G.F.Watts 1875.
'Public controversialist', art collector and railway investor, Wrigley was
strongly critical of the L&NW in Moon's early chairmanship years.
Copyright: Bury Art Gallery, Museun & Archives, Lancs.

37. Branch train at Bedford early 1870s
Example of L&NW branch: train at Bedford St Johns in early 1870s. Opened in
1846 the branch from Bletchley was extended to Cambridge 1862. The engine is a
Trevithick 2-2-2. Bedford Library

becoming at one time a director of the East Lancashire Railway. Though a substantial shareholder in major railways, including the L&NW, he may well have been offered a seat on the company's board to shut him up, but he remained an independent voice. He was later to concern himself in safety matters, taking credit for anticipating the block system by what he called the need for 'affirmative signalling', i.e., keeping signals at danger instead of showing line clear. A Liberal in politics and a Unitarian, Wrigley donated significant sums to charity, rebuilding his parish church and contributing to the local hospital. He died in 1880. He is still remembered in Bury today by the fine collection of paintings he bequeathed to the town.

Moon was on familiar ground when he countered Wrigley's allegation that centralisation was extravagant by quoting the locomotive management of the Lancaster & Carlisle. 'I give you my word ... the arrangements have been better conducted by Mr Ramsbottom at Crewe than was the case under sectional management'. He was understandably more cautious when he added that the company did carry out 'as far as we can ... the divisional system which the honourable proprietor recommends. It is entirely a matter of degree'.

Having reviewed the immediate causes of the company's difficulties, Moon then moved to his second point, the more permanent causes of 'a great deal of what has happened to us'. In considering the position was not as bad as it seemed, he pointed out that 'seventeen years ago, when you got 10 per cent, the concern was a small one. Everybody thought the permanent way would not wear out, and the engines were small affairs of ten or twelve tons. The whole of that is entirely changed ... the permanent way has to be renewed every few years ... our engines also have to be renewed and we have to make provision for that for which no provision was made formerly'. He explained that from 1849, when an annual 5% was paid, the average to the present had been £4.19s.7d. per cent and that included the half year nadirs of 3¾% in 1858 and the first half of the current 1861 year. Over the last four years the dividends had averaged £4.12s.6d. per cent and that did not show they had 'gone back'. 'What is wanted is hard work', and 'if you are not satisfied with your directors ... exercise your right of turning them out ... it is entirely a question of confidence'.

He then turned to the change from no competition to having three companies attacking them. He claimed that since 1852 the company had lost, by the GW, GN and Midland, 'more than £600,000 a year of your best traffic, besides the natural increase of the traffic of those districts'. As a result traffic which had been previously worked at a cost of less than 40% of receipts was now 50%. Rhetorically he posed the question as to why this had been so:

> Because the proportion of the higher class of traffic has come down. You were getting £2.5s.0d. for your fares to Liverpool, now you are getting 35s. You were going at a slow speed. You are now going at a maximum speed. Where you ran one express train from Manchester in the day, you are running three, and your neighbours are running two. I state this only to show you what competition has brought upon us, and how, to a certain extent, it accounts for our present position. That is to say, we have lost £600,000 a year directly in traffic and £400,000 in the increased expense at which the traffic is worked.

Parliament had been 'very hard upon this company when they allowed the Great Northern to go into our main towns in Lancashire, reduce our rates to 5s.0d., and at the same time be free from that competition in their own district'. Warming to the theme, he said that 'whilst our traffic is assailable by many, our neighbours are able to recompense themselves to a great extent in the district which they have free to themselves to charge any rates they choose'. He was over dramatising the position, railways were not free to charge what they liked, but his point was valid in terms of relative rates.

Summarising the immediate outlook, he outlined a policy of 'improving what traffic we have got, trusting to the general increase of the trade of the country, the opening of new districts, and the development of new traffic'. He suggested that 'if we cannot get the long traffic' then they would try 'to make it up in coal traffic, or anything else that will yield a profit'. He had no doubt that by so doing, as the Midland had done, 'we shall bring ourselves into as favourable a position'. The Midland had steadily increased their dividends from a low point in 1850 to 6¾% in 1860, and even for the first half of 1861 it was at the annual rate of 6¼%.

Moon was putting a brave face on things. Clearly he was personally deeply dissatisfied with the company's performance, as evidenced by his 'beggarly' dividend criticism to Chandos. Moon never lost sight of what mattered to him: to be judged from the point of view of the ordinary shareholder. His reference to his family's stake in the capital of the company would have reminded shareholders of his statement at the time of the Blakemore affair. It was confirmation that his investment in the company was just as critical as their own. Neele in his *Reminiscences* recalls streets in London where cards with the letter "D" were placed by residents in their windows when the dustman was required to call and Moon telling him he always had the letter "D" in his window. 'To him it meant Dividend and he could not allow it to be lost sight of in any expenditure that was discussed.'

Looking to the future, Moon concluded by pleading for time and support. In explaining that 'most of our agreements are at an end, so that we are almost unfettered', he said they intended to work the 'traffic ourselves, wherever we have a right to work it'. And although that 'may tend to increase the expense, we shall not be in the position that we have been hitherto, of having gentlemen saying, "The North Western are coming and taking our traffic" which has positively been ours all the while'. The policy would be 'to work in the most friendly competition; and all we intend to go for is this, that we shall all work at equal rates and fares and under equal conditions, to which it must come in the end'. He told them that they 'must not expect that a change will come about in the course of a month; there is nothing to be done but by pure and deliberate hard work and a constant watching of the concern'.

Though regretting the proposal for no more branch lines, he confirmed the board's opinion that 'the concern is more than large enough, and that we should unwillingly see its extension'. Nevertheless he hoped that as nothing would be brought before them which was not clearly to their advantage, they would 'never hear again of resolutions saying this company must not go into extensions'. He had to remind shareholders that there were a considerable number of Acts of Parliament under which certain lines had to made, for example the Eccles and Tyldesley line and the stations in Burton. But 'beyond that we will consider, as early as we can, and report to you in what way the remainder of the work should be done to press as lightly upon the proprietors as is possible under the circumstances'. He looked forward to an increase in receipts as trade improved and to 'the exertion of our officers to reduce the expenses to a minimum. Beyond that we cannot promise you anything. We say that your confidence in the board at this particular juncture is of vital and essential necessity to the interests of the company'. Whether there had been mistakes in the past, shareholders now 'must take those as gone'. In seeking the meeting's acceptance of the accounts and dividend, he concluded:

> Let us in future, as we have hitherto done, most carefully consider what our policy should be. I am sure that if we are not successful it will be no fault of ours, and we say to you that, under these circumstances the accounts will be passed, that the dividend, though distasteful to all of us, shall be received as a necessity of our position. And that we shall see whether we cannot meet Mr Wrigley's difficulties by giving you a better dividend, or by letting him come and see whether he can teach us to work the line better than we do.

The adoption of the report and accounts was carried unanimously. The £1.17s.6d. dividend for the half-year was agreed, as was the £150,698 increase in capital for additional engines and stock. Moon must have breathed some sigh of relief as he sat down after the vital votes had been taken. His frank approach had worked. However it was soon to become evident that, as his first year progressed, his difficulties were far from over.

In the meantime he still found time to pick up on detail. Writing from home in October, he demanded from his office to know who had authorized £10.10s.0d. for the antimacassars for the Queen's carriage and to ask Mr Bore 'to let me know how he came to buy sewing machines at Brighton. I understand Newton & Wilson used to be the best but had been surpassed as I told him by a Glasgow invention giving the sailors stitch without the fatal thread running through'.

That items such as sewing machines could still occupy his mind, as the company faced the rising costs of upgrading lines and trade continuing to be depressed, was to become typical. After a bad winter adding to maintemnace costs, Moon again faced his shareholders, at his second half-yearly meeting in February 1862, with further explanations as to why the year's dividend rate was only 4¾%.

The irrepressible Wrigley again led the complaints, protesting sarcastically that 'every year had its specialty, and if one year they had a frost, another they had depressed trade, the war in America, or some other specialty by which their receipts were affected'. He claimed that over the last five years the company had spent £747,000 to earn £573,000 in additional gross receipts with the percentage of expenses to receipts rising from 63% to 79%. And if the directors could not produce a better dividend than the average of 4½% for that period 'he for one was extremely dissatisfied with their management'.

Criticisms from other shareholders followed, both generally and specifically, on matters of operating practice. Moon was personally accused of forcing decisions which were wrong. A shareholder believed the board had been divided on many issues with decisions taken only on the casting vote of the chairman. The same shareholder, a Mr Haly, criticised the changes in the legal department and the 'policy of taking the collection of goods out of the hands of the great railway carriers' resulting in losses of 232,000 tons a year.

Moon defended himself against Wrigley by saying 'he had not attempted to excuse or apologise for the smallness of the dividend', merely pointing out 'the facts which had occasioned it'. He explained that the expenditure could not be reduced in proportion to the receipts as new lines were 'brought into the account' at the same time as the main Manchester-Liverpool traffic had 'greatly decreased'. The increase in the capital was the main cause of the poor dividend rate and that had been unavoidable. He dismissed Haly's comments on the new law arrangements by saying the board had implemented what the shareholders had previously demanded, and on the goods collection issue Haly had been 'wholly misinformed'. 'Chaplin & Horne and Pickfords were collecting for the company just as they had always done.'

It is interesting to note that it took an attack by Wrigley to bring out the almost throw-away line that the main cause of the fall in the dividend rate was the increase in capital. As with the case over the surge in fixed charges, Moon made little use of these significant shifts in explaining the lower dividend rate.

The attack on the company's policies continued in the press. *The Railway Times* for 1 March 1862 reported that Moon:

> Is at once as elastic and as inflexible as his predecessor. He declines to arrange with the Midland for joint occupation of a new entrance into Manchester but he lends a more than helping hand to adventurers who are striving to plant themselves in various parts of the Principality in the west, and within the eastern counties district in the east! [West Hartlepool]. The "honourable gentleman" admits that the L&NW "is in possession of "the shortest route between most of the important places in England" and yet he has to lament that other companies not so fortunately situated can run quicker trains and earn larger profits than the L&NW.
>
> ... The consolation held out to shareholders in the largest company in the Kingdom - a company, which, if the policy of the board is to be carried out, has not yet arrived at half of its dimensions - is given in these cold if not heartless terms:- "We have not much success upon that question to record, nor have we any desire to raise the rates at present on low or unremunerative traffic. We therefore must be content and see if we cannot work ourselves hereafter into as good a position as other companies seem to enjoy". Mr Moon and his colleagues have no desire to <u>do</u> anything in a right direction, but they are content to <u>see</u> if they can stretch out their vision hereafter into something better than they have yet beheld, and <u>so</u> bring the property into a position which their smaller neighbours already enjoy.

Mounting shareholder unrest led Wrigley and Gartside to head a deputation of Manchester shareholders to meet L&NW directors on 16 July 1862. Wrigley proposed an official association with the object of forcing changes in company policy. And at the company's half-yearly meeting the following month, Moon was inevitably under fire again when, at 3¾%, the annualised dividend rate declared was no improvement over when he took office.

Moon claimed the results were actually better, as they had taken less out of reserves (he brushed over the reduced balance carried forward to achieve this). Giving a mixed explanation of the results, he drew attention to the effect of the serious decline in trade in Lancashire, but stressed the considerable reduction in expenses achieved in working 'a larger area of the country at a reduced cost'. He looked 'forward confidently to having turned the corner and, when things become improved in the country, to improve along with them'. He referred to the further improvements in the permanent way and mentioned the more economical use of wagons as a result of the company's own working of the London goods stations.

However the continuing low dividend led to further attacks by dissatisfied shareholders. At the next half-yearly meeting, in the absence of Wrigley, a Mr Michell moved that 'the present and long-continued depression in the L&NW property is not attributable to exceptional circumstances or insufficiency of business, but to a want of true relation between gross and net receipts, and to the persistence of the directors in promoting extensions, amalgamations and guarantees'. Echoing Wrigley's criticisms, he said that 'the directors always had some drawback to which they attributed the smallness of the receipts. In an undertaking with a capital of 36 millions and having ramifications over 1,000 miles, reverses might always be expected at some points; but their working operations ought to be based on such a contingency'. Scornfully he dismissed the attitude that 'however black and dark their position was, the report always pointed to some stream of light in the distant horizon ... waiting, like Mr Micawber, for something to turn up'.

In responding, Moon commented the board 'might be in the position of Sisyphus in having to roll a stone up a hill, but they had the satisfaction of knowing that they were getting it up the hill'. Moon was frequently to use this metaphor when facing difficulties. He complained that other companies had held meetings 'where no dividend was paid and the shareholders did not say a word'. L&NW shareholders found fault 'but did not give the directors any practical suggestions for improvement, they called over each item and said, "you do not do this right", but they did not state how it could be done better'. He contrasted the dividend rate with other companies, e.g., the Sheffield ¾% last year and this year none, the GW last year

2½% and this year ½%, L&Y last year 5½% and this year 3¾%.

Using averages as he had in his first meeting, Moon reminded shareholders that since 1850 the lowest full year dividend rate had been 4¼% and the highest 5½%, with the average from the last twenty-six half-yearly declarations being £4.18s.10d. So 'he thought there was no reason to despair or be afraid of the value of the property'.

Although Michell was persuaded not to pursue his motion, Moon remained under pressure. The eighty or so shareholders present were not in the mood to respond favourably to a motion to pay him for his services. The matter had been deferred from the February meeting, when Rutson had proposed that Moon should be paid the same as Chandos. It seems that Moon had taken on the chairmanship without any firm agreement to be paid. He had told Chandos that he was 'content without' when considering his work to be only part time. However as chairman he could no longer have seen his duties as other than full time.

It was reported that 'a lengthened conversation took place' on his position. Although some contended 'that the services of a practical man of business, as was the gentleman now filling the position of Chairman of this enormous undertaking, ought to be properly remunerated', others, including Michell, thought the present dividend did not justify such payment. Michell ultimately proposed as a compromise that the present allowance to directors of £4,000 be increased to £5,000 and the directors agree on their own distribution. Michell's compromise received 34 votes and Rutson's 41. Moon had vacated the chair to Brown-Westhead for this debate. It is to be wondered what was going through his mind as the shareholders argued over his value to the company. The £2,000 annual payment eventually agreed remained unchanged throughout his chairmanship and was never questioned by him. It was modest in the context of the size of the operation and the executive role he played, being appreciably less than salaries he subsequently agreed for his own senior management.

In the meantime circulars from Wrigley and Gartside were continuing to urge shareholders to unite in their Manchester association to force changes in company policy. The directors countered by cautioning shareholders against too hastily committing themselves to such action, reminding them that capital expenditure already required their approval. A meeting with other leading shareholders was arranged for early November 1862 in order that the directors could explain the difficulties and the progress being made. Continuing shareholder unrest, however, led to two resolutions being circulated: one simply demanded that a 'stop be put' on capital expenditure except for completion of existing works and maintenance; the other, under Wrigley who headed a committee formed by the Manchester Shareholders' Association, went further.

Circulated on 23 December 1862, the Manchester criticism was reviewed by the L&NW board at their following January meeting. Wrigley had given notice that he was going to put a motion to the meeting severely censuring the directors:

> That the gradual and continuous decline in the value of the property is clearly traceable to the mistaken policy of the directors who instead of relying on the inherent resources of the railway, and a steady developemnt and economicsl working of the traffic, have sought to establish a territorial monopoly by unwise and unprofitable extensions and improvident purchases, leases and guarantees of competing companies whereby the capital has been wastefully expended and the revenue absorbed to meet the losses and liabilities incurred.

Wrigley insisted that 'no further liabilities should be incurred by leasing or in any other way subsidizing competing schemes'. He added that 'the business and working management of a railway require that the whole time, attention, and energy of those engaged in it should be exclusively devoted to the duties' and that the 'mode of electing directors affords no guarantee of fitness for these duties'. He maintained that the social and independent position of directors, combined with their private engagements rendered it impossible to give the continuous attention required. His motion called for the meeting to agree that 'the management should be confined to a paid staff of officers, including a managing director as the chief, who shall be competent to carry out the policy of the directors, and conduct the business affairs of the company', and that 'the directors should confine themselves to initiating and controlling the general policy, appointing the chief officers, and supervising their proceedings by a periodical examination and comparison of the expenses and net proceeds of the various sections of the railway'.

The board had also received notice of a less extreme motion submitted by Edward Smith of Sheffield who was chairman of the Shareholders' Audit Committee. His motion thought it 'not expedient' to refuse to sanction measures for the 'proper development' of the company. Although Smith recorded his 'strong objection to any addition being made to the capital account not absolutely necessary, or to any enlargement of the liabilities of the company by leasing, guaranteeing, or subsidizing lines', he expressed his 'confidence that the policy of the board will be in conformity with these views'.

Wrigley's release to the press of a damaging interpretation of the company's financial position was serious enough for Moon to refute what he considered to be deliberately inaccurate details. He wrote to Wrigley beforehand advising against circulating such information and attempted to head off discussion at the half-yearly meeting by commenting in his directors' report that 'a good deal of misapprehension exists'. He said that the directors were as much opposed as any proprietor can be to adding to the liabilities of the company. He quoted a 'dignitary of the Church' who, when asked why he should join in the opposition to the present board without being acquainted with all the facts, replied 'that what he wanted was dividend, and by that means he hoped to get it'.

Being accused of mismanagement clearly rankled. Moon had taken the trouble to explain in detail the circumstances affecting the accounts, for example showing the effect of the continuing cotton recession on the Liverpool trade, how expenses per train mile had been reduced and the extra costs of delivery in London caused by competition. He had also pointedly drawn attention to what he termed the real cost of competition. 'We are travelling,' he commented, 'at a speed which can not be maintained without an enormous expense to all companies engaged'. He had hoped to have satisfied shareholders and 'redeemed the pledge' he gave in the previous August that, 'so far as we could effect it, the traffic should increase and the expenses should decrease', arguing that the value of the dividend proposed was more than the increased traffic received.

In recommending acceptance of a 5½% dividend rate, he challenged 'any other company in England to show the same results - that they should have earned £112,000 additional, and divided amongst the proprietors all the sum that has been so earned - every farthing!'. He thought the company had seen 'the turn in our affairs' with 'nothing but the fluctuation of trade to interfere with our position'. He sought the usual adoption of the report and accounts before taking Wrigley's resolution. However Wrigley still persisted in having his proposal, which he had modified and softened after talking to some of the directors, taken as an amendment and a lengthy debate ensued.

Before taking a vote on Wrigley's amendment, Moon let Edward Smith, in a long speech, point out that it was not extensions but competition that had reduced the dividends. Some idea of the tenor of the meeting is evident when the report of the proceedings noted that he was hissed at this point. Smith went on to say that it was 'perfectly absurd' to adopt such an amendment committing the directors to 'a bed of iron, in which no man can stretch himself'. Smith thought the amendment wrongly attributed past problems to the present directors and went on to support Moon by saying he was 'convinced that there is not a man in this room who is less desirous of spending capital than the chairman, if he could possibly avoid it'.

Smith put his motion and Rutson seconded it, commenting briefly that 'they were running a race with other railways and...if they tied the hands of the directors they would not have a fair position in that race'. An attempt was made to bring the meeting back to voting on the Wrigley amendment, but Moon let further shareholders have their say before finally intervening to summarise the position.

He conceded that the board was in a difficult position as 'we are the defenders of the company and its policy to a certain extent for many years past', and accepted that it was impossible to separate himself from the past though he did add that individually he had been 'opposed to what is now called this policy of extension'. However he then quickly struck at what he saw as the heart of the matter. 'It is not a question of policy of extension, but in real truth it is a question today of confidence or no confidence.' The association of Manchester shareholders had not discovered anything new. 'If you go back twenty years, when I had nothing to do with railways, nearly all the shareholders were exciting the board to go into extensions. You say that it is a question of extension that has caused you losses. Is there nothing in competition?' He had 'hoped to have seen this question to-day debated upon its merits, and was ready to debate it'. Clearly exasperated, he reiterated that 'it is a question entirely of confidence, and to-day we have, we believe, the confidence of the great majority of the proprietors'.

That Moon was now very angry was evident when he went on to say that the board 'could not put up' with such an insult as Wrigley's motion. 'I say it is such a statement that we cannot take it, whatever you gentlemen may mean. Nobody outside could read that resolution without at once saying that the present board know nothing whatever of railway management.' He believed 'that the directors of this company at this moment deserve the confidence of the proprietors more than is shown even by the resolution which I understand will be shortly proposed [by Smith]'. Significantly, he went on, 'I for one would not remain here with a threat used by an association which is picking holes and finding every fault it can with the management of this concern'. Bluntly he stated that a 'new phase has come over the railway world' and that 'there are certain things which must of necessity be done, and which I distinctly tell you there is no escape from. But I will not do anything which will not be likely to bring you a dividend'.

It is unlikely that Moon's threat to resign was posturing. No chairman confident of his policies could have accepted Wrigley's restrictions. And yet, such was the mood of the packed meeting, which had lasted five hours, that when Wrigley forced a vote, a show of hands was in his favour. Smith and Rutson immediately demanded a poll. Moon declared the poll would open that evening and adjourned the meeting until the following Wednesday 25 February (the meeting had taken place on Friday).

The board had taken their usual precaution of obtaining proxy votes in advance and published over the week-end the state of the poll as at 6pm on Friday, including the proxies lodged. This led Wrigley, with some justification, to complain that the information was released to 'disparage the amendment in the eyes of the proprietors'. Although Wrigley and his supporters held proxies representing nearly £3.3million of stock, those against were an overwhelming

£8.6million. The final poll saw 115 proprietors voting in person for Wrigley and 160 against; by proxy 1,913 voted for and 4,065 against. Out of a total poll representing £13.25million of stock (the total ordinary was £25.6million) the board obtained over 72% of the value, which in number of votes gave them a majority of nearly 69%.

What is surprising is not that Moon carried the day, but that Wrigley managed to obtain as many votes as he did. The publicity generated by the Manchester meeting of his Shareholders' Association and the protests at the company's half-yearly meeting had persuaded over 2,000 proprietors to vote against the board, yet the actual dividend rate declared was the highest since 1856.

Moon was justified in making the issue a question of confidence, not only in the board, but also in himself. That February 1863 half-yearly meeting was only his fourth as chairman, he was still largely an unknown quantity outside the board room, his future yet to be assured.

CHAPTER 14

TURNING POINTS

Moon's difficulties during his early years at the helm of the L&NW have so far been been highlighted largely by reference to his shareholders' meetings, in particular over the issues raised by Wrigley. Despite his confrontational manner, Wrigley did seem to be genuinely concerned over the performance of a company in which he had a substantial shareholding. And Moon must have recognised that his fears over extensions had some grounding in fact. It is worth dwelling on this issue before moving on to other matters that dogged Moon's first years in the chair.

Taking the attempts to penetrate south Wales first, with control of the West Midland passing to the GW, Moon was well aware of the need to reach some understanding with the remaining independent lines offering access to the area. The GW's position had been strengthened by their absorption of the broad gauge South Wales Railway. At his May 1861 board Moon explained the proposal to lease the Shrewsbury & Hereford and a letter was read from George Findlay on the subject. This was one of the first references in L&NW minutes to Findlay who was eventually to replace Cawkwell in the overall general management of the L&NW.

When the contractor Brassey had taken a ten-year lease of the S&H in 1852 Findlay was employed to manage it. With Brassey's lease expiring it was initially agreeed that 50% would be taken over by the L&NW and 25% each by the GW and WMR. The GW/WMR amalgamation consolidated the GW interest as equal joint owners of the line. Also at this time an agreement was considered by the L&NW to lease the Merthyr Tredegar & Abergavenny line based on guaranteeing 6% by a rebate on traffic brought from the line. The Merthyr company however proposed a fixed 5% plus half the surplus profits above this. This was the basis of the agreement for which parliamentary approval was sought together with access

38. Hartlepool dock and warehouse

The warehouse and quay temporarily acquired in 1861 by the L&NW at Swainson
Dock, West Hartlepool. The dock was opened 1854 and the warehouse built in
1860. Courtesy of Hartlepool Museums & Heritage Service

39. L&NW 1860s train at Pontypool Road

Early 1860s L&NW train for Newport at Pontypool Road, Crewe type 2-4-0 with
an 0-6-0 arriving from the Taff Vale extension line (see Map 4).

Painting by Gwyn Briwnant Jones.

over the Monmouthshire Railway to Newport.

By early 1862, with Brown-Westhead, Bancroft and Dean, Moon was leading a company delegation to convince traders in south Wales of the company's intention to develop traffic from the area. He reported to the Special Committee on 12 February that they had visited Swansea, Cardiff and Newport 'and had satisfactory interviews with some of the principal traders in the district'.

At the diagonally opposite extent of their network the L&NW had become drawn into various discussions and negotiations aimed at giving the company access to the north-east of England independently of the North Eastern Railway. It is not clear who was originally behind these proposals but they were to prove embarrassing to Moon. The L&NW had flirted with a proposed Derwent Valley railway. This seemingly local project, running from the Tyne south-west from Newcastle, was seen as a possible link, via Tebay and the South Durham & Lancashire Union Railway, in a route between Lancashire and Newcastle. Although the Derwent Valley Bill was rejected another more ambitious scheme was promoted: the Newcastle Derwent & Weardale, which backed by both the L&NW and the North British, would have had access to a quay on the Tyne.

The South Durham connection at Tebay had also provided another opportunity for the L&NW to avoid being dependent on the North Eastern for the traffic between Liverpool and a new port being developed in the north-east at West Hartlepool. This expansionist policy had so alarmed L&NW shareholders that at the February 1861 meeting they accused the directors of threatening aggression against the North Eastern Railway and wastefully committing £1.1 million on subscribing to these schemes and investing in extensive warehousing at West Hartlepool. Glyn, at the ensuing board meeting, reminded directors of the need to make arrangements 'rendering unnecessary any considerable outlay of capital in that district'.

The West Hartlepool Harbour & Railway Company had promoted Bills which included a connection to the L&NW and for that company to subscribe a quarter of their capital and purchase the quay and warehouse at Swainson Dock. In the meantime Moorsom had died and Moon had become chairman. At his September 1861 board meeting it was minuted that the chairman had 'explained fully' the West Hartlepool agreement which was agreed and the 'purchase moneys paid in terms therof'. The chairman, deputy chairman and secretary were to hold the property as Trustees.

Moon had clearly found himself having to strongly defend the L&NW's involvement with a company which had been promoted to compete with the Stockton & Darlington for the sea borne coal trade and with ambitious plans for owning not only docks but also collieries and shipping. Ward Jackson, the guiding spirit behind the West Hartlepool, was eventually discredited particularly over financial mismanagement and activities contrary to the Act authorising the company (owning coal mines and ships). Moon had personally negotiated with Ward Jackson, having led a L&NW delegation to commit to the purchase of the warehouse and quay, this without the sanction of Parliament.

The L&NW directors' report to their next half-yearly meeting, February 1862, recorded that they had secured 'Station [warehouse and quay] accommodation at West Hartlepool together with the right to use the lines, Stations and conveniences … for £100,000'. However no powers for the L&NW to invest or acquire interests were ever authorized by Parliament. The West Hartlepool company remained financially embarrassed and after restructuring eventually agreed to sell out in 1864 to the North Eastern, which earlier had absorbed both the Stockton & Darlington and the South Durham & Lancashire Union, so killing any further serious attempt at competitive access to the area. But by then there had been no need, the North Eastern obtaining their Acts to absorb these connecting companies by conceding traffic arrangements to the L&NW and the other companies previously opposing their Bills. The property bought by the L&NW though had to be reconveyed. It could be said that there was a touch of face-saving rather than relief when in their report to shareholders in August 1862 the directors 'rejoice to say' that they had now negotiated 'full facilities for the interchange and working of traffic'.

Throughout his first years as chairman the clamour against territorial expansion continued. Leaping forward to 1865 Moon was still finding it neceesary to justify how the company's capital had been spent since he became chairman. In so doing he reviewed where he thought the company's rightful markets should be and his attitude to competition. He began his address to shareholders at their August meeting by saying that 'we have no wish for extension ourselves; the concern is big enough; it is as much as we can manage, and we have no wish to increase beyond the extent that is absolutely necessary to protect your interests'. Incidentally he showed that he was still sensitive to the effects of the GW and WMR merger, pointing out it had 'shut us out of Monmouthshire and that district'. He explained that with the GW 'we took charge of the Shrewsbury & Hereford' and 'took also a small line from Abergavenny up to a point on the way to Merthyr in order to arrive at the different works in that district. That was a very small thing, costing perhaps £300,000'.

His surprising dismissal of £300,000 as a 'very small thing' is a further example of the contrast between his strategic thinking and the penny-pinching attitude that, for example, required gas lights to be turned down. His attitude to paying top salaries for top management has already been noted when originally recommending retaining both Ramsbottom and McConnell, which again contrasted, for example, with the protests he had made against giving staff company coats as it was, in effect, a wage increase.

'We have done nothing more beyond what is absolutely necessary in improving stations, and such like things', he continued in conversational style as he justified, almost light-heartedly, other quite significant additions to the network:

> Then again the Lancashire coal owners would have a way to ship their coal, and they put a pressure on us under which, as I explained to you, we were obliged - under their guarantee, mind - to make a line for the coal from the Wigan district towards St Helens. And that involved the necessity for taking the St Helens line, and that, again, involved our making another line, of a few miles, jointly with the Lancashire & Yorkshire into Blackburn. Then we settled an old squabble with the Lancaster & Carlisle by taking the Lancaster Canal, which is no burden to you. We subscribed £25,000 to the Cockermouth & Penrith. Following that we have been invited to take an interest in that district, and you will see in the report that we have made terms for leasing in perpetuity the Cockermouth & Workington and

Whitehaven Junction lines, that being a new country, which is now developed not only for the making of pig iron but also for enormous exports of iron ore.

We also advised you to come under some traffic arrangements with regard to a short line in communication with Greenore, near Dundalk. Beyond that, out of your capital we have not laid down more than twelve or fifteen miles of line. These are all the liabilities we have come under for you, and therefore you may say, certainly, that for four years we have not put you under liability for lines out of your own country, and we think, have been doing as little as we could consistently with accommodating our district satisfactorily. I ought to say that with the Midland we intended to have had a line from Huddersfield to Halifax, with the co-operation of the local people, but that Bill failed on standing orders, as you know.

His reference to the joint line with the L&Y into Blackburn is of interest for this *was* the result of an attempt to avoid wasteful competition. The Lancashire Union Railways, mentioned earlier, had been promoted and supported by the L&NW for providing extra capacity for shipping coal from the Wigan coalfield to both the Mersey and inland to the towns of north-east Lancashire. However, the L&Y had promoted their own line from Wigan to Blackburn and although both schemes were approved it was agreed that parts of both would be used with sections to be jointly owned.

Claiming generally that developments had not been 'out of your own country' was putting rather a wide interpretation of what was L&NW territory, for example the Greenore proposal was in the north of Ireland for a new route to Belfast. And their lines in Cumberland were to remain isolated from the L&NW main line throughout the history of the company (although they did run all the services except for the through North Eastern company's trains via Penrith).

Moon seemed to have maintained a particularly special interest in the Irish traffic and in the boats providing the service ever since the days when his Stores Committee took responsibility at Holyhead. He was personally to interview candidates for 'Steam Boat

Superintendent' at the end of 1865 when Dent was selected at £400 p.a. (the post had not been permanently filled since the death of his old adversary Hirste in 1861). Cumberland and Irish developments are explained in later chapters.

The Merthyr Tredegar & Abergavenny Railway, leased at the end of 1861, was taken into ownership in 1866. The approach over the jointly owned Shrewsbury & Hereford, and running powers to Abergavenny for Newport and the company's own Merthyr line, ultimately gave the L&NW access to Cardiff. In mid Wales the L&NW absorbed the Central Wales company from Craven Arms on the joint S&H and opened to Llandridnod in 1865, which together with the Central Wales Extension to Llandovery (opened three years later) gave them access to Swansea. This was achieved by jointly leasing with the Llanelly Railway, the Vale of Towy line and securing running powers over the Llanelly company.

The Eccles-Tyldesley line, the first new line opened under his chairmanship, was the 'independent' line he had proposed to Chandos for the Manchester-Preston traffic. Typically he was personally to go over the ground with Cawkwell to select the station sites.

In summary the inescapable fact was that, extensions or not, the L&NW route mileage increased from 950 in 1860 to 1,274 in 1864.

On the overall trading front it had become clear before the end of 1861 that there was to be no upturn in traffic to increase earnings. Moon was reduced to appealing to his officers to second 'by every means in their power, the efforts of the board to improve the working of the trains'. The directors expected from them 'the utmost watchfulness, energy, and perseverance' and suggestions for 'measures as, in their judgement, may appear calculated to ensure the utmost regularity, despatch, and economy in conducting the business of the company'.

Interestingly one of the areas where train services had already been curtailed was over the link to the former OW&W company's line at Yarnton (connecting with L&NW to Bletchley and Euston). As a Worcester resident and regular traveller to Euston, Moon had clearly despaired of an efficient service by that route. At the L&NW's Special Committee meeting on 12 September, the 'manager was authorised to reduce the passenger trains via Handborough Junction on the 1st October, arranging with the Midland for establishing an efficient communication [from Worcester] via Birmingham'.

Throughout these developments Moon continued with the system of board committees esentially set up under Chandos. It had been Moorsom, on taking over as chairman, who had called for a review of the 'general system of management', being concerned with not only the organisation of the officers but also the committee system. Glyn had also supported a review. Earle though, at the March 1861 board meeting, won the day to continue the existing system of committees 'for the present'. And this view seemed to have been supported by Moon, for a year later he instigated only minor changes for improving the working of the traffic and local area committees. He had however forced the change in the working of the company's main goods depots in London. The recommendation he had made in his Investigation review, that the company should run these depots not the national carters Pickfords and Chaplin & Horne, was implemented. This was not to be without fierce opposition from Benjamin Horne.

Moon had never been satisfied with the cartage agents' costs and obtained the unanimous support of the board to give them notice that the company were going to take over themselves the loading and unloading of goods in the stations (not yet though the collection and delivery from and to the customer). This was to be the first step towards the company handling directly the entire distribution service. Although Pickford accepted that their services for handling within the depots could be terminated, Chaplin & Horne refused to recognise the company's right to do so and demanded compensation. Horne angrily attended the board's Special Committee to argue his case. This was to lead to an unpleasant protracted dispute over many years with Horne involving Moon personally. This will be touched on later.

The goods department was further strengthened by the appointment of Charles Mason, who on Bancroft's recommendation vacated the management of the Birkenhead Railway to become General Goods Manager in 1861 when the previous incumbent, Mills, was paid to retire. Mason in effect also became assistant general manager. He was to be held in high esteem by Moon and but for his premature death would have been a strong candidate for the general management of the company.

Complaints over the high costs of the company's legal services had also led the Law Committee under Richard Dean, an Oxford educated barrister who had replaced Heywood as a director in 1859, to recommend the company changing from using outside solicitors to managing their own legal affairs. A sub committee formed of Moon, Brown-Westhead and Dean confirmed the proposal to terminate long-standing solicitors, Carter & Swift, and recruit the company's own legal representatives. Inevitably the solicitors took exception to implied criticism that they had been overcharging for their professional services. They they were assured tactfully that the company's need was for the appointment of a solicitor at Euston 'whose attention might be given uninterruptedly' (an added embarrassment had been that Carter had also represented the Midland). It was hoped that although neither senior partners could be expected to accept the appointment 'one of their junior partners might be retained'. Carter and Swift agreed to continue until Moon himself reported discussions with James Blenkinsop, a partner with Carter and Swift, which led to his appointment as the company's first salaried solicitor [David Hodgkins advises the first in any British railway].

The main outstanding internal issue that Moon needed to address was however the cost and organisation of the locomotive departments. Had Moorsom lived, the outcome of the special locomotive enquiry committee into McConnell's costs may well have been different. Moorsom's death delayed further consideration and it was not until the beginning of 1862 that the board was able to review formally the committee's report.

McConnell had been asked at the committee's meeting on 13 November 1861 to explain in writing the discrepancy between his original estimate of £21,000 and the £78,010 actually spent. The committee met to review on 18 December but was adjourned to 20 December when the engineer, Baker, attended to confirm work carried out at Wolverton and Stafford. McConnell then claimed that some of the additional costs had been sanctioned by the Stores Committee and others by the increase in traffic which was outside his control. At this stage McConnell appeared not to have treated the enquiry seriously enough. He should by then have had enough experience of dealing with Moon to know that the matter would be pursued in ruthless detail, especially after their argument in front of Moorsom.

40. J.E.McConnell

J.E.McConnell (1815-83) locomotive superintendent of the L&NW's
Southern Division at Wolverton from 1847 until his forced retirement in 1862.

Wolverton library

41. 'Bloomer' class locomotive

McConnell's small 'Bloomer' class C 103, coal fired, the first of its type built at
Wolverton in 1857. Harry Jack

The result was that the ten-man committee voted 8 to 2 in censuring McConnell severely.

Although 'unwilling to impute' an intention to mislead the board, the committee found 'that the statements of the probable outlay on capital account have been so much at variance with the real facts of the case as seriously to shake that confidence which the board ought to have in the report and statement of an officer holding so responsible a situation'. Once McConnell realised how critical was his position, he belatedly prepared and circulated on 6 January a far more detailed analysis which threw into doubt the actual unsanctioned sums he was alleged to have spent.

McConnell's new statement gave an item by item account of expenditure, referring in each instance to the authority of Stores Committee or Board minutes, to arrive at a total of £52,846 sanctioned, against which £55,214 had been spent, a discrepancy of only £2,368. He went on to quote the beneficial results of this expenditure which included the ability to turn out fifty-two new engines a year, twenty-six of which had been completed in the last six months. He listed votes taken by the proprietors over the last two years totalling £340,000 for working stock and £88,868 for enlarging workshops and stations. Additional expenditure on the new joint Southern and Northern division engine shed at Stafford he blamed on Baker for having no control over costs, and that he, McConnell, had no responsibility for the Northern requirements.

Unfortunately for him McConnell then spoilt what had been a reasonable defence. He ended his analysis by stating that having been charged with causing large increases in expenditure beyond what was originally contemplated, 'I feel that it would be well to state shortly the advantages the company have gained by the extension and outlay'. He listed savings on engines, miles run, capacity to build, etc., so implying that even if he had overspent his actions were justified by the results.

The board, and certainly its new chairman, could not have one of its officers making judgements as to what should or should not be expended no matter what the outcome. When the committee met for the last time on 10 January their critical draft report had already been prepared. After a discussion the report was approved for immediate submission by 7 votes to 3; Cropper, Birley and Blake wanting the committee to consider further the letter from McConnell. The board at a special meeting on 15 January was more evenly divided. Mangles and Blake sent letters in support of McConnell. Surprisingly a letter from Chandos was also tabled but his views not recorded. Benson and Glyn's amendment to refer the matter back to the committee was only defeated by 14 to 11, the margin by which, after another vote the report was subsequently adopted.

The main consequence was the resignation of McConnell. After the committee's censure his position was untenable. He resigned on 20 February. He wrote that although he did not 'admit the justice of the conclusion' and felt it his duty to protest, he accepted that he could not continue to act and resigned 'the office which I have now held for 15 years'. Moon had won the day and the resignation opened up the far wider issue that had frustrated him for so long: the combining of the locomotive departments under one head.

At the half-yearly meeting of the company that followed, Moon was roused to defend the decision particularly in response to the critical Haly, who quoted 'the question of Mr McConnell's resignation' as an example of a divided board. Moon retorted that 'if one thing could show more clearly than another that the board was right in the way they had acted in the case of Mr. McConnell it was Mr Haly's speech, seeing that matters to which he referred could not have been known outside the board-room except by a gross breach of confidence'.

Though the board accepted McConnell's resignation without comment, it voted him £1,000 to cover a half-year's salary and additional expenses for 'the sudden removal from his present residence'. It was agreed that another special committee be asked 'to report on the future management of the locomotive establishments of the company, and that for this purpose the members of the Stores Committee be associated with that committee'.

Moon, as over Trevithick, was accused at the time and by later commentators of unfairly forcing the resignation. Had McConnell woken up earlier to how vulnerable he was, at least in the eyes of the man that mattered, the defence he eventually presented, suitably modified with contrition, would have been much more difficult to dismiss. McConnell was a respected member of his profession (he had made his reputation with several successful locomotive designs in particular the 2-2-2 Bloomer design) and was to remain so after he left the L&NW. But it was as a manager that Moon had lost confidence in him and once that was lost the die was cast as far as the engineer's future with the company was concerned. Surprisingly the *Railway Times*, not known at the time for its support for the L&NW, agreed that his 'discharge ...ought to have taken place years ago - prior, at all events, to the unmerited dismissal of Mr Trevithick'.

The new committee to consider the future locomotive arrangements met on 6 March 1862 and 'after full consideration' affirmed the principle of consolidating the two locomotive departments into one under Ramsbottom, only Benson dissenting 'in the absence of details of the suggested arrangements'. Reconvening on 21 March they agreed their report to the board which met the following day when it was resolved 'that Mr Ramsbottom be the chief Locomotive Superintendent for the whole line and that until the board decides on further change his headquarters and chief office be at Crewe'. A annual salary at £2,000 was agreed and that he should 'select and recommend to the board the persons to act as his principal Indoor and Outdoor assistants at Crewe and Wolverton'. Moon had finally won his battle over the locomotive departments.

Returning to overal company results, for each of the years 1862 to 1865 the L&NW's half-yearly dividend rate showed an increase over the comparable period of the previous year, from £4.12s.6d. per cent in 1862 to £6.12s.6d. for 1865. However, this should be put in context as most of the other major companies, with which the L&NW competed or were associated, grew at the same rate. Over these four years the L&NW remained positioned, in terms of dividend rate, below the two highest of the major companies, the Midland and the Great Northern.

It should be noted, belatedly perhaps, that the use of dividend rates as a means of measuring a company's performance needs qualifying. They have been used freely in this book as they were the main yardstick by which Moon himself and the market generally judged company performance. It was not only policy variations in the early days of railway accounting that made it difficult to make accurate comparisons. Dividend values declared depended on the extent to which earnings were retained or drawn from reserves;

and the percentage rate on the proportion of a company's capital held by ordinary shareholders. Arriving at a more accurate measure, in particular of efficiency, gives rise, however, to further problems. These will be referred to in a later chapter.

It would be misleading to imply that a sharp pick-up in trade between 1863 and 1865 was the only reason for improving performance. Moon must take some credit for the lead he took in tightly controlling expenditure. He set himself a punishing schedule of inspections, meetings and reviews, which not only set an example to his principal officers, but also enabled him to have a decisive input into all major issues affecting the company's development. He had brought to the chairmanship an unrivalled grasp of company administrative detail and wasted no time in applying this to the overall management of the company.

The irony of Wrigley's criticism was that Moon had, in practice, become the managing director Wrigley wanted and, at heart, Moon would not have disagreed with him over the shortcomings of uncommitted directors. One director who clearly had not fallen into that category was Bancroft. Moon had once suggested to Chandos that he would make a good 'right hand man'. He was in effect to become just that to Moon for many years, his services recognised in February 1865 by being paid £1,000 p.a.

The confidence gained by the more favourable financial climate of 1863 led the board to agree at that year's May meeting to seek the authority of their shareholders for 'a further creation of Debenture Stock' as a means of completing the works in hand. The board subsequently agreed to raise nearly £2.2 million on the fixed dividend of 5% in shares of £100 each, which was proposed to shareholders on the occasion of the half-yearly meeting in August. This brought Wrigley to the fore again.

Wrigley had held another well publicised Manchester meeting of his association and written to Moon reporting their strong objection to raising additional capital and protesting against the creation of preferential capital for any purpose. Moon explained that it was too late to object to raising additional capital as shareholders had sanctioned the work two years ago and Parliament had authorised the construction, which had included the Eccles & Wigan line, Runcorn Bridge, a central goods station in London and extensions at

Holyhead and Liverpool. The only question to decide was 'the best mode of raising the capital'.

Moon justified the 5% preference stock by saying that the directors thought it better to raise the capital in the cheapest and most direct way and be issued on such terms as the money market would give them. 'This would meet the general interests of the company, and be much better than offering a 4% or 4½% stock. The latter rate would place them between wind and water, while the 5% stock would realise about 15% premium.' At a special board the following month a price of £115 was agreed. Moon had explained that the 'money would not be all needed at once, nor for a considerable period, but as the works went on. The directors could therefore take advantage of the state of the market from time to time'. He said that they could raise the money at about £4.6s.6d. per cent which was less than their ordinary dividends had averaged over the 18 years, which he calculated was £4.18s.10d. from July 1849 to July 1862. He expected this to increase in future and 'it was clearly the interest of the company to raise the money in that way'.

The objection to the issue of preference, as opposed to ordinary stock, was the risk that future earning would drop and not cover the guaranteed rate. And for holders of ordinary stock a greater risk was that the preference holders would have priority should there be a shortfall in earnings. Companies of lesser stature than the L&NW, with perhaps a risky reputation or facing an uncertain future, frequently had no option but to raise capital on costly guaranteed preference terms. On the other hand, as a Mr Morgan pointed out to the meeting, even a company the size of the L&NW with all the security it offered could not easily issue £2 million, or even £1 million of ordinary stock, all at one time except at a heavy discount. He put the question that the issue was whether they were likely to get a larger dividend than the preference they proposed to give. He saw no reason to doubt that the increase of traffic would continue and with it an increase in profit. However as 'an abstract question he regretted to see this company resorting to preference stocks; but, upon the whole, he thought the course suggested by the directors was the best, and that the proprietors had better give them their confidence. The company, he considered, was better and more economically managed during the past twelve months than it had ever been'.

Sheward (later elected a director in February 1864) 'confessed that the 5% preference staggered him', but he hoped the shareholders would vote the capital unanimously and 'they ought to have confidence enough in the directors to leave the mode and time of raising it to them'. An attempt was made to adjourn to consider the matter further but Moon forced a vote and the meeting agreed (65 to 18). Also at this meeting, it was agreed to convert up to £5 million of the borrowed capital of the company from debenture loans into 'perpetual' 4% debenture stock. With many different loans outstanding at a range of rates and redemption dates, it was of advantage to lenders to convert to a long-term secure stock giving an attractive yield. And it was of advantage to the company to reduce the cost of capital if the conversion was made at an attractive price; the latter being a reflection of confidence in the company and standing in the market. The extent to which debenture conversions were made became an additional key measure in how Moon personally rated the success of his company's performance.

The improved dividend rate still did not satisfy the Wrigleys of the day. Moon remained under pressure to justify extensions. Countering criticism he presumed that he was not expected to explain that they 'should stand still and be hit. They intended to be peaceable neighbours, but at the same time they were determined to defend their rights and improve their dividends'.

The personal confrontation with Wrigley came to a head the following February. Despite Moon claiming the 6% dividend rate proposed for the second half of the 1863 year was the highest since 1849, Wrigley questioned the accuracy of the accounts. He issued another Manchester circular claiming the company was misrepresenting their position. Through the secretary, Stewart, the company dismissed this as 'transparently and ridiculously fallacious'. Moon and Brown-Westhead then responded with a circular of their own, again cautioning shareholders against committing themselves in support of an association when facts had been misrepresented and a 'fallacious document' issued in 'full knowledge of its erroneous character'. At the company's half-yearly meeting in February 1864, Wrigley repeated his criticisms and attacked Stewart for his 'highly reprehensible' language.

Wrigley said he was not satisfied that the progress made was the result of a change of policy nor that the dividend increase could be maintained and referred to three of the developments covered in the directors' report. He saw no need for the extension in Ireland with the Dundalk and Greenore line, considering the company should be satisfied with handling the traffic at Liverpool. He opposed the takeover of the remaining portion of the St Helens, quoting the dramatic rise in the St Helens company share price with the likelihood of the L&NW guaranteeing their dividend. And he objected to taking an interest in the proposed railway between Chorley and Blackburn saying that the area was already well served [by the Lancashire & Yorkshire]. He thought that unless the company dropped schemes such as these he would continue to doubt that the 'directors were as much against extensions as the chairman would lead them to believe'. He concluded by again referring to the 'delusions' of the accounts and accused Stewart for insulting him by charging him with 'issuing deliberate falsehoods'.

An exasperated Moon 'quite despaired of satisfying Mr Wrigley that what was being done was the best under the circumstances; but for a gentleman to come half-year after half-year and tell them that the accounts presented from time to time were delusive was more than he could bear with composure'. Countering the complaint of uncourteous language, he threw Wrigley's own language back at him. Wrigley had criticised the company's circular for being "not less remarkable for its unprincipled and unscrupulous mis-statements and exaggerations than for the studied brutality of language which pervades the whole". 'After language like that on the part of Mr Wrigley', Moon said, 'it did not lie in his mouth to complain and say the recent remarks of the secretary were not justified by the circumstances'.

Moon then explained in detail the sections in the accounts over which Wrigley had been complaining. Though he then told Wrigley to forget personalities, he went on to say that if Wrigley's association was not satisfied with the directors 'let them try and find others to take their places'. He denied the board had ever accepted a no-extension policy. What he had said was 'that they would not adopt any extensions which they did not believe would prove profitable to the undertaking'. He defended the company's policy in the developments quoted and questioned whether Wrigley's interests lay with another company. Moon concluded by saying 'all he asked for

... was a fair field and no favour. He would undertake to show that Mr Wrigley was wrong in every position he had taken; and he was equally prepared to defend the policy of the board on any point that gentleman might select'.

Wrigley rather lamely countered by insisting that everything he had stated had come from the published accounts and was sorry that Moon had insinuated he wanted to 'promote interests other than those of the company. His stake in the Lancashire & Yorkshire was only £5,000, whereas in the L&NW it was upwards of £20,000; his whole career in the past showed that he was only anxious for the success of this undertaking'. Moon was 'thankful' to hear this but adding it was only natural to suppose Wrigley had other motives when he had put such pointed questions on Lancashire & Yorkshire matters which, with negotiations taking place, should not have been raised at a public meeting.

This last exchange with Wrigley can be said to mark a turning point. In acknowledging the shareholders vote of thanks at the end of 1864's summer meeting, Moon attributed the near half million increase in revenue since June 1861 and only £35,000 in increased expenses, not just to the low price of materials and state of the country, but to 'most of all the energetic exertions of the officers of the company'. Publicly recognising and supporting his managers was to become an enduring feature of his chairmanship. For the first time he was cheered by shareholders when he concluded by agreeing with the recent article in *The Times* calling the L&NW 'a noble undertaking'.

The recovery culminated in a dividend rate of 7¼% being declared for the second half of 1865. At the February 1866 meeting, in hoping the shareholders were satisfied, Moon nevertheless thought it would have been prudent to have kept the rate at 7% (as at February 1865) and, in his words, 'to stop awhile on the platform upon which they had arrived and look carefully about them. Rising from 4¾ per cent in 1861 to 7¼ in 1865 they had taken a greater leap than the shareholders probably ever anticipated'. Though he claimed with some pride that 'there was not one of the large companies that had enhanced its dividend in anything like the ratio this line had done' he sounded a note of caution in hinting that he would have preferred to have held something back. 'The directors would have been glad to have watched patiently to see what could be developed, and also to have looked in the face of those difficulties that were coming upon them.'

He thought the board had 'almost reached the limit of the economy they could practise' and that the railway business was the only trade in the country where prices were not increasing. He complained that on the L&NW the rates and fares were lower but the public were daily expecting services to be improved and that raw material prices and wages were increasing. As an example of the economies realised he quoted the locomotive expenses being increased from the half year in 1861 by only £27,000 whereas the additional traffic earned had been £840,000. He could not help comparing the locomotive costs of 7.825d per train mile with those when McConnell left the company: the Southern division then was 10.82d and the Northern division 9.36d. In cautioning shareholders against expecting the dividend trend to continue they should not 'suppose that 7¼ per cent meant 10 in future and that 10 per cent meant 15, and so on'.

Moon claimed that shareholders he had consulted had persuaded him not to restrict the dividend by keeping the ¼% in reserve. Whether these shareholders included Wrigley is not known. At least Wrigley now admitted publicly that he took some pleasure in the improved dividend, but irrepressible as ever thought Moon's caution, which he described as similar to Lord John Russell's "to rest and be thankful", was 'extraordinary'. He saw no reason why the dividends should not be further increased and treated the meeting to a detailed review to demonstrate that the results to date were only 'an indication of what they might look forward to in the future'. Moon somewhat dryly concluded that there was 'a good deal of truth and a good deal of fallacy' in what Wrigley had said.

One significant change in the company's overall management at this time should be mentioned. The board's Special Committee meeting of 15 December 1865 clarified the duties and responsibilities of senior officers. Cawkwell was to watch over all Parliamentary matters and strategic plans for development, Mason taking the day to day general management of the Traffic department for both passengers and goods, and Findlay the general management of the Goods and Mineral departments. Neele was to take the general superintendence of the Passenger department and Reay was to succeed Stewart. The long serving company secretary, Stewart, had resigned through ill health. Already a confidant of the chairman, Stephen Reay was appointed in January 1866 at a salary of £1,250 p.a. A Liverpool man, he had been with the company since 1842, joining the Grand Junction as a twenty-three year-old clerk and rising through the accounts and audit offices.

And so Moon had survived. Whether expected to or not, by doing so he had proved his qualities. There should never have been any question that a company the size of the L&NW with its trunk routes to the midlands, the north-west, Ireland and Scotland could fail. Nevertheless criticism of performance by dissident directors and unruly shareholders had been so persistent that without some firm hand over its management the business could have fallen further into disarray. Clearly, it had dawned on colleagues and shareholders alike that they had a man for the long haul. His trial was not yet over, the economy of the country fell dramatically into depression, but it was no longer a question of confidence, more now the reliance on a master's eye to oversee the company's profitable survival.

CHAPTER 15

RIDING THE STORM

The uplift in trade that had contributed to the L&NW's 7¼% performance for 1865 was short lived. In the first few months of 1866 a number of finance houses collapsed and when in May Overend Gurney stopped payment a financial panic followed. In an attempt to stabilise the market the Bank rate was moved to 10%, remaining at that level for three months, unprecedented during the whole of Moon's railway career. Peto & Betts, one of the largest railway contractors, failed. And over-stretched railway companies such as the London Chatham & Dover, the Metropolitan District and the Great Eastern, soon found themselves in the hands of administrators. Even the Great Northern had a narrow escape, at one point asking the government for a loan of £1million.

The company's senior auditor, Henry Crosfield, wrote to Moon on the need to reassure shareholders 'at the present time, when the discreditable proceedings of some of the larger railways are naturally drawing down upon this species of property a heavy amount of distrust, that it may be well to look into our own internal condition in order to see whether our position is inherently sound in these respects'. He further suggested that the company:

> Demonstrate the system which prevails and so to prove the perfect honesty of the figures returned as the nett earnings of the L&NW Revenue account - complete confidence may therefore be felt in the inherent soundness of the company's position. The value of its property, the real security for its loans, is in this manner being steadily augmented year by year and with the large surplus revenue which is shown as applicable to the discharge of its debentures and preferential engagements, may be regarded as bona fide security for the financial stability of the undertaking.

As has been seen, Henry Crosfield, as a thirty year old young man, had first known Moon when they were together on the 1850 committee of L&NW shareholders charged with reviewing the board structure. It appears he had inherited a huge holding of L&NW stock, over £100,000, which would have marked him out as an obvious candidate for any shareholder involvement in the company. The standing of L&NW shareholder auditors at that time was more akin to a director and they had to be qualified with a minimum stockholding. Their brief was, independently of the company's officers, to assure the accuracy of the accounts and correctness of the principles applied. In his early days as chairman Moon, had dismissed what he called the 'fashion' for auditors to be outside public accountants as they could never understand the company and served only to check that all items of expenditure were covered by relevant vouchers.

Crosfield's warning was discussed at the L&NW's October board when it was agreed that he and fellow auditor, Hand, should publish a report outlining the strength of the company's financial position. This was not issued, however, until early January 1867.

In the meantime the economic downturn following the financial crisis had seen the bank rate fall to 3½% by the end of 1866. It was to remain at 3% or below over the next two years. Moon referred in early 1867 to 'the collapse' in trade and later in the summer to having 'a half-year of no ordinary anxiety, the trade of the country, as all knew, had been in a state of panic, rumours of all kinds had prevailed and shareholders generally had scarcely known what to believe and what to disbelieve'. He did not think that 'the country ever had such a staggering blow as it had received in the course of the past twelve months'.

Under these circumstances it is not surprising that progress in improving dividends was checked. During 1866 the company was able to hold its dividend rate for the first half at 6%, which was the same as the first half of 1865. However, for the second half of 1866 the rate had to be dropped from a peak 7¼ to 6¾ and for the first half of 1867 from 6 to 5¼ (over the corresponding periods of the previous year). Thereafter the dividend did not drop below these half-yearly rates for the remainder of Moon's chairmanship (although they came near to it in the troughs of 1879 and 1886).

Despite the state of the country the fall to 5¼ led to yet another long complaint from Wrigley. Wrigley did little to enhance his case by referring to 'the working of a railway as the simplest thing in the world' comparing it to his large 'manufactory' where he found 'that as he extended the business the proportion of fixed charges diminished ... but in a railway business it seemed otherwise'. In responding, Moon made no attempt to expose this fallacy, simply saying that it was easy for Wrigley to come to the meetings and make disparaging remarks. 'He should come on this side of the table and try his own hand at it, and let us see if he would do better'. Wrigley, perhaps wisely, never did.

As the economy recovered only the Lancashire & Yorkshire of comparable northern companies was generating a higher dividend rate than the L&NW, although the North Eastern, significantly in its largely monopolistic position, was soon to surpass both. In an obvious reference to Crosfield's work, Moon reminded the August 1867 half-yearly meeting that the audit report, which had been undertaken in response to other companies' financial difficulties, showed the 'accounts were all clear, honest and straightforward'. He went further the following February when he claimed that the outcry in the country had had a 'good effect'. It had 'caused the directors to look carefully through the Accounts, and the more they had done so the better they had liked them'. He claimed that there was nothing which had not been under the consideration of the Special Committee of the board and they had been satisfied that 'everything was above board and safe, and open to inspection and criticism'.

He then went on to make one of many references to what was to be a recurring theme in his half-yearly reviews to shareholders: the value of the security offered by the company. His campaign to convert the bond debt of the company into fixed interest stock had begun to take effect. He believed 'the credit of this company so good, that if it were fairly appreciated, it would entitle them to borrow money at as low a rate as the Funds [Government gilts], and at 4 per cent they were offering a security ... as good as, or better than, any security in the world'. Referring again to the 'late crisis, the like of which this country has never seen before' Moon reminded shareholders that they had in the L&NW 'a security which enabled them to feel comfortable, and to think that whatever other doubtful property they had, the L&NW was not going to be pushed back in a ditch'.

By early 1869 Moon was calling attention to the value of the L&NW debenture stock, whereby they had recently been able to place nearly £400,000 and he had 'no doubt they would gradually get the whole of the debenture stock placed on a permanent basis at 4 per cent'.He again boasted that the rate was the 'best security in the world' and without the 'slightest risk' as the 'margin was so enormous'.

A year later he was reporting that the company had been 'able to get out their debenture stock in larger quantities, and at lower rates, he believed, than any other company'. Reporting that around £1.5million had been issued in the year, he claimed that the company's income was then more than enough to meet all the outstanding bonds if they had to pay them off as they fell due. As recovery continued, Moon progressively reported increases in the placing of this stock. By August 1873 he was sure shareholders would find 'cause for congratulation' in pointing out that the bond debt 'which in old days was a source of anxiety to your directors, is now beyond the reach of the money market or the fear of panics'. He explained:

> We have twelve millions of debenture stock and only six millions of ordinary debentures [bonds], which will be shortly converted into the permanent debenture stock. You will observe today that we offer to the proprietors a portion of this debenture stock at par; those who wish to invest their money safely will get a turn on the market price. The average interest on the bond debt is 2¾d. over 4d. per cent, but we shall come down, we hope, in the course of the year or so to a permanent 4 per cent.

An aspect of accounting, which had dogged railways since the downfall of Hudson, was the allocation of expenditure between capital and revenue. Railway companies were still wrestling over the correct procedure for accounting for depreciation and renewal. An L&NW auditor at the time, Abel Peyton, could have been reflecting some professional disagreement when he had commented on his retirement (in 1860) that 'there were many items now charged to revenue, which in strictness, ought to be placed to capital, but the course adopted had been taken in consequence of the oft-expressed wish of the proprietors, that the capital account should be closed'. No doubt one of the areas Peyton had in mind was the old method of accounting for the costs of renewing and extending the permanent way.

The L&NW could be said to have been one of the pioneers in tackling this problem. Following attempts in the early 1850s to close the capital account, the only way to charge for additional works and stock was to set up a deferred account against revenue. Although it was soon accepted that the costs of additional works could be capitalised, the cost of replacing track originally designed for lighter and slower trains led to further large increases being put to a 'suspense' account. An element in the higher costs of renewal was of course the addition for the improvements made, for example iron for wood in bridges, heavier rails, etc., which some thought could be justified as capital. When the decision was made to charge actual costs, the rate at which the suspense account was cleared became an item for critical review.

A suggestion that the permanent way account had been used 'to put to capital to produce dividends' brought forth this retort from Moon in August 1865:

> I tell you we should not be fit to manage your concern if a paltry consideration of that kind could affect us. Here you are, trusting five, or five and a half millions a year to us; and for the thirty gentlemen who sit here to do such an unworthy thing as for the shabby purpose of increasing your present dividend to depreciate your property hereafter is what, I trust, none of you will think us capable of. I tell you, if you take care to put gentlemen of consideration and honour upon your board such a thing could not occur, and it never has occurred in this company.

He explained that nothing was put to capital 'but the additional weight of iron in the rails'. Rails were originally laid down at a weight of sixty-five to seventy pounds per yard and 'we have now put eighty-four pound rails, and no labour or anything of that kind is put to capital, but only the additional weight of metal'. He thought that was 'fairly chargeable to that account'.

The Railway Companies Act of 1867 laid down requirements for company accounts and gave additional powers to auditors. This led the L&NW auditors, Crosfield and Hand, to report in February 1868 on the 'the subject of constantly adding to capital outlay'. They were 'unable to see how any railway company can refuse to supply the additional accommodation' which the public required and so long as the population and traffic of the country continued to increase they could not see how the capital account could be 'entirely closed'. However they felt strongly that additions 'should only be allowed, under the strict control of the shareholders, and subject to such stringent regulations as shall insure the bona fide nature of the appropriations' which was 'already attained to a very large extent by the system adopted' by the L&NW. They explained further that 'no debit has been admitted to capital in respect of interest on money expended upon unfinished works, or for fish-plating, or for the increased weight of metal put into the line, or for the improvement of bridges. Steel rails to the value of £32,000 have been substituted for iron at the cost of revenue, and the whole of the Law & Parliamentary expenses have been charged to the same account'.

The law and parliamentary expenses had been another controversial accounting area. The L&NW had allowed balances to accumulate in an attempt to even out fluctuating and late invoiced charges, with costs being allocated where relevant to new works capital. In 1861 this account had been £100,000 in arrears. Parliamentary expenses were incurred in not only the cost of preparing and submitting the company's own Bills but also in looking over all the other private Bills that could affect the company's position. 'They did not watch these Bills because they liked it', Moon said, 'or wanted to throw away their money, but because they were anxious the company should become a permanent property. It was the master's eye that kept the property in good order'. When later in 1868 he at last moved from Bevere to a house within a mile or so of Tamworth station and in sight of the company's Trent Valley main line this became literally true!

By February 1869 Moon was able to report that 'for the first time for 18 years the permanent way suspense fund, which in former years used to excite a good deal of discussion, will at the end of this year will be entirely wiped out'. He also added that the 'arrears

42. Tamworth Station

The station at Tamworth, showing main entrance to the L&NW's Trent Valley line
and on the right to the Midland's Derby Birmingham platforms at first floor level.

Warwickshire Railways

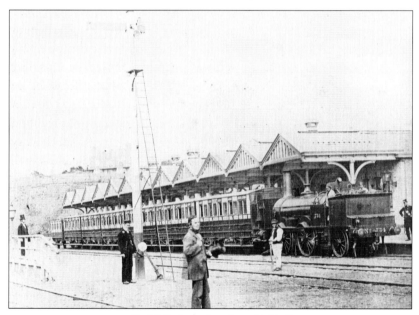

43. 1860s branch train at Solihull

L&NW branch train at Sutton Coldfield in late 1860s showing McConnell 0-4-2
Tank with rake of four-wheel carriages. Opened in 1862 the line was extended to
Lichfield in 1884. LNWR

of law expenses had been wiped off, and the company paying its daily expenditure'.

Although the L&NW board had a finance committee, Moon initially followed the example set by Glyn who, when chairman, had in his words, 'kept out of' being directly involved in financial affairs. Glyn had told Chandos in 1855 that he was never a member of the board's Finance Committee and so could not be accused of working to 'individual benefit'. Glyn's bank was of course the company's bankers; and throughout his long chairmanship years Moon never changed that arrangement. He was to write to Glyn Mills & Co. on his retirement that 'from the day the first Lord Wolverton [Glyn was created Lord Wolverton in 1869] and I made the present arrangement between your bank and the company, I look back with pleasure unalloyed by hitch or difficulty on our connection and trust it may long continue with the same confidence and goodwill'.

When Moon became company chairman he persuaded Glyn to serve on the committee, initially under Robert Benson (who had been on the committee since 1851 and its chairman since 1855) and then under Brown-Westhead who replaced Benson in 1864. Benson's own banking interests were mainly in American railways. Westhead's frequent absence through illness and eventual retirement saw Benson resume the chair in 1872 until his death in January 1875. Moon never seems to have been particularly close to Benson and was occasionally at odds with him, for example over the locomotive arrangements, yet they were of the same age with a Liverpool merchanting background as young men. However by the 1870s, Benson's bank, small by City standards, was already showing signs of being overstretched. When he suddenly died of a heart attack, Benson had not been in good health for some time and seems to have lost his grip on the bank; so much so that by the June following his death accountant Edwin Waterhouse was called in as receiver.

For the first three years of Moon's chairmanship the L&NW board's Finance Committee had as one its members a future Liberal Chancellor of the Exchequer, H.C.E.Childers. Though reported in *The Times* as a 'man of business' Childers appeared to have little impact on L&NW affairs during his three years or so as a director. Of far greater influence on Moon in financial matters was the auditor, Crosfield.

Auditors were responsible to shareholders through their own Audit Committee. This committee elected two members, each for a term of two years, one being voted on each year. In a particular reference to Crosfield, Moon believed that 'the auditing of their accounts was the most important thing they had on their hands, as on that depended the company's salvation. So long as they had such an auditor as they had at present, that could neither be coaxed nor flattered, they never need have any fear as to the accounts'.

Perhaps the best indication of Moon's reliance on Crosfield is shown by the memoirs of Edwin Waterhouse whose firm of public accountants, Price Holyland & Waterhouse, was appointed to the company at the end of 1867. Waterhouse recalled that Crosfield, 'an intimate and valued friend of Mr Richard Moon ... was looked to as a great authority on questions of finance, and occupied a position of far greater influence than that of an auditor generally'. Moon's apparent detailed grasp of the intricacies of the accounts obviously owed a lot to the briefings provided by Crosfield. When many years later Waterhouse briefly took over Crosfields's work on his death, he relates how his L&NW work 'took up much time, as I was desirous of preparing half-yearly books of statistics of the railway, even more comprehensive than those of which Mr Henry Crosfield had somewhat prided himself, and which he delighted should be of use to his friend the chairman'. Waterhouse amusingly records that:

> After the completion of the half-yearly statement of statistics, I handed it to Mr Moon, and he kindly praised my endeavour to make myself conversant with the affairs of the railway, saying my work was 'worthy to stand alongside "Henry's". I took the opportunity to ask whether I had earnt [sic] a gold, in lieu of the leather, pass on the line, a mark of his favour which he had bestowed on Mr Crosfield - and he immediately granted what I subsequently termed the 'order of the Moon', to wear on my watch chain. He generally after this took my half-yearly volumes of account home with him, or on his holidays, to study, bringing back a number of queries to put to me for his further information.

Moon referred publicly to Crosfield's books when, in 1868, he hoped the auditor would long be with them, but 'when he could no longer serve them he would leave behind him a legacy of the valuable books derived from his experience and knowledge of their affairs, and made up by his own hand, that would serve as a check on their accounts'. Crosfield was indeed long with the company but his death when it came, in January 1882, was tragic. This will be touched on later.

Remarkably dedicated as an auditor, Crosfield had been a leader in his field. The actual presentation of railway accounts had varied between one company and another. When the Government insisted on some uniformity, L&NW practice was one of the models used. Despite his own interest in standardising accounts, Moon had recognised the difficulties involved. In February 1869, when reporting for the first time the company's accounts in the 'parliamentary form', he remarked that it 'was very like putting the same sized coat on a little man and a big man'. He did not think it would ever be possible to compare one company with another because of differences in circumstances.

Moon's satisfaction with his own company's auditing procedure was more than could be said for the system for electing directors which had been a contentious issue between the board and shareholders. The thirty strong board was only allowed to re-elect four of the six retiring at the end of their five year terms. The shareholders had insisted on this condition. Moon's views when chairman were initially mixed. His main concern when first elected was to ensure the right calibre candidates emerged, representing the main trading areas and interests of the company. However it soon became clear that he was unhappy with apparent indifference shown by those electing them. Both these concerns were aparent when he sought his own relection in February 1866. 'There was one thing which pressed upon him very much indeed, namely, that every year two of the directors had to retire for the purpose of enabling the proprietors to put in two new members.' He believed that 'they acted as if they were giving a ticket to an infirmary or a vote at a general election; they gave their proxy without considering for an instant that the effect of that proxy would be either to appoint a man of business and experience to manage their concern, or an inefficient person, or, what was worse, an inexperienced or indifferent one'.

He thought the proprietors had never sufficiently borne in mind that the success or mismanagement of the company depended on who they elected as directors. 'As he had told them on previous occasions, the directors inside had a most disagreeable duty to perform. They were required every year to ballot out - nobody knew whom it might be - two of their body, who might have been acting with them ten or eleven years, and against whom nobody could urge anything.' He therefore thought that 'in some way the shareholders should consider what was best to be done' and suggested a committee to consider the question. He agreed that there should be an infusion of new blood occasionally, 'that from time to time there should be some new interests upon the board', but this 'must be made in some way less offensive to the directors and more practically useful to the company'.

After taking soundings with a 'large number of influential shareholders', Moon later reported they could not see a way to improve the present system. It was not until 1870 that the board appointed a sub-committee to review the situation but even then the legality of reverting to a more normal practice was challenged. It was a proposal to merge the company with the Lancashire & Yorkshire Railway that brought the issue to a head, the L&NW's half-yearly meeting in February 1872 agreeing that five not six would retire each year with all five being able to offer themselves for re-election. Incidentally Crosfield thought the old system had worked well and regretted the change.

The enlarged board had in any event become cumbersome and rarely was there full attendance at the regular monthly meetings, with little discussion recorded on the long list of minutes presented for their review from the numerous committees. Increasingly Moon had adopted the system initiated under Chandos, where details were reviewed first by a sub committee of the board which met fortnightly, and only the more important items brought before the monthly board.

This Special Committee had first been set up in 1858 and comprised initially the chairmen of the main committees, in effect forming a cabinet of the most active directors. Under Moon the membership evolved as a mix of some committee chairmen and other senior directors such as Benson, Mangles and Tootal. Mangles never chaired a committee and Tootal only a minor one for hotels. Yet Dean, who been active in chairing the Audit and Law Committees in 1862 and the Southern in 1865, was not appointed to the Special until 1867. In 1868 the Duke of Sutherland, who never regularly attended board meetings, nor chaired a committee, became a member. Over the first ten years under Moon, the committee's membership grew from nine to thirteen.

Widening the membership of the Special Committee brought about the same problems for Moon as an unwieldy board. With his hands-on style of management he found himself forming an even more exclusive group of key directors to direct day-to-day policies and operations. This move to even stronger direction from the centre was to find its ultimate expression in control through one man, viz., Moon himself.

Moon's ability to retain such a masterly grip at a time of further growth in the company's operations was remarkable. Mistakes were inevitably made, as will be seen, and eventually exercising such personal control came to be questioned, but for the foreseeable future financial results fully justified the faith the company placed in him.

CHAPTER 16

NEW ROLES

Though Moon's experience as a reforming director had generally been in the area of cost control, his influence had spread beyond management efficiency into the wider issues of overall company direction well before elected as chairman. Some account of the success or otherwise of how he now handled these issues needs to be followed.

Perhaps one of the most impressive structures built by the L&NW is the bridge at Runcorn over the Mersey. This formed part of a shortened route from the south to Liverpool, which had been considered as far back as early Grand Junction days when that company was looking for an alternative to the Warrington & Newton link for access to the Liverpool & Manchester Railway. The idea was revived in the late 1850s as the 'Huyton and Aston' project; Huyton being on the original L&M and Aston on the ex-GJ line south of Warrington (near where the eventual junction was made). As the estimated cost of this proposal was half a million pounds the L&NW's Special Committee appointed Moon and Bancroft in October 1858 to review a shorter and cheaper alternative by using the St Helens Railway. This would have been from Moore, nearer Warrington, to Fidlers Ferry on the St Helens line from Runcorn Gap (Widnes) to Garston.

Aware that negotiations to use the St Helens would first be necessary as would an extension from Garston to Edge Hill for access to Liverpool itself, Moon and Bancroft reported that no action needed to be taken 'at present'. A year later Locke, still the company's consulting engineer for the area, recommended crossing at Fidlers Ferry with two swing bridges. The Admiralty insisted however that any swing bridge would have to be kept open for two hours at high tide so an alternative fixed bridge was discussed. A Bill for the Fidlers Ferry route, described in the L&NW's half-yearly report as from

44. Runcorn Bridge
L&NW's bridge over the Mersey at Runcorn opened in 1869, designed and built
under the supervision of the company's engineer William Baker. LNWRS

45. W.Baker
William Baker (1817-78), the L&NW's civil engineer who took over all new
construction when consultant Joseph Locke died in 1860.

Huyton to Moore, was submitted in early 1860 but was thrown out on objections from the upper Mersey navigation interests. Cawkwell and the company's engineer, Baker, were then promptly asked to review a high level crossing at Runcorn Gap itself. In June they were later joined by a large committee of directors which again included Moon and Bancroft who, after inspecting both sides of the river, reported favourably but at an estimated cost of £550,000.

With the Admiralty agreeing a 75ft clearance and three spans of 300ft, a new Bill was drawn up. Locke died in September and it was Baker who presented the plans and estimates for authorization in the 1861 session. The project together with the connecting lines was enacted on 11 July 1861 when Moon had been in the chair for less than three weeks. The bridge was to be Baker's most notable work and it is worth recalling Moon's earlier opinion of the engineer in the row with McConnell over Haydon Square machinery. Moon had thought Baker lacked the 'master's eye' for repairs and 'no genius for details'. This view is remarkably at variance with a memoir of the Institute of Civil Engineers. 'Mr Baker possessed a singularly retentive memory, was methodical and exact in all things, fearless in the expression of his opinion, matured in the knowledge of men and business.' It would appear that Moon's judgement over the Haydon Square dispute had been unduly influenced by Baker's lack of enthusiasm for routine maintenance and the strong personality of McConnell. Moon clearly changed his mind over both men: his distrust of McConnell and his view of Baker softening. In suggesting that Francis Stevenson become Baker's clerk of works to handle more routine work, (ten years younger and succeeding Baker on his death in 1878) Moon had clearly recognized where Baker's real worth lay.

The company had used costly consultants Robert Stephenson and the Locke & Errington partnership for handling major new works. After Stephenson died in October 1859 the company had separated engineering functions into four maintenance districts but Baker was made responsible, at a salary of £1000 p.a., for implementing new works over the whole of the line. His wide experience well qualified him for this changed responsibility.

Born in 1817, the son of an officer of the East India Company and educated privately, Baker began his training as a civil engineer in 1834 articled to G.W.Buck. Buck had acted for Robert Stephenson

on the construction of the London to Tring section of the London
& Birmingham Railway. On the opening to Tring in 1837 Buck
moved to Manchester where he was to engineer the Manchester &
Birmingham Railway. Baker went with him and, at the age of twenty-
one, was given responsibility for a section of the line (Neele attributes
the Stockport viaduct to Baker). He then subsequently became chief
engineer for the construction of the Manchester, South Junction &
Altrincham Railway, which opened in 1849. During the building of
the latter he was also engaged on railways in the Staffordshire area,
engineering the Shrewsbury & Birmingham line to Wolverhampton
and the Shropshire Union from Shrewsbury to Stafford; both these
railways opening in 1849 when he became responsible for the
L&NW's Stour Valley line from Birmingham to Wolverhampton. In
the latter capacity he became personally involved in the infamous
battle between the L&NW and the Shrewsbury & Birmingham.
MacDermot, the historian of the GW, refers to him leading a party
of navvies to prevent a connecting siding being built and 'thenceforth
known in the district as "General Baker"'. The Stour valley line
completion was protracted by the dispute with the S&B, not opening
until 1852 when Baker took over the engineering for the southern
division of the L&NW.

Within a year of being given responsibility for new works
Baker was presenting plans and estimates to the L&NW's Special
Committee (October 1860) of nearly £1.5 million, which in addition
to Runcorn Bridge included £300,000 for the Eccles-Tyldesley-
Wigan line. With major projects such as these the responsibility
on Baker was formidable and, with Errington's death in 1862, all
construction was placed under him. It is typical of Moon that, despite
his apparent earlier misgivings, once he trusted the man he gave him
his full support. A £1,000 annual allowance in addition to salary was
agreed, charged to capital, backdated to cover the additional 1861
parliamentary work and for as long as the heavy work load continued.

The lattice-girder bridge over the Mersey at Runcorn was to
prove Baker's finest memorial. Earthworks were started for the
approach lines to the bridge in the summer of 1862 and by the end of
the year all land purchases were in hand. The main contract for the
line was let to Brassey & Ogilvie the following March. Construction
took five years, with the bridge ready in May 1868, but the whole

line was not opened until February 1869 for goods and 1 April for passengers. As has been noted, it gave access from the south to the Warrington-Garston line of the former St Helens Railway.

The L&NW's eventual absorption of the St Helens had been on the cards even before they jointly leased the Warringon & Stockport company in 1859 (this company never actually built the line beyond Timperley to Stockport). The following year the L&NW leased from the St Helens their Warrington to Garston line, thereby giving them control of the whole of the St Helens route from the MSJ&A at Timperley to the docks at Garston. In 1861 the L&NW bought the Warrington & Stockport and in 1864 full ownership of the St Helens company passed to them. The L&NW's own extension from Garston to Edge Hill for Liverpool was also authorised that year. Though the rival MS&L had run the trains on the jointly owned MSJ&A and had running powers through to Garston, the L&NW succeeded in blocking their access to Liverpool. This policy was to prove shortsighted, Moon adopting the very same tactics he had criticised Huish for, i.e. denying the MS&L a share of the traffic for 'the temporary profit of the moment'.

The MS&L's association with the Great Northern, that brought the latter to Manchester, had taken a further step forward in 1862 when the two companies agreed to develop jointly a number of separately authorised lines in Cheshire with the object of obtaining access to Chester and Merseyside. This was confirmed by the GN's Cheshire Lines Act of 1863. In 1865 the Midland became the third partner in what became the Cheshire Lines Committee (incorporated as such in 1867) when the more direct threat to the L&NW of an alternative route between Manchester and Liverpool was authorised, despite strong opposition from both the L&NW and the Lancashire & Yorkshire. This further challenge to the long established monopoly of the L&NW's original Liverpool & Manchester Railway (the L&Y route via Bolton had not been opened until 1848) was given added thrust by the re-emergence of Edward Watkin.

Watkin had been lured in 1861 to Canada. Ever ambitious, he accepted a challenge offered by the London board of the near bankrupt Canadian Grand Trunk Railway to help resolve that railway's funding problems. Though resigning as general manager of the MS&L, he had continued to maintain contact, increased

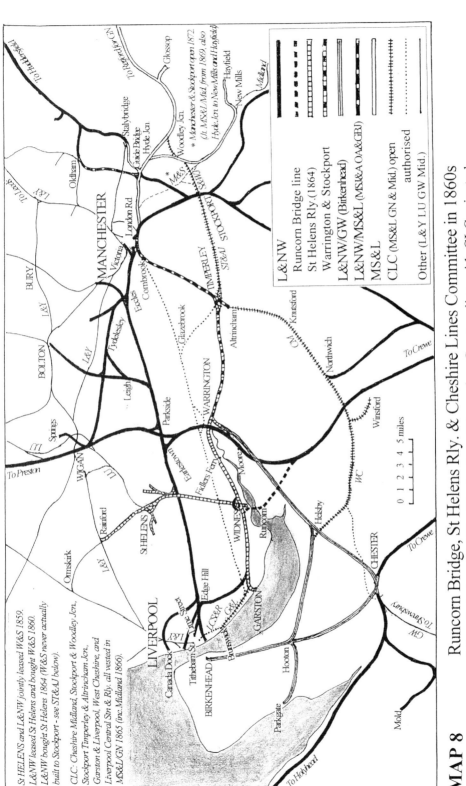

MAP 8

Runcorn Bridge, St Helens Rly. & Cheshire Lines Committee in 1860s
Moon's belated 1868 offer to share Timperley-Garston line with CLC rejected
(Manchester-Garston lines opened 1872-3 & Liverpool Central 1874)

Legend:

L&NW

Runcorn Bridge line
St Helens Rly. (1864)
Warrington & Stockport
L&NW/GW (Birkenhead)
L&NW/MS&L (MS&A OA&GRJ)
MS&L
CLC (MS&L GN & Mid.) open
authorised
Other (L&Y LU GW Mid.)

St HELENS and L&NW jointly leased W&S 1859.
L&NW leased St Helens and bought W&S 1860.
L&NW bought St Helens 1864 (W&S never actually
built to Stockport - see ST&AJ below).

CLC: Cheshire Midland, Stockport & Woodley Jcn.,
Stockport Timperley & Altrincham Jcn.,
Garston & Liverpool, West Cheshire, and
Liverpool Central Stn & Rly. all vested in
MS&L/GN 1865 (inc.Midland 1866).

To Huddersfield
To Retford for GN
Glossop
Stalybridge
Guide Bridge
Hyde Jcn
Woodley Jcn.
Hayfield
New Mills
Midland
Oldham
MANCHESTER
London Rd
Victoria
M&S
S&W
* Manchester & Stockport open 1872.
(1. MS&L/Mid. from 1869, also
Hyde Jcn to New Mills and Hayfield)
TIMPERLEY
ST&J STOCKPORT
ST&J
Eccles
Cornbrook
Patricroft
Glazebrook
Altrincham
C.M. Knutsford
BURY
L&Y
BOLTON
L&Y
Leigh
Northwich
To Crewe
SPRINGS
M
WIGAN
LU
LU
Parkside
WARRINGTON
Winsford
WC
To Preston
Ormskirk
L&Y
Ramford
L&Y
S HELENS
Earlestown
Fidlers Ferry
Moore
WIDNES
Runcorn
Helsby
CHESTER
To Crewe
GW
To Shrewsbury
Mold
Edge Hill
LIVERPOOL
Canada Dock
Tithebarn St
Brunswick
L&Y
L CS&P
GARSTON
Hooton
Parkgate
To Holyhead
BIRKENHEAD
0 1 2 3 4 5 miles

his shareholding and, with his broader experience of moving in both British and Canadian government circles, had manoeuvered successfully to return to the MS&L in January 1864 as director and chairman.

With Watkin now the driving force behind the CLC, Moon should have been well aware of problems ahead. It need not have been too late to counter the threat, as construction of the CLC's new line was seriously delayed as a result of the trade depression. Moon did shift from aggressive tactics to compromise but it was not until 1868 that he offered the CLC the alternative of a 50% share in the ownership of the former St Helens route to Garston and access to Lime Street. As an alternative Liverpool-Manchester route, the St Helens line was never critical to the L&NW, its main purpose being to tap the lucrative local coal trade to Garston docks and to provide the Runcorn Bridge link into Liverpool.

Moon reported to his shareholders in February 1869 that the MS&L had actually agreed his offer, 'but their partners did not see their way to accept it'. The Cheshire Lines main line from Manchester to Garston was completed in 1873 and by the following year their new Central Station in Liverpool was open.

A far more serious accusation of misjudgement by Moon in attempting to deny competition at this time was the dispute over the Midland's share of the Scottish traffic. The Midland, centred on Derby, had then no directly owned lines to either London or Scotland but relied on others for access. The extension of the 'Octuple' agreement in 1856, as the 'English Scotch Traffic' agreement, had continued to ignore the alternative Midland route to Carlisle via Leeds, Skipton and Lancaster; their share of the pooled Scottish traffic still being based on only the old Normanton to York route.

With the opening of the Midland's extension to Hitchin and their agreement with the Great Northern in 1858 for through running to Kings Cross, the prospects for a real 'middle way' to Scotland were enhanced. It had led the Midland to lease permanently the local Skipton company, the so called "Little" North Western Railway, from January 1859. The Midland had worked the North Western since 1852, the Lancaster line being a natural continuation of the Skipton extension from the Leeds & Bradford Railway which the Midland had absorbed in 1851.

Though the North Western had opened from Skipton to Lancaster as early as 1850, their original main line had been projected northwards as a more direct route to Carlisle, joining the Lancaster & Carlisle line at Low Gill, five miles south of Tebay. However the main line had been opened only as far as Ingleton and subsequently abandoned. When attempts were made to resurrect the project the Lancaster & Carlisle successfully promoted the line as their own branch southwards from Low Gill, opening in 1861, as a means of controlling any intention to use it as a competitive route. This left Ingleton an isolated exchange point between the two companies: a link which the L&NW, through their control of the L&C, had little interest in developing. Limited to a fixed share under the 'English Scotch' agreement based on Normanton, the Midland had seen no point in declaring any additional Scottish traffic they were routing through Skipton and Lancaster. With the significant improvement in potential that the L&C opening to Low Gill offered, the Midland rightly claimed that to continue allocating pooled receipts on the basis of past traffic flows was outdated. Their case was strengthened the following year when the North British Railway, in extending to Carlisle, offered the prospect of an additional share of the Edinburgh traffic.

The L&NW and the other parties to the agreement not only did not agree, but succeeded in having the Midland receipts frozen by the Railway Clearing House pending resolution of any new apportionment. The Midland and North British eventually had to resort to the courts to have them released, but not until mid 1866. In the meantime the Midland's attempt to run a service from Kings Cross to connect with the main west coast route was dependent on L&NW cooperation at both Ingleton and Tebay. Inevitably each side blamed the other for delays or problems. Seeking a more secure route to Scotland had by then become a priority for the Midland. In the south their dependence on the GN to Kings Cross was ended with the opening of their London extension to St Pancras in October 1868.

The most natural route for the Midland to reach Carlisle from north of Leeds was the existing direct line from Skipton to Low Gill. Given sensible cooperation at Ingleton and Tebay and agreed rates, through running by Midland trains over the whole route made economic sense. The L&NW were paying a high price to lease the

L&C and having the Midland bear a share of that cost was attractive. Discussions to this effect had begun as early as the autumn of 1863.

Although leased in perpetuity to the L&NW, the L&C still remained an independent entity with its ordinary shareholders enjoying a minimum guaranteed annual dividend of 8%. When the L&NW paid its own ordinary shareholders over 4%, payment to the L&C shareholders was increased proportionately. In July 1863 the annual payment had risen to 9¼%. Out of the fifteen directors of the L&C only five could be nominees of the L&NW, which gave the company some independence in determining any change to their financial position. With the Midland willing to participate a basis for compromise between all three companies should have existed.

The Midland however were determined to improve their share of the Scottish traffic, even to the extent of building their own independent line to Carlisle. Moon wrote to Edward Hasell (chairman of the L&C since the line's opening) in the summer of 1863, suggesting giving the Midland running powers: 'it is probably a less evil than allowing them to make a competing line'. It was in the interests of the independent L&C directors to protect their guarantee should the impact of competition reduce the earnings of the L&NW. And it was in the interests of the L&NW to share the high cost of their L&C lease. So why was agreement not reached?

Moon met a number of independent L&C directors and suggested that the guarantee could be raised to 9½% if they agreed to a joint lease with the Midland. The local directors though, led by the experienced Hasell demanded 10%. With Moon's high hopes for his own company's dividends this should not have been a problem (by 1865 the L&NW was paying the L&C 11%). Moon was keen in his report to L&NW shareholders in February 1864 to demonstrate his 'peaceful intent' towards their neighbours. He described negotiations with the Midland as having 'practically agreed with them to join in the lease'. He told them that 'instead of compelling them to make their own line into Scotland the directors said, "come and use this line, be joint owners with us, and let us work together"'. By August the L&NW had obtained powers to admit the Midland over the L&C and later that year the Midland sought confirmation in their own Bill. By the end of 1864 the Midland board had approved a draft agreement for joint use of the L&C.

46. E.W.Hasell, chairman Lancaster & Carlisle

Edward Hasell (1796-1872), chairman of the Lancaster & Carlisle Railway since its enactment in 1844. From a portrait by Francis Grant. Robert Hasell-McCosh

47. James Allport

James Allport (1811-92), Midland general manager 1853-57 and (after a period in shipbuilding) from 1860-80. On retiring he was presented with £10,000 and elected to board. Knighted in 1884 for improving 3rd class travel. NRM

Moon's counterpart on the Midland at the time was Samuel Beale. Moon maintained, from the very first meeting with Beale, that mutually agreed rates was always the basis of their negotiation. It seemed unfortunate that Beale subsequently resigned in July 1864 through ill health and in October his deputy Hutchinson took over as chairman, with Price as deputy. The new Midland leadership together with James Allport, their formidable general manager, met Moon in January 1865 to finalise arrangements. It was then that Moon seems to have overplayed his hand, failing to remind himself of his own plea to Chandos in previous negotiations with the Midland that 'we will never get more money out of a fight than by making a fair bargain'.

Whatever he considered had been agreed with Beale seems to have been lost in subsequent negotiations. It became clear that arrangements were far from finalised. Moon had demanded that the Midland should meet half the L&C rent regardless and that the L&NW should control the rate to Carlisle. The Midland's use of the line was unlikely ever to reach 50% and to accept a limitation on the right, effectively, to set their own through rates was unreasonable. Moon had insisted on Carlisle, the gateway to the Scottish market, being treated no differently from all the other stations on the L&C line where rates would be mutually agreed to protect local traffic. He later claimed that he had been prepared to submit the Carlisle rate to arbitration. But the damage had been done. Hutchinson reported to his board in February that negotiations had failed. To quote historian Peter Baughan, when the Midland gave the L&NW a month to re-consider, there seemed 'no relaxation in Euston's grim determination to get the last ounce out of the Midland'.

If Moon had banked on the Midland being forced to return to the negotiating table economic circumstances worked against him. The improved trade of the country not only enhanced companies' abilities to pay increased dividends, but also provided a more favourable climate for encouraging speculative schemes, one of which was for a potential new route to Carlisle. The first hint of this came to light in the summer of 1865 when the L&NW learnt that Midland surveyors were reported in the area. By November it had become obvious that a Midland alternative to the whole of the L&C, from a junction on their Skipton-Lancaster line, near Settle, direct to Carlisle, was planned.

Outspoken shareholders with a stake in both companies saw the failure in negotiations as a disaster. One attacked Moon at the L&NW half-yearly meeting in February 1866 for refusing to allow the Midland 'a just participation in the profits of the north'; adding that 'the Settle and Carlisle was nothing more than robbing the shareholders of both companies'. Moon defended his company's stance by saying that they were prepared to reconsider the Scottish traffic agreement and, 'with regard to making a line to Carlisle that was not an affair of this company, but the Midland'. He explained that they had 'offered to give them entire possession of a part of the L&C line, and full use to Carlisle on the other part, on fair and reasonable terms, to be fixed by arbitration. He did not know they could do more'. He concluded, rather lamely, that, 'while the board regretted it, they could not help it. He was sure they had done all in their power by offering such terms as they thought would bring the Midland to their view, and they believed the terms offered were more favourable than any that that company could make for themselves, but it seems they did not think so'.

At the Midland meeting in May 1866, despite continuing strong objections from a body of powerful shareholders, it was agreed to proceed with a Bill for building the new line. At the Parliamentary Committee hearing, the L&NW's objections were put by general manager Cawkwell. He was far from convincing when claiming that existing services via Ingleton were satisfactory and blaming the Midland for delays. Supported by the North British, Glasgow & South Western, L&Y and local Carlisle interests, the Bill passed quickly and was enacted on 16 July 1866.

The financial panic of 1866, however, meant that any hope the Midland may have had of a quick start on placing contracts was dashed. Instead, as the recession began to bite, the company came under renewed shareholder attack to rein back expenditure. And in the L&NW, under pressure from his own shareholders, Moon attempted further to wave aside any responsibility his company had for bringing about the Midland decision.

At his February 1867 half-yearly meeting, Moon recalled his meetings with the previous Midland chairman Beale when 'three distinct offers' were made for the Midland's use of the L&C: firstly to become joint owners by paying half the rent and each company using it 'free of toll', secondly joint ownership by both companies paying into a joint fund the mileage proportions of agreed rates on L&C lines, and thirdly to lease the Ingleton branch to the Midland for 5% of its cost and for the Midland to have running powers to Carlisle on mileage rates subject to arbitration if differences arose.

Throughout 1867, when it became clear that hardly any progress was being made on the proposed line, Midland shareholders at meetings in Manchester and Leeds demanded an ending of the project and called for negotiations with the L&NW to be re-opened. Midland capital was already stretched by the cost of extending, from Bedford, their own line to London and improving access to Manchester through the Peak district. At this time the Midland were also seeking amalgamation with the Glasgow & South Western Railway (Hutchinson was chairman of both). Although Midland shareholders agreed this merger, they continued to object strongly to the Carlisle line and formed a committee to meet the L&NW. Ironically, when the Midland and G&SW Bill failed, one of the grounds given was that the two companies' lines were not directly connected.

At the L&NW half-yearly meeting in August 1867, Moon, stung by continued criticism of his negotiations, retorted vindictively that 'the Midland directors insisted on the power to fix the rates to Carlisle which practically would have given the power to ruin the rates for the Scotch traffic. To this the L&NW could not agree. If they were to have power to destroy the traffic, the Midland had better expend the £4million on the Settle & Carlisle line and bear part of the burden themselves rather than at the cost of the capital of this company'.

This outburst certainly confirmed where he stood and made nonsense of the view at the time that the L&NW were only protecting their local traffic to Carlisle. An outspoken shareholder of both companies persisted in pleading for a settlement by sharing the cost of the L&C, commenting that their (L&NW) dividend was only 5¼% yet they paid £254,322 p.a. rent for the lease. He proposed that an effort be made to agree with the Midland 'on the basis of doing away with the Settle & Carlisle line'. Moon tartly responded by hoping 'the proprietors would not inflict that resolution on their directors'.

However the Midland's own directors, now faced with a total requirement for all new capital of around £5million, of which the estimate for the Carlisle line was £2million, accepted that the position had to be reconsidered and by the end of 1867 stopped all work on the line. And early in 1868 the Midland's Leeds shareholders were in direct contact with the L&NW. Despite his public reaction to his own shareholders, Moon then wrote to their representative, Baines, suggesting that terms for through working could be agreed including the critical right for the Midland to set their own rates. Baughan refers to this as a 'complete climb down' by the L&NW. It appears that Moon had at last accepted that it was in the interests of both companies to compromise.

Throughout the summer of 1868 the two companies met to re-negotiate terms, agreement eventually being reached in November for the Midland to pay for the use of the Ingleton to Carlisle line and for the L&NW to support the Midland in a Bill to abandon the Carlisle project. Even then Moon still tried, unsuccessfully, to extract some contra benefit by obtaining running powers over the Midland's Birmingham to Bristol line.

For the Scottish companies however, in particular the North British, the abandonment would have meant continuing to be subject to L&NW control of their traffic south of Carlisle. Despite their close ties with the L&NW, the Lancashire & Yorkshire was also against the abandonment. They saw not only increased prospects for their existing connection with the Midland at Colne, but also the potential for resurrecting their original idea to extend their Chatburn branch to Hellifield (authorised in 1871), which would give them a more direct access to the new route.

The Settle & Carlisle Abandonment Bill came before the committee of the House of Commons in April 1869. Despite evidence in support from Hutchinson personally, Baines on behalf of the Midland shareholders, and Cawkwell for the L&NW, the petitions against the Bill from the North British and L&Y were upheld and the Bill rejected. Cawkwell's evidence, as in 1866, does not appear to have been particularly telling. Moon always seemed to have delegated representation before parliamentary hearings to his principal officers. With abandonment legally rejected the Midland had no other option but to resume work on the line.

It took over six years to complete the Settle & Carlisle line, the £2million estimate swelling to £3.5million. The line provides not just a lasting memorial to its builders, but also a dramatic reminder of the folly of nineteenth century railway politics. Immediately the abandonment Bill failed, Moon tried to restrict the Midland's use of the Ingleton line although he was soon offering to reconsider this.

With the Midland then committed to its own direct route to Scotland, and the flouting of the pooling arrangements under the English & Scotch Traffic agreement, the renewal of the latter became increasingly uncertain. The pooling arrangements terminated six months before its renewal date at the end of 1869 and were replaced (as far as the west coast companies were concerned) by an agreement only to review regularly rates and fares by the formation of the West Coast Conference.

It was not only in the competition for the Scottish traffic that the L&NW faced threats from the Midland via their Skipton line. The industrial development based on the Cumberaland iron industry had attracted railway development and offered new markets for potential connecting lines.

In 1862 the Midland were projecting a link to the Furness Railway, who had just acquired the Ulverston & Lancaster Railway, a line that had connected the area to Carnforth on the L&C. This link would give them direct access to Barrow and the iron districts, breaking the monopolistic postion of the L&NW to the south and the Maryport & Carlisle to the north. Peter Baughan in his *North of Leeds* history writes that Moon personally intervened in February 1864 to try and prevent this. Clearly he did not succeed: the joint Midland Furness line from Wennington opened to Carnforth in 1867.

Before the Ulverston & Lancaster opened the only rail link to the Cumberland coast had been the Maryport & Carlisle Railway. When a more direct line to Workington for the mineral traffic was authorised from Penrith to Cockermouth (Cockermouth Keswick & Penrith Railway) Moon was not slow to show his company's interest. Jointly with the North Eastern, who had just reached Clifton (south of Penrith) via an extension of their Stockton & Darlington line, the two companies obtained powers to subscribe and work the traffic. This co-operation with the North Eastern effectively meant the ending of Moon's flirtation with extending into the north-east.

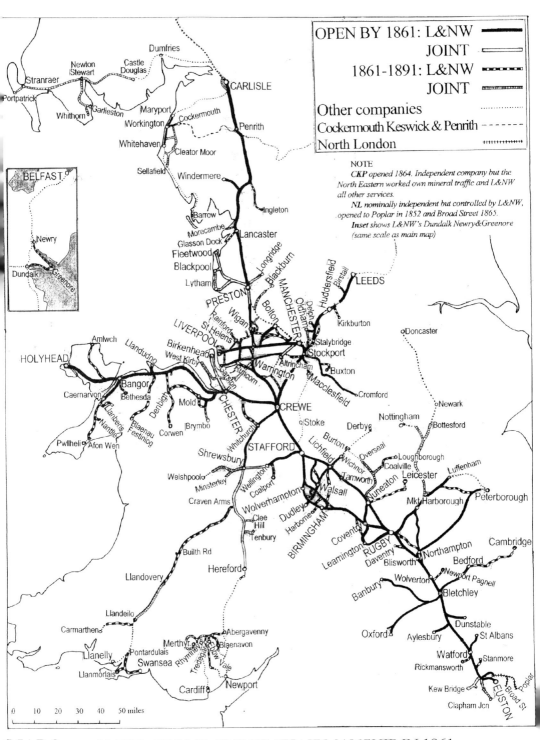

MAP 9 L&NWR: FROM MOON'S CHAIRMANSHIP IN 1861 TO RETIREMENT IN 1891

The line to Cockermouth was opened at the end of 1864 and connected directly with the Cockermouth & Workington Railway, a small independent company which not only gave access to Workington but also to Maryport and Whitehaven through another independent line, the Whitehaven Junction Railway. At Whitehaven yet another separate company provided the link to the Furness Railway's lines from Barrow, the Whitehaven & Furness Junction Railway. Into this cocktail of companies and arrangements, Moon appeared to have moved skilfully in personally negotiating with the Duke of Devonshire and the Earl of Lonsdale (chairmen respectively of the Furness and the two Whitehaven junction companies) for ownership to be shared between the two main companies. The L&NW took control of the WJR and the C&W; the Furness the W&FJ.

Despite further complications involving additional competing lines in the area (primarily mineral) and the opening of the joint Furness Midland line, relations between the Furness and the L&NW remained good. This probably reflected the long tenure held by both Moon and James Ramsden (Furness managing director) of their respective companies. Younger than Moon by some six years Ramsden, knighted for his services to Barrow in 1872, first joined the Furness as locomotive superintendent in 1846 and remained with the company until he died in 1896.

The trade recession that led the attempt to abandon the Settle & Carlisle affected all companies. Moon reported to his shareholders in February 1869 that the previous year 'had been a period of as much depression in trade as was ever known in this country' but that he believed the company 'to be as solid and good as ever it was'. By the summer he was reporting signs of economic recovery and thought 'the dividend had been depressed to as low a point as it was likely to touch'. In this he was right. Under the remaining years of his chairmanship the dividend never fell below the 5¼% annual rates of the half years ending the summers of 1867 and 1868.

By February 1870 Moon was reporting 'they were now on the move upwards, and had returned to a point at which they were earning at the rate of 7% per annum for the past half-year, or 6¼% for the year'. He 'positively' assured shareholders that the dividend was 'honestly earned' and that the accounts were even better than they looked as he had advised going 'prudently and slowly forward rather than pay a larger dividend with the chance of coming back again'. At the end of the first half of 1870 Moon was reporting even more confidently and 'thought it right to take advantage of this period of prosperity to execute a great many necessary works, and to renew, as it were, the face of the concern'.

CHAPTER 17

FITTING REWARD

Moon's reference to renewing the 'face of the concern' was also relevant in terms of senior personnel. In 1869 both Glyn and Earle were honoured. Given a peerage for his work in the City, Glyn took the title Wolverton, recalling his formative years as chairman of the London & Birmingham Railway. Earle was awarded his baronetcy for services to the Liberal party in Liverpool. He was to continue as a L&NW director until his death aged eighty-five in 1877. Glyn did not enjoy his peerage for long, he retired from the L&NW in the summer of 1870 following a period of poor health, and died three years later. Glyn's exchange of correspondence with Moon showed that he had wanted to resign earlier but Moon had been reluctant to accept it. Glyn finally resigned on 3 August when he wrote, with some emotion, to Moon:

> I think the time is now arrived when you should act upon the resignation which I have from time to time tendered to you and replace me at the board ... by one who can devote his time and his influence to the service of the company. I appreciate most highly the kindness which has kept me so long as a member of the board, but it must not be abused by me. Of course in writing to you on this subject, old feelings and recollections crowd upon my mind, but they are all of the same character and bear testimony to the uniform kindness which I have received from every one connected with the service of the company. ... Let me close by requesting you to convey to my old and kind friends my sincere thanks and earnest wishes for their prosperity and that of the great undertaking administered by you and them. I am the only survivor of the original direction, though my old friend, Sir Hardman Earle, comes very near me.

Glyn was replaced by Lord Richard Grosvenor. Proposed by Moon and Tootal at the next board meeting, Grosvenor was in many ways as surprising a choice as the selection had been of the previous nobleman, Lord Chandos. Not an obvious City candidate, the younger son of the Marquis of Westminster, Grosvenor was educated at Cambridge and had apparently spent his early years roaming North America and China before settling, at aged twenty four, as Liberal MP for Flintshire where his family had estates and mining interests. He had first come to prominence in 1867. When still only thirty, he was appointed chairman of the British committee formed to promote with the French a channel tunnel rail link. He had come to be seen as sufficiently well connected both socially and politically to bring value to the commercial world. He proved to be a dedicated and long serving L&NW director and, as Lord Stalbridge, was eventually to become Moon's successor as chairman of the company.

At the same board which elected Grosvenor, the resignation of the locomotive superintendent, John Ramsbottom, was accepted. Ramsbottom had written to Moon on 20 September 1870 resigning his position 'on account of fading health'. He gave the company the year's notice required by his contract and the board expressed its 'great regret they feel at the severance of a connection which has existed for so many years' and they trusted his 'health may speedily be restored'. He was requested to return his gold pass but £500 was voted for 'some momento' to be presented in recognition 'of his long and able service'.

Under Moon, Ramsbottom's annual salary as overall locomotive superintendent had advanced from £2,000 in 1862 to £5,000 by January 1869, the highest paid officer in the company. Despite Moon giving him his head in running the locomotive department and rolling mills, Ramsbottom had apparently been affected by the weight of his heavy responsibilities and the strain of meeting his own exacting standards, if not the demands of his chairman. Although it seems that in his last year at Crewe he became genuinely ill, Ramsbottom recovered quite remarkably after he left the company. He took up private consulting work, which subsequently included advising the Lancashire & Yorkshire in the planning of their new locomotive works at Horwich and, before finally retiring he was, for a brief period, a director of that company.

48. F.W.Webb as Crewe works manager 1864

F.W.Webb with some of his foreman in 1864 when Crewe works manager. He was
to succeed Ramsbottom as L&NW's locomotive superintendent in 1871. NRM

49. Locomotive *Bevere*

Ramsbottom's 2-4-0 Newton class no. 1746 *Bevere* built in 1869 for express
services north of Crewe. Webb was to continue the design but with modifications
that included a cab. LNWRS

A natural successor to Ramsbottom could have been T.Stubbs, who at age thirty had been appointed effectively Works Manager in 1866, having been previously head of the drawing office. However he had died from an illness at the time of Ramsbottom's resignation. Moon moved quickly to make replacements. The appointment of Francis Webb not only marked the beginning of a legendary thirty-one year reign at Crewe (he gave notice to retire in November 1902) but also provides a fine example of Moon's willingness to pay high salaries for good management. When defending the cost of appointing solicitor Blenkinsop, Moon had affirmed the principle by asserting that 'if they chose to employ counsel they must pay him, and if they employed counsel they had better have the best'.

Born in May 1836 Webb was a generation younger than Ramsbottom. The second son of a Church of England rector in Staffordshire, Webb had gone to Crewe in 1851 as an apprenticed pupil of Trevithick. He was promoted in 1859 to be head of the drawing office when still only twenty-two at a salary of £140 p.a. Brian Reed, the historian of Crewe works, wrote that he came to prominence by doing the design work on the changes to the locomotive *Cornwall*. In September 1861 he became foreman at £180 a year and the following month his salary as 'Indoor Assistant' was increased to £220. Still only twenty-five, Webb was then the Works Manager responsible for production which included the rolling mills where he oversaw the installation of the Bessemer steel plant. This experience led him to be attracted away from Crewe in 1866 to manage a steel plant in Bolton.

Webb must have kept in close touch with Ramsbottom and Crewe for within two weeks of Ramsbottom's resignation, Moon had met and agreed terms with him to rejoin the company. After formally obtaining the approval of the Special Committee, Moon wrote to Webb on 8 October confirming the appointment; the annual salary being £2,000 for the first year and £3,000 thereafter. It was subsequently agreed that Webb would start 1 July 1871. He took up his post only on 1 October as Moon sent him on a tour of US steel making plants during the summer. Moon had waited for his return before confirming with him the appointment of T.W.Worsdell to take over Stubbs's responsibilities. Worsdell had met Webb in the States and was to remain at Crewe for ten years before moving on to follow his own career as a successful locomotive superintendent, firstly with the Great Eastern in 1881 and then the North Eastern in 1885. He was incidentally a son of N. Worsdell who had been the carriage superintendent at Crewe who Moon considered too old for the position at Wolverton when Bore was appointed.

The following month the chairmanship of the board's Locomotive Committee also changed, J.P.Bickersteth taking over from J.T.Chance. Bickersteth was to chair the locomotive committee for the remainder of Moon's time in office, becoming a deputy chairman of the company under both Moon and his succesor Lord Stalbridge until his death in 1909. Much comment has been made on Webb's dominance of Crewe and controversial locomotive designs, but little reference has been made to the board's committee of directors who in theory set the policy.

John Pares Bickersteth was first elected to the board in February 1867 at the age of forty. Born in Liverpool, he spent his early years in India before settling in the London area. He appeared to have had no railway experience before joining the L&NW although he subsequently also became a director of the London Brighton & South Coast Railway. Bickersteth died an exceptionally wealthy man, his estate valued at over £275,000, yet he accepted paid employment as virtually a full time director of the L&NW.

Moon was also without his official deputy chairman during most of this period. Brown-Westhead had become ineffective throughout 1870 and 1871 as the result of poor health and resigned in January 1872. He had attended his last board meeting as far back as November 1869. Poor health too finally led Cawkwell to consider his future. Was the seemingly inexhaustible Moon setting too demanding a pace?

Cawkwell wrote to Moon on 17 March 1871:

> I regret having to inform you that in consequence of my failing health and inability to apply that active supervision which is absolutely necessary to manage a large railway like the L&NW, I feel bound in justice to myself as well as the interest of the company to intimate that I can not continue to hold my present position longer than the twelve months ... necessary to give notice for its termination.

50. W.Cawkwell
William Cawkwell, replaced Huish as L&NW general manager in 1858 and
appointed director from 1874, becoming one of two deputy chairman in 1881
until his death in 1897. NRM

51. G.Findlay
George Findlay, joined L&NW in 1862, becoming goods manager in
1866 and general manager in 1881. Knighted May 1892 but fell ill
in December and died early 1893. NRM

Thanking you for the many acts of kindness conferred
upon me during my service with the company as especially
the consideration shown to me of late.

The board accepted Cawkwell's notice to retire and trusted 'that
his health may soon be re-established'. Significantly it was agreed to
defer a decision on replacing him.

It is difficult to assess the relationship between Moon and
Cawkwell and the contribution the latter made to the development
of the L&NW between his appointment in 1858, when he replaced
the authoritarian Huish, to the notice he gave in 1871 to retire.
During this time Moon had increasingly given more responsibility
to Cawkwell's principal lieutenants Mason and Findlay for traffic
and goods management respectively, leaving Cawkwell freer to
handle the parliamentary business and negotiations with competing
companies. With his experience as a former manager of the L&Y,
Cawkwell should have been well placed to take the lead in resolving
any differences between the two companies. However whatever
succession plans Moon had for the management of the L&NW were
upset by the premature death of Mason.

As Neele put it, Mason was a 'shrewd and indefatigable man of
business, after the chairman's own heart'. By the end of 1864 Mason
had become assistant general manager at a salary of £1,500 p.a. In
October 1867 this had been increased to £2,000.

Mason's high standing with Moon was reflected in the unusually
generous tribute minuted at the September 1869 board when the
death of 'the trusted manager' was reported. Moon and Brown-
Westhead were authorised to 'present to his family in such a way
as they think best ... a sum equal to one years salary'. Mason's loss
was particularly keenly felt as Cawkwell had already begun to be
frequently absent through illness.

Mason's early death in 1869 brought George Findlay to the fore.
However with Cawkwell retaining an overall brief he was not to be
officially designated general manager until 1881, when Cawkwell
was appointed one of two deputy chairman of the company. Findlay
had shown talent from an early age. He had been only twenty-one
in 1851 when contractor Brassey gave him the job of overseeing the
building of the Shrewsbury & Hereford Railway and, on Brassey

taking the lease to operate the company, Findlay became his local manager. It was on the expiry of Brassey's lease in 1862 that he joined the L&NW as their local representative in the joint L&NW and GW takeover. Further recognition of his skills led to him being selected in January 1866 to manage under Cawkwell the overall company's goods and minerals traffic; and in 1874 he was promoted further as chief traffic manager to relieve Cawkwell of more routine details. Some commentators have suggested that on Moon's retirement Findlay, then sixty-one, declined a directorship to be his successor. As it was he did not live long to enjoy the knighthood given him in May 1892, the first of what became a traditional award for L&NW general managers, becoming ill and dying in March 1893.

Cawkwell's role in the L&NW had been shifting and it is not clear whether this was as a result of his own inclination or whether contrived by Moon. At the November 1871 board meeting, recognising that Cawkwell's resignation notice would soon expire, it was proposed to recommend him as a director at the forthcoming February half-yearly meeting. However the motion explained that when elected a director Cawkwell would:

> Continue to superintend the working of the line, or perform any duties which the board may desire until 31 December 1872 receiving his present salary of £3,000 p.a. After that period Mr Cawkwell will receive as director £1,000 p.a. for which he will attend to parliamentary work, arbitrations, plans of works, contracts with other companies and any other matters in which the board may need his assistance.

Although this was agreed by the shareholders, incidentally proposed by Wrigley, Cawkwell did not take his seat on the board until two years later (at the end of February 1874), continuing in the meantime to act and be paid as the manager but in the limited role as described above.

Meanwhile the company was recovering strongly from the recession. In February 1871 Moon had boasted that the annual rate of dividend at 7¼% was the highest for twenty-three years (although he added the same rate had been achieved for the second half of 1864). He commented 'we do not need eloquence, that it is not necessary to use enticing words to beguile you into thinking that things are pleasant'. He appealed to the 'stern logic of facts and the figures of the accounts for the record of our stewardship'. And when in August he declared a half-yearly rate of 6¾% p.a., this gave the company 7% for the year. He believed that 'no one, ten years ago, who was then present anticipated that they would ever get a 7% dividend. The directors at that time told the proprietors that they did not want merely to achieve a temporary success, but to place the concern on a solid basis of increasing value'. He said that they 'had done everything they could to make the property of solid intrinsic value, without indulging in fanciful anticipations for the future, but with a determination to make it a splendid concern to hand over to the proprietors some day'.

He concluded that August address by reminding shareholders that it was '25 years that day since all the concerns were amalgamated as the London and North Western Railway Company, and he believed it would be found that the average dividends ... were not far from 6 per cent per annum. No railway accounts looked better than those of the company; and the more they were examined the better they would like them'.

Most companies however were showing similar recoveries, none more so than the Lancashire & Yorkshire. Both companies had seen their dividends increase steadily; the L&Y had recovered from under 4% in the trough of 1862 to rise to almost 8½% in 1872. The L&NW had at first recovered more strongly but by 1866 had fallen a ½% or so behind.

With competition from the Cheshire Lines Committee, the L&Y and L&NW had been driven to protect their interests in Lancashire with a series of traffic agreements, bringing some order to their competing interweaving lines. At one time the L&NW had feared a possible combination of the L&Y and Midland, but the Midland joining the CLC had changed that. Despite the L&Y's objection to the Midland abandoning their Carlisle line, this closer cooperation with the L&NW was to prove a critical shift in railway politics. A progression from traffic agreements to total amalgamation was now on the cards. Previous attempts at such an outcome had foundered on both an inability to agree terms and opposition from traders fearing monopolistic control of local markets such as Liverpool.

It seemed that changes in management at the L&Y and untimely deaths of successive chairman, as well as the CLC threat, had hastened the renewal of merger discussions. J.Smithells the L&Y manager, considered by Tootal in correspondence with George Wilson to be another Huish, had resigned at the end of 1867 to become general manager of the Caledonian. He was replaced by W.Thorley who had been a colleague of Cawkwell in their early days together on the Manchester & Leeds Railway (predecessor of the L&Y). Tootal, as ever, had retained a close relationship with Wilson, deputy chairman of the L&Y and chairman when Wickham (chairman since 1853) died at the end of 1867. And when Wilson in turn died in December 1870 and the L&Y chair passed to the veteran T.Dugdale it seemed timely to press again for an amalgamation.

New discussions to agree terms then quickly progressed and both companies called their shareholders to special general meetings on 20 October 1871 to approve a merger. Moon explained that the two companies had had for many years more intimate relations than any other in England, 'their lines being very closely interlaced, and the two companies dividing an immense amount of traffic between them. In fact, they had stations side by side in all the most important towns in the county of Lancashire'. He referred to many agreements between them over a period of thirty years, the last of which was the fourteen year traffic agreement expiring at the end of 1875. He said that the proposal had stemmed from discussions by the companies' managers who had concluded that as the ramifications of the two systems had increased, the difficulties of renewing 'were so great that it was evident either that still closer relations between the two companies must be adopted or else their interests would become in many instances conflicting, perhaps largely so'.

Moon further explained that the proposal was not a new subject, having been discussed on many occasions. He said he had personally made 'arrangements' with Wickham 'which circumstances prevented being carried out'. These were similar 'to what he was about to propose'. He also referred to the fact that the L&Y's late chairman, Wilson, had made 'other proposals having a similar object, which were frustrated by his untimely death'. He went on to say that 'with the present chairman they had been on very intimate terms, and he believed it was the unanimous opinion of both boards that it was for the advantage of both companies that they should be united. The only remaining question, therefore, was one of terms'.

Uncharacteristically for Moon, the terms announced were based on permanently conceding to the L&Y shareholders a higher dividend rate. He confirmed that the L&Y was to have '12s.6d. per cent per annum more on its ordinary stock' than L&NW shareholders.

Despite criticism of the rate difference, the meeting approved unanimously the amalgamation into 'one united undertaking' and the directors were authorised to apply to Parliament and, pending the application, 'to enter into any agreement or arrangement they may deem expedient ... with respect to the working and management of the undertakings of the two companies'. It seemed that the delay in Cawkwell taking up his board appointment could have been the result of awaiting the outcome of such discussions.

At the following half-yearly meeting on 22 February 1872 most were in celebratory mood. The 8¾% dividend rate declared for the half year ending 31 December 1871 was the highest to be paid by the company under Moon's chairmanship. Moon boldly opened proceedings by asserting 'this was the last occasion on which the shareholders of the London and North Western Railway would assemble to discuss their separate interests; according to the vote of a previous meeting they were now partners in a great concern to be hereafter called the "London Lancashire and Yorkshire Railway Company"'.

Later in the meeting Moon admitted it had been a hard bargain for the company. He was satisfied though that 'if the Bill did not pass there would be no end to internecine war between the two companies; that this company would have to spend an enormous amount of capital to accommodate the districts its lines went through'. When the anomaly was pointed out to him that the L&Y had just paid 8% and the L&NW 8¾%, Moon said that the L&Y usually paid in two equal halves whereas the L&NW generally paid more in the second half. Over the last five years the L&Y had averaged 10s.6d. per cent more.

Moon further justified the premium by explaining that 'although the bargain was not a cheap one for this company, still in the long run it would be advantageous, because it would enable them to do what they could accomplish otherwise only by a large outlay of capital, and it would make their future dividends much more secure'.

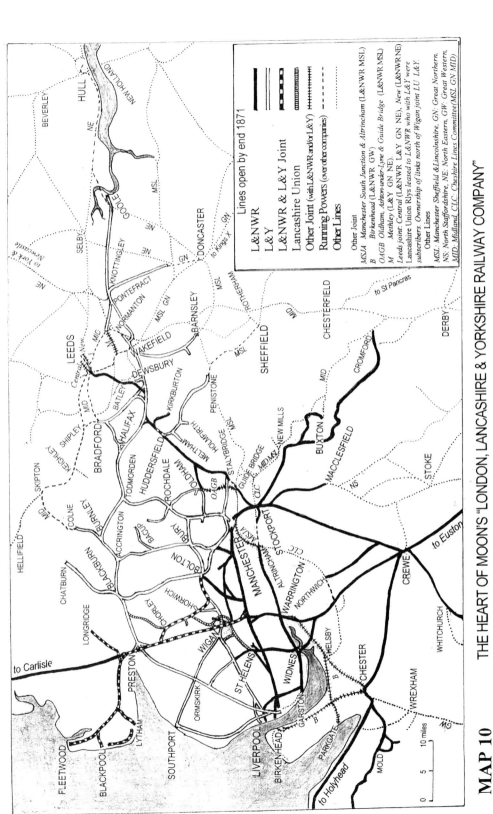

MAP 10

THE HEART OF MOON'S "LONDON, LANCASHIRE & YORKSHIRE RAILWAY COMPANY"

Position at end of 1871 when L&NWR and L&Y negotiating to amalgamate

Lines open by end 1871

L&NWR
L&Y
L&NWR & L&Y Joint
Lancashire Union
Other Joint (with L&NWR and/or L&Y)
Running Powers (over other companies)
Other Lines

Other Joint
MSJA Manchester South Junction & Altrincham (L&NWR MSL).
B Birkenhead (L&NWR GW)
OAGB Oldham, Ashton-under-Lyne & Guide Bridge (L&NWR MSL)
M Methley (L&Y GN NE).
Leeds joint: Central (L&NWR L&Y GN NE), New (L&NWR NE)
Lancashire Union Rlys leased to L&NWR who with L&Y were
subscribers. Ownership of links north of Wigan joint LU L&Y.

Other Lines
MSL: Manchester Sheffield & Lincolnshire. GN: Great Northern.
NS: North Staffordshire. NE: North Eastern. GW: Great Western.
MID: Midland. CLC: Cheshire Lines Committee (MSL GN MID)

He thought 'it was better to yield the 2s.6d. per cent which they stood out for, than to lose the advantage of union'. However John Marshall, in his L&Y history, has described the financial success of the L&Y at that time as 'the result of "cheese-paring" methods of operation' and control by 'short-sighted, money-grabbing tycoons'. He noted that 'the year of the record dividend, 1872, marked the nadir of L&Y services' with minimum expenditure being spent on locomotives, rolling stock and the permanent way. If the L&Y directors had in mind a deliberate policy of boosting dividends by deferring expenditure to improve merger terms then they succeeded.

It is to be wondered to what extent Moon and his colleagues were aware of the log jam of expenditure needing to be released, which was shortly to reduce L&Y profitability, or whether they expected the merger to render some of the work unnecessary as it would have duplicated facilities. By the end of 1873 the L&Y annual dividend had already fallen below the L&NW and was to remain significantly so for the remainder of Moon's chairmanship.

Nevertheless any doubts over the terms of the merger on the part of a few shareholders were not allowed to detract from Moon's justification. And he used the occasion of the February 1872 meeting to highlight the progress that had been made in bringing the L&NW to its pre-eminent position. It is worth quoting his review in some detail as they can be said to mark a peak in his own career.

As the capital of the merged companies would be about £105million and the amount which the company had to earn to pay the dividend and interest was so considerable, Moon quite rightly thought that 'they ought to take some pains' in asking for a second vote to approve the amalgamation:

> He proposed, therefore, to show them that when he and his friends began the resuscitation of the company in 1861 they divided among the shareholders in the half-year ending Dec. 31 £599,000 in dividend, being at the rate of 4% per annum. They now proposed to divide £1,350,000 in dividend, being at the rate of 8¾ per cent per annum.
>
> The ordinary capital in 1861 was £25,000,000 only, and in 1871 £31,000,000. They were in arrears for their law

expenses about £100,000, and had one year's bills not sent in, and also £100,000 owing on renewal account [permanent way]. They were also in arrears £25,000 upon their compensation account. If proprietors would compare how they stood that day, they would find that they had no arrears whatever upon their law account. The lawyer's bills did not come into reserve accounts - they paid them every week, and all their law expenses were paid up to 31 December last. Their compensation account was square, and they had put by £27,000 to meet contingencies accruing up to that date. The renewal of the road account had been written off for some years.

They had re-arranged their locomotive, their carriage, and their waggon departments, and had set aside such large sums every year as were amply sufficient to meet all depreciation of their property. They could say that their line and works were as intrinsically valuable as they were on the day when they were made. He did not believe it was possible, considering the enhanced prices of labour and materials, the higher prices of lands, the extra accommodation, and works now required, to construct lines cheaper, or as cheap as those which the company now possessed. They therefore stood in the race of competition better than any company in England.

He could, if it were worth while, show that they had honestly and industriously worked out for the benefit of the concern all that they had promised and undertaken at the celebrated meetings when they had unusual disturbances, and shareholders who would not believe in anybody. It was not by cleverness or by any particular policy, or by making five quarters out of one year, as the Chancellor of the Exchequer did, but by sheer hard labour, that the change in circumstances had been accomplished. In 1861 the whole amount of debenture stock issued was about £1,800,000. It was on 31 December, £8,717,000, as stated in the accounts; and since 1 January last a further sum of

£1,800,000 had been tendered for, leaving only between £7,000,000 and £8,000,000 of loans or debentures which were not converted into perpetual debenture stock. The rate of interest was down nearly to 4 per cent on the whole, and they were at present getting 102 per cent for their debenture stock, which had never been done before.

That fellow directors and shareholders agreed with him was evident by the motion that followed. It had been agreed beforehand by a group of influential shareholders that he should be formally recognised by being granted a testimonial for his contribution to the success of the company over the twenty-one years he had been a director. It is not known if Moon was aware of this beforehand. In any event the meeting recorded their conviction that it was 'to his great talents, indomitable energy, unwearied exertions, and high and honourable character, they are largely indebted for the pre-eminently sound position of their property, and the highly satisfactory dividend declared today'.

A sum of 5,000 guineas was voted 'for the purpose of presenting some fitting acknowledgement to Mr Moon and his family for the social sacrifices entailed upon them by the devotion of his entire time to the duties of his position'. Although even larger sums have been voted by other companies for recognising outstanding contributions none could have been as well deserved as Moon's in terms of dedicated service to one company. A committee was formed, which included Bancroft, H.Crosfield and Tootal, to arrange a suitable presentation 'in the manner most agreeable to Mr Moon and his family'. In acknowledging 'the compliment' Moon referred to the time when he joined the company. 'It was many years before he could get a hearing' but 'those who had been most opposed to him were now his best friends'. He added that 'if he could have had his way this company and the Midland would have been amalgamated [the L&NW and the Midland had discussed merging in Moon's early years as a director]'.

Moon remained confident that the L&Y merger would be authorized despite the Bill deposited in the 1872 session being withdrawn on the 23 July. Hearings had been suspended while a joint Select Committee of both houses of Parliament reviewed railway amalgamations generally. The Bill was to be deposited again in the next session. At his summer half-yearly meeting he was cheered on rising. He reported that in agreement with the L&Y their dividend would be at the rate of 7% and the L&Y at £7.12s.6d. 'He trusted that that would be the lowest dividend that would ever be paid by the combined undertaking, and that they were about to enter upon a course of long and uninterrupted success.'

Later in the year, on the evening of 22 November 1872, the shareholders held a presentation dinner for Moon. *The Times* newspaper called it 'a banquet on a scale of more than usual splendour'. Their reporter described the silver and jewellery presented as:

> A service of plate comprising three candelabra, two large and two small flower vases, two claret jugs, two sugar vases, four salt cellars, and a complete set of spoons, forks, and knives, all in silver, richly gilt. Accompanying this service was a lady's dressing case, a magnificent set of diamond and sapphire ornaments, and two sets of bracelets and brooches, composed of amethysts and pearls, intended as gifts to Mrs and Miss Moon.

Held in the shareholders' meeting room at Euston, the dinner was a formidable gathering chaired by the Duke of Sutherland who had been a director of the company for almost as long as Moon. The duke had on his right Mrs Moon, the Duke of Buckingham, the Duchess of Sutherland, Lord Richard Grosvenor, Miss Moon and Earl Vane; and on his left the Duchess of Buckingham, Moon, Lord Powis, Lady Grenville, Mr Lowther and Lady Stanley. Among the many other guests were colleagues including Earle, Tootal, Cawkwell and Reay.

In toasting the queen, the chairman said he was happy to hear of her safe return to England and raised a laugh when he added there was no better place to rest than a L&NW railway carriage, whether in coming or going to Scotland. Speakers included Lord Powis, Earl Vane, Admiral Evans, Colonel Bourne, the Duke of Buckingham, Childers and Sir Daniel Gooch. In toasting Moon, Sutherland said that twenty years had elapsed since he had first met him and he believed there had but very few hours of those twenty years in which he (Moon) had not been occupied in thinking of the welfare of the railway and the best mode of promoting the interests of the shareholders. In referring to the gift he said what made it more pleasant to receive as well as more agreeable to present was that Mrs and Miss Moon had not been forgotten.

In his response Moon said he could not feel otherwise than proud at the honour which had been paid him and, as *The Times* reported, he thought:

> That next to the approval of a man's own conscience there was nothing more valuable in life than the esteem and good will of those by whom he is surrounded. Since he began, twenty-two years ago, to take part in the management of the company's affairs he had done everything in his power to promote its prosperity. There were some who thought that the effort could not be successful, but he had received much kind aid and encouragement from such men as the Duke of Buckingham and Lord Wolverton; and though many of his colleagues had succumbed in the struggle, he was glad to think their ranks had been filled up, and that the direction still presented a united band ready to achieve even greater success than had hitherto been attained. As for the magnificent testimonial which he saw before him, he could not too cordially thank the shareholders for the kindness which prompted them to give him such a proof of the estimation in which they held such services as he had been able to render them.

52. Testimonial 1872

Part of service of silver plate presented to Mr & Mrs Moon at a testimonial dinner given by L&NW shareholders on 22 November 1872. ILN

53. Board Room Euston

L&NW Board Room at Euston in 1897 where Moon had hardly missed a meeting for forty years from being elected a director in 1851 to retirement as chairman in 1891. NRM

CHAPTER 18

SOME PERSONAL ASPECTS

Moon was fifty-eight when feted by his company in 1872. A generation had passed since the young man, unknown outside the commercial world of Liverpool, had taken his family out of the environs of an unhealthy city and retired to rural Worcestershire. It seems timely therefore to pause at this high point in his career to attempt some details of his personal life, a task made difficult by the absence of family papers and, as the *Liverpool Courier* noted, Moon's 'almost morbid objection' to divulging any facts concerning himself.

His three children when he left Liverpool in 1847 were all under six: Edward, Richard and Eleanor. By the summer of 1854, he was to have three more: John Arthur, Edith and Ernest. These completed his family. All had been born in the first fourteen years of his marriage to Eleanor; the first in June 1841 nine months and a week from their marriage day, with the subsequent children following at two to three year intervals, all born in the summer months. He was elected L&NW chairman the day after the seventh birthday of Ernest, their youngest.

Despite the inconvenience of not living on his railway, Moon seems to have settled happily at Bevere. And certainly Eleanor must have done so for they were to remain there until the children were well into their teens. His reservations in the autumn of 1858, telling Chandos he could only take on extra duties temporarily ('to give as much time as I do at present is not fair to me and would alter the whole course of my life'), is only understandable in the context of loyalty to his immediate and wider family. No other interest has been traced to suggest some other time absorbing activities were pressing.

It is possible that at this time Moon was concerned for the health of his elder daughter Eleanor who, as has been seen, died in January

1859. And there could have been conflict with his eldest son. The sixteen-year old Edward had been in his second of only two years at Edinburgh University (1857/58) when his records show his home address was changed from Worcester to Liverpool. Descendants of Moon's second son believed there had been a rift. When Edward died in middle age on a fishing holiday in April 1893 (recuperating with his family after a winter's illness), his brothers attended the funeral but his sister Edith and their widowed seventy-eight year old father did not. Whether this was a result of Moon's own health is not known.

Richard, the second son, was fifteen when he also was sent to Edinburgh for further education. Though it was not uncommon for English boys to be sent to Scotland it was usually for non-conformist reasons. This seems unlikely with Moon, given his subsequent duties in the Claines parish and his brother Robert's career at Cambridge. No details of Liverpool schooling have been found, but it could be that being dissatisfied with local progress, Moon took advantage of the low standards for university acceptance, the first year being the equivalent of secondary schooling, to improve his boys' prospects. And it had been a course his own father had pursued with him.

Family commitments would have included Moon's joint trusteeship with brother Robert over investments for their sisters. Moon had the business background to take the lead in this. Additionally his uncles in retirement may possibly have looked to him for advice, particularly over railway stock. Moon and his brother were named as executors for their Uncle Edward's estate in 1880.

Moon's work for the Claines parish could have fed the rumour that he wished to join the church. But even when he became active in many of his railway company's committees, he never joined the one responsible for churches and schools; although he had chaired one in 1860 to ensure that, in working Sundays, all employees were given time for attending divine service. In his later years, especially in retirement in Coventry, he contributed generously but anonymously to his church. Incidentally his brother Robert also proved to be a generous benefactor to his Cambridge college.

Robert Moon had a long association with Cambridge, being a fellow of Queens' from 1839 to 1858 and an honorary fellow from 1868. He met the cost of restoring the hall windows with new stonework and tracery and the fireplace with new decoration. Admitted to the Inner Temple in 1838 he was called to the bar in 1844. He published a study of the Old Testament *Light Explained: The Pentateuch and Joshua Considered*. He was forty when in 1857 he married Mary, the daughter of Robert Pacy of Rio de Janeiro and Liverpool so maintaining the family link with Brazil. They also had six children. He died in Paris in 1889.

Neither Edward nor Richard graduated at Edinburgh. No record has been found of where Moon sent his third son, John Arthur. By the time youngest son, Ernest Robert, was of age, Moon had changed from Scottish university education to the English public school (Winchester). He seems to have regarded the two systems as comparable alternatives, once referring to himself and his colleagues as having 'the benefit of old institutions both in England and Scotland and of the public schools and other facilities'. Moon's brother also sent his sons to Winchester.

Maintaining a contented family base at Bevere had clearly been important to Moon. However an eventual move was almost inevitable once it became clear that his career as full time chairman of the L&NW was secure and the ties of family began to loosen. Only the seventeen year old daughter Edith was still at home when they moved to Tamworth in October 1868 immediately after the marriage in Worcester the previous month of their second son, Richard, to local girl Sarah Blakeney. And the fourteen year old Ernest had started his first term at Winchester. Edward, the oldest son had married two years earlier. The other son John Arthur would have been around nineteen at the time, already embarked on a commercial career.

The previous April Moon had written to his L&NW colleague Stephen Reay saying that 'we are going to look at a house near Leighton on Wednesday'. This certainly would have been more convenient for London and perhaps made the later move to Harrow unnecessary. However they eventually chose a more central location for the railway as a whole. From the addresses given in subsequent railway correspondence, Moon probably moved to Wigginton Lodge, Tamworth, around the weekend of 12/13 October 1868. He wrote to Reay a week later thanking him for his good wishes. 'We are in a sad mess still but things are righting themselves gradually.'

54. Robert Moon

Robert Moon (1817-89), Moon's brother, fellow of Queens' College Cambridge and called to the bar in 1844. Canon Moor

55. Wigginton Lodge, Tamworth

Wigginton Lodge, Tamworth, first house bought by Moon. He moved from Bevere in 1868 to be more centrally located for the L&NW after over twenty years in the Worcester area. Tamworth Library

Reay, a fellow Liverpool man, had been running the L&NW's Audit department for over ten years when Moon made him company secretary in 1866. Not only a close confidant, Reay seems, unusually for a company officer, to have become a personal friend. Both he and his wife Emily were staying at Wigginton Lodge when the 1871 census was taken. On Reay's death in 1888 Moon showed a side of his character that was far from coldly unemotional. He made the L&NW Board record a glowing tribute. This not only referred to 'irreparable loss' and 'conspicuous ability', sparing himself 'no labour' in the best interests of the company and employees, but by 'his kindness, courtesy and ability, and by his constant readiness to assist in every difficulty he had endeared himself to every member of the board'.

This minute, as will be seen clearly written to reflect Moon's personal views, continued, 'and they feel by his death they have lost not only an invaluable officer but a personal friend on whose fidelity, sound judgement and cordial cooperation they could always rely. They trust that his example will not be forgotten while any remain who have served the company with or under him'. This tribute was sent officially to Mrs Reay and Moon had her reply formally minuted when she thanked the board for an appreciation 'so beautifully worded and such a joy to her to know how greatly he was beloved and valued by those whom he has been so long connected'. Even allowing for the rhetoric of grief, this view of how her husband was perceived was markedly at odds with what Neele recorded. In noting that Reay had been secretary for twenty-two years and the confidential friend of the chairman during all this time, Neele wrote that 'by the outside public, he was considered very cold and unsympathetic, and while admiring the strict justice he displaced, the officers at headquarters coincided very generally in the public verdict'.

Moon led the strong L&NW presence of directors and officers at the funeral. It was one of the few such events where he attended in person. If Neele was correct in his views then there could well have been the necessity for a three-line whip to ensure the unprecedented number of company officials listed as attending. Neele's comment on the death of Moon's other close confidant and friend, Henry Crosfield, could not have been in greater contrast. In his account of a visit by L&NW directors in 1881 to the railways of Canada and the United States, which had been enthusiastically organised by Crosfield, Neele refers to the 'dark shadow' thrown by his death.

He wrote that 'those of you who knew Mr Henry Crosfield will be aware what a chatty and genial man he was, he won golden opinions on the voyage, and was the most popular man on the ship'. Neele quotes the example that following the birth of a baby to an Irish immigrant, 'Mr Crosfield's fatherly kindness was at once elicited and he managed to collect a very handsome sum for the benefit of the woman and baby. On the Sunday afternoon prior to our reaching New York this baby ... made, by Mr Crosfield's arrangement, a triumphal procession through the saloon and was received with loud applause'.

The 'dark shadow' Neele referred to was indeed tragic. In January 1882, after weeks of depression and a visit with his doctor to London, Crosfield returned home to Liverpool and committed suicide by cutting his throat. He was buried on 1 February in the graveyard of the Society of Friends chapel at Penketh, near Warrington. Though a report mentioned six coaches of mourners no names were given. It is not known if Moon attended, nor if Henry was related to the Crosfields of Warrington who founded the soapworks there. A clearly shocked Moon called a special board meeting for the following day in London to pay tribute; thirteen of his directors were present including George Crosfield. It was at this meeting that Waterhouse was formally appointed to succeed Crosfield. At the company's half-yearly meeting, a little over two weeks later, Moon opened by telling shareholders that no doubt 'you will notice with great regret that the signature of Henry Crosfield is no longer appended to your accounts. The correctness of those accounts has been testified by him for more than 30 years'. Then under great emotion he was only able to continue by saying, 'I am not going to trust myself to say more. Our friend has gone away from amongst us, but his work remains, and the best memorial you can raise to him is to see that the accounts of this company over which he has so long watched, shall be hereafter, by ourselves and our successors, as honestly and truly kept, and show everything as faithfully as before'.

In fact a more physical memorial was raised to him, a bust placed in the half-yearly meeting room at Euston which read:

Henry Crosfield
This bust embodies the unanimous vote of the proprietary
of the London and North Western Railway in grateful
acknowledgement of more than 30 years distinguished
services, especially as their Auditor, to which Mr Crosfield's
singular gifts gave an exceptional prestige and power.

In contrast to the isolation of Bevere, Moon found himself at Wigginton Lodge quite literally overlooking his railway and within a mile or so of Tamworth station. The house of Georgian origin stood on the slopes above the Trent Valley main line in forty-five acres of park land. Unlike his tenancies in Worcester he bought Wigginton Lodge, the first property he actually owned. The value at the time has not been found but it failed to reach a reserve of £9,500 in 1862, but in 1878 the estate was sold for £14,300. Moon's holding of L&NW stock, as listed in the company reports, had been increasing progressively at this time: £16,512 in 1861, £25,000 in 1866, and £28,049 in 1871. Whatever funds he realised to purchase property obviously did not come from his personal stake in the L&NW. Wigginton Lodge still exists but with housing developed on the estate and the actual house used by a local rugby club.

The contrast between the outskirts of a cathedral city such as Worcester and the small borough of Tamworth must have been as great for his wife in her personal life as it was for Moon in access to his railway. Having previously considered Stafford further north and then Leighton nearer London, Moon's choice of Tamworth could well have been a compromise pre-empted by its central position for both Euston and the prospect of the Lancashire & Yorkshire merger.

The 1871 census shows his house servants as a butler and six others; in addition there would have been a coachman and gardeners as there was a entrance lodge and a home farm forming part of the estate. No account has been found to show whether the two women then in his life, his wife Eleanor and unmarried daughter Edith, found Wigginton Lodge, or life in Tamworth, enjoyable. Within five years they had moved again.

It is possible that the failure of the merger and the inevitable logic of a home-counties base for the Euston offices drove the move to Harrow Weald in the autumn of 1873.

Moon was still shown at Wigginton Lodge on 25 August 1873 when his uncle William's will was proved. However he was listed at Woodlands, Harrow Weald by the following February's L&NW half-yearly meeting. Woodlands was one of a number of imposing large houses off Clamp Hill. Thought to have been built around 1780 and extended in the 1840s, the house at one time had grounds of about twenty acres. In the 1940s it was bought by the then Harrow UDC but sold in 1972 to the local hospital board for possible re-development. However, badly vandalised it became derelict and subsequently demolished.

At one time the home of Lord Catto, Governor of the Bank of England, Woodlands with its Georgian ceilings and mouldings, marble fireplaces, carved wooden panelling and grand staircase must have provided a fitting home for the chairman of what was once Britain's largest company. Typically Moon is not recorded locally in contemporary records as being a noteworthy businessman, but as one of the chief donors to the building fund for Holy Trinity church at Wealdstone.

At the time of Moon's move to Harrow Weald, he was fifty-nine. It would be surprising if he had not seen this as a final move to be more conveniently located for his office in Euston and possibly to see out his final years in retirement. Although his constant travelling over the line would still have kept him frequently away from home, it made sense for him to be based within daily commuting distance of his headquarters. But apparently either he or his wife, or both, or even his daughter, did not take to living in the home counties.

Within two years of moving to Woodlands, the Moons lost their twenty-six year old son John Arthur. One of only two occasions Moon missed a board meeting in thirty years as chairman was on 20 November 1875. With Bancroft in the chair the board expressed 'its heartfelt sympathy with the chairman and his family in this crushing blow which coming from a distant land has struck them in their nearest affections'.

John Arthur Moon, merchant, died in Valparaiso on 14 November. His death (the certificate does not give the cause) was reported by Archibald Roxburgh, who was shown as a merchant living there. No information has been traced on his business. It is possible they were in partnership. Before 1914, when the Panama Canal opened,

56. Woodlands, Harrow

Woodlands at Harrow Weald, Moon's imposing residence where he moved in
1873 after only five years in Tamworth. Harrow Library

57. Copsewood Grange, Coventry

Copsewood Grange, Coventry, the multi-bedroomed mansion in 200 acres Moon
bought for the last decade of his chairmanship and into his retirement years.
Warwickshire Record Office

Valparaiso was a key trading and staging port for European shipping rounding Cape Horn for the west coast of the Americas.

How much his son's death affected the Moons' life in Harrow Weald can only be speculated upon. He was unmarried and was the closest brother in age to his sister Edith who never married. Why Moon chose to move back to the midlands, to a town with no evident family or business connections, as with so many other aspects of his personal life, is not known. Although at the 1881 census, Moon, Eleanor and daughter Edith were still shown at Woodlands, it is likely he moved that year, for by then he had already negotiated the purchase of Copsewood Grange at Stoke near Coventry. It looks as if he had bought the property by the end of 1879 or early 1880. The house was built on the site of an older house, which had been demolished by a Coventry ribbon manufacturer, James Hart, whose mills and the large mansion became known locally, when his business declined, as 'Hart's Folly'. The following details are taken from an estate agent's auction particulars after Moon's death.

Located 'about two miles from Coventry on the road to Binley and Combe, the estate comprised an 'imposing family mansion, in the Italian style, built at a large cost in 1872'. The approach from the main road was 'by a carriage drive through an avenue of fine old elms with picturesque lodge at entrance and standing in delightful pleasure grounds of considerable extent'. The grounds were 'laid out with much taste, adorned by noble cedars of Lebanon and other handsome timber, and surrounded by several enclosures of undulating park-like pasture and meadow lands, studded with fine timber and interspersed with plantations of well grown oak, ash, beech etc.'.

There were 'excellent ranges of horticultural buildings' and 'a large and highly productive walled-in kitchen garden', stabling for six horses, a coach-house and harness-room. Included was a 'suitable farmstead, placed at a convenient distance from the mansion, two ornamental cottages for bailiff and gardener and labourer's cottage, the entire estate embracing an area of about 145 acres in a ring fence [207 acres in the 1897 *History of Stoke*]'.

The mansion itself was described as standing 'upon a gentle eminence, commanding fine views over a well wooded country, and affords every accommodation for a family position. ... Exceedingly well appointed, admirably arranged', the accomodation included 'a vestibule, spacious hall and three noble reception rooms, billiard room, boudoir or morning room, and about twenty bed, dressing and other rooms'. There were 'capital cellars and the customary out-offices' with gas laid on and 'an abundant supply of good water'.

What made the then sixty-five year old Moon purchase a muli-bedroom mansion in 200 hundred odd acres for only himself, wife, thirty year old daughter and a modest complement of servants in an area where he had no previous association is difficult to understand. It is tempting to conclude that, given his own lack of ostentation, it was his wife who made the choice; that she saw the opportunity as no more than fitting for a man in his position. Even more splendid than Woodlands, the estate was a residence to rank with those of the grandees with whom her husband had for so long been associating.

In such a large house it is mischievous to speculate whether Moon ever chastised his servants, or even his wife or daughter, over the number of rooms he allowed to be lit by the gas. However from what can be gathered from several references it does appear that Moon and his wife made generous use of the facilities in welcoming visitors to stay, not just from their intermingled Moon and Brocklebank families but also colleagues from the railway world.

All of Moon's surviving sisters had married, some very well financially, none more so than the eldest, Eliza. Seventy-four when she died in 1885, Eliza had no need of any watching care from her brothers. Her husband Ralph Brocklebank's estate was valued at over £790,000 on his death in 1892. Ralph had not only been the senior partner in the family trading and ship owning business, but also chairman of the Royal Insurance Company. For over thirty years he had been an active member of Liverpool's Dock Committee and subsequently the Mersey Docks and Harbour Board, serving as its chairman for six years. He contributed generously to the Royal Infirmary and to charities in particular the Seamen's Orphanage.

In 1864 Brocklebank's eldest son, also Ralph, became a partner in T&J Brocklebank and established a name for himself in the commercial community of Liverpool, which led to him being proposed for a vacancy on the L&NW board. Whether Moon was in favour of having his nephew on the board, he was careful to ensure that his election in 1883 was proposed by Liverpool shareholders and not from fellow board members. The vacancy arose through the illness of James Bland who had effectively resigned in October 1881. A Liverpool timber merchant, Bland had been elected by shareholders to the board in 1869. Moon had agreed that he could retain his seat until someone suitable to represent Liverpool interests could be found to replace him. Bland wrote to Moon in January 1883 saying 'I am truly pleased to hear that Mr Ralph Brocklebank Junior is now strong enough to take a seat on the L&NW board'.

Brocklebank was elected at the half-yearly meeting the following month. One of the committees he joined was Moon's old one, the Stores, which he subsequently chaired. Whether his uncle's single-minded example of dedication had any influence or not, Ralph severed his partnership in the family business in 1886. He never married and his most notable work in Liverpool was as honorary treasurer and donor to the Royal Infirmary where he was largely responsible for raising the funds to rebuild the hospital. Incidentally his youngest brother, born in 1842, the year of his maternal grandfather's death, was given as first names Richard Moon. The connection between the two families was obviously a close one.

Although he was not to retire for another ten years Moon, in moving to Coventry, does seem to have put the uncertainties of Tamworth and Harrow Weald behind him, with Eleanor and Edith apparently settling more contentedly.

As will be covered later, it seems that Eleanor or Edith, or both, could have been instrumental in persuading Moon to accept his baronetcy in 1887. However as Lady Moon, Eleanor had not long to enjoy her title. Little is known about her character. Their marriage lasted for over half a century. No evidence has been found to suggest that they had ever been other than devoted to each other. Not only must she have been a loyal wife and mother, but with his numerous absences from home, a capable manager of their household. Her illness in 1890 was probably the deciding factor that hastened Moon's retirement. As Neele was to write, her death must have devastated him and strengthened the ties with his unmarried daughter Edith.

Edith was to remain Moon's faithful companion throughout his retirement years. She lived to be ninety-eight, dying in Bath in 1947: a grandniece remembering her as a 'good and kind person'. She had out-lived a lease on a flat in London and moved with her faithful maid Hughes into a hotel in Bath.

Although his L&NW stock holding at the time of purchasing Copsewood Grange was still exceptional, Moon had in fact reduced it to just under £41,000. What other investments he held has not been determined, but at some stage he had investments in the Great Western Railway company (possibly from his uncles) whose dividend record, although never matching the L&NW, had been on a rising trend since a low point in 1878. However he must have spread his investments widely, the gross value of his estate on his death was over £394,000. His inheritance from his father's personal estate and his relatively modest L&NW chairman's fee could not account for the accumulation of such a large sum. It is possible that the original winding up of the Moon Brothers' business in the 1840s gave rise to a larger capital disbursement than thought at the time, but the most likely sources of his additional wealth were inheritances from his uncles.

It will be recalled that John in Brazil had appointed Moon as one of his executors; and on 5 August 1873 his uncle William died, with administration of his estate granted to Moon on 25 August.

Moon was one of four executors named for William's estate, the others being William's wife and his two former business partners. The others renounced in November leaving Moon to establish various trusts and legacies for William's family and charities. William had property and a merchant's business in both Liverpool and Rio de Janeiro and flax spinning and scutch mills in Antrim. The extent to which Moon personally benefitted from the disposal of William's businesses is not known but the total estate was valued in a category that would have taken it to £300,000. On the death of another uncle, Edward, Moon's inheritance is clearer.

Dying on the 10 August 1880, Edward was the last of the original brothers who formed the Moon Brothers partnership. By then well into his nineties and living in his twenty-five acre property called The Lawn at Aigburth in Liverpool, Edward had continued in business in his own right, trading with the United States, including the private banking firm Drexel Morgan in New York, which had been formed to channel European funds into North American markets. Outliving his wife and unmarried daughters, he appointed Moon, his brother Robert and Ralph Brocklebank Junior his executors. He gave all three substantial legacies, £35,000 each to the brothers and £10,000 to Brocklebank, and left the residue to Moon and his brother.

58. William Moon
William Moon (1789-1873), one of Moon's uncles, a wealthy independent
Liverpool merchant. Canon Moor

59. Stephen Reay
Stephen Reay, L&NW company secretary (1866-88) and confidant
and friend of Moon. LNWRS

His estate was valued at almost half a million pounds. An interesting reference to his youth in Lancashire is made in the local history of the area. When the Kirkland free school, the oldest in the parish of Garstang, had a new building opened in 1876 it was paid for by Edward Moon who was reported as being a former pupil.

With assured wealth, advancing years and a changing railway world, what is perhaps the most remarkable about Moon's life is that he chose to continue in gruelling full time employment. Although his company's difficulties were never to go away, the days had long gone when he needed personally to remain so dedicated. His work had clearly become not just a way of life, but what he regarded as a duty.

The banquet that honoured Moon's service to the L&NW seemed a rare occasion for him to relax and for his wife and daughter to enjoy with him the acclaim. There had no doubt been many times when both Eleanor and Edith had questioned his need for long absences on railway business or even during his hours at home to be distracted by studying reports and accounts. But there was to be no let-up in the intensity with which he resumed his duty.

CHAPTER 19

SETBACKS

There seems little doubt that Moon was genuinely convinced in 1872 that the proposed merger with the Lancashire & Yorkshire would be authorized. However, as will become obvious, he was also well aware of the fickleness of relations between Government and the railway interest.

The creation of Britain's railway network had been a piecemeal development, financed and built by private initiative. Though railway companies had to be authorised by Acts of Parliament there was no state planning of routes or services. As a result competing lines were allowed to be built and in many cases facilities duplicated. From the point of the view of investors the proliferation of new projects was seen as either a speculative opportunity or a threat to established companies. Parliament was lobbied both to promote and throw out Bills. As early as his second half-yearly meeting as chairman, Moon had controversially challenged the system when he commented on the 'grievous injustice which is done to us' by the 'bête noire of all railway management, that is, Parliament and its proceedings'. The costs in seeking parliamentary approval for new lines and agreements, or, even more critically, opposing competitive developments could result in, to use Moon's word, 'fabulous' expenditure. His outburst at the time indicates his frustration:

> No general principle has been laid down by Parliament; there has been nothing to guide us as to what their policy may be. One committee upholds one principle; another committee is under no necessity to follow it, and may uphold another principle. The only principle they seem to act upon is that, having encouraged us to undertake large works, and to bring our undertaking to a successful result, Parliament encourages somebody else to come and

knock it down. Even where railway companies have been attacked wrongfully, the railway company has no remedy. The committee throws out the Bill, but there is no penalty that the wrong doer should pay the costs of both parties, as in common law cases. We are fleeced on both sides.

In his February 1865 meeting reference had been made to a Royal Commission announced by Gladstone (then Liberal Chancellor of the Exchequer) being set up to enquire into the "railway system". A shareholder hoped any such enquiry would 'be upon more practical principles than those which have hitherto been enunciated by Government'. He thought it 'bad in principle for the Government to issue a commission to inquire into the details of a trading company like this or any other company'; concluding that it was 'the thin edge of the wedge ... for the purpose of getting the railways into their own hands'.

Moon's response could be said to be pragmatic. It was 'entirely a commercial question' he said and 'if the Government would pay a fair price, or guarantee them a 10% dividend in perpetuity, shareholders would no doubt be ready to deal with them. But this was not at all likely, because the House of Commons would never allow any Government in this country to do such a thing'.

Moon's reference to 10% had substance in that this was the return guaranteed under legislation enacted in 1844. A young Gladstone, then at the Board of Trade under the Conservative Peel, had headed a committee charged with reviewing railway Bill procedures and the role of the state in future development. Opposed by the railway interest, his resulting Act (August 1844) nevertheless had given the Government an option for twenty-one years of purchasing newly authorized companies. Any valuation, depending on past profitability, could be based on capitalising over twenty-five years a maximum of 10% profits. However by the time the option period expired in 1865, talk of nationalisation was no longer a major issue.

In view of his strongly held views in opposing any attempt by Government to interfere in how companies were run, Moon nevertheless thought that if railway development 'had been properly regulated, the public would have had all the accommodation they had at present, at much less cost to the country and with greatly reduced rates and fares, more so indeed than they could ever hope now to see'.

He had returned to this theme in the summer of 1866. Referring to the impact of uncontrolled speculation that preceded the financial crash earlier that year, he reckoned 'Parliament seemed to be a sort of self-acting machinery for the encouragement of speculative schemes and the expenditure of capital, without license or bridle, not only by railway companies, but by steamboat companies, water companies, and gas companies'. All were borrowing and 'offering to pay in thirty years or something of that kind, and the result was it locked up more capital than could be spared. The House of Commons had ten or twelve committees all authorising the spending of money without reference to the general result; but there was not a single committee looking to the general result, nor a shred of design or policy in the whole arrangement'. He had continued that 'as long as that went on they would have an enormous waste of capital, depression of the railway interest, dissatisfaction of the public, and, what they might call this year, parliamentary panic; for it neither arose from bad trade nor bad harvest, but purely from the involvement of the money of the country'.

The following year he was again attacking the Government for a lack of what he called 'a proper system' of railway legislation and for 'some uniformity of decision, that which was done one year not being undone the next'. This criticism was confirmed by the Royal Commission findings published in 1867, particularly in reference to the lack of consistency in the conditions imposed on railway companies for raising fresh capital.

Moon's scepticism should have made him wary of the outcome of his L&Y merger. The subject of railway amalgamations generally had excited both the political and commercial world in 1872 in view of the large number of Bills submitted. The L&NW and L&Y Bill had become a national issue, as had the Midland's proposed merger with the Glasgow & South Western, which was resubmitted when it was known the lines would be physically connected by the Settle & Carlisle project.

Parliamentary views had ranged from outright state ownership to unrestrained competition. As early as 1853, a committee chaired by the then President of the Board of Trade, Edward Cardwell, had been set up to determine a policy on amalgamations. However it served only to spawn the 1854 Railway & Canal Traffic Act. It is as well to be reminded of this Act as the principles it established were to be enforced in 1872 and were fundamental to understanding later the rates and charges agitation that so dogged Moon's final chairmanship years. The Act required railways 'to afford all reasonable facilities for the receiving, forwarding, delivering of traffic, and to make no unfair distinctions between their customers'; in short, comparable mileage rates for all through traffic.

However with the continued lack of a policy on mergers, a joint Select Committee of both houses of Parliament was appointed in early 1872 to 'enquire into the subject of the amalgamations of railway companies ... and to consider whether any and what regulations should be imposed'. Sitting in the summer, again under a President of the Board of Trade (Fortesque), the Select Committee reviewed evidence from a range of experts. One of the Commons members was Childers who, from historian Cleveland-Stevens's comments, appeared to have had little empathy with his former company when questioning Cawkwell and other leading railway managers on the effect of competition. Although the committee came to no conclusion on amalgamations generally, it did refer to the favourable benefit of the mergers that had led to the formation of the North Eastern Railway. They recommended a Permanent Committee of both houses to review all amalgamation Bills, but also, more ominously, the appointment of a tribunal of three Railway Commissioners to administer more effectively the 1854 Act with the right to examine the companies rates and charges and replace existing arbitration procedures.

The Committee's report came out immediately before the L&NW's half-yearly August meeting in 1872. Moon, not having had time to appreciate the wider implications of the additional recommendations, seized on the favourable North Eastern reference and thought 'therefore Parliament would not next year refuse its assent to their Bill [L&Y merger]'. It was not to be. Nearly half a century was to pass before a merger was agreed between the two companies (the final year of their independent existence).

Moon's optimism over amalgamations was not only misplaced but soon turned to anger over the wider issue of rates and charges.

The companies had been slow to appreciate the implications of the report. Moon's dismissive reference to the 'notion' that 'some silly people had got into their heads - namely equal mileage rates', was to prove a prelude to a long and bitter struggle.

Powers to review railway operations were incorporated in a government Railway & Canal Traffic Bill which went beyond the recommendations of the Select Committee. Unfortunately when the first occasion came for Moon publicly to condemn the Bill at his February 1873 half-yearly meeting, he was confined to bed with bronchitis. It was the only such meeting he missed in all his long years in the chair. He insisted that Bancroft handle the meeting, not the senior director Benson who had been voted to chair the board meeting in his absence.

Moon clearly knew his Bancroft. He proved an able deputy, launching into an attack as fierce, if not more so, than any that could have been made by Moon himself. Although the object of his wrath was the proposed authority over railways to be vested in the Railway Commissioners, Bancroft also had his own axe to grind. Arbitration was a business in which he personally specialised. His main point however was that such action by Parliament was an unjustified interference rather than conciliatory or helpful in the management of railways. It was a view increasingly epitomized by Moon in defending the rights of companies to manage their own affairs.

The essence of the railways objection to the tribunal of Railway Commissioners was that, in Bancroft's words, it transferred to them 'the power of control, whilst the responsibility is still continued on the companies'. He thundered that the Bill proposed 'to refer all your interests, all your rights, all your arrangements and everything that affects you to a tribunal so created from which there is no appeal. And this body is to determine rights as between companies, the mileage rate that they shall take, in fact, it does what Parliament has, up to the present time, never allowed anybody to touch - namely, to fix a tariff for railways or other bodies'. The legislation, he said, 'amounts to confiscation'.

Throughout the Spring and Summer of 1873 the railway interest pressed hard to revoke what they considered penal clauses in the Bill by adopting a policy of amendments rather than outright rejection. The companies eventually succeeded in obtaining concessions, in particular a House of Lords amendment that allowed them to appeal all decisions. At a meeting of the Railway Companies Association on 11 June, Moon was prepared on this basis to compromise and urged railway MPs to support the modified Bill. However matters soon changed dramatically when, under pressure from traders, the Commons rejected the appeal amendment. The Association met again on the 3 July under Leeman of the North Eastern when Moon demanded they petition the Lords to insist on the railway companies' absolute right of appeal. It was agreed to send an immediate delegation to the Lords, which included Moon, to meet members of the Government.

The delegation was successful in that when the Board of Trade's Bill (under President Chichester Fortescue) was passed as the Railway & Canal Traffic Act on 14 July 1873, it gave the companies an unconditional right of appeal. Moon reported to his shareholders in August that Fortescue had acknowledged that the Government's original intention did "go beyond and outside the recommendation of the Joint Select Committee". Nevertheless Fortescue had justified his proposals by saying that "nothing in any special Act contained shall be construed so as to prevent the Commissioners from ordering and apportioning a through rate under this section". Moon then indignantly pointed out that the "special Acts" were 'in fact the charter of the Railway Company, and its compact with the Nation on the faith of which the lines have been made'. He then quoted a member of the Select Joint Committee who had admitted that 'if they were to hand over to the Railway Commissioners the power of revising rates that would practically amount to confiscation'.

Although the Act setting up the Railway Commissioners was a critical step along the road to enforcing the rights laid down by Cardwell in 1853, it initially contained many loopholes which the companies were not slow to exploit. Although the so-called 'permanent' committee on amalgamations met only once, in 1873, it nevertheless summarily dismissed both the L&NW/L&Y and the Midland/G&SW merger proposals. After that, as Cleveland-Stevens put it, 'the amalgamation question continued to shape its own course'.

Moon hoped that 'if the companies act together and consult each other as to what will be for our mutual advantage, the Bill may not have a very serious effect'. Clearly cynical however over being able to co-ordinate effective protest action, he warned that the Commissioners 'are capable of most seriously affecting us, and it will depend, first of all, on the prudence of the Commissioners, and on the other hand upon the mode in which we ourselves act towards each other, whether it is to be injurious to our property or otherwise. At this moment it is a lottery'.

Moon was referring to the difficulties within the RCA of not only reaching agreement but in ensuring that individual members implemented accordingly. The lack of an effective independent body, to which disputes could be referred, had led (as seen in the Chandos Watkin fracas) to leading companies attempting to mediate amongst themselves. In October 1858 delegates from some twenty companies had met under H.S.Thompson, North Eastern chairman, with the object of forming a more permanent association. Moon had tried hard then to convince Chandos that this association should be used to lobby for a Royal Commission to put some order into railway legislation. Despite the chairmen of some leading companies, including Chandos, agreeing to a committee to set up a formal body nothing of consequence resulted. Nearly ten years were to lapse before the concept of a railway companies' trade association took shape and even then not all companies were convinced of the benefits of joining.

It had been in June 1867 that representatives of the Great Northern, Lancashire & Yorkshire, L&NW, Midland and the North Eastern agreed to form a standing committee: the United Railway Companies' Committee. This comprised the chairman, deputy chairman, general manager and solicitor of each member (the GW and the MS&L were later invited to join). They resolved to 'meet from time to time to consider questions affecting specially these companies, or generally the whole "railway interest", and if practicable, to recommend to their respective boards some uniform course of action with reference thereto'.

Thompson was again voted chairman; Brown-Westhead, Cawkwell and Blenkinsop were the L&NW delegates with Blenkinsop appointed honorary association solicitor. Although Moon joined his delegates for the next meetings, he was not hopeful of their success, especially 'the difficulty that existed in companies coming to any general arrangement among themselves'. He commented that it often happens that 'although many of the companies agreed to adopt a certain course of action, one company dissented therefrom, and reserved entire freedom of action, the result necessarily being that the good that was suggested could not be carried out, and all the companies suffered'. He thought that 'in matters of this sort the minority should adopt the views of the majority'.

Though Moon's attendance at these meetings was irregular, other chairmen and senior directors continued to meet regularly and the membership grew as the benefit of becoming a focus for exerting pressure both in and out of Parliament was seen. Directors who were MPs also routinely attended. In 1870 the membership assumed the name of the original proposal, the Railway Companies' Association. Moon had proposed Leeman as chairman in 1873 with Gooch of the GW the deputy; and the pair acted together until 1881.

Originally a director of the York & North British (a constituent of the North Eastern), George Leeman, MP for York, had been deputy chairman of the North Eastern for nearly twenty years and from 1874 chairman until his retirement in 1880. It is worth noting that although Gooch and Moon were elected chairman and deputy respectively for 1881, Moon declined the following year to be re-elected, refusing to be considered as Gooch's replacement as chairman (voting for M.W.Thompson of the Midland). Despite his standing as chairman of the largest member company Moon resisted any further moves to appoint him to a leadership position until near retirement. However he frequently chaired meetings in the absence of the elected chair or deputy. In 1887 he relented, accepting the deputy position by typically commenting that 'he should not be doing his duty in the present serious state of affairs if he altogether declined to accept' and that 'he would be happy to serve them'.

One of the issues at the time of the 1873 Traffic Act over which the RCA failed to agree was on the question of taxing passenger fares. A duty had initially been imposed in 1832 on the basis of ½d. per four passengers carried, but in 1842 it was simplified to 5% on all fares. Some relief was given two years later in Gladstone's 1844 Act. The concept of 'cheap trains' was introduced, aimed at encouraging companies to run at least one train a day for third class passengers paying fares not exceeding 1d. a mile and stopping at every station. Fares on these third class trains were exempted from duty. Discretionary powers were given to the Board of Trade in the Act to dispense with any conditions except the 1d. a mile, provided any alternative arrangements made were more beneficial and convenient to 3rd class passengers. As services improved, the condition that the exemption applied only to trains stopping at every station appears to have been, by default, waived. The authorities apparently had accepted the companies' view that as the original intent had been to offer better facilities for third class travel then the provision of additional faster trains was in the spirit of the Act. This view was later challenged by the Inland Revenue who prepared a test case in the late 1860s against the North London Railway, claiming six years back duty on passengers not travelling on trains stopping at all stations (the NL did not have third class but charged only 1d. mile on second).

In the meantime the Government considered simplifying the duty further by levying a flat 2% on all passengers (or even 1% on all *traffic* which would have considerably increased the tax burden on companies). Moon, in optimistically responding to a query on the passenger duty at his shareholders meeting in August 1870, had explained that there 'were a great many difficulties connected with that question, because the interests of the different companies and the mode in which it affected them were very different - some companies' traffic being chiefly passenger, and others nearly all goods or minerals'. He conceded that 'in their own case it was not so serious a thing as in some others, though they paid a considerable portion of the total passenger duty - perhaps 1/5th or 1/6th'. He thought it 'was not fair to say that the company had shifted the tax on to the shoulders of the public. No doubt the case was different with some of the other companies; but inasmuch as the Chancellor of the Exchequer had acknowledged practically that the tax was untenable, there was no doubt that sooner or later he would have to abandon it'.

The Government did not abandon the duty and it was thirteen years before any significant concession was made. The 'many difficulties' to which Moon alluded weakened the combined companies' efforts to present a united front, for example the southern companies, handling mainly passenger traffic into London, demanded more extreme action to repeal the duty.

The North London case eventually came to court in 1872; the point at issue being whether the Board of Trade had the right to dispense with the requirement for trains to stop at all stations in order for duty on 3rd. class to be remitted. The North London was closely associated with the L&NW who was the largest shareholder, appointing six of its own directors to the thirteen strong board, with the L&NW's Bancroft in the chair. Moon brought the Inland Revenue claim before the Railway Companies Association and demanded a meeting with the Chancellor of the Exchequer. Following correspondence between the chairman of the Association and the Prime Minister (Gladstone since 1868), a delegation from sixteen companies met Gladstone and his chancellor in December 1872. Leeman presented the case for the companies pointing out the unfairness of railways still having to pay duty on passengers when other forms of transport had been relieved of the tax. He asked for the abolition of all duty as soon as an opportunity arose or when the chancellor had a surplus. Moon was the other main speaker.

Moon maintained that there had been 'no intimation of the claim for duty upon traffic earned during the six years antecedent to 1869 when the Board of Inland Revenue first made the claim'. The companies had 'divided amongst their shareholders the amounts claimed, and ... had, therefore no fund at their disposal to meet such an emergency'. He stressed the 'great importance of the question to the companies and trusted the Premier would relieve them altogether of the passenger duty'.

The North London joined the RCA in early 1873 and Bancroft became a member of the association's Parliamentary committee lobbying against the duty (although he was not an MP). Leeman and Moon proposed another meeting with Gladstone. A written submission was made but Gladstone's reply in August regretted he could not see how the duty could be remitted. Moon however was telling his shareholders at the time that pressure to remit the duty on all 3rd class was 'irresistible'. A Railway Shareholders' Association had begun to be very active and a Railway Passenger Duty Repeal Association formed.

In March 1874 a concerned Moon was raising at the RCA the Revenue's claim on the North London and reported that the tax officials had already written to the L&NW demanding that duty be paid on all their 3rd class trains not calling at every station. His earlier view that the North London case would be decided in their favour, and that total abolition was a real possibility, was now looking increasingly unlikely. The RCA sought a meeting with the new administration (Gladstone had given way to Disraeli) and a deputation headed by Leeman and Moon met Northcote the new chancellor.

Moon reminded the chancellor of the reasons for the original 3rd class exemption. He pointed out, that following the 1846 amalgamation that created the L&NW, their fares had been reduced. He called it a 'a bargain made with Parliament' (rates per mile for 1st, 2nd and 3rd classes of 3d., 2½d. and 2d. respectively, had been reduced to 2d., 1½d. and 1d.) and that 'we should be entitled to charge a part of the duty on our passenger fares' and that with regard to 3rd class there was a 'special exemption made in the interest of the working classes'. He argued that it was out of date to assume 'that a train which was to carry the cheap passenger should stop at every station all the length of the line. To day we enable a third class passenger to get from London to Carlisle in seven or eight hours, and if it took him a day and half his labour for one day would be lost'. And he reiterated the point that the companies had 'not provided against the contingency which has now arisen ... nor did any one dream that such a claim as has now been set up ... would be ever put forward'. He claimed that 'not only has the policy of the company benefited the working classes, but since the universal adoption of the third class carriages on all trains the Board of Trade has sanctioned the principle'. He protested that 'we ought not to be put to the expense of fighting this question which the Government has been afraid to try with us for several years, but that for the future it should be settled upon some clear and tangible basis'.

But the real issue had now become not the 3rd class remission conditions, but the abolition of duty altogether. Moon aggressively concluded 'it is in the interest of the country that there should be no tax upon locomotion. It is amongst those taxes which are injurious to the prosperity of the country'. The tax 'presses upon' railway shareholders as 'an income-tax, which no other class is subject to'. He believed that the 'proper conclusion to come to is to abolish and abandon the tax'. This view was echoed by Samuel Laing, the London Brighton & South Coast chairman, whose company had the highest proportion of passenger revenue to total receipts, and C.H.Parkes, who though chairman of the Great Eastern Railway was speaking on behalf of the Railway Shareholders' Association. Laing neatly, if somewhat misleadingly, put the cost in perspective: his company had paid a 'miserable' dividend for three consecutive years of 12s. per cent (£50,000), whereas in the same three years had paid £60,000 in local tax and £40,000 in duty (these were not the last three years).

The Government whilst not unsympathetic was not prepared to make changes in the duty without obtaining some concessions from the companies, which they in turn were not prepared to offer. Gladstone had earlier suggested, for example, more favourable 3rd. class return fares. However no changes were made and the matter came to a head in the summer of 1874 when judgement in the North London case was given in favour of the Revenue. Duty would not be remitted on 3rd. class fares other than those on trains stopping at all stations.

At the 14 July RCA meeting called to discuss the implications, Moon's first reaction, as was that of Gooch and Parkes, was to propose the withdrawal of all the other trains carrying 3rd. class passengers. However calmer views prevailed and the general managers were asked to report. The meeting did not convene again until 23 September, presumably as a result of the holiday period. An impatient Moon thought the companies should have met earlier in order to agree a policy. Annoyed that some had agreed to pay the 3rd. duty, Moon hoped the Association's members would not agree to any compromise before sending another deputation to the Prime Minister. On a vote however, Moon's motion pressing for an interview with Disraeli was lost. Leeman suggested passing on the duty in the fares and his proposal that the companies should now pay the duty from 1 November was carried. They agreed however to Moon's further proposal to wait two weeks for each company to review the matter.

Moon's strong stance against any compromise was not backed by his board. Dramatic action by the Midland had added a new dimension to the situation. It was not until 13 October that Moon was able to convene a special meeting of his own board. He summoned them not just to review the 'passenger tax' question but the Midland's dramatic decision to reduce all fares, abolish the 2nd.

class and upgrade the 3rd.. The board, whilst thinking Moon's stand at the RCA was 'politic', agreed to support Leeman's resolution provided all the other companies agreed. At the following day's meeting of the RCA Moon had to back down and explain his company's conditional acceptance of Leeman's policy. All companies then agreed in principle to pay and pass on the duty with the one exception: the Midland. Their board voted unanimously not to add the 3rd. class duty to their fares.

In the following March, Moon told the RCA that he thought the Government would be prepared to remit duty on all fares at or under a rate of 1d. a mile and fare values of whatever class under 10d. Allport of the Midland believed they should concentrate on securing only the former. It was agreed that Leeman should see the Chancellor and also that members would support the North London in appealing against the judgement. The L&NW were then paying about £130,000 annually in duty of which, Moon told his shareholders in August 1875, 'one third came out of their pockets, and was practically an additional income tax. Instead of giving them any relief, the Chancellor of the Exchequer had turned the screw on them, and had more than doubled the loss they previously sustained'. In urging his shareholders to protest, he 'hoped and expected that the North London Company would ... win their cause against the Government - a result which would alter the whole status of that duty'. However 'if they were afraid, and stood like sheep ready to be fleeced, they might anticipate that [the Chancellor] would take advantage of the opportunity afforded to him'.

The appeal, heard in the Lords in 1876, failed and the RCA members agreed to meet North London's costs. The Government however conceded that a Commons Select Committee should consider the future position. Moon explained to his shareholders that although 'we have no right to object to any tax which is general throughout the community', when they 'were taxed as an additional income-tax upon those fares which, being under one shilling, are too small to have the duty added on, we say we have a fair claim and are entitled to be relieved'. He asked them to 'think for a moment that the average fare of passengers over your line is only 1s.5d. per head, you will see that a very large proportion of the duty falls upon yourselves'.

60. Trains at Bushey water troughs 1870

L&NW in the late 1870s: train taking water at speed from the Bushey troughs (one of eventually seventeen installations on the L&NW). The 2-2-2 locomotive piloting a Webb 'Precedent' 2-4-0 is Ramsbottom 'Problem' class *1431 Psyche*, one the last batch of eight built in 1865 which included *1427 Edith* and *1428 Eleanor*. The passenger train is overtaking a goods headed by a Webb 0-6-0 '17" Coal Engine', his first wholly new design, introduced in 1873. NRM

Moon privately seems to have accepted the futility of further public protest, leaving it to his directors who were MPs to continue to press the matter. He did not attend the RCA meeting when a sub committee was formed to handle the evidence to be given to the Select Committee. It was not until 1883 that any significant concessions were made by the Liberal Government (Gladstone had defeated Disraeli in 1880) when the chancellor, Childers, finally abolished the duty on 1d. a mile fares and reduced the duty to 2% in urban areas in return for the companies improving cheap workmen's trains.

Moon's personal attempts to obtain relief from the passenger tax had little or no impact on Government policy. His initial reaction to confront rather than compromise had to be toned down by his own board. And it was a far cry from the enlightened attitude adopted by the Midland. Such reactionary posturing was not of course confined to only the L&NW, but it was to become increasingly typical of Moon's views on other taxes and regulation.

In his early days as a director it has been noted that Moon never missed a meeting, over the six years or so he was a member, of the L&NW's Rates & Taxes Committee. Part of that committee's brief was to protest against unduly high rating assessments imposed on railway companies by local authorities. At the time these were generally based on mileage in the area and frequency of trains. His experience on that committee no doubt influenced his later complaints over the costs. He told shareholders in August 1870 that he felt 'rather annoyed' at the way rates and taxes had increased and that it was 'shocking to see large towns wasting their money and spending it without taking any account "of how it was to be got"'. Four years later in an outburst against the rating system in general, he expected the Poor Rate to be 'alleviated' as a result of the prosperity of the country 'but somehow or other we get new inventions, we get Health of Towns Acts and every conceivable mode of rating'.

In 1878, he supposed rates and taxes would continue to grow, 'partly owing to the increased expenditure of towns and I was very much amused in my own parish, Harrow, to find that they were rejoicing in having a school board. That will certainly tax us to the extent of £400 or £500, although we have not a yard of line in Harrow [with the L&NW running through Harrow this quip is difficult to understand]'. A year later he was referring to local rates as a 'bottomless pit' and that 'the Government was going to be bothered, and they ought to be, for having allowed the towns to borrow immense sums of money, to be nominally repaid in a number of years'. He added that the 'burdens on the great towns in consequence of this borrowing were enormous [and] that the country was going to be eaten up with its local rates'. In 1885 he was to claim that Bond debts 'are all piling up for a day of evil reckoning'. A year later he was resigned to facing further increases: 'it was of no use grumbling at the rates and taxes, for although they did not pay more than they could help, they were in the hands of philistines'. Within a year or so of retirement he was still despairing on the same theme: 'you must remember that every town through which we go is trying to find some fresh means of spending money for sanitary or other purposes, and they get it so easily by *borrowing* [sic] that they do not care what we ratepayers have to pay'.

Following through on Moon's protests over passenger duty and rating has introduced more of a thematic approach to this book. In the later chapters, marking the second half of his long chairmanship years, this will be increasingly used, covering subjects rather a strict chronology. Before doing so, however, it is necessary to show how Moon dealt with the approaching economic recession that followed the celebratory mood that peaked in 1872.

CHAPTER 20

INTO RECESSION

At the beginning of 1873 agitation had been voiced over the surging increase in prices. For example Bancroft, when lambasting the government over the powers of the Railway Commisioners referred to the 'deranged affairs of the country at large' and the 'extraordinary and sudden advance in the price of materials as well as labour'. And at the following summer meeting Moon was inevitably complaining over the 'enormously increased' working expenses offsetting the large increase in traffic.

Coal prices for example had more than doubled between 1871 and 1873. Moon reported in February 1874 that 'the greatest cause of the advance of expenditure is a very simple one, and patent to everybody. It is the advance in the price of materials and in the wages of labour'. Putting this into perspective six months later he told shareholders that the company's costs had increased from 46% of revenue, 'the normal state they were in a few years ago' to 56%. He claimed that if they had been able to keep the expenses down to the former level, the dividend would have been at the rate of 9% instead of 6½%, and that though expenses had increased they had not been able to alter rates. 'The jealousies of the [railway] companies are so great - some are too rich to care, and some are so poor they don't care - that very little has been done in that way, but we must live in hope. We are like Sisyphus, though we do not deserve his fate; we are always rolling the dividend stone up the hill and it is always coming down again.'

Although by the end of 1874 the price of such key materials as coal and iron had begun to drop, Moon was still reporting early the following year that 'there has been no such wonderful change in the prices of the last half year as the world outside has supposed'.

In analysing the increase in working expenses to 56%, Moon blamed firstly costs, in particular the 'block system', and the 'state of the labour market'; secondly the 'diversion to the Midland line of a part of the Scotch traffic'; and thirdly 'the "spoiling" of the traffic by the reduction of the first-class fares throughout the country'. By the 'block system' he meant improvements in signalling and control of train running. This was to embroil him in further conflict with the government and will be covered later.

By August 1876 Moon was again having to explain a further drop in the dividend rate. He commented 'they were all aware, however, that the difficulties of the labour market and the action of the trades unions had brought on a depression of trade in the country which even the influence of an unprecedented cheap money market had been unable to overcome'. The bank rate of discount had been reduced progressively from 5% at the beginning of 1876 to 2% by the end of April and was to remain at that level for over a year. At his summer 1877 shareholders' meeting, Moon had to report 'a less rate of profit per train mile' than in any year since he had been chairman. 'If you look at the losses we have sustained by the reduction of rates and fares' and the 'enormous losses we have sustained by the abstraction of traffic through new competitive routes, I think you will say it is only marvellous that we are able to show you today receipts for the half-year which are £23,000 in excess of the corresponding half of 1876'. And, he continued, 'if you will look further at the general depression of the trade of the country, I think we ought to be thankful that we are able to divide today the same dividend we did a year ago'.

In early 1878 Moon thought there must 'be something grievously wrong in the commercial state of the country, when we find that we are, in our own home markets, undersold in glass, manufactured iron, slates, paper, screws, and many other things by the foreigner'. He attributed this mainly 'to the regulations of the Government and the restrictions of the trades unions'. He said 'the country has righted itself before, and I hope will come right again'. Although he expected trade to revive he said 'it is going through a dangerous crisis' and concluded, gloomily, 'the threads of the trade of the world seem to be broken, and how to piece them [together] no one knows'. A year later Moon was 'as anxious as the shareholders to spend as little money as they could in the present distressed state of the country' and that shareholders could not 'expect the country to suffer and that their railway should not'.

By the summer of 1879 he was having to apologise for yet another drop in the dividend rate saying 'it has been gradually going down since 1873 at an average of about a ¼ per cent per annum; in 1873 it was 7 per cent, today it is 5½'. The cause was 'not a depression of one interest only. You will find that the agricultural interest, the manufacturing interest - cotton, iron, and everything - and the shipping interest, are suffering most grievously'. In particular he referred to the 'great loss' on the Holyhead line and the Irish traffic generally:

> The trains must run whether full or half full ... the whole of the stock is beautifully maintained and only wants work. ... We have preparations made for everything. I have been over the line and the conclusion I have come to is that the North Western is like a man who has been ill in bed two or three months and gets up and finds his clothes too large for him. ... He never remembered such a period as this, when money was of no value, when there was no profit in trade, with agricultural distress, and with the shipping interest of the country nowhere.

Nevertheless despite these economic circumstances there were still some shareholders ready to criticise the company's performance. Bluntly Moon told one that he did not know what he was talking about, reminding him of the impact of competition and the state of trade generally. He drew attention to the 'enormous amount they had lost by the competition of the Midland. The company's receipts were reduced in one morning by £200,000 a year by the reduction of the fares, and in the face of that fact they could not get the same dividend'. And he blamed competition for the drop in the Liverpool and Manchester traffic, also from Birmingham and the midlands, but, he stressed, 'they must accommodate the traffic that came to them'. He made passing reference to claims that the price of materials had gone down. 'And so it had,' he said, 'but there was no great change in wages, except to a certain extent, and in certain departments. They were paying the same wages in Liverpool, and there was very little change in London and Manchester'. He posed the question: would shareholders want the company to pay the same dividend as last year, and 'starve the concern'? He claimed he had asked his colleagues, "must we stand still and pick our traffic, or provide for the traffic?" and they told him that "you must provide for the traffic". He explained that they had. 'They had spent half a million on Holyhead, and they were spending a quarter of a million in Dublin, and though the amount of that traffic had temporarily gone down, and though the distress in Ireland was perhaps greater than in this country, still it was not lost altogether:

> If they were to stand still they would regret it hereafter. They were not prepared for the rush of traffic which took place after the American war, and suffered in consequence; and they might depend upon it, the rush of traffic would come over again. They wanted, therefore, without greatly injuring the dividends to be prepared for it. They were borrowing money as low as they could - they would never be able borrow money lower than they could that day; they were buying their materials lower, and all the contracts they were letting were at very low prices. If they suffered he would suffer, for his holding in the company was a very serious item.

By the autumn of 1879 there was some improvement in trade and the crisis for the moment was over. Throughout this difficult period Moon was frequently at pains to point out that as unfavourable as the results were they were not tempted 'to depart from our usual course' of firstly 'giving a liberal service to the public' and secondly 'maintaining the efficiency of the works and the line'. He regarded it as an important principle to leave both 'in as good order as they were in the beginning of the last half-year'. He strongly believed in the need for timely renewal and improvement to maintain the financial security of the company. He made this point perhaps most clearly in 1882 when he advised, 'always bear this in mind, that if you once let down your concern, and if you do not carry out our principle, that on the 31st of December the property shall be as good, as well maintained, and as valuable as at the beginning of the year, you never can or will overtake the depreciation'.

London & North Western Railway of England.

ROYAL MAIL ROUTE.

Passengers from the United States intending to visit Europe are informed that

THROUGH TICKETS

For the portion of the journey across England by the London and North Western Railway (the direct route from Liverpool to London) are obtainable **AT ANY OF THE OFFICES OF THE TRANS-ATLANTIC STEAMSHIP COMPANIES IN NEW YORK AND BOSTON.**

LIVERPOOL TERMINUS.

At Liverpool (one of the termini of the line) arrangements of a most complete character have been made for dealing with passengers to and from America, as well as their baggage. On arrival at Liverpool, carts will be found in readiness to convey passengers' baggage to the Lime Street Station, the scale of charges in operation being regulated by a tariff laid down by the municipal authorities. The Company have representatives appointed to meet the steam vessels on arrival at Liverpool, and to act on the instructions of the passengers with reference to the conveyance of their luggage.

A MAGNIFICENT HOTEL, "THE NORTH WESTERN,"

Containing upwards of 200 bedrooms, with spacious coffee room available for ladies and gentlemen, and replete with every accommodation, adjoins this terminus.

EXPRESS TRAINS,

at frequent intervals, leave for London (which is reached in five hours) Manchester, Birmingham, and all parts of the kingdom.

At Liverpool (Lime Street terminus) Through Tickets can be obtained for all parts of the United Kingdom, either for tours or single journeys. Passengers wishing to make arrangements for Continental journeys can obtain every information at Messrs. Gaze & Son's Branch Office at the Lime Street Station, and No. 4, Parker Street; or at the Head Office in London (142, Strand).

Passengers desiring to obtain information in Liverpool respecting the London and North Western Railway, should apply to Mr. James Shaw, the District Superintendent at Lime Street Station.

IRISH MAIL TO LONDON.

The Atlantic and other lines of steamers put in at Queenstown, and by alighting at this place, American passengers can avail themselves of the Irish Mail Trains by the Great Southern and Western Railway to Dublin, and thence proceed to Kingstown, the port from which the magnificent steam vessels of the City of Dublin Company, leave for Holyhead, where on landing the passengers can at once seat themselves in the splendidly-equipped carriages of the London and North Western Company's celebrated Irish Mail Train for London.

The Mail Train completes the journey from Holyhead to London (264 miles) in seven and a-half hours, there being only three stoppages on the way. The engines are provided with an apparatus by which they are enabled, as they travel, to take up water from horizontal troughs which are laid between the rails. Sleeping saloons are attached to the Night Mails both from and to London.

KENILWORTH, WARWICK, STRATFORD-ON-AVON.

The Irish Mail Trains from Holyhead, and the Express Train from Liverpool, afford a rapid service to Birmingham. Kenilworth and Warwick are easily reached by the trains from New Street Station, Birmingham.

A new line of railway has been opened through from Stratford-on-Avon to London, *via* Blisworth, by which quick trains are run daily.

LONDON TERMINUS.

The London terminus of the London and North Western Railway is at Euston Square and there are two hotels for the accommodation of families and gentlemen immediately adjoining the station—the "Victoria," on the western side, and the "Euston," on the eastern side of the entrance.

The London and North Western Railway Company have Central Offices in Manchester and Birmingham, with complete arrangements for through bookings. The Company's Superintendents will afford all information to visitors in those districts.

For information respecting trains, fares, &c., apply to Mr. G. P. Neele, Superintendent of the Line, Euston Station.

The London and North Western Railway Company have also through booking arrangements for parcels and goods traffic from Liverpool and Holyhead to all the principal towns in the kingdom and on the Continent. Full particulars as to merchandise can be obtained of Mr. Thomas Kay, Chief Goods Manager, Euston Station.

GEORGE FINDLAY,
Chief Traffic Manager

Euston Station, London.

Feb., 1877.

In September 1879 Moon was sixty-five. At the previous months half-yearly meeting, he had made passing reference to his age in a light-hearted exchange with Bancroft. The company's report of proceedings recorded him admitting that 'his friend on his left and himself were getting old'. However Bancroft, then into his eighties, had apparently rejoindered, "You speak for yourself!". Moon nevertheless maintained that 'they were getting older, and the concern was getting bigger, and it was as much as they could do to manage it'.

Although never formally recognised as such, Bancroft had been effectively deputy chairman of the company since the illness of Brown-Westhead in 1870. It was Bancroft who generally seconded the adoption of reports and accounts until the deputy chair position was re-established in 1881, with Cawkwell and Bickersteth being appointed jointly. Despite the reference to his age there seems no evidence to suggest Moon ever contemplated retirement then, nor eighteen months later at the end of his fourth five-year term as a director.

It had been in the summer of 1873 that Moon first made open reference to an inner core of directors who, in effect, exercised executive control of the company. In making the case for paying J.P.Bickersteth, as well as Bancroft, £1,000 p.a., Moon explained that himself, Bancroft, Bickersteth and Cawkwell 'took together upon themselves more than the ordinary duties of directors; and though other directors helped them, they were unable to do as much as those he had named, and could not feel the same responsibility as those who had special sums voted to them to retain their services'.

Moon said that 'he himself devoted all his time to the company, Mr Bancroft had not much time for anything else,' and that Bickersteth would be paid to 'look after the works on the distant parts of the line'. This 'continually required someone's presence because they knew the difference between working without the master and under the master's eye'.

Cawkwell was in a somewhat anomalous position. He had not actually taken his seat as a director at that time, continuing in a managerial role. However on several occasions Moon had publicly stated that 'it was no longer possible for one general manager to work the concern as Mr Cawkwell did'. His remarks could be implied as criticism, yet on the other hand may simply have been a justification for his policy of working through a team of executive directors. He had said that the position was 'too onerous', that there was 'a sort of mythical opinion that the general manager should be responsible for the whole working of the concern, but for a long time past it has been practically impossible, and has been putting a burden on the general manager which he never was able and could not bear'.

What Cawkwell thought of all this is not known. According to Neele he was a man of few words,. It does seem however that Cawkwell was sufficiently in tune with Moon's own thinking on matters of practical detail to provide reliable support in the quest for economy and control over capital expenditure.

Justification for control by a foursome of directors had been given by Moon to the shareholders in February 1874 when it became clear that there was no hope of the L&Y merger going through. He confirmed that his executive directors 'will be a sort of consulting centre to advise with the officers under the authority of ... the Special Committee, who will be the guiders of the policy of the board'. However as has been noted, he also announced the further promotion of key officer, Findlay as Chief Traffic Manager at £2,500 p.a., with Kay from the Lancashire district replacing him as Chief Goods Manager at £1,500 p.a.

Moon was always prepared to pay for good management, but what has not been evident is that he had no apparent prejudice in appointing women. In 1876 he had called and chaired a special meeting of the Hotel Committee following the illness of the hotel manager in Liverpool. The monumental 200-bed hotel at Lime Street station had been opened in 1871. The Committee resolved that the manager's wife, Mrs Bisserot, 'be placed in full charge of the hotel at a salary of £500 per annum'. Subsequently her successor was also a woman, promoted from running the company's Holyhead hotel.

With the heady days of 1872 over, Moon was perhaps overly reacting to criticism when he told shareholders in February 1874 that he trusted the new company management arrangements would be successful and that 'the strain will not be unbearable', and that we shall 'more easily watch the concern, because, although we are amongst the best-abused people in the country, and considered to be amateurs and indifferent, and have no care for our work people, and no eye to anything except for your dividends, yet we are workers, and know our business, and intend to have it managed so that the master's eye shall be over every part of the line'.

However dispensing with both an official deputy and overall general manager, Moon was, despite his executive directors, clearly putting immense pressure on himself to maintain the control of detail which was his style. Whilst his health never seemed a major problem it must have become clear to his colleagues that he could not continue in this manner. Some serious behind-the-scenes discussions must have taken place for, by the by the end of 1880, the long serving and independent director, the Duke of Sutherland, was deputed to raise the matter formally at the board. Sutherland gave notice (actually given on his behalf by Bancroft as the Duke was absent owing to his wife's illness) of 'a resolution in reference to the very heavy duties now devolving on the chairman'. And at the 22 January 1881 board Sutherland moved and it was resolved that:

> It is highly desirable that a greater amount of assistance should be afforded to the chairman by other members of the board and especially that he should be relieved of some of the detail which at present comes before him. That with a view to effect this object the office of deputy chairman so long in abeyance should be again filled up and that Mr Bickersteth and Mr Cawkwell be now appointed deputy chairmen, which was seconded and approved unanimously.

Although officially appointed in 1881, it seems remarkable that not until the August 1884 half-yearly meeting did either Bickersteth or Cawkwell publicly fulfil the role. In formally seeking a seconder for adopting the report and accounts Moon was reported as saying "Mr Bancroft (the Deputy Chairman) [sic] is not in his usual place today and has asked our friend Mr Cawkwell to second the resolution for him". What a stoical Cawkwell thought can only be imagined. Bancroft was then well into his eighties and although re-elected a director the following year gave up his committee work and thereafter became an irregular attender at meetings. He died in 1888, thought to be aged ninety.

When seeking re-election as a director in February 1881, Moon was in bouyant mood in summarising his thirty years with the company, giving no hint of any change in his role, nor any thought of retirement. Driven as usual by dividend performance he summarised the company's position as follows:

> For the years from 1851 to 1860 inclusive the average dividend was £5.0s.9d. In the next decade, from 1861 to 1870 the average £5.15s.6d.; while in the last ten years, up to December 31 1880, it has been £7.0s.6d., and your shares have gone up accordingly. That no doubt, is to a certain extent due to the fall in value of money, but not so much in proportion. On February 13 1861 your £37,000,000 of stock was not within £200,000 or £300,000 of par, while now, in February 1881, your £92,000,000 of stock is worth £119,000,000, so that we have in our pockets not only the average dividend of £7.0s.6d. for the last ten years, but an increased value of the property to the extent of £27,000,000 sterling. (Cheers). Let us hope that will continue, and that from year to year, as time goes on, this company will see its way to pay steadily improving dividends.

The value of his own stock holding (as shown in the detail given for his re-election) had increased dramatically from £21,000 in 1876 to nearly £48,000. Whilst prudent buying and increased valuation may have resulted in some of the gain, a more likely factor was the significant inheritances from his uncles.

Moon's doubts over any single officer being able to handle the overall management of the company may well have stemmed from the sudden death of Mason and the illness of Cawkwell. However with a strong man, Webb, responsible for Crewe, and effective officers in supporting roles, he finally accepted that he had in Findlay the right man for the general management of the rest of the company's operations. Findlay was appointed General Manager by the board's Special Committee on 20 February 1880. Ironically the appointment of Findlay and the elevation of Cawkwell and Bickersteth the following year served only to strengthen Moon's personal position as a modern managing director. With their executive role diminished and the eventual demise of Bancroft, Moon's inner core ceased to function as a coordinating body, leaving him in sole control of his senior managers. This structure was to remain basically unchanged for the remainder of his chairmanship.

In many explanations to his shareholders during the difficulties of the 1870s, Moon had pointed out the adverse effects of competition, arguing that as this was outside the control of the company there was little he could do about it. Though whether this was true over the Cheshire Lines incursion into Liverpool is a moot point and it is certainly questionable in the case of the Midland Railway's threat to Scotland. Moon, in his initial negotiations over the Settle & Carlisle line, could be said to have directly contributed to the building of the alternative route.

The Midland had already shown their ambitious intent with the opening of of their own extension to London in 1868. In 1872 they set the pace in 3rd class travel by revolutionarily introducing this class on all their passenger trains, and in October 1874 stunned the railway world by their decision to abolish all 2nd class with effect from the following January. They were preparing the way for an aggressive onslaught on Scotland (construction of the Settle to Carlisle line was then well under way). As has been seen their October bombshell had come at a time when Moon was already on the back foot with the Railway Companies Association over the passenger duty question.

After a lengthy discussion, Moon's 13 October emergency board meeting had 'unanimously deprecated' the Midland's policy and a committee was formed to obtain support for keeping the 2nd class. With the Midland proceeding as planned, the L&NW directors' report to their shareholders in February 1875 said that the 'exceptional course taken by the Midland' had received their 'anxious consideration' and 'in common with every other railway board' had agreed that this was 'foreign to the wishes and convenience of the public generally'. They therefore had decided 'to retain the three classes of fares and carriages, and to give some greater facilities than hitherto to the middle class, which it is hoped will ultimately prove a truer policy, though the reduction in prices necessitated by the Midland competition may cause considerable loss of profit'.

The Midland's Carlisle line opened for passenger traffic on 1 May 1876. After a year experiencing the impact of their fares policy, Moon found himself having to defend his company's decision to retain

2$^{nd.}$ class. He calculated from an analysis of Midland accounts that 'about four-fifths of their second-class traffic has gone into the third-class, and only about one-fifth into the first-class'. From this he argued that 'we do not see why we should inconvenience the 3,500,000 passengers who are desirous of travelling in something better than the ordinary third-class carriage'. Therefore, he concluded, 'we believe we were right in the retention of the second-class'. He was to continue at subsequent meeting to justify his policy culminating in 1880 with a detailed analysis of both companies' returns comparing 1879 with 1874. He concluded that despite the increased mileage, the Midland had received no more increase than the L&NW and 'thought, therefore, they had satisfied themselves that they were quite right in retaining the three classes ... and they did hope still that a sound policy would show their neighbours that, sooner or later, they would have to go back to where they were about six years ago'.

The Midland never did revert to the old three class system. Though not publicly admitting it, Moon must have realised that had the Midland not adopted such a pricing strategy they would not have been able to increase their business at the rate they did. The Midland's policy was gradually vindicated as other companies, including eventually the L&NW, were forced to follow suit in not only improving facilities to meet the surge in demand for 3$^{rd.}$ class travel but also in the eventual abolition of the 2$^{nd.}$ class.

Despite Moon's complaints over the loss of traffic to the Midland, the L&NW's response was eventually positive. With the advantage of shorter routes they met the new competition head on with improved services and facilities. And the burden of new construction weighed heavily on the Midland. Although there was some recovery in their dividends, the Midland never reached the percentage returns declared by the L&NW; and in the trade depression of the eighties they fell even further away in comparison.

Moon personally never relented from his policy of maintaining the traditional three classes. He commented, for example in 1882, that 'he could never see, for the life of me, why we should do away with our second-class, who represent two million of travellers, inconveniencing them, and depriving ourselves of the extra price which we receive'. Speaking to shareholders in 1884, he complained that 'everyone has said you ought to have third-class trains, and we have provided them, but they were intended for the working classes. We find, however, that gentlemen of the first position take third-class tickets; sometimes I have been tempted to wish they might have a sweep or a navvy for company'. Prejudiced of course, but the remark had a practical viewpoint. Two years later he commented amusingly on always now having a compartment to himself. 'Some one was sure to air a grievance and try to get some concession from him. The first day he had a compartment to himself, the station master at Bletchley asked him if he would allow an old clergyman and his wife to share it with him. He of course consented, but the lady had not been in the compartment five minutes before she asked him to enlarge their station.'

It was not until after Moon retired that the L&NW first began to abolish 2nd. Class, when the new joint-West Coast stock was introduced in 1893. Total abolition on the L&NW though still took almost another twenty years.

CHAPTER 21

TERRITORIAL EXPANSION

Though the main railway routes in England were substantially in place by the last quarter of the nineteenth century there were exceptions, the most notable of which was the MS&L's line to London which became the Great Central. However in the main they were improvements to existing lines or extensions to tap new markets and the L&NW had not been slow to pursue this policy.

In 1880 Moon was proudly reminding shareholders that the L&NW had 9% of the country's total railway mileage yet 15% of total traffic (*Bradshaw's Railway Manual* showed 9.35% and 15.15% respectively for 1880). As this had been substantially the position in 1875 (*Bradshaw* 9.27% and 15.66%), Moon could also have argued that investment in additional facilities and extensions had been necessary simply to maintain the company's overall position. The old arguments against extensions had not gone away, and in some cases with justification. Not all were successful, for example, the venture in the north of Ireland was never profitable, but overall they clearly contributed to the L&NW maintaining its dominant position. Some of the major developments, therefore, need explaining.

The developments that gave access to Nottingham arose from a proposal backed by the Great Northern for a new north/south link from the West Riding to Leicester, not only to compete with the Midland for that traffic but also to tap the east Leicestershire iron stone deposits. GN access to Leicester, from their main line in the south, would also then be possible if links could be made to use the L&NW's branch from Rugby via Market Harborough to Luffenham. It was from the latter, with running powers over the Midland, that the L&NW had provided their service to Peterborough as early as 1851.

The GN Bill for a Newark to Leicester line was only partly successful in the 1872 parliamentary session; landowner and Midland objections restricting the line southwards only as far as Melton Mowbray. With a Watkin inspired rival scheme being promoted jointly by the MS&L and the Midland, the GN looked to the L&NW for support with a new Bill to reach Leicester. Moon played his cards well in giving this support. It should be noted that he had successfully taken advantage of earlier schemes to serve the coalfield (centred on south Derbyshire and Leicestershire) by agreeing in 1866 not to renew support for an independently promoted line. The L&NW had participated jointly with the Midland in the Ashby & Nuneaton line, which had opened in 1873. Also in that year the L&NW's alternative route from the south to Rugby was authorised. The new line from Roade to Rugby via Northampton was part of the doubling of the main line which not only avoided the cost of duplicating the Kilsby tunnel, but gavee more direct access to the Market Harborough line.

Moon demanded from the GN access to both Nottingham and Doncaster in return for contributing towards the joint lines to be built by the two companies (the north/south line between Newark and Market Harborough and a branch from Melton to Bingham to link with the GN's Grantham/Nottingham line). The GN would give the L&NW running powers from Bingham to Nottingham and from Newark to Doncaster, the L&NW reciprocating by giving the GN running powers over the L&NW from Market Harborough south to Northampton and east to Peterborough. The L&NW agreed to build their own link from the Luffenham branch to the Peterborough line. Such an arrangement would give the L&NW not only a route to Nottingham, but more direct access to the coal traffic from both the Nottingham and south Yorkshire fields, in some cases to collieries in competition with the GN; the only real benefit to the GN being the reduced capital outlay on new lines.

However, when the joint Bill was first presented in 1873, only the GN line from Melton to Leicester was agreed. Still conscious of Watkin's threat for a rival MS&L line, the GN pressed for the Bill to be submitted again the following year. In agreeing Moon further strengthened his hand by insisting on the GN building themselves the first section south from Newark (to Bottesford) but retaining L&NW running powers over it. The joint lines authorised in 1874 consequently ran from Bottesford (where the GN's Grantham to Nottingham line was crossed) south to the junction with the L&NW

just north of Market Harborough; these also included the direct link from the south (avoiding Bottesford) to the Nottingham line.

Moon was reporting to his shareholders in August 1874 that the new joint committee with the GN had convened. By the following February the company's engineer, Baker, was reporting that the land was being purchased and plans prepared for the new lines. Baker did not live to see his lines completed. He became ill in 1877 and although still working into the following year died, aged sixty-one, on 20 December 1878. He had been connected with the company for over forty years, nineteen of them as chief civil engineer. Moon paid generous tribute to him at the January 1879 L&NW board. Baker was succeeded by his deputy Francis Stevenson, who saw the lines open by the end of the year.

Moon's initial negotiations with the GN over the Nottingham line had followed in the aftermath of the failure to merge with the Lancashire & Yorkshire. Despite Parliament's apparent hostile attitude to railway company mergers generally, serious consideration was given at the time to another proposal involving the L&NW which is worth noting. That involved the North Staffordshire Railway where there already had been close working arrangements. In addition to covering the Potteries, this company provided an alternative route from Birmingham and the Trent Valley line to Manchester. The L&NW was the natural partner for developing this traffic.

Struggling to reach even a 2% dividend, the North Staffordshire was ripe for a takeover at the end of 1874 when its chairman publicly agreed with shareholders that 'it was desirable to negotiate for a lease or sale ... to some or any of the neighbouring companies'. Possibilities for a joint lease by the L&NW and the Midland were discussed but in 1875, led by the ever-scheming Watkin, the Cheshire Lines became involved. As no agreement could be reached between the partners Watkin attempted to go it alone. He succeeded in 1876 in having the NS shareholders vote for a proposed MS&L and NS amalgamation Bill. Financially however the MS&L was in no position to pursue such a merger and Moon ensured that in any event his company's favourable traffic arrangements with the NS would have to stand. No agreement could be reached and the company was to remain independent until the grouping in 1921.

Developments in Ireland had seemed to hold a special interest for Moon ever since his first involvement under Chandos in the Chester & Holyhead negotiations and later when his Stores Committee became involved in shipping. Since 1860 the L&NW had provided the rail service between London and Holyhead for the then current Irish mail contract; the City of Dublin Steam Packet Company providing the sea link. The Dublin company's mail boats also carried first and second class passengers on the crossing to Kingstown (Dun Laoghaire). In the meantime the L&NW worked their own shipping service for goods, cattle and passengers directly to Dublin's North Wall quay on the Liffey (originally with the vessels inherited from the C&H). The service was initially very much a poor relations one for passengers, as sailings were dependent on the tide. However in the early 1870s improvements began to be made when dredging enabled a regular schedule to be maintained.

A quay on North Wall had been rail connected since the opening in 1864 of the Liffey branch of the Midland Great Western railway. That company's main line ran from Dublin's Broadstone terminus to Galway and the west.

One of the problems of the premium mail service through Kingstown for the rest of Ireland was that connections had to be made by cart and coach across Dublin. The Kingstown railway's terminus was isolated at Westland Row and it was not until after Moon retired that an extension from the terminus to the other railways was officially opened. The L&NW had therefore seen the opportunity to exploit their position at North Wall by encouraging the two other railways serving Dublin to build branches to the quay: the Dublin & Drogheda (part of the Great Northern Railway of Ireland from 1876) and the Great Southern & Western which served Cork and the transatlantic port of Queenstown (Cobh).

In 1872 the GS&W obtained powers to build an extension from just short of its terminus at Kingsbridge (on the west side of Dublin) to connect with the MGW's Liffey branch. With running powers over this branch, the GS&W reached North Wall by an additional short extension to link with the branch authorised for the Dublin & Drogheda. The L&NW took an active part in supporting the GS&W in not only negotiating more favourable rates for the use of the MGW line (the GS&W's own parallel line was not opened

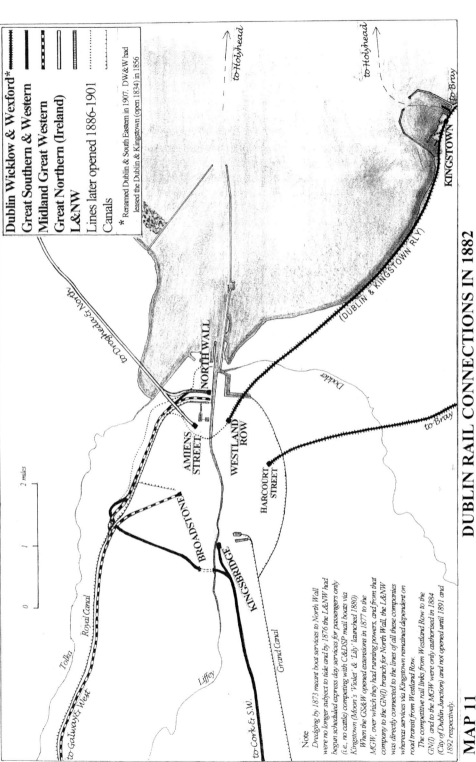

Legend:

- Dublin Wicklow & Wexford*
- Great Southern & Western
- Midland Great Western
- Great Northern (Ireland)
- L&NW
- Lines later opened 1886-1901
- Canals

* Renamed Dublin & South Eastern in 1907. DW&W had leased the Dublin & Kingstown (open 1834) in 1856

to Holyhead

to Holyhead

to Bray

KINGSTOWN

to Bray

(DUBLIN & KINGSTOWN RLY)

to Drogheda & North

NORTH WALL

Dodder

AMIENS STREET

WESTLAND ROW

HARCOURT STREET

BROADSTONE

KINGSBRIDGE

to Galway & West

Royal Canal

Tolka

Liffey

Grand Canal

to Cork & S.W.

2 miles

0   1   2

Note

Dredging by 1873 meant boat services to North Wall were no longer subject to tide and by 1876 the L&NW had begun scheduled express day services for passengers only (i.e., no cattle) competing with C&DSP mail boats via Kingstown (Moon's 'Violet' & 'Lily' launched 1880)

When the GS&W opened extensions in 1877 to the MGW, over which they had running powers, and from that company to the GN(I) branch for North Wall, the L&NW was directly connected to the lines of all these companies whereas services via Kingstown remained dependent on road transit from Westland Row.

The competitive rail links from Westland Row to the GN(I) and to the MGW were only authorised in 1884 (City of Dublin Junction) and not opened until 1891 and 1892 respectively.

MAP 11

DUBLIN RAIL CONNECTIONS IN 1882
WHEN L&NWR BID FOR NEW IRISH MAIL CONTRACT

until 1901), but in investing capital in the actual building of the extensions and the Dublin & Drogheda branch. These lines and the L&NW's North Wall passenger station were opened in 1877, giving the three local companies direct rail links to their respective terminuses in Dublin.

In anticipation of an earlier opening, the L&NW had started a new London-Dublin express service the previous summer using vessels, as Neele put it 'free from the taint of cattle traffic'. The L&NW's marine fleet then comprised thirteen vessels, or rather, as Moon wryly told shareholders, 'twelve steamers afloat and "one at the bottom"'. He added that the latter 'would have been raised in the autumn but a stupid captain went out of his way and ran down the pontoon'. In looking forward to the opening of the connecting line, he believed that the company 'paid something like one-fourth of the harbour dues of the port of Dublin and their Irish traffic was the largest foreign traffic they had over the line in one continuous stream'. By "foreign" he meant traffic originating from other companies. He believed 'Ireland was going to improve and they had all the great companies in Ireland working with them as one system of traffic'. And as soon as the links at North Wall were completed 'nothing could ever touch' their Holyhead and Dublin service. Also in 1877 the L&NW had embarked on a series of improvements to the inner harbour at Holyhead, which would give them a new station with separate rail connected quays for arriving and departing services and a hotel.

In 1880 Moon used the contacts of both the Duke of Sutherland and Lord Grosvenor to have the Prince of Wales inaugurate a grand Holyhead opening. Following the years of depression, Moon had told his shareholders at the beginning of the year that they had contributed £500 to the relief of the Irish people. This was at a time of famine and mounting agitation in Ireland and in Parliament for land reform. Remarking that it was 'an unusual thing for them to do', he explained that they 'were so mixed up with Ireland' and had 'such an enormous income from their traffic to and from that country - that they had thought it only right to do something in the direction he had mentioned'. He then claimed that they thought the company:

62. Holyhead new harbour 1880

Holyhead new harbour from hotel in 1880 with *Earl Spencer* left and *Lily* right,
probably taken at opening ceremony cruise for the Prince of Wales (among group
on *Lily's* paddle box?). NRM

63. PS *Violet* at North Wall, Dublin

Moon's 'magnificent' *Violet* at Dublin North Wall after being refitted in
the 1890s, one of two vessels launched in 1880 for the L&NW's
express Holyhead-Dublin service. NRM

Had done more to improve Ireland, and make that country prosperous than all the legislation of the century. There were more people passing over to Ireland by the Holyhead route than went over to the Continent. The only thing in which they found their Irish friends deficient was self-dependence. If they would only leave politics alone and depend on themselves they would never hear of anything but prosperity in Ireland. They frequently visited that country and nothing was wanting except settled quiet.

The L&NW's key role in opening up North Wall, to both the GS&W and Dublin & Drogheda companies, led to an arrangement in 1878 whereby the L&NW took ownership of the half mile or so of line from the junction of these companies at Church Road to the quay and the facilities there. All three Irish companies, i.e., including the Midland Great Western, were then running services to connect with the L&NW steamers. The GS&W did not open their own independent branch to the quay until 1886.

North Wall was not the only railway property in Ireland to be owned by the L&NW. Negotiations within the country to develop a more direct route to the north-west of the island had led to early proposals for developing a port at Greenore and a railway to Dundalk. Promised support from the L&NW was eventually to lead the L&NW becoming deeply and unprofitably involved in the project.

Moon seems to have personally championed the Greenore venture despite objectors, particularly from Liverpool shippers interested in maintaining a direct sea link to established ports, and others who considered the company had no need to invest in an Irish railway to protect its northern Irish traffic. The latter were probably right, the railways from Greenore made little if any money for the L&NW. This could be said to be one of the few examples where Moon seems to have let his heart rule his head. D.M.Barrie, in his history of the local railways, refers to Moon personally contributing to funding school and religious services in the new township subsequently built at Greenore.

In only the second year of his chairmanship the L&NW Special Committee had minuted 'that it appears expedient to arrange for the daily service between Holyhead and Dundalk or Carlingford, and to aid the Irish North Western company in extending their railway to Carlingford'. That same committee also considered extending the company's 'steam boat powers' to Irish ports other than Dublin and to find out what support the Government was prepared to give to the Portpatrick company to make 'proper harbour accommodation at Portpatrick' (the line from Castle Douglas to Stranraer and Portpatrick had been promoted as the shortest 'sea passage' to Ireland).

In January 1863 the L&NW had estimated the Greenore development would cost £150,000; and at the following February half-yearly meeting the directors told shareholders that no 'outlay of capital by this company' would be required to build the twelve miles of line from Dundalk to Greenore Point on Carlingford Bay. In the event the Irish company proved incapable of financing the development on its own; and no agreement was reached with the Dundalk Steam Boat company who had written to the L&NW 'willing to unite in performing the sea portion of the service'. Two separate local companies were authorised in July 1863, the Dundalk & Greenore and the Newry & Greenore, with joint responsibility for the harbour and works at Greenore. The L&NW appointed three members to the initial board of the Dundalk & Greenore. The chairman of the company was the chairman of the Irish North Western, the Earl of Erne.

From what looked like a promising start, little actual progress was made. Matters came to a head in 1867 when the Newry & Greenore company failed and Moon was forced to admit to his shareholders that it would be necessary to subscribe to the 'short link' between Dundalk and Greenore. The shareholders sanctioned the authorised £130,000 in August 1869.

When in 1870 construction work at last got underway, Moon was not above mixing some pleasure with business. He took the opportunity of a ceremonial opening in Caernarvon (of the link between the Llanberis and Bangor lines) in July to invite 'as many of the directors with some of the ladies of their families as could make it convenient' so they could accompany him afterwards on a jaunt to Ireland 'to look over the Dundalk and Greenore works'. Eleanor may well have welcomed the chance of an outing without too much distraction from business. It is apparent from company records that a steady stream of paper from Euston always seemed to follow him on their regular holidays, for example in Windermere.

Although still nominally independent, the local Dundalk & Greenore company was heavily reliant on its two partners. With the Irish North Western however in financial difficulties too, when the line was eventually opened in April 1873 it was in all but name a L&NW operation including the shipping service. Was it just a coincidence that the first L&NW paddle steamer allocated to the service was the *Edith*? *Edith* took part in the grand opening ceremony by providing a cruise on Carlingford Lough when Moon, accompanied by the Duke of Sutherland and Lord Richard Grosvenor (and no doubt Eleanor and Edith) welcomed the Lord Lieutenant of Ireland, Earl Spencer.

The L&NW eventually found themselves committing nearly half a million capital to what was renamed, in 1873, the Dundalk Newry & Greenore Railway. The more direct link for Belfast, originally projected by the failed Newry & Greenore, was incorporated in the new company and opened in 1876, giving a connection to both the lines to Belfast and Armagh (in 1879 the Newry & Armagh company became part of the Great Northern of Ireland which had absorbed the ailing Irish North Western three years earlier).

Whatever Moon's aversions were to personal publicity, he had little as far as promoting his company was concerned. And presumably he had no objection to using his ladies' names for the steamers (as he had for two locomotives in 1865). The first new paddle steamer specifically built for the Greenore service was the *Eleanor*; later when two more were built, *Earl Spencer* and *Isabella*, the latter was the name of one of Moon's sisters. Built in 1877 the *Isabella* was the first of the L&NW's fleet to be built of steel, steel made in Crewe.

The vessel 'at the bottom' in 1877 was the *Edith*. The following summer Moon was having to defend the cost of raising and refitting her. 'She will cost nearly as much as a new ship but then she is just as good as ever and will do you service for many years to come'. His continuing close interest is shown by the detailed reference in the directors report for February 1881 when they regretted the loss of the *Eleanor* 'which went ashore during a dense fog near the entrance of Carlingford Lough on the night of the 27 January last'. The report claimed that every effort had been made 'to get her off, and until the severe gales of Sunday and Monday last they were in great hopes of success. The severe weather which then set in has, however, disappointed these expectations and she has since become a complete wreck'.

It seems Moon had more feel for his ships than he ever had for his locomotives. No locomotive was ever named after him during his chairmanship, whether this was because he did not allow it or no one suggested it is not known (however after he left Worcester his house *Bevere* was so commemorated). He made little public comment on locomotive design or performance, usually restricting his remarks to economy of working. In marked contrast he was to comment with pride on the two new steamers built in 1880. In the summer of 1889 he reminded shareholders that:

> They have two beautiful steamers, the *Lily* and the *Violet* - most magnificent models. The time had arrived, or it will shortly arrive, for the renewal of their boilers; and we discussed this ourselves whether we should build new vessels or whether we should adapt these vessels to modern requirements. The conclusion we came to was that we should fit them with modern triple-expansion engines, steam steering gear, and everything that would make those vessels what they were formerly - the fastest vessels afloat.

With the improvements at Holyhead and the connections at North Wall, the L&NW considered they were in a good position to bid for both the rail and sea service for the Irish mail contract when the Post Office invited tenders for the renewal of the contract in 1883. It had always been the intention in the days of the C&H to bid for the through service to Kingstown. The company now had the option of bidding for both that service and an alternative to North Wall. In reporting to their shareholders in August 1882 that they had submitted tenders, the directors thought 'the company's new steamers, now running between Holyhead and North Wall, are unequalled for speed, punctuality and comfort'. At the subsequent meeting Moon confirmed they had offered to run between London and North Wall in 10½ hours. However a shareholder commented presciently that the contract 'was causing immense stir on the other side of the water and he was sure that it would be very unpopular if the contract went away from the City of Dublin Steam Packet Company, who had had it for the last twenty years and done the service admirably'.

The L&NW sent two offers, to Kingstown and to North Wall. They were awarded the rail and sea service between London and Kingstown, with, as the directors reported, the option of transferring to North Wall if the Postmaster General 'shall hereafter see fit to do so'. In explaining further to his shareholders in February 1883, Moon told them that two additional steamers had been built and would be ready in May for cattle and goods and that two more would be required for the contract to carry the Irish mails. 'One of these would be ready in February, and as soon as the House of Commons had confirmed the contract the other would be got ready.' He explained that 'they would have preferred that the mails should have gone to North Wall rather than Kingstown, but they hoped that with the appliances they had in their inner harbour at Holyhead the community would derive great advantage from the shortening of the time and the improvement of the communication'. However clearly aware of Irish opposition he went on to say:

> A good deal has been said about their not being an Irish company. They paid one-quarter or one-fifth of the Dublin harbour dues. They had half a million of property there, and the people they employed got the highest wages of any in their service in their particular capacity. They had as many Irish officers and men as they had English on their steamboats, and they had a large number of Irish shareholders.

Unfortunately for Moon a great deal more was said about the local Irish company losing the shipping contract. Strong parliamentary lobbying by the City of Dublin company led to the Post Office reconsidering the L&NW bid and inviting fresh tenders. Moon called a special meeting of his board on 11 July, the day the new tender was due, when 'after full consideration' it was agreed to withdraw the shipping service. The directors reported to their shareholders the following month that their 'tender for the land service alone, on terms identical with those which the company had previously offered to perform that portion of the service', had been accepted (this was half an hour quicker than the old contract). In discussion Moon commented somewhat resignedly 'that looking to the tone of the House of Commons we came to the conclusion that an English company would go to the wall'.

A contract for twelve years was subsequently agreed with the Post Office from the 1 October with the C of DSP performing the sea service from Holyhead to Kingstown. But the L&NW had made its point and renewed efforts were made to promote the rail connection from Westland Row station to the remainder of Dublin's railways. It took until 1891 however before the City of Dublin Junction Railway was opened to bring this into effect.

The additional steamer the L&NW had committed for the mail service proved an embarrassment. Moon was complaining in 1884 that it 'is rather a heavy loss and she is not able to show the great power she possesses, but has been relegated to take her turn in the slow services we have been condemned to'. He reckoned that if their original offer had been implemented it 'would have given an advantage to the whole of Ireland by about one hour over anything that can be done today'.

Also during this period the L&NW had a stake in the shipping from Fleetwood to Belfast through their joint ownership with the L&Y of the Preston & Wyre railway. The two companies had been authorised in 1870 to take over the vessels of the North Lancashire Steam Navigation Company which they did in 1873. However as Moon was at pains to point out the company never had any interest in the docks at Fleetwood. Much less straightforward was the L&NW's involvement with Portpatrick.

The Portpatrick Railway from Castle Douglas had opened to Stranraer in 1861 and the following year to Portpatrick but with no satisfactory harbour as promised by the Admiralty. As a result of leasing the Lancaster & Carlisle, the L&NW found itself with an interest in the company. In August 1864 they reported that the Portpatrick had obtained powers 'to establish communication, by means of steam vessels, between Portpatrick and Stranraer, and Donaghadee and other Ports on the north-east coast of Ireland; also, to increase their capital, and to make working arrangements with the L&NW and Caledonian companies'.

Moon had objected earlier to the Portpatrick attempts to attract 'a great number of English and Irish companies to contribute funds for the purchase and working of steam boats between Portpatrick and Larne'. It was the Caledonian who eventually entered into an agreement (twenty-one years from 1864) to work the line. However it was not until 1872 that a regular shipping service was established by the Larne & Stranraer Steamboat company in which the Portpatrick had a major holding. The earlier attempts to establish the Portpatrick Donaghadee service had been in expectation of a mail contract and assistance in improving the harbour at Portpatrick; neither came about despite protracted negotiations. Moon was to publicly rail against the Government for what he perceived as their default on an obligation to develop the harbour.

With access to the line from Dumfries dependent on the Glasgow & South Western railway and the arrival of the Midland at Carlisle in 1876, the struggling Portpatrick company saw the opportunity to seek wider support when the time came to negotiate a new working agreement. As a result, a joint committee of the four companies (L&NW, Caledonian, Midland and Glasgow & South Western) was formed and agreement eventually reached for them to take over the local company and its shipping investment. This also included another struggling local company, the Wigtownshire (opened progressively from Newton Stewart to Whithorn by 1877). Discussions were protracted and it was not until August 1885 that the two local companies were officially transferred to the four partners as the Portpatrick & Wigtownshire Joint, two directors from each partner forming the directing committee.

Initially Moon joined the joint committee with M.MacInnes (a Carlisle based director) as his L&NW colleague. Representatives from the other partners also included their chairmen. However Moon must have quickly reconsidered his direct involvement. The L&NW board minute, noting his appointment, was followed by a further minute stating that from the following month he was to be replaced by J.J.Hare. Hare and MacInnes were to remain the L&NW representatives for over ten years. Hare was an interesting appointment. He lived in Chorley, Lancashire, and was a former L&Y director, but had resigned from that company and been elected to the L&NW board only the previous February to 'strengthen the good feeling' between the two companies and for his 'knowledge of the Lancashire district'.

With the Belfast & Northern Counties Railway eventually joining the four British companies in managing the shipping interest, a five partners' Larne & Stranraer Steamship Joint Committee was established in 1893, but by then Moon had retired from the scene.

Before leaving developments within the L&NW during this time, further reference needs to be made to Moon's policy of sourcing goods and services from in-house facilities. For example, under Webb the vast Crewe works not only built and repaired the company's locomotives but an increasing range of components and equipment, even artificial legs to individual requirements by the 1880s. Full details of production at both Crewe and the company's other principal works, Wolverton, have been the subject of separate studies and are not included here (see source notes). However it is of note to record that Moon's personal involvement in distribution services came to a head when the work of the carting and goods agencies was brought under the direct control of the company.

Ever since the Grand Junction and London & Birmingham days there had been differences of opinion over the role of goods agents. Moon was firmly of the school that felt the company should take into its own hands as much of its operations as could economically be justified. Neele was in no doubt where he thought Moon stood when he wrote: 'all agencies or at least payment to agents were equally disliked by him. Boating agents, canal agents, parcel agents, excursion agents were in his view parasites to be got rid of and the duties performed by the company's own staff'.

After the controversial ousting at the end of 1861 of the agents from the company's London goods' stations what is surprising is that it took Moon so long thereafter to complete the process by establishing the company's own carting and collection business.

To put the L&NW's carting business in perspective, at the end of the first ten years of Moon's chairmanship receipts from merchandise traffic had exceeded those from the total of all classes of passengers. Even ten years later, despite the dramatic over 150% increase in 3rd class receipts, merchandise still accounted for the greater income and these figures did not include minerals or livestock traffic.

64. Crewe new 1882 iron foundry opening
A variety of Crewe built products exhibited in the new iron foundry during the
opening ceremony in 1882. LNWRS

65. Horse and dray at Camden goods station
Carter posing with his horse and dray at L&NW's Camden goods station in
early 1900s. F.H.Dent, the London district goods superintendent named on
the dray, subsequently became SE&C general manager and knighted for
special war services in 1916. NRM

Two of the main agents, Chaplin & Horne and Pickfords, had long been established in the cartage business. Pickfords had grudgingly accepted the loss of the handling inside the London goods stations and eventually established a carting and collection service to complement the railway's own service (particularly to and from the outer suburban areas). Benjamin Horne however had resorted to legal action in trying to prevent L&NW men from taking over his work inside the stations. David Stevenson, the L&NW officer given the responsibility for managing the 1860s change in London, later wrote of Horne's reaction as follows:

> Mr. Horne pursued me with unrelenting persecution. He left nothing undone, no vituperation unsaid, to ruin me with the directors and the management. The goods establishment in London was transferred to the company, giving me nights and days of labour and anxiety; the chairman alone in any way helping me with advice, assistance or authority. The general organisation was soon brought into form although Pickford & Co carried away nearly all the best men. ... After the removal of the agents a few years of tolerably regular work ensued, always accompanied by Mr Horne's never ceasing attacks.

Of concern to Moon were the costs. In 1871 expenses paid to agents for collection and delivery were running around 12% of gross merchandise receipts. Horne died in 1870 and under Chaplin their cartage agency continued with less rancour and not until 1877 was a further change implemented. With the contract due for renewal, the opportunity was taken in negotiations to buy out the agent's business. Perhaps conscious of still lingering loyalties amongst his older directors, Moon called a special board to review Chaplin's offer to sell for £100,000. Findlay was instructed to offer half that amount. Chaplin refused. This negotiation took place at the time of the summer half-yearly shareholders' meeting and the board reassembled afterwards when Chaplin was given until October to reconsider. In the meantime Findlay was further instructed to plan for the 'contingency of the company having to take the business into their own hands on 1 January next'.

At the following February half-yearly meeting negotiations were reported as ending in 'friendly arrangement', under which the staff were transferred, the offices, horses, carts, etc., taken at valuation, and the business 'conducted wholly by the company's officers'. The report added that the 'directors take this opportunity of expressing their sense of the zealous and honourable manner in which the Agents have acted during the long years the agreements have existed'. And Moon thought he was not a politician! Stevenson wrote tellingly:

> I found the town offices in a very confused and irregular condition as regards charges, check and discipline. The cartage irregularly and expensively worked and the canvassing department unsystematic. Five or six years of incessant labour and attention absorbed the offices into the railway method of audit and supervision. The cartage and canvassing were organised into districts. New premises in several parts of London were opened and the old offices improved. The agency was altogether made to cover the Metropolis ... and advertised the L&NW more prominently than it had ever been previously.

Stevenson reported through Findlay to a Cartage & Agency five-man sub committee of the board, which met every alternate month in Moon's office for the remainder of his chairmanship. Stevenson estimated that the savings in cost in London paid off the purchase money in the first three years. Not all goods agencies had been absorbed by that time; it was not until early 1888 that negotiations with Carver, in Manchester and Liverpool, led to that business being taken over; and Pickfords were to continue their carting agency until 1901. For the last half-year before Moon retired agency expenses were still running at almost 5% of merchandise receipts.

CHAPTER 22

CONSOLIDATION

The shareholders' acclamation of Moon in 1872 can be said to have marked a turning point in his career with the L&NW. The year not only fell roughly mid-term in his forty years as a director, but also the dividend, as measured by the percentage paid on ordinary shares, reached its highest point: an annual rate of 7¾% for 1871 and 1872. This rate was not matched until the 8% paid in 1922, the last year of the company's independent existence. The relevance of dividends as the indicator of success has been touched on in an earlier chapter and it will be necessary to comment further on other measures. Before doing so however, some national background should be noted, as the years 1872-73 also marked a turning point in the economic trends of the country.

S.B.Saul, in his *Myth of the Great Depression* booklet, notes that wholesale prices steadily declined, with only short term uplifts, from this time to almost the end of the century. Using an index of 100 for the four years 1871-75, prices had declined to 68.3 (63.6 for coal and metals) for the 1891-96 period. The boom of the early seventies gave way to a long period of relative decline that provides the background for the remaining years of Moon's chairmanship.

It is convenient therefore at this point to summarise the financial trends in L&NW performance, not only for the first half of Moon's career but also over the remaining decades to his retirement.

For purposes of comparison Moon's forty years can be grouped into four periods: firstly, the years as a young director from 1851 to 1861; secondly, the difficult early years of his chairmanship to the acclamation in 1872; thirdly, the years of territorial expansion and financial consolidation to 1879; and finally, his so called increasingly reactionary years to his retirement in 1891. Trends in company results covering these periods are summarized in Table A.

In 1851 when Moon joined the L&NW the company's route mileage was just over 500 and total receipts around £2.6 million.

Over the following decade there was a near doubling of the mileage and an almost seventy percent growth in receipts. Yet this period saw the ratio of traffic expenses to receipts increase dramatically, so much so that the actual amount of the dividend was less in 1861 than it had been in 1851. It was no wonder that so many shareholders had been agitated in the late 1850s, none more so than Moon himself.

TABLE A
L&NW Trends in Receipts, Expenditure & Dividends 1851-90

L&NW TRENDS IN RECEIPTS, EXPENDITURE & DIVIDENDS 1851-90
Annual figures based on the tables in M.C.Reed's *The London & North Western Railway*.

	Year	Route Mileage *Miles*	Traffic Receipts *£million*	Traffic Expenses *£million*	Ratio %	Capital# Expenditure *£million*	Dividends *£million*
	1851	518	2.63	1.07	40.7	29.51	1.12
	1861	1030	4.43	2.33	52.6	36.41	1.08
% change *1851-61*		+98.8	+68.4	+117.8		+23.4	-3.6
	1872	1539	8.04	3.85	47.9	58.49	2.96
% change *1861-72*		+49.4	+81.5	+65.2		+60.6	+174.1
	1879	1713	9.29	4.80	51.7	83.76	3.61
% change *1872-79*		+11.3	+15.5	+24.7		+43.2 (+26.1*)	+22.0
	1890	1876	11.58	6.23	53.8	101.02	4.41
% change *1879-90..*		+9.5	+24.7	+29.8		+20.6	+22.2

*Capital expenditure is net cumulative outlay*

***** *Percentage increase if £10 million capital deducted for Chester & Holyhead, Lancaster & Carlisle and other leased and guaranteed lines not included in pre 1878 L&NW accounts*

The success of Moon's policies, once he was in the chair, in controlling costs can be seen in the figures for his first decade. Although capital expenditure increased by over sixty percent between 1861 and 1872, the reduction in the ratio of expenses to receipts reduced from almost 53% to below 48%. This was one of the lowest so called operating ratios for any major railway company at that time. It can be argued that this was the main reason for the almost threefold increase in the value of the dividend. That this ratio was not held in later periods was to be a common problem with most major companies and the reason for this has been the subject of much debate among economic historians.

Despite his tight control over costs, Moon was unable to prevent expenses from rising again above 50% and to remain so for the remainder of his chairmanship. Explaining the reasons for this became a constant theme in his reports, both from the point of view of the need for more capital, and justifying increases in costs. The need for better facilities, additional and improved lines to handle increased traffic and items such as new signalling and interlocking, all increased costs and required further injections of capital. His turn of phrase in addressing shareholders frequently caught the imagination, none more so than in February 1876 when describing the line as being 'manured with capital'. And if he appeared grudgingly to accept this need, he put it well when adding that in generating a £135,000 revenue increase in the half year, shareholders had to expect to spend some capital if they were to 'provide for the wants of the community in the district allotted to the company, for if the company did not, others would'.

The peak of the early 1870s followed the pattern set by the economic cycles of the country. In the downturn that followed, the L&NW emerged as the least affected of major comparable companies. All declined steadily in dividend performance, the L&NW falling to a low point of 5½% for the first half of 1879 (significant recovery however in the second half boosted the total dividend for that year). And in 1880 a recovery nationwide saw dividends increased again, but only to fall back again steadily to 1886. Fortunately for Moon an upturn at the end of the decade saw out his chairmanship on another high (if only temporarily). It may be opportune therefore to illustrate these trends over the whole period of his tenure by comparing L&NW's dividend performance with major companies either in direct competition or serving the same main markets.

TABLE B
L&NW Dividends Compared with Comparable Companies 1861-91

L&NW Dividends compared with Comparable Companies 1861-91
Turning points in the Economy marked: P peaks & T troughs.

	L&NW	NE	GW	MID	GN	L&Y	MSL
1861	4.250	4.625	2.625	**6.625**	5.750	5.250	1.000
1862T	4.625	4.250	1.750	6.000	**6.500**	3.875	0.000
1864P	6.375	5.875	3.125	**7.375**	7.125	5.875	2.625
1865P	6.625	6.125	2.000	6.750	**7.125**	5.875	2.250
1868T	6.000	5.250	1.375	5.375	5.875	**6.750**	1.250
1872P	7.750	**9.000**	6.000	7.250	7.125	8.375	3.500
1876	6.625	**7.375**	4.000	5.375	5.500	5.875	2.250
1879T	**6.500**	5.875	4.125	5.625	5.125	4.625	2.125
1880P	7.375	**8.250**	5.125	6.125	5.125	5.375	3.000
1883	7.500	**8.250**	6.375	5.875	4.625	4.375	2.875
1886T	**6.250**	5.375	5.250	4.625	4.375	3.500	2.000
1889P	**7.375**	7.250	6.750	6.000	4.875	4.500	3.375
1890	**7.250**	7.250	6.500	6.250	4.750	4.250	2.750

Annual dividend rates in pounds as listed in Bradshaw's Directory for 1892.
*The figure in **Bold** for the year is the highest paid by the companies shown.*

From Table B it can be seen that taking annual ordinary dividend rates from Moon's first year in the chair, 1861, to his last full year, 1890, the L&NW emerged as the leading performer among its contemporaries.

From the peaks of 1871 and 1872, the L&NW dropped no lower than a 6¼% full year annual rate and displacing as top performer even the largely monopolistic North Eastern during his last five years.

Over the same period the once lauded Lancashire & Yorkshire fell from over 8% to well under 5%. In the year of his retirement the L&NW led the field of major English companies north of the Thames in being able to declare a 7% dividend.

As mentioned in an earlier chapter, Moon's use of dividends as a measure of success needs qualifying. Dividends paid to ordinary stockholders need not necessarily be relevant if a company's capital structure is such that ordinary shareholding is not representative, or when dividends are topped up out of reserves (or infamously in Hudson's case out of capital). For Moon the dividend was always the most straightforward way of relating a company's performance and was well understood by the market. There were of course other companies paying higher dividends, most notably the largely coal carrying Taff Vale Railway in south Wales, but that company had a route mileage of not much more than 6% of the L&NW's.

Relating revenue (whether gross or net of expenses) less fixed charges and interest to capital expended has been quoted as perhaps a more useful indicator, but the difficulty remains of calculating working capital using only published trading statements. Differing interpretations within the industry over allocating costs between capital and revenue have been referred to earlier and remained so, as were company policies over reserves and depreciation. Moon would have been all too familiar with the effect of such decisions on not only performance but, as he frequently put it to shareholders, the value of their property. The clamour at one time for closing the capital account was never far from some shareholders' minds.

So given Moon's detailed involvement in operational management, should some further analysis be needed to demonstrate just how efficient was the L&NW under his leadership? The problem remains, however, that published figures alone cannot provide satisfactory answers without further study which is considerd to be outside the remit of this book. In reviews that have been made in calculating other measures of efficiency (see references to *Economic History Review* articles in source notes), the L&NWR still comes out favourably; though it is again the Taff Vale that led the field. Expressing profit as a percentage of estimated capital employed in 1892, the Taff Vale generated a return of over 5.9% as opposed to the L&NW's under 5.2% and the NE's just over 4.9%.

Suffice to say that Moon was as well aware as any of his contemporaries of the need for tight control over costs and investment. And the L&NW had been analyzing figures in a reasonably sophisticated way, e.g., locomotive costs per train mile, since the days of Chandos. And Moon's detailed Stores Committee briefing to his new horse superintendent can still stand as a model of its kind. It was only in the declining years of his chairmanship that such vigilance could prove counter-productive, especially when faced with requirements imposed by outside regulation for safety, signalling and braking, which will form the basis of the next chapter.

The capital structure of the L&NW had grown somewhat haphazardly as a result of the numerous associated and subsidiary companies absorbed. Original shareholders of these companies, depending on the strength of their negotiating position and market conditions at the time they were taken over, had been guaranteed various rates of return. The L&NW themselves had also raised new capital through both stock issues and loans. Moon, from his early days in the chair, was conscious of the company's vulnerability to repaying large amounts of maturing loan debt at fixed dates in the future regardless of the state of the company's finances at the time. He had therefore pursued a policy in periodically taking advantage of the company's standing in the market to replace this old debt with new 'open-ended' stock.

In 1867 Moon had told his shareholders that out of a total capital of around £70million (which he claimed was the largest of any concern in the country) the loan debt was £19million. A high proportion of this loan capital was in the form of debentures. Debentures were issued by companies to guarantee the repayment of loans made to them. They provided a regular income to holders in the form of interest. Repayment was made at the end of a fixed term. Interest rates offered to attract lenders would generally reflect the risk. Where the risk was perceived to be low, as would be the case with solid well managed companies, then the company could raise capital this way at a moderate cost, with investors looking for longer term secure income (as is the case with Government bonds) rather than speculative high short-term returns.

As Moon explained to his shareholders, 'it was the debentures of bankrupt concerns that had tended to injure debentures generally, but there was no ground for apprehension in sound undertakings'. The problem was that debentures issued at times of uncertainty may have had to be offered at interest rates subsequently seen to be penal. And the commitment to pay back in full a substantial loan on maturity could be an untimely burden on a company's finances. So Moon was anxious to assure shareholders that 'net revenue in the past half-year was five times the amount of the debenture interest, and nearly sufficient to pay off all the debentures of the company as they become due'. And he was in no doubt that 'the time would come when they should be able to convert the whole of their debentures into 4% debenture *stock*'.

The importance of debenture stock as opposed to debentures was that, although the company was committed to pay a periodic fixed rate of interest, the stock did not have to be repaid unless the company defaulted on its interest payments or was wound-up. In liquidation the stock had the status of equity, not debt. It could also be said to be similar in status to preferred stock whose holders have priority over ordinary shareholders if ever there was a shortfall in the distribution of dividends.

As well as converting loan capital the company had also begun to tackle the problem of replacing the preference stocks of acquired companies with standard L&NW shares. However it was not until well into the 1870s that the problem of replacing the varying guaranteed stocks of these still legally existing companies was seriously addressed. Difficulties over converting had remained outstanding and matters were further delayed when in 1875 Benson, the Finance Committee chairman, died. Moon himself then decided the matter was so critical that he would have to take over the Committee himself. This was despite his previous decision to follow the precedent set by the company's first chairman, Glyn, of not being a member to avoid possible accusations of working for personal benefit.

Further emphasis was given in January 1876 when the shareholders' Audit Committee (then chaired by Glyn's son, the second Lord Wolverton) drew attention to the large number of separate stocks in the L&NW and affiliated companies. They reported 'that a consolidation of these stocks into L&NW "guaranteed" and "preference", according to their several rights, would be of advantage to their holders, and simplify the accounts of the company'.

The Committee 'accordingly suggested to the directors that the subject should be considered with a view to the preparation of a scheme of consolidation to be submitted to the respective proprietors at an early date; which, when sanctioned, should be confirmed by Parliament'.

At the following half-yearly meeting Moon referred to both the preference and guaranteed stock. He thought the problem with the various preference shares was a relatively simple one: holders 'never know what year's preference stock they purchase ... and it has got rather in a state of confusion in the minds of the community and there is no good reason for its continuance'. He quoted the example of a Government bond where the old "three per cents" commanded a higher price than the new issues although they were equally good, 'but in the one case you have a very large stock with which you can deal, and in the other you have a comparatively smaller market and people don't know so much of it'. He thought that by 'putting all these stocks into one large amount' there would be a better price than when 'divided into a great many separate stocks'. However in the case of the guaranteed stock he admitted that the problem was 'much more difficult'. But he assured them that the company would 'endeavour to see if any plan can be arrived at which will bring that into some sort of shape'.

It seems that getting the guaranteed stock into "shape" took longer than anticipated. The bulk of the administrative work fell on Reay the company secretary, who with Moon and the Finance Committee, recommended that the fifty three different stocks be consolidated into only four. Parliamentary approval was obtained the following year, 1877.

The 3½% debenture stock was converted into the L&NW 4% and, in February 1878, the directors trusted 'that all the remaining stocks of the company may at an early date be consolidated into either guaranteed, preference, or ordinary, according to their respective rights'. Moon seemed to take some personal pride in adding that 'the amount represented by debentures expiring at various periods during the next three years is now less than one million and a half, and as they mature they will be replaced by debenture *stock*, the issue of which now amounts to nearly twenty millions'.

The consolidation offer was sent out in July 1878 to all holders of the various preference and many small guaranteed stocks (whose rates varied from 2½ to 10%) in the expectation that agreement could be reached at a series of special meetings to be held in August. Spread over the week beginning the 19th., Moon and Reay then went through the formalities of holding the special shareholder meetings legally required to obtain acceptance. All were recorded as accepting unanimously except the Lancaster & Carlisle whose meeting was adjourned.

Not without a sense of humour, Moon recorded, after the last of the week's meetings:

> I can only say we held something like sixty of these meetings and I am sure the shareholders are greatly indebted to the reporters for nobody else came. One gentleman looked in; he found us sitting in great glory; he said, "I have not come to oppose: I have no hostile intentions; I only came to see what a North Western meeting was like; I will go away;" and he went.

The problem over replacing the Lancaster & Carlisle paper lay in satisfying their holders of the guaranteed minimum 8% ordinary stock. The L&C had been guaranteed an even higher return if the L&NW's own dividend exceeded 4%. The minimum 8% was arrived at by adding 4 percentage points to a base L&NW dividend of 4%. If the actual L&NW dividend was 4¼ then the addition was also 4¼ making the payment 8½, if the L&NW was 4½ then the addition was 4½ making the payment 9. Thereafter, whatever the higher L&NW dividend, the addition would be a fixed 4½; for example if the L&NW paid 6% then the L&C received 10½%. As a result, since the lease in 1859, the L&C holders of their ordinary stock had enjoyed a dividend rate averaging around 10¾%: an exceptionally good return.

The L&C's original chairman, Edward Hasell, had stood firm against Moon's previous attempts (at the time of the negotiations with the Midland for a line to Carlisle) to fix the dividend at a guaranteed 9½%. Hasell had demanded a minimum 10%, and now the current chairman, Henry Garnett (Hasell died in 1872), adopted an equally tough stance. Although accepting Moon's offer of £200 of L&NW guaranteed 4% stock for £100 of L&C ordinary (to cover the minimum 8% guarantee), he rejected the £44 of L&NW ordinary stock for every £100 of L&C as compensation for the fluctuating potential dividend above this rate. Based on a minimum L&NW dividend of 4%, the £44 would have given the L&C holders an additional 1¾%, i.e. a total of 9¾% (8% of which being guaranteed as above).

Moon and Henry Crosfield had met Garnett beforehand and, not unreasonably, taken the actual average L&NW dividend of 6¼% over the term of the lease to demonstrate the L&C should get their previous 10¾%. However with the deep depression in trade at the time showing no signs of lifting, Garnett and his colleagues stood out for more additional L&NW ordinary stock to give them a better chance of achieving the higher dividend. At a meeting in December the two sides compromised, the £44 additional L&NW stock was increased to £47.10s.0d. At a minimum 4% L&NW dividend this gave the L&C almost 10%. As the foreseeable prospects of the L&NW ordinary dividend dropping as low as 4% were considered remote, the L&C had effectively won what Hasell had asked for when Moon had originally offered to buy out the guarantee with the Midland.

In reporting at the following February's half-yearly meeting Moon thought the overall consolidation had gone, 'on the whole, tolerably satisfactorily. The only strong fight they had had was with their friends of the Lancaster & Carlisle who ... drove rather a hard bargain'. The directors' report summarized the position as follows:

4% Debenture Stock and Loans	£23,256,555
4% Consolidated Guaranteed Stock	£15,100,406
4% Consolidated Preference	£21,328,120
Consolidated Stock [Ordinary]	£32,724,377
	£92,409,458

With another £6.5million of capital powers to be exercised (around £5million for new lines and improvements) the total authorised capital of the company was then almost £99 million. And this did not cover the near £7.5 million which represented the L&NW's responsibility for the Shropshire Union and the Birmingham canals; and their joint interest in the North Union, Shrewsbury & Hereford and Birkenhead companies. As Moon told shareholders 'therefore the total real capital of the company would be £106,500,000'. Loan stock had then been reduced to under a million.

Moon must then surely have paused to reflect on the magnitude of the concern he was presiding over. No wonder he revealed in his aside to Bancroft that it was 'as much as they could do to manage it'. Could he ever have imagined this was to be his destiny when over thirty years before he'd retreated from a family business in Liverpool?

The security offered by the L&NW to investors undoubtedly reflected the soundness of Moon's financial management. However the very solidity of the structure he had created was to bring its own problems when faced with new challenges for change. In attempting to deal with these with the same cautious approach that brought financial success, Moon makes it difficult at times to appreciate that in his younger days he had been such a driving force for progress and reform. Unfortunately it is this shift to a more conservative attitude that he is largely remembered for today, in particular his handling of new technology and reaction to regulation. His defence that his policies were always in the best interests of the company is understandable, his life was the company, but what is more difficult to appreciate was his continued obsession with detail.

In his last years he was still approving such items as the water supply for a drinking fountain in Stafford 'subject to the corporation agreeing to pay for the water at the rate of 6d. per 1,000 gallons', and amending rules for the collection of gas accounts. Remarkably it was at one of his last board meetings that a decision was solemnly taken to agree 'the provision of a lavatory adjoining the Billiard Room at the Greenore hotel at an estimated cost of £32'. No wonder a frustrated Findlay wrote in his book on management, in discussing the company's approval procedure, that the chairman 'who keeps a watchful guard over the company's purse strings, has to be convinced that the expenditure is not only desirable but actually unavoidable'. On reading this, standing on the desolate Greenore point over a century later with the waters of Carlingford Lough swirling past the quay, it was not envisaging the *Eleanor* alongside that brought a lump of nostalgia to the throat of this author, but the imagined click of billiard balls from the empty shell of the hotel [subsequently demolished] behind him. Was it Moon stooped over the table?

To return to technology and regulation, the challenges facing the aging Moon were many. By technology is meant the basic signalling and braking systems that enable a railway to operate safely. In looking back to mid-nineteenth century practice it is hard to appreciate just how crude early systems were on all railways. Interlocking of points and signals was not at first regarded as essential, the merits or otherwise of automatic braking were debatable, accidents were accepted as inevitable and liability for compensation considered a burdensome expense. All were concepts held generally by railway officials at the time, none more so than by Moon. Demands for greater safety came from both the public and from the government; consequently pressure for regulation grew: a concept familiar to the twenty-first century but strongly resisted by the powerful independent companies of the nineteenth. And when the government attempted to interfere in the rates and charges from which the companies were dependent for their income, no chairman protested more strongly than Moon, claiming such a policy amounted to no less than 'confiscation'.

A firm believer in the rights given to companies by their Acts of incorporation, Moon not only fought outside interference from such bodies as the government and trading associations, but any organised attempt from within to determine his policies. Driven by old-fashioned ideas of paternalism, Moon was not alone among leading employers in also seeing no need to concede to the growing demands of trade unionism. However with a labour-force the size of Crewe's it was not surprising that such attitudes would inevitably lead to conflict. Moon's handling of all these matters and his final years into retirement form the subjects of the remaining chapters of this book.

CHAPTER 23

SAFETY

Railways when first envisaged were thought to be no different from toll roads and canals in that owners assumed responsibility for only the track leaving others to provide the services. Even when the impracticability of having uncontrolled access was soon accepted, it did not necessarily follow that any system introduced should take away responsibility for individual trains from the drivers and guards; an over-reliance on mechanical means only encouraging a slackening in vigilance on their part. Moon was strongly of this view.

Concepts that are obvious today, that signalling and points should be inter-locked, that a signal to proceed could be given only if the appropriate junction or switch in the rails had also been set and that no train should enter a section, or 'block', of line until the preceding one had been cleared, were not acknowledged as critical; neither was a system of fail-safe braking, or even if it were, agreement would not have been reached over the most effective means.

The Board of Trade inspectors, whose approval was required before a new line could be opened to the public, were also responsible for inquiring into accidents. Their reports in apportioning blame and recommending remedial action could demand, but not necessarily enforce, changes in methods of working. In August 1867 Moon had typically complained to his shareholders over. 'how often upon a change of officers of the Board of Trade were they to change their system of signals?'. He said that 'as a matter of course accidents could not be prevented entirely'. He thought that 'this new plan of Saxby and Farmer [for interlocking] would fail, but on the whole they thought it advisable to adopt that plan. They could not, however, build Rome in a day, and from that time to the present they had altered 182 junctions, and so had done a very great deal towards accomplishing what the Board of Trade recommended'. He couldn't help adding however that another reason why he was doubtful about their success was that 'many of the companies did not adopt it; and he believed that up to the present time the Midland had not done so, or at all events, till very recently. Mr Allport [Midland general manager] was a man of great experience, and certainly his experience was greater than that of any theoretical officer of the B.of T.'. Moon was being too dismissive: accident inspecting officers were all ex-Royal Engineers and well versed in railway technology. Clearly what really rankled was resentment at being told by a Government department what to do.

An 'interlocking' system had been patented in 1860 by J.Saxby and, following an earlier B.of T. condition for approving the opening of a new junction, the L&NW had subsequently agreed to some trial installations. Largely on the potential for L&NW work, Saxby then set up manufacturing facilities with J.S.Farmer and their partnership was to become the leading supplier of such equipment.

Moon's scepticism stemmed from his attitude to expenditure which could not be quantifiable in terms of financial benefits. For him it seemed that the matter was one of being convinced that the expense could be justified on economic as well as safety grounds. He was complaining in February 1870 that the company 'had spent for the protection of the public £48,000 in the single item of concentrating and locking points'. Neele recalled that Moon's urging of 'economy in all departments made the necessity for improved signalling go much "against the grain" with him, and had it not been that Saxby and Farmer by their concentration were able in various cases to show the possibility of reduction in the number of men employed at stations, the improvement would I fear not have made the progress it did'.

These improvements had not prevented one of the most horrific accidents of the century in the summer of 1868 on the Chester & Holyhead line at Abergele. It had been a very shaken chairman who found himself, at the half-yearly L&NW meeting on 21 August, rising before his shareholders 'under very depressing circumstances, owing to the accident which occurred on our line yesterday, whereby above twenty of our fellow-creatures have been hurried into eternity'.

The events leading to that accident began at Llandulas where some goods wagons, loaded with barrels of highly inflammable oil, had been shunted on to the main line where they had run away on a falling gradient into the path of the Irish mail express. The collision cascaded broken barrels of oil over the front part of the passenger train, which instantly caught fire from the hot coals of the engine. The driver had jumped clear but the fireman and all thirty-two passengers in the front carriages perished. The accident happened in the early afternoon, and although Binger, the area superintendent and his engineer Lee, were quickly on the scene it is unlikely that Euston would have had the full details even by the following morning. Yet, shaken as he was, Moon instinctive reaction was to defend the company's position.

> We have looked with pride upon our Irish Mail as the finest service in the world - punctual to a proverb - and yet this awful catastrophe has overtaken it. All the consolation that remains to us is to know that nothing which money, ingenuity, skill, or ability could provide has been left undone for the safety and comfort of our passengers. Our line was in splendid order, our engines and rolling stock in the best possible condition, our signals the most perfect that could be devised. In a word, there was nothing which has been proved to be good or useful that we have not without hesitation or regard to expense, adopted. ... All this, I know, is but poor consolation to those who have suffered from this calamity, to their relations and friends. With them we can only sympathise; and I am sure I shall have you all with me when I say with what pain we have witnessed so grievous a calamity - the most awful that has yet happened in this country.

To add to the tragedy the immediate public inquest was a shambles: the coroner had little idea how to handle proceedings as the dead could not be identified and it took unilateral action by the bereaved to force a mass burial of the charred remains and the appointment of 'an assessor' to complete the inquest. There is no evidence that Moon publicly attended the inquest or funeral, Cawkwell was the senior company man listed as present. The inquest was the subject of national interest with *The Times* writing several leaders and publishing daily reports. Among letters to the paper one, from "C.L.S.", was particularly prescient in advocating the general adoption of the block system. The correspondent ended by saying that to prevent accidents entirely was impossible 'but to diminish them is possible; but this duty is not sufficiently appreciated by those at the head of railway management'. The *Illustrated London News* had engravings showing scenes of the disaster.

Although signalling failure was not the cause of the accident the fact that shunting was taking place on a main line only minutes in front of an express raised serious questions on the efficiency of the train control system. Moon's old adversary Wrigley used the occasion to write a long letter again advocating the keeping of signals at danger until a positive indication was confirmed that it was safe to proceed (which is the modern practice, the reverse was still then the general method). Moon's unfortunate claim that the signals were perfect led Wrigley to remind *The Times* readers that the L&NW had paid compensation for accidents and losses over the previous twelve months of almost £150,000. He witheringly commented that 'it is difficult to believe that if there had been no attempt at perfect arrangements matters could have been much worse'. In making the point that shunting had taken place on the line within two minutes of the time when the train was due, he asked, 'what are we to think of the perfect arrangement theory?'.

It was at the following shareholders' meeting that Wrigley was nominated as a L&NW director but he declined to stand.

Although the L&NW had introduced the telegraph as an aid to regulating trains on a section, or 'block', of the line between stations or junctions it was slow to be widely used. During Moon's early chairmanship years the train control system was still based on a time interval system. Trains were allowed to follow each other after a given lapse of time. Under this system the method of working was known as the 'permissive block' system. Despite the availability of the telegraph to notify train movements and the opportunity it gave to control 'absolutely' the entry of only one train at a time into the section, this was not deemed necessary providing the time interval between each train was maintained. However this meant that the signalman at the receiving end of the section had no control over the trains approaching him. Yet this was the system that Moon and others were still defending in 1870. He told shareholders that

66. Abergele accident 1868
Artist's impression of scene at Abergele after L&NW's disastrous accident on 20
August 1868. ILN

67. L&NW train for 1875 Newark brake trials
L&NW train comprising a section of four carriages and a chain brake van, headed
by a 'Precedent' class 2-2-2 loco, preparing for the Newark trials in June 1875.
LNWRS

under pressure from the B.of T. 'they were trying the experiment of the absolute block upon 14½ miles of a most difficult portion, the Stour Valley, and had worked 91½ miles of single line upon it'. But he made the point that 'they had also 310 miles of line worked upon their own telegraph caution system and they believed that to be the best and most effectual'.

In August 1871 Moon reported that 150 miles of line were 'on the block system, 400 miles on their own telegraph system, and 550 miles were, in deference to public opinion, mind, I say in deference only to public opinion, in course of conversion to the block system'. A year later he was complaining that 'the insistence of Parliament upon the block system had involved them in a cost of £120,000 a year'. And he took the opportunity to rant generally on other demands being put upon them, the B.of T. for example changing their minds on the 'cord communication' and 'there were also smoking carriages to be provided and some persons had proposed foot warmers. Next they would be expected to supply dinners!' The L&NW were to introduce their first dining car two years before he retired.

By 1873 over half the lines of the L&NW were covered by interlocking and the 'new-fashioned mode of signalling', which, Moon complained, had cost £500,000. Although most companies had by then adopted the *absolute* system, he still personally believed the 'permissive block' was the best 'because it leaves a larger amount of responsibility on the driver, who is the captain of the ship'. His continued reluctance to accept the superiority of the absolute system was not just over costs, but in reduced flexibility. He was to touch on both these considerations when countering the Chichester Fortescue (President of the B.of T.) circular in November 1873 to all company chairmen, enclosing Captain Tyler's general accident report for 1872 which criticised the companies for not doing enough to improve safety.

Amongst the many criticisms the report asserted that 'methods of working and mechanical contrivances, the value of which has been thoroughly ascertained, have been too slowly introduced; and there is great reason to believe that sufficient provision has not been made for the safe working of the increased traffic'. John Bright, Fortescue's predecessor at the B. of T., had written personally at the time to Moon's fellow railway chairman Watkin assuring him that the government had no intention to be unjust to the railway interest and telling him not to show bitterness and hostility against the Board. 'If you have the facts let us have them. It is in your interest not to exhibit temper, but to show that you are as anxious as the Board and the newspapers to secure the safety of those who travel'. Moon certainly responded with the facts as he saw them and not a little temper. His vigorous rebuttal of all the criticisms ran to over 3,500 words and was published the following February with the proceedings of his shareholders' meeting. It seems, however, that Moon was more concerned to defend his company's position than appreciate the force of public and press opinion.

On the question of block working and interlocking Moon claimed that the L&NW began 'before any other to work the trains on part of their line by telegraph, on what was afterwards termed the "Permissive Block System" which was considered a great improvement at the time'. He claimed that the L&NW was the first to introduce the Saxby interlocking patent and the many modifications and improvements since, with 13,000 new signals and corresponding apparatus installed by the end of 1872. Moon then quoted the House of Lords Committee's report on the evidence that had rejected a proposed Bill to enforce interlocking. 'A perfect system of interlocking requires many complicated arrangements, such as refuge sidings, alteration of signal stations, and other changes which, especially where the junction unites two lines under the management of differing companies, involve matters of difficult adjustment.'

Though only 135 miles of L&NW's line were then being worked on the old system, Moon still couldn't resist commenting that they had made the change 'under the pressure of public opinion - which you know I do not share in, believing our own permissive system is far better'. He went further by complaining that the new system 'has brought about a sudden and great difficulty in the management of the traffic ... which is a very serious matter and always weighs heavily on my mind'. He said the company 'had not sufficient people trained and experienced in the working of those scientific instruments - the telegraph and the new system of interlocking'. And that they had 'to train an immense number of people. In addition to that, not being able to go on gradually as we were doing, your arrangements for sidings and other facilities for carrying the traffic on this system have not been completed'. Still complaining six months later over the expense, Moon hoped that shareholders would derive in the future some advantage; 'but it is not yet at an end. For the next two or three years you will still continue to have a large item charged every half-year to the revenue of the company'.

Moon was to return again and again to the cost, the uncertainty of the benefit and how difficult the system made the management of the line. It took him until the summer of 1875 before he admitted publicly that there could be benefits. Even then he qualified his admission by saying that however much safety the absolute block secured 'it was purchased at a very considerable cost. Not, indeed, that they grudged the cost if they could thereby obtain safety'. He claimed that 'out of two or three and twenty million passengers whom they had carried during the last half-year, only one person had been killed'.

Even when in early 1877 there were only 55 miles of the old system remaining, Moon still thought 'it is the best'! A year later he told shareholders 'you must not suppose that even the block system can ensure absolute safety. The human eye and the human hand will also be responsible to a certain extent. We have always told you that if the block system fails, which it will occasionally do, the catastrophe is likely to be worse than it would be under the old regime, when the driver was always on the watch for fear he should come into a collision'.

In addition to signalling control Fortescue had been critical over the general lack of a fail-safe braking system. Here the answer was not so straightforward. Opinions varied widely over the most effective system. Moon in his response to this issue had commented that braking had recently been 'brought prominently before the public, and is a good example of the difficulty with mechanical inventions on a large scale'. He claimed that the L&NW had been carrying out experiments for many years and had 'given every facility to inventors to use our plant and lines to try their experiments whenever there seemed any prospect of success'. However 'it is left to us to find out their defects and that can be done only by long trials under the varying circumstances of our traffic'. He pointed out that the L&NW had 'some 4,000 vehicles, exclusive of engines, used in passenger trains, all, or nearly all, of which would have to be fitted with the apparatus to make it generally applicable, it is obvious that this cannot be done - especially in the face of a constant supply of new inventions and improvements - without much time and consideration'. But his main objection was clearly deeper than that. He went on to say:

> It should be observed with regard to all these mechanical appliances, whether brakes, or interlocking, or any others which are believed to meet some particular danger, that they are liable to create a feeling of confidence in the men, who are therefore naturally induced to risk more than they would otherwise do. Hence an accidental failure in one of them may produce more danger than their absence, and they should never be generally adopted until after the fullest trial of their certainty of action, not only of trains specially prepared for an experiment, but under the varying circumstances of general traffic.

Gooch, as chairman of the GW, had implied similar consequences in his company's response, warning 'that grave and serious dangers may arise from too great a reliance on mechanical appliances as substitutes for manual labour'. However Neele recorded that this view was not one generally held by more progressive management. In noting what progress had been made with the absolute block and interlocking he wrote 'but we never failed to hear from the chairman that these mechanical appliances were all inducements to inattention on the part of signalmen and drivers'.

Moon's seemingly perverse resistance to introducing continuous and automatic brakes must be seen in the context of not only then current practice but the practical difficulties of implementing a common system At the Railway Companies Association meeting in June 1871, leading managers had not been able to agree on a solution. All were experimenting with 'continuous and other brakes'. And the Government was reluctant to impose any particular system, being mainly concerned to ensure that companies improved their standards of safety and that accidents were reduced.

The traditional way of braking trains was by the engine or its tender, supplemented by brake vans interspersed between, or in, the carriages. Following the failure of a private attempt in 1873 to legislate for the enforcement of block and interlocking, the mover was more successful the following year when he proposed a Royal Commission on accidents to examine the railways' safety record. The chairman appointed for this commission was none other than the Duke of Buckingham, formerly the Marquis of Chandos, ex-chairman of the L&NW.

Buckingham's brief was wide: including such aspects as reviewing signalmen's hours as well as braking systems. Whether Buckingham's own idea, it appears that the Commission was the first to propose running trials to compare different systems. The request was made through the Railway Companies Association. Moon was not on the committee appointed by the association to arrange trials and was not present when details were agreed, but he accepted that the L&NW should participate as did six other companies. All agreed to provide complete trains (except the North Eastern who did not use their own engine) to demonstrate various systems being used or proposed.

The trials took place in June 1875, on a stretch of the Midland's Nottingham to Lincoln line west of Newark. However it appears that although useful information was gathered, and the interest shown by the railway world was considerable, no firm conclusions were drawn. Each company remained convinced that their system was satisfactory. Whether the outcome would have been different had Buckingham remained its chairman is an interesting point. He left for India in the autumn of 1875 before any conclusions could be published. Under a new chairman the Commission was to take another three years before finishing its work and left the question of brake recommendations unresolved.

In writing to Buckingham before he sailed, Moon gives a rare glimpse of another side of his character. Whatever he thought of the Royal Commission's work Moon showed personal warmth for its chairman. In July he had written that it would be very agreeable if 'before you leave for the honourable appointment of Governor of Madras you would favour myself and colleagues with your company at dinner. We have so long been associated together that before parting from England for a term at the end of which many may be gone or separated in all directions, it will be very pleasant to have one more social gathering'. Buckingham of couse was present at the shareholders' dinner given to Moon in 1872 but it is clear that they had kept in touch socially beforehand. In the summer of the previous year for example, Buckingham had written to Moon saying he would like to entertain old colleagues at Stowe after a board meeting, hoping that 'you will close the minute book early and you will come yourself with Mrs Moon'.

For their passenger trains the L&NW had by then adopted a long established chain brake, originally designed by John Clark, but subsequently modified by the company's locomotive superintendents. The brakes were sectional, covering only a group of carriages rather than the whole train. The carriages comprising a section were connected by a chain, which ran from the furthest one to a revolving shaft in a specialist brake van. This shaft was connected by a friction drum to the wheels of the van which, when engaged, tensioned the chain and applied the brakes. A weighted-lever in the brake van triggered the drive. Though operated directly by the guard the lever could also be remotely triggered by the driver through a connecting cord. It was a simple system, crude in its application and could not be applied gradually. However it was effective in stopping a train in an emergency providing the chain did not brake. For a standard length train at least two brake-vanned sections were required. And as originally conceived it was not automatic: if the chain broke then the brakes could not be applied. Although the system was subsequently adapted to fail-safe, the brake levers kept in the off position by compressed springs maintained by keeping the connecting chain in tension, it was not continuous as it could not be applied to the whole train.

The systems used at the Newark trials were all meant to be continuous and it was originally intended to test them at sixty miles an hour. Over fifty experiments were initially carried out using complete trains. However the varying weights of the trains and locomotive power meant that, over the distance set, speeds much above 50 mph were not possible, so from the actual stopping distances achieved a theoretical distance was calculated based on a standard speed. Although a chain broke on the first run, the L&NW's brake performed well in a subsequent group of experiments, the stopping distance being bettered amongst air and vacuum systems by only the Midland's Westinghouse automatic air brake.

Although it appeared that the Westinghouse system performed

the best the issues were not clear-cut. For example Westinghouse relied on a critical control valve system which gave rise to operating difficulties. Their problem was that the valve could not apply and release the brake gradually. It could apply the brake to any desired degree but not the release. Once released the brakes could only be applied again when the whole system was recharged (see Rodney Weaver's article in the *Journal of the R&CH Society* for November 1981).

Some eighteen months after the Newark trials Moon summarised the L&NW's position as follows:

> It is nearly twenty years since we bought the first continuous break [sic] - Fay's patent. We have a large number of carriages arranged with that break, and I don't know a better break that has yet been introduced, as far as convenience is concerned; but it is not put on so quickly as the new continuous breaks, which are self-acting. When Clark's break was brought out eight or nine years ago, we purchased the patent, and our late superintendent, Mr Ramsbottom, did a great deal to improve it, and our present superintendent, Mr Webb, has completed the improvement, and we believe it is the best break yet produced. It is not only the best break in itself, but it enables other carriages, not adapted to it to be introduced into the train, and if you have a break on the first and last portions of the train, it is more than ample for all the purposes of a continuous break. With regard to the application of it, I think all our suburban trains and all our express trains out of Euston are supplied with it, and we are increasing the use of it every day. A certain additional number of carriages are provided weekly with the break, but in addition to this, in a short time other carriages will also be provided with chain or rope which can be used on all the trains provided with the continuous break.

Moon then went on to make the point that the brake was used only for bringing the train to a standstill. His distrust of any system which reduced the care and watchfulness of the driver and guard was apparent when he explained 'you must bear in mind that except for stopping trains, we dare not let Clark's break be used as the ordinary break, but simply as supplementary. To let it be used as an ordinary break would be to incite men to come within danger, to come within the distance in which the train can be pulled up'. By ordinary brakes he meant primarily those on the locomotive. However at his next shareholder meeting Moon did admit 'the brake power has enabled our drivers to avoid some difficulties that might have resulted without it'. At that time, August 1877, Moon complained that although the chain brake was applied to 'about half of the whole stock' he thought it odd that 'although we have done this at very large cost ... nobody seems to be aware of the continuous brake on the North Western line'. He boasted that 'you see all manner of brakes named; but the one we use we think is the best - I think there is not the smallest doubt about it - and it is more largely used than any other'. He said it had a 'pre-eminent advantage above all others, that anybody's carriages may come into our train, and still the continuous brake may be used on the train; and I don't think that would apply to any other brake in the country'.

Despite Moon's rhetoric the L&NW's system was *not* continuous. Criticism of its working increased, even from the L&NW's own staff. Neele's comments were scathing. After referring to the 'incumbrance' of the chain brake with its 'jerks' and 'stoppages' at roadside stations accompanied 'by a sharp shock', he wrote that very few of the other companies followed our lead, the 'Caledonian being loud in their condemnation of the arrangement'. And the 'system completely failed to comply with the Board of Trade requirements, promulgated in 1876, viz., that the brake should be applicable to all the vehicles on the train; that its control should primarily be in the hands of the drivers; that the guards should also be able to apply it; and that it should act automatically on the vehicles in case of break-away'.

Nevertheless Moon persisted in justifying the company's system. In February 1878 he told shareholders that '£50,000 had been spent and a further £50,000 was necessary to complete the fitting of the brake'. Moon believed the company had done 'more in applying this continuous brake than all the companies in the country put together'. And stung by persistent sniping over safety generally, he was provoked to comment, 'It has been said that railway directors thought first of the dividend and then of the safety of the public, but whoever it was that said that, it was a scandalous libel'.

A year later Moon reported that the subject of brakes was the 'chief item of expenditure' and 'a subject which had given them an immensity of anxiety'. But he dogmatically stuck to his defence of the chain brake. 'He did not believe that any man in his senses would say that they ought to trust their trains to a self-acting brake. It might sometimes act when they required it, but it was more likely to involve them in a new class of accidents, of which they had no experience. They set their faces against self-acting brakes, and held that it must be in the hands of the driver and the guard.' He argued that all their through trains were 'supplied' with engine and tender brakes, the two guards' brakes and the 'supplemental brake, one put on by the guard and one by the driver, and further there was the power of the engine driver to reverse the engine, so that, practically ... they had six powerful brakes, such as were never used before in the history of railways'.

The L&NW was not alone in failing to comply with the ideal of the continuous and automatic principle. In June 1880 the Board of Trade asked all the main companies to report their position. One of the main alternatives to the complicated Westinghouse air brake was Smith's simple vacuum, the term "simple" meaning that it was not fail-safe. The brakes were applied by the force of the vacuum, which of course meant if a pipe leaked or fractured the brakes were inoperative. The L&NW's reply sent by Findlay, fell back on Moon's 1873 response and explained the developments which had led to the adoption of 'a brake which can be applied by both the engine driver and guard, and is otherwise in conformity with the conditions named by the Board of Trade ... and no time will, therefore, be lost in extending its use to the whole of the carriage stock of the company'.

But the writing was on the wall for the chain brake. Criticism now grew apace and Moon's public utterances on the subject became strangely muted. Neele wrote, in recalling 1882, that 'all Mr Findlay's special pleading, and all the chairman's determination, could not get over the Board of Trade report that the brake was sectional, was not continuous throughout the length of the train, and was not self-acting'. Neele quoted as an example the 9.0am train out of Euston in 1880. It had 'two engines and seventeen vehicles behind them, brake in three parts, seven vehicles for Liverpool, six for Holyhead, and three for Birmingham, each section with separate brake communication, but all of no service as a continuous brake'. Although he went on to say that an 'automatic cord' was subsequently introduced to link all the sections and a 'double gear' brake van used to work the flanking sections simultaneously, the Government inspectors would not approve the system: the brake was not continuous and not automatic. He recalled that 'case after case arose in which these points came under notice, and the half-yearly reports issued by the Board of Trade are far from pleasant reading'.

Moon's belief in the mechanical simplicity of the chain brake was at a time when the theoretical advantages of the early vacuum and air brakes were plagued by technical problems in practice. However his thinking would also have been influenced by the expenditure committed to the chain brake and the additional costs of radically changing to another system. It has been suggested that Webb would have developed an automatic vacuum system but for Moon's opposition. This may well have been the case, yet Webb was also committed to refining the chain brake and it would have been entirely in character for Moon to have publicly backed his faith in Webb by supporting his engineer in justifying the continuance of the old system.

However when it became inevitable that a proper continuous system had to replace the outdated chain brake it does appear that Moon influenced Webb in his choice of one based on the least costly to adapt to existing brake linkages. At a conference of twelve company locomotive superintendents held at Euston in April 1881, Webb persuaded nine of them to adopt the simple vacuum, instead of what they should have done (and eventually had to do) install the fail-safe automatic system where the vacuum kept the brakes from being applied. It seemed that low cost ease of conversion had outweighed any other consideration.

Moon later explained to his shareholders that although he still thought the chain brake satisfactory the company had, after 'interviews with the chairmen of the Great Northern, Great Western, Midland, Lancashire & Yorkshire, Manchester Sheffield & Lincolnshire, and the North Staffordshire railways' agreed to change. 'All these companies with whom they interchanged a large amount of traffic used the vacuum brake, and they found they could apply the system to their own brake gear, without materially altering it, and thus render interchange easier.'

In August 1884 Moon reported that they had begun 'to a considerable extent' the change from the chain brake. In responding to a question from an anxious shareholder he quoted failure rates to justify his company's choice. From a Board of Trade return covering the four years to 1883, he showed that the Westinghouse air brake had been used for 71 million miles with 3,900 failures, the automatic vacuum 42 million miles with 519 failures, and the non-automatic vacuum 62.5 million miles and 555 failures. He further justified the simple vacuum by quoting from senior inspector Col. Yolland's accident report.

Yolland had referred to the Westinghouse automatic air-pressure brake as 'a very clever and ingenious piece of mechanism, made up of a very great number of separate parts to give it automatic action; but, as is well known, the greater the number of parts in any piece of mechanism the greater is the liability to failure'. And he rather dryly considered that 'the liability to apply itself when not required and when there is no accident, and to fail to act or go on when absolutely required by the engine driver, constitute two grave defects in its present construction'.

Despite Moon's comment that the company had improved the simple vacuum principle 'so that if there is a break-away the automatic van will come into action immediately' the brake still failed to provide the obvious safety of a fully automatic system over the whole length of the train. Moon remained adamant in not changing to automatic, answering criticism at the company's February 1885 half-yearly meeting by a terse 'we are not going to alter it at all'. But in fact he had already conceded the principle. As Neele wrote, in recalling the company's 1885 regulations, 'they lay down the fact that carriages and vans are now fitted with the vacuum brake, which can be applied by the driver. The [brake] van is also provided with an automatic brake, held off by a small vacuum, which must be constantly maintained in the train pipe'.

In October 1884 correspondence over competing claims between Westinghouse and the Vacuum Brake Company (simple vacuum) had been published. In pushing their automatic system Westinghouse

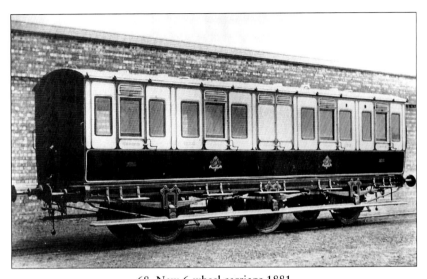

68. New 6-wheel carriage 1881

L&NW 6-wheel tri-composite carriage introduced in 1881, one of first to be fitted
with the simple vacuum brake. LNWRS

69. Armagh accident 1889

Great Northern Railway of Ireland 1889 accident: disconnected carriages ran back
on the bank out of Armagh crashing into following train. With 80 killed, worst to
date, the accident made automatic brakes and block telegraph compulsory.

referred to Moon as once telling shareholders that 'no man in his senses would trust his life to an automatic brake', yet he had now so far abandoned that opinion that he has since informed his shareholders that, whilst applying a non automatic vacuum brake to his trains, he has fitted his brake vans with an automatic system, which 'however useless this may be' indicates that he has at least taken a 'step towards automatic'.

Unrepentant the seventy-three-year old Moon was still defending even the chain brake as late as February 1887, complaining that the cost of coverting to the vacuum would be £110,000 and that 'more than half of their stock is already fitted with it ... [and] in deference to the wishes of some of the neighbouring companies, they had also agreed to instruct their officers to make the brake automatic, and that they were doing at a cost of £45,000'. He emphasised that he would not like shareholders 'to run away with the idea' that the continuous brake was to do away with all danger. On the contrary, it had its own special dangers. He was not in favour of it, but in deference to the general desire of the community and the wishes of the Board of Trade they were adopting it'. A year later his final public comment on the subject, when reporting progress on replacing the 'old Clark brake' with the vacuum and the fitting of the automatic vacuum, was that 'it is however a very expensive work'.

Legally no enforcement of a continuous automatic system on passenger trains was enacted until near Moon's retirement when the Armagh accident in 1889 made the fitting compulsory. That accident cost eighty lives, the highest number up until that time on any British railway. Taken over by the Great Northern Railway of Ireland ten years previously (no connection with the English Great Northern), the Newry and Armagh line was still operated on the time interval basis and the brakes the simple vacum. The engine of an overcrowded excursion train for Warrenpoint had failed on a steep gradient out of Armagh. In attempting to continue over the summit the train was divided. With the vacuum broken the brakes were released on the carriages temporarily left behind, which then ran away down the gradient and crashed into a following train.

However by then the threat of compulsion and the obvious benefit of improved safety had been sufficient for most companies to make the changes required for effective braking and signalling.

Nevertheless in the twilight of his chairmanship Moon was still protesting internally. In October 1890 the L&NW board noted a meeting held by Moon at which more time was sought under the then mandatory order to apply continuous brakes to engines and tenders and that the 'company carries out the order under protest'.

By the time Moon did retire there were still around 700 L&NW engines and 500 vehicles fitted with the chain brake and it was not until over a year later that the automatic vacuum was fully installed on the L&NW.

It is easy to ridicule Moon for opposing for so long the introduction of a modern brake. Resistance to change, lack of technical vision, in-built opposition to Government pressure and too great an emphasis on capping costs, are all accusations that are difficult to counter. However given the lack of common purpose among his contemporaries and the undoubted shortcomings of alternative systems, Moon was at least consistent in backing a system, albeit outdated and cumbersome, that had practical advantages. The matter was not resolved unanimously by railways themselves until long after he retired. The technical advantages of the competing systems all had their limitations. The chain brake was crude, but it did work and its safety record was good. The authorities never did recommend any one system to be used. Although Moon appeared to have been suffering from amnesia when referring to the lack of complaints over the chain brake, he had a point when alluding to the low cost and incidence of faults. The failure rate of the early vacuum and air systems was high: the most popular Westinghouse air being over four times worse than the automatic vacuum and over six times the simple vacuum. The Midland, which in so many ways had taken the lead in innovative change, became so seriously dissatisfied with Westinghouse's air system that they changed to vacuum.

The legacy of the nineteenth century 'battle of the brakes' was the complete lack of standardisation which lasted until the advent of British Railways in 1948. No better example of the folly of maintaining different systems had been the need to fit both the Westinghouse air and simple vacuum to the L&NW and Caledonian West Coast joint carriage stock; the Caledonian, with most of the other Scottish companies, adopting the air brake. When Moon first announced the change to the vacuum system he thought 'no doubt all the companies would be eventually of one accord with regard to the adoption of the vacuum brake'. Whilst most of the main English companies did so there were some notable exceptions, for example the North Eastern, Great Eastern, and the southern companies L&BSC and London Chatham & Dover all stuck with the air brake.

C H A P T E R   2 4

REGULATION OR CONFISCATION?

It has been argued that by 1873 Britain reached her peak as a major player in world markets with increasing competition from abroad beginning to erode the returns of manufacturers and traders. Inevitably such traders looked to their inland carriers, principally of course the railways, for matching reductions in freight charges. That it was not in the railways' interest to do so inevitably led to conflict. Having invested heavily in providing the improved services and facilities demanded by such users, the railways naturally resisted attempts to reduce their own returns. The effect on relations between the railway companies and their trading customers was to come to a head in the battle over freight rates.

The tribunal enacted in 1873 that set up the Railway Commissioners, proved limited in scope and had been given powers for only five years. Their failure to make an impact on reducing rates led to further attempts to legislate against the railway interest, which in turn strenghtened the companies resistance to such moves.

By early 1875 Moon had launched into a typical tirade against the pressures building for reductions, telling his shareholders that:

> The public are daily expecting more and more from the railways; they also want us to reduce the rates, and we find we cannot put them up again, so that the contingencies are all against us; our expenses go up, but we cannot get the traders to pay more money; they say "give us whatever you can, but we don't want to pay anything for it." That is the course of things throughout the country. .... This railway interest is very badly used, if you look at the tyranny of Parliament, the tyranny of the Board of Trade, the tyranny of the Inland Revenue department, and the tyranny of the public. No interest in the country has done so much as the

railways for the prosperity of the country. It has brought
its mines into play and developed its ironworks, yet no
interest is so poorly remunerated.

He claimed that there was not a trader in the country who would
take so low a rate of interest on their money as his shareholders took
in dividends. 'We.must prevent any further interference with our
rights and privileges.' He said they were 'knocked about on all hands
before we can stir; we cannot put in a junction without consulting
somebody first. If railways are to be managed by first-rate people,
they must be dealt with in a first-rate way, and not in the shabby way
in which they are dealt with today'.

The Commisioners, in recognising the weakness of their position,
sought to renew powers to exercise greater control, but it was not
until February 1881 that a Parliamentary Select Committee was
specifically proposed to look into railway rates and charges. Although
only seven of the twenty-seven-man membership represented the
railway interest, the Committee, when reporting their findings in July
1882, was reasonably favourable to the railway companies. Basically
they recommended the following: one uniform classification of
goods; the conditional recognition of terminal charges; the Railway
Commissioners to be permanent but their through rate powers not to
be such as to reduce current lowest rates; appeals were to be allowed;
and (on the subject of Irish railways) any proposals for amalgamation
could be considered.

Moon however was quick to label the Railway Commissioners
as a 'standing menace to this great property'. Although the Ralway
Companies Association accepted the Select Committee's findings it
was not until towards the end of the following year that members
began a detailed review with the Government of the new goods
classification and proposed rate changes, including the recognition of
terminal charges. Early in 1884 however the Government proposed
an omnibus Bill linking the issue of rates and charges to safety
matters, in particular the brakes question.

The right to make additional charges to cover the costs of
handling within the terminal stations had become an emotive issue
with traders, who resisted it, and the companies who maintained it
was within their enacted rights. The Commissioners had disagreed,

maintaining that the charges for the use of goods' stations and sidings were an integral part of the maximum rate. The Government now saw the opportunity of using the threat to disallow such charges as a bargaining chip with the companies to impose other conditions. Moon found himself chairing a long meeting of the Railway Companies Association on 4 March 1884 to consider these conditions. Watkin put the hard-liners' view that the question of terminal charges should be dealt with 'without condition'. On the wider rates issue Moon had sufficiently compromised to obtain agreement on a somewhat woolly amendment that the companies 'will not object to some provision in the Bill which shall make it the interest of the railway companies to adopt the classification'.

A deputation of railway managers met the Board of Trade officials to review the Bill but could not reach agreement. Continuing to insist on a more favourable Terminals clause the companies eventually rejected the proposals. Though the Commons passed a motion by Samuelson (a leader of the traders' interest) allowing local Chambers of Commerce to petition against the Bill on the grounds that rates could be injurious to trade, the Government withdrew the Bill. It seems that they were torn between the two factions. In effect they compromised by asking the railway companies to bring in their own Bills. The companies agreed; the L&NW, GW, Midland, North Eastern, Great Eastern and the three main southern companies each undertaking to submit identical bills.

At a time of worsening recession railways were already under considerable pressure to reduce their charges. Moon had reported in the summer of 1884 that trade was 'now worse than ever' and that the dividend was the 'greatest drop this half year that has ever occurred'. Early the following year the companies agreed to a conference with the traders and for the Board of Trade to attempt mediation.

As the eighties progressed the railway companies were only slowly waking up to the shift taking place in the country as a whole in attitudes to railways. Gone were the days when they were accepted as being no different from any other private company free to make profits as best they could. They were now expected to have social responsibilities, to provide facilities and services for the convenience of the community and trade, almost irrespective of cost. In protesting so publicly against such demands, Moon would have considered that he was only doing his duty to his shareholders, yet already he must have known that some change was inevitable.

When first reporting to his shareholders on the railways' own Rates & Charges Bill, Moon found himself having to use the excuse that in agreeing to the proposal it was to their advantage to have a simplified common system. But at a special shareholders' meeting called in March 1885, Moon had to explain that though the Bill would 'enact the maximum tolls beyond which we shall have no power to charge, it does not mean that it fixes the charges we are to make to the community'.

Objections to the railway companies' Bills grew, the Board of Trade committing to oppose them. The companies were then forced to re-examine their stance and in April they announced that their members would withdraw their proposals. One of the objectives of the company Bills had been to have the terminal charges allowed as an addition to the maximum rates. The issue had come to a head when one of the leading southern companies, the London Brighton & South Coast Railway, challenged a judgement given in favour of a customer, Hall & Co, who had refused to pay a terminal charge. The Railway Companies Association agreed to back the LB&SC in appealing and they won their case in June. With the withdrawal of the companies' Bills the whole issue of reclassifying and simplifying rates and charges was now back with the Government.

Traders were additionally accusing the railways of giving preferential rates to importers at the expense of domestic trade. At his February 1886 shareholders' meeting Moon denied this, but claimed, somewhat ambiguously, that if his company did not offer competitive rates the trade would be lost to them. Moon at this meeting was at the end of his fifth five-year term as a director. Had he known what lay ahead he may well have decided not to offer himself for re-election. The following month the freshly elected Gladstone Government, through the President of the Board of Trade, A.J.Mundella, introduced their controversial Railway and Canal Traffic Bill.

Mundella's Bill would give the Government strong powers over setting rates and charges. An ultra Liberal (and a manufacturer) Mundella had reacted favourably to the trading lobby. However he claimed that his Bill was based on the draft inherited from his predecessor in the short-lived interim Conservative Government. The RCA met on the 23 March to agree their response. Moon was prepared to back extreme protest action to mobilise opinion. Together with the Midland the L&NW published an alarmist manifesto proclaiming the damaging effect on railways' profitability. When *The Railway Times* reported four days later that this had 'startled stock markets', prices of railway stock plummetted. Leading RCA members each agreed to call special crisis meetings of their own shareholders. The L&NW's was held in the Great Hall of Euston station on the 31 March. *The Times* was to recall the scene a few years later (on Moon's retirement) 'when, from the pillared gallery at the end of the great hall at Euston, looking down over the colossal marble shoulders of George Stephenson upon the sea of faces beneath, he [Moon] urged the assembled shareholders of British railways to join together and defeat the measure of confiscation - for he did not mince words - which has now become law under the name of the Railway and Canal Traffic Act 1888'.

The company's official report of the meeting estimated that over three thousand were present. Neele wrote that they had to be addressed by director Thomas Brooke as Moon's voice was too weak. A questioner afterwards said he had not been able to hear some of the points Moon made which would suggest he did try, at least initially to make his own speech. The account of the speech as circulated showed that this was no tedious repeat of so many of his harangues against government interference. It was a call for direct action.

He opened by saying the company could not bear the responsibility of resisting the attack made on it without their assistance and advice, an attack 'which has been made with the consent of the Government ... upon your charter, that charter being the right to fix your own rates and charges within certain limits which have been enacted by Parliament for many years ... that right forming the basis of the faith of which this great railway property has grown up, and being in fact the only basis and security for the property'.

In referring to previous attempts to regulate rates, from 1844 to the Select Committee of 1881 and 1882, he claimed that the railways had been acquitted of 'any grave dereliction of their duty to the public' and that it was 'remarkable that no witnesses have appeared to complain of preferences given to individuals by railway companies

70. Great Hall Euston

The Great Hall of Euston station designed by P.C.Hardwick was completed in
1849. Board and meeting rooms faced the top of the staircase and offices led
off the galleries. NRM

as acts of private favour or partiality'. Then making a disparaging comparison with landlords in Ireland he said that:

> It has oozed out that her Majesty's advisers reckon they can purchase all the land of Ireland for about 200 millions sterling. But that is a very small matter compared with this railway property, which has cost more than the amount of the national debt: it has cost 800 millions of money sterling, and of that amount you yourselves have found between 100 and 110 millions, and at present moment you are employing over 60,000 people in your service, and paying wages equal to about four millions a year. I ask whether this is a property to be lightly interfered with.

In accepting the need to update the classification and revise rates he referred to the attempt to introduce their own Bill 'for a settlement on fair principles between Parliament and the trading community and ourselves'. He claimed this had included more than 2,000 articles in the classification and they had tried to make them 'suitable tolls to that new classification'. He explained that at present these were contained in about eighty Acts of Parliament and they proposed to combine them under one Act with one set of tolls and a suitable classification. 'All we ask is that in any such consolidation and revision due regard shall be given to the existing powers of the company and that any settlement should be final and by agreement.' This was to be 'before a fair and competent tribunal'. However he protested against the prejudging of the case by the clauses of the present Bill:

> I ask you to say we will not be oppressed in this way and we will not sit down quietly, like Egyptian fellaheen, and have your property robbed from us but will exert ourselves and say to Parliament they must do what is reasonably right, and if the Government want to do what they like with the property let them purchase it. That is what the Government of Italy have done, and then they make what ducks and drakes of it they like. But they must purchase it before they confiscate it.

Support for the company's stance was unanimous except for two speakers. Sir William Herschel 'deprecated' the language used saying 'we are identical with the interests of trade' and 'ought not to use such words as "confiscation" when we are really only contending for our interests in a matter which we hope and trust will be settled by compromise'. Herschel (son of the astronomer) pleaded 'let us meet our opponents and meet Parliament in a rational spirit'. John Patterson similarly objected and urged the company to adopt a more conciliatory approach in arguing its case.

Moon responded by saying it was his 'own private opinion' that 'expediency has driven out the old-fashioned words "honesty" and "justice" from the House of Commons'. He accused Patterson of being unaware that the Government's Bill was not going before a Select Committee 'but a committee of the whole house. Where are you going to be heard? We have not the power to appear'. Moon wanted an impartial Select Committee before whom their case would be made by counsel. He added that "confiscation" was not their 'word at all, it is a word used by the Joint Committee of the Houses of Lords and Commons' when admitting 'if that which is going to be done is done, it would amount to confiscation of the property'.

In his letter covering the circulation of the report of the proceedings, Moon drew attention to Mundella's assertion that his Bill was 'practically the Bill of his predecessor'. He pointed out that the late President of the Board of Trade (Chamberlain) had written to *The Times* to say that he had not sanctioned the Bill as he had wanted to receive deputations from both traders and railway companies first.

It has been alleged that Moon overplayed his hand in the extent to which he led outright opposition to the Bill. It is evident that he was at odds with his own RCA members who, in the following months, agreed not to oppose the Bill but to adopt the view taken by Lord Colville (Great Northerrn chairman) in negotiating an amendment to take out the compulsory powers clause. Although the Bill was given its second reading it was subsequently withdrawn when Gladstone's new administration was defeated on Irish Home Rule. At his own company meeting in August 1886 Moon was to prove over optimistic in believing favourable modifications would have been made anyway. He was also at this time on the defensive over his company's results.

The decline in trade had meant that the profitability of all major companies had continued to fall. One of the reasons Moon gave for the drop in receipts was the reduction in first and second class travel, explaining that there had been a loss of nearly 10d. per mile in passenger traffic since first class fares were reduced and facilities for third improved. Between June 1874 and June 1886 they had carried half a million fewer first class passengers, 800,000 fewer second but over six million more third. The total number carried in the respective half years had increased from 20 million to 25 million yet the receipts were down by £5,000: 'the whole difference having gone into the hands of what he might perhaps term "the ungrateful public"'.

The re-election of Salisbury's Conservative administration did not mean that pressure for a revised railway rates structure was reduced, in particular from accusations that differential rates were favouring importers. In an attempt to head off this criticism the railway companies met Lord Stanley (the new President of the Board of Trade) at the end of 1886 to seek a full parliamentary enquiry before any legislation on import and export rates was introduced. They believed that the principle of differential rates was not understood by the public. Stanley refused and committed to proceed with a new Bill.

Moon devoted practically the whole of his February 1887 address to shareholders to the issue, re-iterating that if their rates were 'put under the control of any commission or court whatsoever ... they would not hesitate, if necessary, to call together again the railway shareholders of the kingdom'. However Stanley brought in his Bill the same month and on 10 March a deputation from the railway companies met Lord Salisbury.

Moon was one of the main speakers explaining that they 'would be very sorry not to assist the Government in carrying out a fair Bill. What they objected to was that their earning powers should be interfered with'. He looked to Salisbury 'to say that he did not mean anything in the Bill to take away the powers granted to the railway companies'. Salisbury, at one time a railwayman himself (chairman of the Great Eastern from 1868 to 1872), agreed and invited the companies to submit proposals for modification.

During the following months detailed discussions took place. In May, Lord Brabourne (deputy chairman of the South Eastern Railway) acting on behalf of the Railway Comanies Association obtained amendments to the Bill in the Lords whereby the proposed scale of maximum rates should, on the whole, be equivalent to the existing statutory powers. It was then the traders turn to object claiming this was too conciliatory to the railways. It was at this time that Salisbury announced the Queen's Jubilee Honours. Having adopted such an aggressive stance in defending his company's interests, Moon could well have been genuinely surprised over his name being put forward for a baronetcy. More of this will be covered later. That he ultimately accepted is of course history, but it clearly made no difference to the tenor of his opposition to the government.

In the event, through pressure of other business, the Bill had to be withdrawn. A revised Bill was introduced to the Commons on the 14 February 1888, the day of the L&NW's half-yearly shareholders' meeting. Once again Moon gave a long exposition warning of the dangers, again a lot of it repetitive. He began by effectively chastising those in whom it was 'difficult to arouse any emotion' and those 'who have no care whatsoever for the earnings of your railway property', and appealed for shareholders to ensure the Bill 'is fairly dealt with'. 'We do not like crying "wolf" but the thing has been postponed year after year and now probably it is coming to a settlement.' He warned against 'very strong and active opponents who are looking out to get from you all they can to put into their own pockets' and reminded them that the Bill was going before the Houses of Parliament who 'did ruthlessly take away the property of the Irish landlords in 1881 and gave it to another class'. The Irish Land Act had given rights to tenants looking for security of tenure, fairer rents and the free sale of their interests.

> You can only say you are not racketeers, that you are within your powers, that you are not overburdened with debt, that you are able to spend money on the improvement and maintenance of your property. You can refer to the enormous advantages you have given to the community, you can show that the business of the country could not go on a day without your railway, you can show them you have spent your money on the faith of parliamentary clauses which are now the statute law of the country, that you have a statutory right to what you now possess.

But perhaps more conscious of past criticism of his rhetoric, Moon concluded his tirade by hoping his shareholders would take 'seriously' what he said and 'pardon me for not having put it in the best form. It is a difficult thing to weigh one's words so exactly that no one shall feel hurt or that they shall not irritate or set up the backs of anybody interested against us'.

The accusation that the railways were giving undue preference to the carriage of imports was far from straightforward. Moon, in strongly denying there was preference, was not entirely convincing when he said the matter depended on 'port to port rates and other matters than the railway rates'. And that if there had to be an Inquiry it must 'not only be in the interest of the individual manufacturer, but in the interests of all classes of the community, including the consumer and the ports ... and their relative interests'.

In the spring and summer of 1888 events gathered pace. Though J.C.Bolton (Caledonian Railway chairman) succeeded in having the previous amendment included in the new Bill, which passed the second reading in the Commons, strong lobbying at the final Committee stage for "equal" rates led to the amendment being struck out. At the 11 April meeting of the RCA Moon suggested rousing the ports to protest against equal rates as a 'ruinous' measure. But the railway interest in Parliament was in the minority and on the 10 August 1888 the Bill was enacted as the Railway & Canal Traffic Act 1888.

The hand of Moon was very evident in the dramatic words of the L&NW Directors' Report circulated for the ensuing half-yearly meeting: there is 'now no security that such new scale will enable the Railway Companies to earn their present revenue. The power over private property costing upwards of eight hundred millions of money, now practically left in the hands of the Board of Trade, subject to confirmation by Parliament, is the largest ever granted to a department of the Government'. In thanking Bolton and Brabourne for 'their efforts to preserve the statutory rights ... and to mitigate the injury which has been inflicted upon railway property', the report pointed out that 'the public also will suffer ... owing to the practical withdrawal from the Companies of the power, by special rates, to meet' local requirements 'which every Royal or Parliamentary' enquiry 'has reported to have been fairly exercised'. Moon then in his subsequent address to the meeting concluded that the decision 'has been left to the trading interests of the country, they have been plaintiff, judge and jury, and like a great many greedy people, perhaps they have overstrained the mark and done rather too much'.

Under the Act the railway companies were compelled to revise the goods classifications and maximum rates schedules for submission to the Board of Trade for approval. Geoffrey Alderman, in his study of the political aspects of the growth of railways, wrote that as there were then 'about 900 separate railway Acts dealing with the charging powers of 976 companies, and involving millions of separate rates, this proved a gigantic task, not made easier by the vague wording of the 1888 Act, which gave little guidance as to the principles which should govern the new schemes'.

Naturally at the L&NW's meeting many shareholders aired their frustrations. For the first time since his early difficult years in the chair Moon was faced with a largely hostile audience in having to explain how the industry found itself in such a position. Seemingly undaunted Moon let his critics have their say and, despite being one month off his seventy fourth birthday, responded with humour and vigour.

The strongest attack came from J.M.Bennett, a director of the Manchester Sheffield & Lincolnshire, who complained:

> If you, as the leading chairman of all the railway companies in the kingdom, had only joined, as you were invited to do, the Railway Shareholders' Defence Association, I believe that railway companies would not have been in the position they are in today. But you did not choose to join that association, and other railway chairmen, following your example, did not choose to join, and you tried to do what you could singlehanded. You were like a rope of sand and the consequence was, when the grand committee was formed, I believe there were only seven gentlemen connected with railways upon that committee, whilst there were ten times seven, or 70, connected with the trading interest of the country. If anyone is to blame, it is you, Sir Richard Moon, and therefore you need not complain now that it is too late.

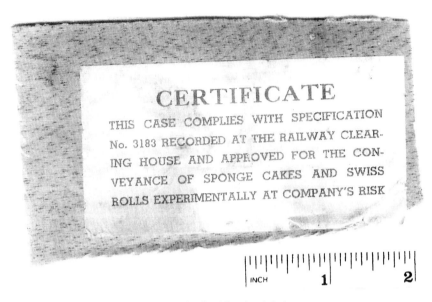

71. Goods classification label
The extent to which classification of goods could be taken: a 1930s carton
label referring to a Railway Clearing House specification for carrying sponge
cakes and Swiss rolls. Author

72. L&NW delivery vans
Some L&NW vehicles for collecting and delivering parcels in early 1900s. NRM

A Mr Griffith also protested, saying he would be 'happy to support you in anything for our benefit, but I must say I do think that we are taking a somewhat extreme and indiscreet view of our position'. He thought it would be wise not to 'agitate a question in which the public are undoubtedly against us, though we may feel somewhat strongly on the point'. He thought therefore that 'instead of agitating the public mind any longer by a case which, though legally right, is somewhat hopeless, we should rather support our board in endeavouring to obtain what is just and reasonable from the Board of Trade than agitate and make public attack on the Government, which is doing the best they can for the country at large'.

And with with reference to agriculture a Mr Adams reminded Moon of a previous warning he had given. Quoting Milton's *Paradise Lost* he invoked the devil Belial 'whose office was to "make the worse appear the better reason". I would like him to make the farmers believe that it was to their interests for railway companies to carry foreign produce double the distance for one-half the rate that they carried their produce. That is what had been tried in the House of Commons to do'. He further accused Moon of circulating only his own chairman's remarks and not those against him.

Moon countered Bennett by saying that had he 'and his friends', instead of breaking away, supported the Railway Companies Association 'we should have been able to do more than we were able to, because we were a rope of sand largely by the defection of those very gentlemen'. He countered the charge of fighting the Government by saying he had been at most of the parliamentary committee meetings and debates in the House, 'and no one knows better than we how Sir Michael Hick-Beach [President of the B. of T.] struggled in that committee to do what was right, and how he was overwhelmed by the votes of the traders'. On the equal rates issue he simply said that that was why they wanted a Special Committee appointed, 'to show what a grievous misunderstanding there is with regard to it'.

Though perhaps missing the point of the complaint over not having speeches against him circulated in his company's reports, Moon caused laughter with his put-down to Adams:

Then a gentleman said we have omitted his speech. All I can say is, I am sorry we omitted the piece of poetry; but I have not a bit of poetry in me, and it does not depend on us, but on these gentlemen of the press in the room who have the power to put it all in. All I can say is, every now and then ... they leave out that which I was most anxious should have been put in. These things happen - you cannot help it. ... They might say to him as they did once to a member of the House of Commons when he complained that they had reported him badly. They sent him a message to say if he was not satisfied with their report they would report what he did say.

The tedious task of not only reviewing and revising rates but also attending the meetings to give evidence was to absorb a significant proportion of the time of senior management of all major railway companies. Neele, although responsible for only passenger traffic, gives a revealing insight into early political correctness when he wrote that 'the whole of the Clearing House Coaching Arrangements Book was overhauled in order to remove anything that in any respect might have been construed into an "undue preference" for any traders or individuals; the recommendations were carried almost to absurdity, thus - books of tailors' patterns, the word "tailors" to be deleted; gentlemen's vegetable and linen boxes to read "families" vegetable and linen boxes, etc.'.

Once in the hands of the Board of Trade, the new proposed schedules were then published and objections invited. In order to review these over 120 meetings were arranged throughout the UK between traders and the railway companies. Traders' associations were set up and, to co-ordinate their activities, leading merchants in London formed the so-called "Mansion House Association". The Government was forced to set up another enquiry to resolve the differences. Evidence to this enquiry and subsequent cross-examinations were to drag on until May 1891; Findlay for example being examined and cross-examined continuously for eight days. Moon referred to the 'endless difficulty' at his February 1889 half-yearly meeting stating it was his 'private view' that parliamentary legislation ever since the formation of the Railway Commission 'has been a mistake' and that 'old existing laws were sufficient'. However there were now 'new circumstances' and 'new people'. Resignedly he concluded that in the meantime 'the community, in all probability, will be disgusted with the change'.

Moon had disagreed with fellow members of the RCA when they accepted a *standard* charge for recovering terminal costs. The principle of having these costs allowed, as an addition to the maximum rates, had been one of the few points the railways had won, but Moon had insisted on *actual* costs being used. He reluctantly agreed to subject his stand to review by his own board. They disagreed with him and supported the association's acceptance of a standard charge.

Moon believed he could settle with the 'practical trader' but not with 'theoretical bodies' such as Chambers of Commerce, municipal authorities, etc., where we 'do not expect these theoretical people to agree with you'. Commencing his last year as L&NW chairman in February 1890, Moon claimed he admired the 'patience and grasp' of Lord Balfour and Courtney Boyle (Government Secretaries heading the enquiry), but complained of the time taken up by the involvement of the company's officers and solicitors. He thought there would no satisfactory outcome to the problem: the traders looking for rates reduction, the railways simply to codify schedules. As Alderman succinctly put it, 'during June and July 1890 the Board of Trade embarked upon the task of drawing up schedules of charges, to be submitted to Parliament, which would satisfy both sides. It was an attempt to reconcile the irreconcilable'.

When members of the RCA met to consider the first of the company schedules submitted (L&NW and GW) which had been amended and returned by the Board of Trade, they predictably rejected them. Moon in particular reacted angrily, claiming that the amendments, for example, 'had largely reduced the rates for coal and other traffic without being asked to do so by the traders'. At his own shareholders' meeting he said it was a 'curious and trying time' for the Board of Trade to revise tariffs and he exhorted every proprietor to lobby against the proposals as the 'property is at stake'. Somewhat wearily he concluded 'we have had a very hard six months but still if we can get your dividend I shall be very thankful'.

It was Findlay who led the RCA delegation of officers and solicitors to the Board of Trade in October arguing that railway companies could not possibly accept the proposed schedules. But the

Government was determined to implement them. By then Moon had lost his wife and no longer had the stomach to continue the battle. At his last shareholders' meeting he gloomily referred to the effect of the rates negotiations as a 'great deal worse'. Complaining bitterly he referred to the current proposal 'to leave to a Select Committee really to confiscate your property - it is neither more nor less than the confiscation of the property. ... We shall resist to the best of our ability ... will do our very best to fix such figures as cannot be argued against. ... In many cases they are absolutely reducing our rates when nobody has asked them. It is a gratuitous piece of folly'. He pleaded for everyone to 'exert' themselves and 'show the Government and show all these dilettante gentlemen in Parliament that we really do not intend to be put upon if we can help it'. It was his final shot in a war that the companies could not win. The following month Moon's successor Lord Stalbridge threatened, in a retaliatory mood, to withdraw all his company's Bills for new works. A new round of battles over rates had begun.

Although it is unlikely that the outcome would have been any different had the leading protagonist of the railway cause not been so single-mindedly antagonistic, the means of revising and agreeing changes may well have been less confrontational. Nevertheless the many years of protracted protest that led to the 1888 Act were followed by four more years of argument before the new classification and revised charges eventually came into effect from 1 January 1893. Initially each company had been given six months from the 1888 Act to submit proposals but it was not until the sessions of 1891 and 1892 that the new rates were confirmed by each company or group of companies by their own Acts.

Acceptance by traders though soon turned to protest once it was realised that only about a third of the rates had been reduced. The railways argued that they had not the time to complete the thousands of changes required. The traders claimed the railways had taken the opportunity to offset decreases by uplifting elsewhere. Another Select Committee was appointed to review the complaints which basically found against the railways and led to a new Railway & Canal Traffic Act in 1894. Under that Act railways had their powers further restricted. Where competitive rates had been offered to take business at below the maximum the railways were not allowed to raise them again without having to prove it was "reasonable" to do so. Paradoxically this was not necessarily beneficial to traders, railways quickly learnt that in many cases it was better not to offer reductions in the first place. But by then Moon had long retired from the scene.

CHAPTER 25

PATERNALISM

During the thirty years Moon was in the chair of the L&NW he was not faced with a major challenge from dissatisfied employees until his last few years. Even then the issue was a political one although sparked by a demand for increased wages.

Until the involvement of his Crewe management in the town council elections in the 1880s Moon had succeeded, at least publicly, in keeping politics out of company business; and in the area of labour relations generally the L&NW had been relatively troublefree. Of course there had been isolated incidents. Pressure for improved conditions of work had first manifested itself as far back as the boom summer of 1872 which had led to a strike at the company's Broad Street goods station. Moon then had referred to labour unrest affecting the scarcity of iron and coal. Moon claimed the company 'endeavoured to have no grudging service'. A year later though he had referred unsympathetically to trades unions when explaining the 'enormously increased working expenses'. He believed in 'a fair day's work for a fair day's wages' but 'we don't get it - the great parties in this country have patted the working man on the back till he has gone to the trades' unions, and now he says "I will do as little as I can for your money"'.

In 1876 he had bluntly blamed the unions for causing a depression in trade. Believing he was a benevolent employer Moon saw no reason why his work force needed to resort to representation by unions. In this he was typical of most traditional employers at the time who considered that the setting of wages and conditions should be entirely the prerogative of local management. Though he was never averse to paying the highest rates to obtain the best management, his attitude to the lowest paid was less clear. Rather like his obsession in saving gas by having station lamps turned down Moon's insistence on keeping a tight lid on hourly wages and conditions (for example the cost of uniforms) illustrates the apparent anomaly. On the other hand he was well aware of the need to recognise loyalty and hard work.

He had told shareholders at their August 1877 meeting that 'we ought to be thankful that our people, during all these trying times, have worked well with us, because, after all, upon them in the end depends the economy of the whole concern'. At Crewe he agreed that the company should contribute to a testimonial organised by fellow workmen for Dingley, the foreman of the erecting shop, when he had completed his 2,000[th] engine (similarly to Ellis, the boiler shop foreman who had completed his 3,000[th] boiler). 'If we can keep our people with us, I believe we shall continue to see the line worked as well as it has been hitherto.'

Without a detailed anaysis it is difficult to assess the trend in L&NW wage levels over the period of Moon's chairmanship when compared to either the country as whole or rival railway companies. Some studies have been made, for example by R.J. Irving (see Sources 2.6), which suggest that L&NW wage costs as a percentage of gross revenue rose at a time of lowering prices. However no evidence has been found that there was any concerted pressure from the company's large labour force for increased pay, or that the early trade unions had any direct influence on L&NW wages policy. Long hours of work for low basic rates of pay have to be seen in the context of the relative security of railway employment. Moon's own work ethic too, which if uncompromising at times, could have had a signficant influence on his managers' attitudes to labour relations.

Moon could be said to typify the nineteenth century paternal approach: only the good intentioned and well meaning company can know what is best for their employees. He had personally shown commitment to staff welfare when working in his own time to devise an officer's superannuation scheme and was concerned to ensure that good housing, schooling and religious facilities were provided at his main centres of employment. He saw no need for interference from either Government or the newly emerging trades unions.

One of the first issues seized upon by the unions for reform was one to which he particularly objected. His dedication to the company was such that he had little sympathy for the agitation for a reduction in working hours. In attacking both Government and unions in February 1878 on this issue, and more generally, he was espousing the cause of pure market economics that became so fashionable a century or so later:

> I calculate that a loss of the labour of something like a million or a million and a half of men has followed the restrictions which the trade unions put upon their members with regard to the work they do and the hours they work. The only fear I have with regard to this country is that ... their interference with every act of the manufacturers in the country, will do that which has been done all through the world's history - viz., in their attempts to regulate trade which cannot be regulated, they will drive that trade out of the country, because capital is of no country and will not stay anywhere to be regulated. You cannot regulate prices and unless the difficulties and differences between the workpeople and their masters can be settled by working cordially together, every man doing his work with all his might and to the best of his ability (because the men of today do little more than half they can do), the foreigner will come in and do the work.

A year later, in complaining of the unprecedented distressed state of the country and the imports of foreign food, he seemed not to have forgotten he once supported a protectionist cause, yet remained blinkered to the wider effect of applying such a principle and its consequences. He said that:

> They heard a great deal about free trade, and there was free trade for the foreigner in this country, but there was no free trade for the English people, for our ships were curtailed in their voyages, our manufacturers were met with most prohibitive duties; and it was very clear that between the interference of the Government and trades union regulations and restrictions and short hours, there was no free trade in labour in this country. It was equally clear that trades and trades unions could not live together - one must die.

But it was not only over hours of work and wages that labour agitation developed. One of the costs Moon had consistently complained about since his early days in the chair had been the amount paid in compensation to passengers resulting from accidents. Costs would have been even higher had payments been made to employees. However it was traditional in most industries, not just railways, that employers could not be held responsible for accidents or losses to their own employees if caused by fellow workers or even by supervisors: the so called defence plea of 'common employment'. It is not the place here to review in detail the progress made by both unions and Government in enforcing changes to the law covering employers' liability, especially in the area of fair compensation, but it is relevant in any study of Moon to examine where he stood in defending the traditional policy.

Taking a lead in instigating legislation for employers to accept increased claims for liability was Thomas Brassey. It must have been more than a little irritating to Moon, as may have been the case when facing Childers over the passenger duty question, to find another former company director an adversary. Brassey, the son of the railway contractor and a Liberal MP, had been a director of the L&NW from 1868 to 1875. In March 1878 he led a deputation of the Amalgamated Society of Railway Servants (ASRS) to the Government to seek better compensation for employees for accidents and injuries. Draft proposals of the ASRS union, which would deprive employers of the 'common employment' defence, were introduced by him as an Employers Liability Bill the following year, although this was soon superseded by a Government Bill. As with other national issues such as the passenger duty and freight rates the opposition was led for the railways by the Railway Companies' Association. At a meeting taken by Moon in the absence of the chairman, the association agreed to meet other employer organisations in a protest deputation to Prime Minister Disraeli (by then Lord Beaconsfield).

At the meeting with Beaconsfield in May 1879 the other employers were led by Thomas Knowles in his capacity as leader of the Mining Association. Knowles was also a director of the L&NW (elected in June 1875 as the "City" director to replace Robert Benson). A self-made man who had started work in the coal industry as a nine-year old, Knowles had been elected a

Conservative MP in 1874 and was on the L&NW board until his death in 1883. Knowles told Beaconsfield that his delegation was unanimous in believing 'that further legislation between employers and employed was undesirable and unnecessary'. On behalf of the railways the principal speakers were Gooch and Moon. The personal relationship between these two great railway company chairman, close contemporaries in age and office, has not been determined but by background they were very different.

Apprenticed as a fourteen year old in an engineering works Gooch had by the age of twenty-one been appointed by Brunel as the Great Western's locomotive superintendant. Though resigning in 1864 and taking a leading role in laying the Atlantic cable, for which he was awarded his baronetcy in 1866, he rejoined the GW as director and chairman in 1865. The following year he was elected Conservative MP for Cricklade of which the GW's Swindon works was a significant part of the constituency. He never spoke in Parliament. There should have been a connection over the Gooch family burials in Claines and they were alike in that they both shunned personal publicity but exercised autocratic control over their companies.

Gooch claimed that the 'the measure was likely to create unpleasant feelings between masters and men. Railway companies had hitherto managed affairs with their men very well, and on the Great Western line there had not been a strike for 40 years'. He said his company had always tried to assist 'their men in the associations which had been established to help themselves, and that was a much better plan than to have legislation forced upon them'. Gooch claimed the GW voluntarily subscribed about £15,000 annually to employee funds, but 'if the Bill should be carried, and the company became liable for actions for every disaster occurring to the servants, and mostly resulted from want of care on their part, they would be unable to bear the additional charges which legislation of this kind might place upon them'.

Before meeting the Prime Minister the RCA had agreed that they were prepared to accept liability where management was responsible. 'Management' they defined as anyone holding the office of manager, superintendent or engineer (or similar) and entrusted with the management or control of the railway, or of the traffic or of any works for the manufacture or repair and no other person.

They refused to accept liability for uncontrolled acts by other employees. Moon reinforced Gooch's view and further argued that railways were being discriminated against. 'Seeing that the Bill did not propose to touch the shipowner, or the farmer, nor Her Majesty's Government as being directors of the royal dockyards and arsenals, he could not see why there should be an exception made in regard to private companies.' However in accusing the government of 'taking upon themselves paternal cares', he did little to dispel the image of a hard man of Victorian business when commenting that 'workmen were well able to take care of themselves, they could leave at any time, and they fully understood the nature of the work which they were engaged in'.

Moon's railwaymen may well have had the option of pleasing themselves, but there would have been little prospect of alternative employment in 1879, a year of one of the greatest depressions in trade. And he admitted that it 'was the worst time at which such a Bill could be introduced, when trade was never in a worse condition, when competition was such that they were beaten not only in foreign but also in home markets'.

Beaconsfield's administration gave way to Gladstone's and the following year the Liberal Government's Employers' Liability Bill was a repeat of the earlier one which basically gave equal rights to compensation for railway company employees as for outsiders. So in June 1880 the RCA once again found itself with other employers protesting and seeking the appointment of a Select Committee in a meeting with the new Prime Minister. Moon persisted with the view that the companies were 'quite willing to be responsible for the acts of a manager or some person in authority' but not for the individual workman. He found himself in agreement with his old adversary Watkin, by then a fellow member of the RCA, who called the Bill a 'barrel of gunpowder' prepared by the Government mainly to conciliate the trade unions.

Railway companies tried to get acceptance of the mutual insurance principle instead of their own compulsory liability. The unions resisted as they did not want to encourage any links that strengthened employees' ties to management. The railways refused to negotiate and at his August 1880 half-yearly meeting Moon devoted a good third of his address to the subject. He told shareholders that he 'spoke with some diffidence on the subject because he felt deeply that it was a matter of great importance to them, not only as railway people but as English people also. Of all the difficult questions in the world the most difficult to solve was that which related to the position of employers and employed'. He claimed the present Government had brought in the Bill with the Commons passing the second reading 'without any discussion whatever'. They had been 'led to this step, not by the wishes of the great masses of the working people of England but by a few who pretended to represent railway servants. They knew that the majority of railway servants did not want the Bill. It was simply a clique representing about one per cent of the working people'.

He went on claim that the L&NW directors 'had always worked well with their people' but if the Bill was passed 'it would alter the whole relations of master and servant'. He quoted a judge who thought the proposed law 'would produce litigation, quarrels, ill-will, fraud, and other mischief among them, probably the discontinuance of accident funds'. Though he admitted the Bill raised questions which required settling, 'but settling fairly', Moon had pressed Gladstone 'that the delay of a year was nothing as compared with the importance of getting the matter settled satisfactorily' and criticised sections of the Bill as 'unintelligible' and, where specifically aimed at railway companies, as 'an objectionable piece of class legislation'. He told shareholders that the Bill would be 'nothing but litigation and trouble and would break up the friendly relations which existed between the railways and their servants'. He had 'had the pleasure of meeting ten of their drivers the other day, and other work people, some of whom had been with them fifty years, all of whom would rather remain as they were'.

Despite all Moon's pleading, and from others like him, the following month the Bill was enacted. With the onus placed with employers either to comply or contract out with comparable or better conditions of their own, Moon's public reaction was bitter. At the next L&NW half-yearly meeting, February 1881, he told shareholders that 'before the last session closed, in a hole-and-corner fashion, when only the placemen of the Government were present, they passed what is called the Employers' Liability Act'. This was despite the employers' appeal 'that proper arrangements might be made which would satisfy both masters and workmen. But they would not hear us, and passed, in the objectionable manner I have said, one of most important bills that the legislature of this country ever sanctioned'.

In believing the Act would be 'from its engendering litigation and trouble, one of the most injurious' ever passed, Moon then summarised the action taken by the company to contract out of the government's scheme:

> We have made a settlement with our people in this way: we have nearly 46,000 people on our wages-sheet, of whom nearly 14,000 are in the locomotive department. Of the latter we have agreed with 13,500, 140 have dissented, and 91 have still to decide; so that we may say that the whole locomotive department have agreed in a settlement which will bring them outside the Employers' Liability Act. Of the other 32,000, 29,000 have agreed, 1,000 have said "No" while the other 2,000 have not yet decided.

Moon went on to dismiss a small core of supporters of the Act in Liverpool led by Samuelson as trying 'to set the people wrong'. He was sure common sense will 'bring them to us' in a short time and explained further his objection. 'If it had been with us a mere question of money', they would have stood by the Act because they would in effect have less to pay apart from the ill feeling and litigation which brought about the payment. So we 'have sought to benefit our employees by extending certain existing beneficial arrangements in their favour'.

To what extent the L&NW would have introduced such a scheme if it had not been for the pressure of imposition is impossible to say, but it is worth noting Moon's further comment that the Act had 'somewhat interfered with what they had intended to do in establishing a system of mutual assurance', which 'would discriminate in the case of men with families and ... provide something in the shape of superannuation for worn-out men, as it was the intention of the Board to have the best service in the world by identifying the interests and sympathies of their army of workmen'.

73. Moon with engine drivers at Crewe
Moon (left) on wall with ten engine drivers at Crewe in 1880, two of whom
had fifty years service, with Webb (right) and in foreground Running
Superintendents, G.Whale (left), Northern, and A.L.Mumford,
Southern. Whale succeeded Webb in 1903. NRM

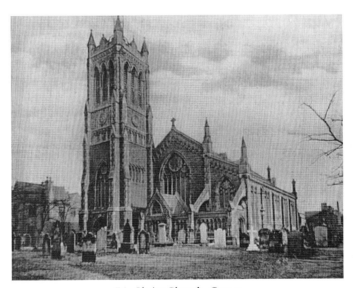

74. Christ Church, Crewe
Christ Church, Crewe in 1930s before partial demolition in 1977. Built by
the railway in 1845 it was enlarged with new tower 1877, chancel 1898 and
Lady Chapel 1906. Moon laid an extension foundation stone in 1884.
Timothy P.Prevett and Christ Church

The railway companies had accepted that the Act did not prohibit them from contracting out provided other support, basically insurance, was provided. One result of the L&NW contracting out was that membership of their own insurance scheme became obligatory. The unions had resisted this on the grounds that it maintained the control over the work force by the company. The L&NW directors' August 1881 report to their shareholders said that of the number of people on weekly rates, 45,444 had joined the insurance society and that the question of a servants' pension fund was now under consideration. Moon at the meeting referred to the 'equanimity and quietness' with which out of 50,000 men scarcely 150 had not joined. However as P.S Bagwell, historian of the National Union of Railwaymen, records, the unions alleged that at meetings throughout the country 'official influence' or intimidation was applied.

How much pressure was brought to bear on men to join the company schemes is difficult to determine. What is likely however is that Moon genuinely believed in the necessity of providing benefits for his work force. That he was not quite so coldly indifferent to labour as has been depicted is evident from his remarks at his February 1883 half-yearly meeting. In reporting that the company had contributed £15,000 towards insurance against accidents, he regretted 'that they could not get their people to take more care of themselves and their lives; but people got accustomed to risk and were continually meeting with accidents which a little care would avoid'. They now proposed 'to establish a pension fund for those worn out in their service, to enable them to support themselves during their old age. Some might say these people ought themselves to provide for their declining years; but it was very difficult out of the wages they got to do so'. This latter admission semed to have provoked little or no reaction from agitators pressing for wage increases. And, as if to head off any such criticism, he claimed, when reviewing the company's activities in Dublin, 'the people they employed got the highest wages of any in their service in their particular capacity'. He later reported that £10,000 per annum had been agreed as a contribution from the company for the servants' old age pension fund.

It is convenient to note at this point Moon's public concern also for his men's spiritual wellbeing. Though, as has been noted, never a member of his company's Church Committee, he frequently appealed to shareholders for funds to support churches and schools. In February 1874, for example, after receiving only a poor response from a previous appeal he asked for more contributions for Crewe, Wolverton and Earlestown 'where we have an enormous number of workpeople. ... We don't ask it as charity ... your workpeople are well-to-do people, and well conducted people'. He believed that there was not 'a better conducted town in England than Crewe; but as we ourselves have the benefit of old institutions both in England and Scotland, and of the public schools and other facilities, so some kind friends must step in and help these people in doing what they require to promote their own good in life':

> It is no use bringing a great body of workpeople together and have nothing for them to employ their leisure time in. It is no use having them and their children there without the means of education. I know there are great differences of opinion on that point, and I know some people say you shall have no religious education in school. I feel discouraged because our previous appeal met with so slight response. You must bear in mind that you, the proprietors of this company - the ordinary and preference and debenture holders - derive an income from this company and its workpeople of about four millions a year, and it is little they have asked you to do for them. But we do say you are in duty bound to do it. I know it is difficult; but we want you to open your hearts as well as your purses.

He claimed that in Liverpool 'two or three thousand persons alone support all the charities of that enormous town'. And he quoted the example of one little village chapel which 'on Hospital Sunday, raised more money than St Paul's, with all the grandees of London and the Prince of Wales together'. He 'would rather have £1,000 from 1,000 people than for one alone to do the whole thing and the others to take no interest in it'.

It seemed that Moon's appeal fell largely on deaf ears for ten years later he was to recall the occasion when 'out of their 35,000 shareholders and 10,000 debenture-holders only 1,500 responded, the amount obtained being £5,000'. In telling them that they had been assisting in the building of churches, chapels, schools, coffee taverns, reading and recreation rooms, etc., it was not clear whether he meant by their donations or from the company directly. He added that the 'last thing had been to build what was called a "Bethell" at Garston, where there were many coal workers and sailors. They were gathering together those people, and the effect had been very good, and brought a better class of men into their service'. With appeals for funds 'from places all over their system', he now hoped 'they would assist in sending him £20,000'. Clearly intending to widen the appeal to all faiths, he somewhat anomalously added: 'setting aside the question of religion - we are Protestants and belong to the Church of England - we will do our best to facilitate everyone who is doing his duty to his neighbours and his country'. That appeal eventually raised just over half the amount he asked for. It would be in character for his personal contribution to have been appreciable.

In seeking to give his employees such benefits there seems no doubt that Moon was displaying a genuine interest. Of course it made economic sense to have a contented work force, to provide some relief from long hours of work frequently in harsh conditions, but on the other hand he would not have expected any more from his men than he did from himself. With the example set by how he saw his own duty, work rate and attention to detail, it is not surprising he expected a similar performance from others at every level in the company. Laxity was not a quality he tolerated, nor sloppy supervision. What is difficult to appreciate is where the balance lay between a concern for the welfare of his men and a fearsome reputation for rooting out inefficiencies at the most detailed level of working. No better example of the latter is his written instruction to the Birmingham and Shropshire Union Canals superintendent J.R.Jebb on 13 October 1884:

> I have to request that you give notice to Thomas Arnold, the foreman bricklayer in your No.4 district who also acts as time-keeper for his men, to leave the service. I will explain when we meet but meantime I may say there appears to be a laxity over the allowance for sick pay for I find that this man after meeting with an accident, through

being drunk, drew half pay from the company and sick pay at the rate of 10s.0d. per week from the men's sick fund for two or three weeks. We do not seem to get that control over the people that we ought to have but we will discuss this when we meet - meantime Arnold must go. You must take care to get a good man for a successor.

And in an aside to the above he had added 'you ought not to have passed this [a coal invoice!] without calling my attention to it ... you must not allow prices to go up without calling attention to them'.

After a surfeit of robberies in 1881 he advised one of his officials 'you must endeavour to get a better staff around you and people of more reliable style in the better positions. We have had so many of these robberies of late years that I can not help thinking a good deal is owing to the low-classed people we have been taking. I would rather pay a little more than have these constant deficiencies occurring'.

Moon was never slow to appreciate or give support to men he trusted. He was to make generous tribute in the last years of his chairmanship when referring to difficulties of working in a bad fog. 'It was impossible to see and everything was done by hearing, and these men were out during all that miserable weather'. 'If you look at the devotion of the people - of the drivers, guards, fog signalmen, platelayers, and all the staff of the company - we ought never to regret the amount of money we pay those people for what they do for us'. Having said that, Moon and most of his contemporaries took it for granted that railwaymen had to work long hours without any falling off in performance. When it had been suggested at a shareholders' meeting in 1871 that overly long hours caused accidents, Moon firmly rebutted the charge by saying that 'the men were not too long on duty'.

That excessive hours under trying condition gave rise to fatigue which could result in accidents ought not to have been disputed, yet in his last year in the chair Moon was still defending the company's hours of work. In taking questions at a half-yearly meeting, after stating that a spate of accident liability claims had helped reduce the dividend and reserves, he claimed 'there is nothing wanting in the appliances of the company or anything which we could do, which would have prevented any of these accidents. They have been wholly due to the mistakes of the servants'. On being asked if these were the result of too extended hours, Moon replied tersely 'not in a single case'. And when pressed over whether he was 'reducing to any extent the hours of such men as the pointsmen', Moon had dismissively responded: 'there are regular hours, and the Board of Trade inspects and then reports'.

It took the first damaging strike by the unions in Moon's last year in office to awaken railway management to the realities of a new era. Even before he retired the general secretary of the Amalagamated Society of Railway Servants, Edward Harford, for example, was reporting that his union were adopting 'robust and even aggressive' methods. 'We are a trade union with benefit funds, not a friendly society with a few mutual protection benefits, and this cannot be made too clear to members of the railway service.'

The unions had forced the powerful North Eastern company to the negotiating table, held mass meetings in Scotland which led to the strike against the three main Scottish companies and more dramatically taken on the profitable mineral carrying lines in south Wales, bringing the Taff Vale, Rhymney and Barry Docks to a standstill.

The success of the unions in reducing hours was the beginning of a long road of agitation for improvement in wages and conditions. A few weeks before Moon retired the outcome of the Scottish strike was a House of Commons debate on powers for the Board of Trade to fix hours of work, which led to the appointment of a Select Committee to investigate the extent of overwork. The Railway Companies Association, whose L&NW representative then was the Liberal MP Miles MacInnes, had agreed by the end of January 1891 to support the Select Committee. Moon had retired when the real effects of changes in labour relations were felt: the passing of the Railway Servants (Hours of Labour) Act in 1893.

Moon had little if any personal contact with the representatives of the "new unionism". The nearest he came to it was over the outcome of the political situation that had developed at Crewe. By far the largest of all the company's facilities, with its locomotive works, steel mills, miscellaneous manufacturing and engine sheds, Crewe was employing around seven thousand at the time of his retirement. By any standard it was one of the largest engineering works in the country. In the town of Crewe, created by the railway, the L&NW was estimated to be paying a third of the town's rates. Not unreasonably the company expected to have some say in the efficient working of the borough. Direct control over a non-unionised work force had been a feature of the company's management and there had been no better exponent of this approach than Francis Webb.

Brought back into the company by Moon to replace Ramsbottom, Webb had taken up his duties in 1871 and reigned supreme over Crewe for even longer than Moon had over the company. Once satisfied that Webb shared his vision of ordered economy and efficiency of working, Moon appeared content to leave him to run Crewe with little interference. J.P. Bickersteth, the director who chaired the Board's Locomotive Committee, appeared to have taken little part in the day-to-day management of the works. None of the quartet of directors effectively running the company in Webb's heyday had an engineering background, consequently the development of the works and design of the locomotives were left almost exclusively to him.

Webb's strong personality, organising ability and technical competence allied to a commitment to economy and an awareness of the need to make a return on the capital employed, were all characteristics which found favour with his chairman. Unfortunately his controversial small engine policy and in particular the problems experienced in introducing compounding, have tended to detract from his achievement in building Crewe into such a formidable manufacturing unit. Webb is mainly remembered today for his perceived shortcomings, not for the strength and success of the organisation he spent such a large proportion of his life creating and maintaining.

The deepening trade depression that affected the company's results over the three years to the end of 1886 had led to short time working at Crewe and men being laid-off. Inevitably unrest followed. Protest found a ready voice among those trying to establish union representation. This same voice also found an outlet in the local municipal council where objections from Liberals against company sponsored "Independents" had grown. Webb had been persuaded in 1880 by his friend Dr Atkinson to become more involved in council affairs by supporting a committee of company officials to establish a party 'independent' of politics. Atkinson was the company's Crewe medical officer who had been ousted as leader of the local Conservatives. By apparent agreement with the Conservatives the so-called "Independent" candidates began to make gains against the local Liberals and by 1885 had effectively replaced the Conservatives as the opposition. With the latter they secured a majority control of the council at the November 1885 local election.

Whale, Webb's locomotive running superintendent for the northern division (Whale was to succeed Webb at Crewe in 1903) became Mayor and, to quote W.H.Chaloner, the social historian of Crewe 'from that moment until 1891 Crewe was ruled from the general offices of the Locomotive Department'. Liberal protests accused the company of intimidating employees to vote against them. An anonymous letter published by the *Manchester Examiner* in September 1885 alleged that the company had been coercing the workforce on both religious and political matters since 1870. Moon found himself drawn into the controversy when the Crewe Liberal Association complained formally to the L&NW board. This was considered at their October meeting and a reply agreed. At the 20 November board a similar letter from 'certain members' of Crewe Town Council was also considered but Moon's earlier reply was thought to have made the company's position clear enough. Moon wrote:

> I am able to assure you that there is not the slightest foundation for what has been said. Our board has nothing whatever to do with the political opinions of its individual members, nor of its officers, and, as nearly as possible, we are equally composed of Liberals and Conservatives. Probably I cannot do better than send you copy of a report of a meeting held spontaneously by our workpeople at Crewe - at which neither official nor foreman was present - when the men entirely repudiated the allegations which have been made, and, in my opinion, made by interested persons for purely political purposes. Your suggestion that I should go to Crewe and address the men with the Liberal candidate is entirely out of the question, nor do I consider it reasonable that you should ask me to do so. Such a proceeding would

be a departure from the line of strict neutrality which has always been followed by the company in such cases.

Chaloner believed that both Atkinson and Moon had refused to stand as Conservative candidates at the general election that year. It has also been said that at one time Moon was asked to stand in Liverpool as a Conservative. It is unlikely that he ever considered such steps given his pronouncements on politicians in general and the need for his company to be seen to be independent of both main parties. However what is less clear is the extent to which his and Webb's innate conservatism unwittingly provoked the accusations of discrimination at Crewe. A member of the Crewe council, W.McNeill, a leading Liberal, alleged that Webb told him in a conversation over local politics that some of his men 'come and ask me, "How am I to vote?" and I say to them "Please yourself"'. Now that is admirable, but he follows this up by saying, "I say to them, keep off platforms, do not make speeches; do not write to newspapers; I don't want to know your politics". Now, why should it be wrong for a man's politics to be known? Why should he suffer on that account?'.

Attendance at St Pauls's Church, opened in 1869, one of the four C. of E. in the town endowed by the L&NW, was also apparently boosted in 1879 when Webb's brother, the Rev. A.H.Webb, was appointed vicar.

Though Moon himself made play of his public impartiality, his fellow directors were not so restrained. The Conservative's eventual choice to stand for the parliamentary constuency at Crewe in the 1885 general election was O.L.Stephen. Formerly a brewer in Burton, Stephen had moved to London and had been an active director of the L&NW since 1866, becoming a member of the board's Special Committee and taking over from the aging Bancroft as chairman of the North London Railway. Stephen lost to the Liberal. Significantly he did not stand again on his rival's death the following year, when the new Liberal candidate, Yorkshire woollen manufacturer W.S.B.McLaren, was elected.

The Crewe accusations were to continue to fester before erupting again in 1889. Before reviewing the final outcome at the company's half-yearly meeting in January 1890, the Jubilee celebrations of 1887 need to be covered.

CHAPTER 26

JUBILEE & POLITICS

Stories abound of Moon's reluctance to accept the baronetcy awarded him in the 1887 Queen's Jubilee honours. Neele later recalled that it was not known until the directors and officers met in the company's Westminster offices on Jubilee Day that such a distinction had been conferred. In his 1904 *Reminiscences* he wrote:

> Sir Richard subsequently told me that it was far from his wish to have accepted the title; but it appeared that the letter conveying the intimation of the intended honour arrived during his absence from home, and was opened by some member of his family. Had the letter come to his own hands he should have declined the honour, but the members of his family deprecated any such course.

The *Liverpool Courier* had in 1899 published a slightly different version of the event:

> Some years before the Queen's Jubilee the chairman of the London & North Western Railway was offered the title but declined it with the remark that he was quite content to be known as Mr. Moon. The offer was not formally repeated but when he opened the newspapers on the morning of June 20 1887 he saw an announcement in the list of Jubilee honours. "Here my dear" he said to his wife, "I'm down for a baronetcy. But I won't have it. I'll write and return it." During that and succeeding days however telegrams and letters of congratulation came in so thickly that Mr. Moon came to the conclusion it might be less inconvenient to accept the title.

That there could be some truth in such stories is the tenor of Moon's response to a note of congratulations from the Duke of Buckingham. In thanking him 'heartily' in a letter dated 2 July 1887, he wrote 'we are quiet people and these honours are not quite in our way but all my friends seem pleased'.

At aged seventy-three Moon was the first to be honoured with a baronetcy specifically for services to railways. As has been noted Gooch of the Great Western received his for Atlantic cable laying and the self-seeking Watkin for undefined political service.

The honours were announced in *The Times* on 21 June 1887. The review made by the paper two days later said 'it cannot be said that the list of persons selected ... was peculiarly well-chosen, but no exception can be taken to the names of the four members of the House of Commons who are to go to the upper house'. When the details of the individual baronetcies were given in the 26 June issue, Moon's was one of the briefest. It simply noted that as chairman of the L&NW he had 'done much to develop that great railway enterprise, and to give it the foremost position among the railways of the United Kingdom'. Pearce of Fairfield Shipbuilding was given the longest with a mention of the first iron ship built in royal dockyards and the current Atlantic liners and that his works employed up to 6,000 men. Moon employed over 50,000, 7,000 at Crewe alone.

It seemed appropriate at the time that Webb himself became mayor of Crewe in 1887 as it was not only the fiftieth year of the Queen's reign but also of the Grand Junction Railway's opening through Crewe. The company celebrated both events by donating land and granting £10,000 to create what became Queen's Park.

The land at Crewe had been part of a large purchase the company had made some years previously to provide for the extension of the works. Twenty-eight acres were surplus and with another twelve given by local landowners a forty acre site was developed and handed over to the municipality to maintain. However even this gesture was not without controversy. When Moon first publicly announced the proposal, a shareholder asked what 'particular merit the inhabitants of Crewe had over other communities in other parts of the company's system and that they could be in danger of having to agree other projects'. He amusingly added that in fact 'it was within the range of possibility that some

75. Moon Queen's Jubilee 1887
Photograph probably taken at the 1887 Crewe Jubilee for the newly honoured Sir
Richard Moon. LNWRS

day they might even be asked to contribute a powerful ironclad to the navy!'.

Moon justified the gift of the park by explaining it was 'not altogether as a present to the town or in relation to the Queen's jubilee but in the belief that they would get an advantage back in the good conduct and well-being of their own people'. There were 'no better workmen or more civil people in this world'. He won unanimous backing for the idea when he surprisingly admitted it 'was really a very small thing out of their enormous receipts and would never be felt by anybody'. Incidentally in so saying he had not been able to resist having another dig at the Government 'who could not manage the navy and could not get a ship built until it was time to break her up'. He went on to make another interesting remark, which seems so much at odds with his whole approach to business that it is worth quoting. 'If they were managing a commercial undertaking they must manage it on commercial principles, and he would undertake to say that there was not one transaction in a hundred thousand which was strictly legal. They must go on the give-and-take principle if they were to succeed.' Given his reputation for integrity it is difficult to know how to interpret what he meant by "legal". Was he being flippant, insulting or demonstrating there was a little more flexibility in his approach than that recorded in so many of the dry minutes of company meetings?

The park at Crewe was well advanced when the actual jubilee and dedication to the town was celebrated on 4 July 1887, officially recorded as being presided over by Sir Richard Moon. After decades of being known simply as Mr Moon it must have been difficult for his workforce to regard him as anything other as such. *The Times* on his retirement neatly put its finger on the matter:

> "Posterity", said Lord Macauley, "in defiance of the Royal Letters Patent, has obstinately refused to degrade Francis Bacon into Viscount St Albans"; and the railway world may be forgiven if they too have declined to sink the individuality of Mr Moon, and to think of him or speak of him by a name by which a score of other persons are known, that namely of "Sir Richard".

It seems in character that he chose as his armorial motto '*vincit omnia veritas*' (truth overcomes all things). His shield was an eagle (perhaps the master's eye!). He no doubt learnt to live with the title, but it seems out of place to refer to him as such in completing this story of his life. The company at Crewe honoured him with a silver gilt casket. Included in the engravings were the words "Progress" and "Prudence". At the other main works, the carriage manufacturing facilty at Wolverton, he was to receive a commemorative embossed memorial in book form signed by all the senior staff.

Among the principal events at Crewe for Moon were attendance at the borough council meeting and the formal opening of the park. At the council he received the first honorary freedom of the borough. At an earlier council meeting this had been proposed by Webb as Mayor and seconded by Alderman McNeill. In a report of the presentation McNeill received the loudest cheers when he said, in a flattering reference to the beneficial effect of the L&NW on the town, 'Sir Richard Moon as chairman of that great company had nourished and brought up children in that town. They had never rebelled against him or the company, and he was quite sure they never would.' It was ironic that it was the same McNeill who less than three years later was to publicly attack the company for its policy towards employees.

Moon in his amusing acceptance speech emphasised again that he was no politician:

> He had lived nearly seventy-three years. He had seen the three great leaders of parties in this country. He saw Sir Robert Peel for many years encouraging the maintenance of the Corn Laws, as they were at that period, and all sorts of crotchety things, but in the last part of his life he so changed his mind that he undid all he had done in the early part. He saw Mr "Dizzy" begin his political life as a very Liberal member and he saw him end his life as a thorough Conservative. He saw Mr Gladstone - who was a Liverpool man like himself, and a little older - begin as a fierce Tory. He did not know now exactly what he called himself - (laughter) - but he did not call himself a Conservative (renewed laughter). Now, he wanted to know which of these gentlemen was right. Were they right in the early part

76. F.W. Webb when Mayor of Crewe
F.W. Webb when mayor of Crewe in 1887. LNWRS

77. 3000th Crewe locomotive
L&NW compound tank locomotive no. 600, the 3000th engine built
at Crewe and displayed, when built in 1887, outside Queens Park
for the opening ceremony. LNWRS

of their lives or at the end; but, whichever it was, he had never been able to pin his faith to any leader of any party. He could tell them of another case, still more remarkable, of a Minister who for nearly twenty years represented one of the largest towns in Lancashire in the Conservative interest, and he believed he polled every vote. But he and his constituents turned round and for nearly twenty years they all went in for the Liberal side, so he said to himself when he came to Crewe that he was not a politician.

In concluding his address Moon must have raised a few local eyebrows when he said that 'in their municipal affairs no party ought to be brought into play at all'. He told them that as chairman of the L&NW 'he had taken care to keep out of politics because it was their duty, and his especial duty, to work with the Government of the day, of whatever party it might consist ... and the L&NW never could have any politics'. He was no doubt reinforcing the company's objectivity as stated at the time of the 1885 intimidation affair. But was it staying above politics to challenge a government, of whatever persuasion, on so many issues as he had done? No wonder the further storm that was to break over Crewe before he retired found him so much on the defensive.

At the formal lunch which followed the council meeting, Moon with his wife and daughter entertained four hundred guests. Eighteen other directors were present who together with the borough aldermen hosted the separate tables laid out in the company's drawing offices. In addition several other members of his family were present.

In proposing the health of Moon, the Midland chairman, M.W. Thompson, paid fulsome tribute to his knowledge of railways, saying 'he seemed to have every detail at his finger's end' and 'possessed marked capacity for investigation and for looking not only into the affairs of his own concern but on railways in general'. Thompson had 'frequently noticed, both at meetings at Euston and also in connection with the Railway Companies Association', that Moon took the 'greatest care to master the details' of the various questions considered:

> No man had given so much time and thought to the study
> of the intricate problems of railway management as Sir

Richard Moon. He was about the only chairman who regularly read all the minutes of every committee, and was thus in a position to talk over matters with his chief officers if anything went wrong. He could not only fulfil the duties of chairman of the board of directors but take the part of general manager as well ... Combined with his great administrative ability he had succeeded in keeping the company out of many difficulties. It was a great thing not to get into difficulties, but to know how to get out of them was a greater achievement. ... Although other railway companies may not like it, they recognised the L&NW as the premier railway company in the country, and it had achieved that position because Sir Richard Moon had put his back into the concern and lifted it up.

In responding, Moon was brief. He modestly used the occasion to thank his officers, most of the senior ones being present, 'for their cordial co-operation. It had always been the aim and desire of the company to get the very best officers they could'. He then quoted a maxim of his that he was to repeat on retirement, that his managers 'were first gentlemen and next officers of the L&NW company, and must, therefore, perform whatever they promised'.

Local MP McLaren was also on the guests' list, but not recorded as one of the speakers. Presumably as with McNeil he was enthusiastic over the celebrations. However like McNeil he was to feature later in the campaign against the company, stirred by further unrest over insurance and pensions.

Surprisingly Moon's admission in February 1883 that some of the lower paid men could not afford the pension fund contributions had not really surfaced as a major political issue at Crewe until the revival of the Liberals in the November 1888 local elections. Discontent then grew and by the following February the company's national pension fund delegates voted narrowly to ballot members on whether or not to abolish the Crewe scheme. Webb was present at the L&NW's March 1889 board meeting when Moon had to explain the difficulty with certain men in the Locomotive department pension fund. Webb though reported that the foremen, with one exception, were unanimous in their wish to continue.

78. Moon family group at Crewe 1887

Moon with family at Crewe, probably taken during 1887 jubilee, daughter
Edith standing behind and wife Eleanor on his left. Others are thought to be
his sons Ernest, Richard and Edward and their wives. Webb second from right,
Ramsbottom(?) left. LNWRS

79. Crewe in the 1890s

Locomotives at Crewe North Junction in late 1890s with Webb improved
Precedent class 890 *Sir Hardman Earle* in foreground. Note horse shunting
at top right. LNWRS

It seems that neither Webb nor Moon anticipated the extent of the men's rejection when the result of the ballot was known. The main objection from members was the relatively high cost of 'compulsory' contributions deducted by the company ahead of other dues such as those paid to friendly societies and unions. Taking advantage of both the pension issue and low wages a large public meeting at Crewe had been addressed by a company workshop employee, William Urquhart, who was one of the leading local activists promoting unionism. Moon had to call a special meeting of his board the following month to review the result of the ballot: 930 for continuing the pension scheme and 11,485 against. The decision was taken to wind up the fund although it was subsequently agreed to continue it for the foremen. The fund had been set up in 1883 with four separate divisions: foremen including inspectors, running divisions, workshops, and the "aged men" [55 and over].

In the summer of 1889 Webb received deputations from his men claiming their wage rates were less than in 1872. However, being asked by the board to review this, Webb reported in October that the 'wages of mechanics and artificers were paid at an average rate quite equal to that paid by other large railway locomotive works throughout the country'. Findlay reported the Traffic department's position and Moon conceded that 'he had considered with some of his colleagues with regard to the wages question'. Moon then held a series of meetings with key officers and agreed increases, but at Crewe further difficulties arose for Webb.

Urquhart had succeeded in setting up a Crewe branch of the new General Railway Workers Union, which embraced all grades of workers including those in the workshops. And at the same time the established branch of the older ASRS, a union which primarily covered traffic rather than workshop men, was given a new lease of life. [The Amalgamated Society of Railway Servants together with the General Railway Workers and the United Pointsmen & Signalmens Society became the NUR in 1913.] As with other local union representatives, Urquhart was a member of the local Liberal party and used that party's platform to protest against the company. Meetings were held in the town and over a thousand passed a resolution 'to affirm and endorse all the charges which have recently been made against some of the Crewe works officials: that Liberal workmen have been threatened and harassed at their work, degraded, and dismissed on account of their political actions'.

Agitation intensified and the unrest attracted national attention when Urquhart himself together with other union colleagues were discharged by the company. The matter came to a head locally at the Crewe council meeting on 27 November 1889 when leading Liberals, Dr W.Hodgson and C.H Pedley, proposed to petition L&NW shareholders over what Chaloner called the 'state of political serfdom in the works'. Hodgson wrote to Moon on 17 December 'alleging improper interference by the company's officers at Crewe with the political liberty of the workmen'. On 20 December a letter from Gladstone (then in Opposition) was published in *The Times* as a follow-up to the Crewe Liberal councillors' protests to him. At the L&NW board meeting the same day, Gladstone's letter was noted and, after Webb had given a full statement, a draft reply to Hodgson was approved. This reiterated the 1885 rebuttal that 'the directors have never interfered in any way with the political opinions of their employees nor do they desire that any such interference should take place. That with regard to the charges made in the memorial against the officers at Crewe, the directors have to observe that they are absolutely untrue and without foundation'.

Further correspondence ensued and at the Board meeting on 17 January 1890 Webb handed in a 'memorial' from all the foreman, except two from the Locomotive department. Not surprisingly this re-affirmed that the foremen had 'never coerced nor intimidated any of the workmen employees under them or interfered in any way with the free exercise of their political opinions'. Moon ordered the memorial to be recorded. However it was by then clear to Moon and his senior colleagues that at the forthcoming shareholders' meeting they could be facing a serious challenge to their authority and in particular to Webb's position.

The 88th Half-yearly General Meeting of the London and North Western Railway on 20 February 1890 was indeed an acrimonious affair: probably the most difficult of all the fifty-six such meetings Moon chaired. In order to qualify to speak, the principal protesters from Crewe (McLaren, Hodgson, Pedley, Urquhart and McNeill) had become shareholders in the company. Led by McLaren, the Crewe contingent with the support of other shareholders, tried to force two amendments to the Directors' Report. The first demanded an impartial public enquiry into the 'serious charges' that the company's Crewe officials 'have dismissed some workmen and tried to intimidate others because they were active Liberals'. The second resulted from the resolution passed by the employees that they should not be 'interfered with': that 'any official or other person who infringes the spirit of this declaration shall be liable to be dismissed and a ballot of the workmen be taken as to whether the charges are true or not'.

Discussion on the call for an enquiry was opened by J.Tompkinson, a banker from Tarporley, who was to alternate in future with McLaren as the Liberal MP for Crewe. He was followed by Hodgson, one of the most active of the progressive Liberals on the Crewe council. Both gave specific cases of men either allegedly dismissed or discriminated against. Hodgson explained that Urquhart was secretary of the Liberal Club and had 'served the company for thirty-three years [and] during the whole of that period no complaint has been registered against him, either for loss of time, or for bad work, or for misconduct ... yet he was discharged at a week's notice, without any reason given to him whatever'. Continuing on the same theme McNeill, a local draper who had played a prominent part in the incorporation of Crewe as a municipality, referred to a man being 'deprived of his rights' and, quoting his past conversation with Webb, asked 'why should it be wrong for a man's politics to be known?'. He alleged that 'every active politician on the Liberal side feels afraid. Every man on the other side, it is no matter what his character may be, if a prominent Tory, he can do almost as he likes'.

McLaren attempted to obtain Moon's reaction to McNeil's accusations before speaking himself, but Moon insisted on hearing all the protests first before responding. Two days before the meeting McLaren had written personally to Moon in what appeared to be a last minute attempt to avoid conflict. He asked that the company at least concede that an Inquiry was warranted. However Moon had peremptorily replied that 'not only do we know that the charges made are not true, but we believe further that the men themselves do not place any belief in them and that there is no such ill-feeling or irritation existing between us and the men you represent'.

At the meeting McLaren claimed 'there was no party element' in what he had to say as he held proxies from over a hundred large shareholders including Conservatives and Liberal Unionists. He argued 'we have cases which will prove that the chief officials at Crewe have been participators in intimidation'. Quoting the resolution in which 1,200 workmen agreed they had been threatened, he demanded an Inquiry. He said the foremen had not signed a collective denial, but only issued a 'shrewd' qualified statement that they were 'each willing to declare for ourselves that we have not intimidated anyone but we are not willing to make such a declaration for our fellow-foremen'. He repeated the charge that 'no Liberal has any chance of promotion, and that if any of the foremen are Liberals they must never go to a Liberal meeting, or become members of a Liberal association'. He had warned Moon that there was 'a feeling of intense irritation between the workmen and their superiors … and implored him to take some notice of it'. He claimed that when a similar situation occurred at the Great Northern's Doncaster works the directors had held a public inquiry and reinstated two Liberal workmen who had been dismissed. McLaren continued by saying he had received many letters from shareholders and quoted one from John Crosfield who wrote 'Tory intimidation by Crewe officials is a fact'. Crosfield owned the Warrington soap works and was the brother of George who had been a director of the L&NW until his death in 1887. Concluding, McLaren appealed to the floor: we have 'only come to you, the shareholders, as a last resort'.

When the last speakers had had their say, Moon immediately challenged McLaren by quoting him. 'He has told you that this is not a political question at all. Now, this is the first time that politics have been discussed in these half-yearly meetings and I trust it will be the last.' In explaining that the company was 'not unaccustomed to these complaints', he reeled off a number of examples: stopping trains to allow Gladstone to address meetings at stations, Conservative accusations of bias by the Earlestown management and allegations in the Dublin press of 'having boycotted our Irish servants'. Explaining the latter Moon said this had arisen from the dismissal of three of them and not 'any of the English servants', but forgetting to add that they had been 'helplessly drunk' and actually 'replaced by other Irish servants'.

Angrily he denounced the protesters at the meeting as 'outsiders'. Against a background of interruptions, attempting to explain how

Pedley had purchased £200 of shares, he went on contemptuously: 'You say they are shareholders. I am entitled to state their interest in the company. Mr McLaren, Dr Hodgson and Mr Urquhart have each purchased £100 of your stock in January; and Mr McNeill purchased £120, and in right of that they are here today'. Moving to the specific intimidation issue he asked rhetorically what was the meaning of ballot boxes? 'How could it be told how any man had voted. ... no one knows and it is nonsense to come here and say that there is this intimidation of the men'. He dismissed Crosfield by asking 'how could he say that he knew it as a fact what he knows nothing about?'.

He went on to deny again 'that there was any irritation or ill feeling in our works at all' and 'did not believe there is an honest workman in Crewe who thinks anything of the sort'. When heckled over the meeting of the 1,200 who had complained, he fell back, for the moment, on his Board's official response at the time that the allegations were 'absolutely untrue and without foundation'. He refuted the claim that as a result of the meeting the directors had issued a notice on the need for free elections and that the officials at Crewe had refused to post it. He quoted his board's Minute at the time: "Some conversation took place as to a suggested issue of notice to the company's employees with regard to the parliamentary election, and after again reading the reply sent to the Liberal Association ... it was resolved that no further action is necessary or expedient in this matter". On the matter of the foremen's statement Moon aggressively countered McLaren:

> Now listen to this. This is dated January 14th 1890. "We the undersigned foremen of the L&NW company's works at Crewe, hereby individually affirm that we have never coerced or intimidated any of the workmen employed under us, or interfered in any way with the free exercise of their political opinions". I ought to say this was signed by 55 of the foremen out of 57. The other two were ill at the time. I do not know what more you can want from the foremen.

He then went on to defend what had happened in the cases of the individuals named. Taking Urquhart first he said, 'Mr Webb had nothing to do with this. Urquhart was especially dismissed by order of a committee of this Board for North Western reasons and not for any political reasons whatever'. In the case of another, Jones, where the case was that a skilled man had been put on boy's work, Moon explained the man had 'spoiled piecework', his eyesight was 'supposed to be failing' and he had been given easier work. But 'would you believe it, from what you have heard, that during the whole time, in consideration of his long service Jones's rate of pay was never altered?'. Another allegation he dismissed as again having nothing to do with Webb: the man worked for the Shropshire Union and was discharged for 'disobedience to orders'. With another he said the case 'is not worth going into. He was discharged properly for being in business which was entirely contrary to the rules of the service'.

Jumping ahead to the second amendment for a moment Moon, perhaps unwisely still smarting from the result of the vote on pensions, somewhat undid the point he had made on ballots when he said. 'I have been always against the wretched ballot system. I say if a man is not equal to standing up and saying so-and-so he is not entitled to have a vote'. Urquhart was to pick him up on this later. Moon then went to the heart of the demand for an enquiry. 'The serious question you have to discuss today, and to decide upon, is whether your works at Crewe are to be managed by an outside political clique or whether they are to managed by your own directors and confidential partners.' 'It wants no reconsideration whatever ... and no power on earth can induce us to delegate the power you have given us to any public enquiry whatever.'

He then reiterated his non-involvement in politics theme by saying that on the board every variety and shade of political opinion was represented. 'I have myself, for the sake of the company, kept out of politics. I believe I have only given four political votes in all my life, and I am seventy-five years of age.' He did not care for politics and did not believe 'so much as some people do in the wisdom of Parliament. Let me go further and say that the strongest assurance we can give you is that it would be worse than a crime - it would be a blunder - if the company allied itself with any political party whatever'.

Before concluding his argument against a public enquiry Moon referred to Hodgson raising the fact that 1,200 had voted to protest. He reminded shareholders that the meeting in question was a public one, held in the Corn Exchange and was open to all Crewe.

He said they did know who was there but afterwards a company group 'voluntarily summoned a meeting of your own workpeople in the Town Hall ... and at that meeting passed certain resolutions emphatically repudiating the charges'. He asked for the resolutions from that meeting to be read out by the company secretary: the first stated that the "time has now arrived that we, the employees of the L&NW Locomotive Department, Crewe Works, should speak with a loud and unmistakable voice in condemnation of the action which is now being taken by our so-called friends"; and the second that the "meeting desires to express in the most emphatic manner possible our unabated and entire confidence in the directors and especially the officials". With evident emotion Moon then went on:

> I am now going to speak for myself. I say this deliberately to you: that I am sure if the work-people knew as well as I do the care that Mr Webb has taken to hold the balance rightly and fairly, the trouble he has taken and the anxiety he has had to keep them all employed and to keep them satisfied, they would with one voice condemn those gentlemen for their disgraceful attacks on Mr Webb.

The vote for the enquiry went on a show of hands 39 in favour and 73 against which (on the basis of the second vote to come) meant that there were at least almost fifty abstaining. The second motion was then put, which called for a ballot of the work force and Urquhart for the first time spoke.

Confirming he had been thirty-three years with the company at Crewe, Urquhart began by saying he had been dismissed by a resolution of the board. He stood corrected when Moon promptly, if pedantically, reminded him his dismissal was not by the Board but by order of a committee. Urquhart then explained how he had been "spotted" and first moved from his job for no apparent reason and affirmed that 'the majority of the workmen are in fear and cannot go about free in political or social and, to some extent, in religious matters. So long as I did my duty to you, and earned my wages, I had a perfect right to use my leisure time in advocating the rights and liberties of my fellow-workmen, and I have acted on that'. On the need for a ballot he asked 'can men come forward and speak openly when they know that there is no other employ in Crewe for them?'. So 'how can you expect men to put up their hands and vote in the manner that the chairman says? I say give us this ballot and you will have an enthusiastic majority ... and we will prove to you whether what we say exists or not'.

Saying he had advised Urquhart not to speak, Moon simply commented that Urquhart had shown 'that there is a great deal of political interest in the whole transaction'. Interestingly neither of them had elaborated on the specific reasons for Urquhart's dismissal. In refusing to accept the resolution for a ballot Moon left no doubt in the shareholders' minds what the real issue was. Srongly defending Webb and his officials, he said. 'I would not be a party to having a slur cast on your superintendent or foremen'. He stated categorically that he did not believe Urquhart. 'I have assured you it is not true. *I will not, therefore, have it* [authors italics]. You must again vote yes or no'.

Hodgson tried to speak again but after constant interruptions Moon forced the vote. The motion for a ballot was lost: 109 against and 51 in favour. McLaren demanded a poll, which would have meant reconvening the meeting after valuing the respective shareholdings. However McLaren quickly conceded when, after he had said he had proxies for £198,000, Moon told him he held nearly £6,000,000. The meeting concluded with perhaps honours shared after McLaren asked 'whether the directors will, although they deny that our charges are true, take measures to prevent the possibility of any such charges being made in future?'. Moon responded that 'the disturbance which has been made today under imaginary conditions will, you may rely on it, prevent any chance of its occurrence. Nothing will induce me to put a slur on our superintendent and officers'.

In an attempt to relieve the tension Sir James Ramsden proposed a 'hearty' vote of thanks to Moon, claiming that in forty years he had 'never known him have to undertake a more trying duty than he has discharged today, and he has gone through it in a way that must be gratifying to all concerned'.

In thanking Ramsden, Moon said he had 'taken great pains with this concern. I should be sorry for anything to happen at the end of my career to disturb the harmony that has existed between us during the thirty years that I have had the honour of being your chairman'.

What Moon may have said privately to Webb afterwards, the Crewe superintendent having been present throughout the meeting, needs little to imagine. Suffice to say that no further talk of intimidation at Crewe arose in future and both Webb and Whale resigned from the Crewe council in the summer. As Chaloner put it, 'the election in November 1891 finally annihilated the Independent Party. The new Council consisted of 20 Liberals and 4 Conservatives'.

A year later, in a leading article marking Moon's retirement, *The Times*, incidentally not referring to him as Sir Richard, wrote:

> Only on two occasions, of late years at least, has Mr Moon come prominently before the public - once, when ... he urged the assembled shareholders of British railways to join together and defeat the measure of confiscation ... and once when, this time last year, the shareholders' half-yearly meeting was turned into a political conflict in reference to the alleged interference of North-Western officials with the political rights of the Crewe workmen. Mr Moon's unflinching determination on that occasion to support an official who had, he was absolutely sure, been unjustly accused, even when it looked almost as though the chairman might be left in a minority by his own shareholders, should go far to explain the success of the North-Western system. A chief who, while perhaps over-ready to mark what is done amiss, yet trusts wholly and supports loyally his officers when he believes they are acting rightly, deserves, and may look to obtain, loyal and devoted service in return.

In marked contrast to the above was the view of the weekly *Railway Herald*. Its comments column in the 28 February 1891 issue included the snippet that although Moon was 'no doubt a friend of the shareholders ... the railway servant has seldom seen such a bitter opponent of the rights of labour to recognition at the hands of the capitalist. "A red herring is quite good enough for a working man's dinner" was one of the dearest and most frequently quoted mottoes of Sir Richard Moon. "Allez au diable" is our verdict'. No reference has been found to any occasion when Moon used the alleged motto.

However the paper had a point. Whether such vindictiveness was justified or not, the twin evils, long hours and low wages, that lay behind the comment, were never seen as such by Moon and most of his contemporaries: *The Times* for example concluding, 'but, rigid disciplinarian though he might be, Mr Moon has never wished to be other than a generous employer. Few companies employing 60,000 servants can boast to have seen as little of labour troubles as the North Western'.

It is easy from the perspective of a later century to condemn as reactionary the attitude of men like Moon. However in concluding this chapter a further quote from *The Times* is perhaps worth dwelling on. 'As for Crewe, the North Western capital as it has been termed, a country village when the Grand Junction first came there, and now a town with a mayor and corporation and an MP of its own, from its first church to its last park, it owes practically every public institution in the town to North Western liberality.'

CHAPTER 27

INTO RETIREMENT

Moon was seventy-one when he first publicly considered retirement. In reminiscing at the February 1886 L&NW shareholders' meeting, after being elected for another five year term as a director, he said it was the eighth time he had been re-appointed and his shares had been held for fifty years, first by his father. He had been a director thirty-five years and chairman twenty-five. He said he 'had doubts whether he ought longer to serve the company on the directorate; but as the shareholders seemed to desire that he should continue in his position, he was willing to retain it, and endeavour to do his best for their interests'.

As the events of his last five years unfolded he may well have regretted his decision to continue. Well before he did retire there were internal rumblings of discontent. Findlay's comment that change had to be actually unavoidable before expenditure was approved was clearly made with some feeling. And if Neele is to be believed, Moon's stance on defending the outdated chain brake verged on ridicule. This may have been so, but probably worse was Neele's claim that Moon had sat on a list of improvements. In referring to the period after Moon retired, Neele wrote, somewhat convolutedly, that 'many of the plans which had received most careful cogitation at the instance of the late North Western chairman, and by him had been cautiously postponed, were now brought under notice ... with the result that plans were approved'.

Neele would seem to have had a point. Average annual capital expenditure over Moon's penultimate five-year term was £2.02 million. Over his last term it averaged only £0.71 million (after allowing for the capitalising in 1888 of the L&NW's share in the North Union and Preston & Wyre). And from a low of £0.69 in Moon's last year expenditure jumped to nearly £1.08 and £1.14 million in the first two years of his successor. Major projects such as new marshalling yards, signalling and the improvements to the lines through the Crewe junctions were then approved. However to suggest that these would not have gone ahead had Moon remained even longer in the chair is perhaps unfair. It would surely have been a matter of timing for him. He had never shirked from spending capital to improve facilities, but he probably would have needed more persuading than his successor. Service to the public was paramount and, once convinced of the necessity for maintaining this, Moon never hesitated to approve the necessary expenditure and forcefully defended it in front of his shareholders.

The veteran London goods manager David Stevenson perhaps put his finger on the frustration felt by some when he wrote of Moon's 'belief in a personal examination of every person and place on whom or which a decision was necessary'. Such a process of decision making may not have pleased some of his managers. However his repeated complaints over the cost of signalling and interlocking are more difficult to defend. And his public posturing against the last competitor to threaten his territory, the Manchester Ship Canal, did little to show him in any other than a blinkered light. Even his old adversary Watkin, an equally strong champion of railway interest, was advocating cooperation rather than confrontation.

It seems ironic that for one, who in his early days had championed their advantages for bulk carrying, Moon's last battle over territory should be against a canal. The L&NW's own canal interests were extensive and despite his despair in later years of ever making an acceptable return on the investment in them, Moon had remained personally involved with the separately constituted Birmingham Canal Navigations. Early in the twentieth century, the BCN, with over 160 miles of waterways, was still carrying 7.5 million tons annually, nearly half a million passing through L&NW wharves.

The first Bill for a Manchester Ship Canal involved channelling the Mersey. Submitted in 1883 it was savaged by Moon as 'probably one of the wildest schemes that it ever entered into the mind of man to conceive'. Although thrown out a new scheme was proposed and an 'astonished' Moon reiterated his 'wildest ever' comments and derided the promoters in saying 'London had taken its docks down to the sea, Manchester was trying to bring the sea up to Manchester ... ships were never likely to go to Manchester'. When this second

Bill was rejected Moon confidently told his shareholders that he did not think they would hear any more of it.

Again it had been the long suffering Findlay who gave the railway evidence appearing six times before the Committee reporting on the Bills. It was with their third Bill in 1885 that the promoters finally succeeded with a canal from Eastham to Salford. By then Moon had accepted the need to temper outright opposition by obtaining adequate protective and compensation clauses. It took another two years for the promoters to finance the necessary purchase of the Bridgewater Canal and for construction to start. The canal was not opened fully until January 1894. Moon had then been retired for three years and may well have ruefully contemplated on the sea being indeed brought to Manchester.

Another area where Moon was frequently criticised in his latter years was the L&NW's locomotive policy. He has been accused of holding Webb back on heavier engines, for seeing punctuality and reliability as more critical than speed, that standardisation and economy of working were the keys to profitability. That Webb was of like mind however is clearly evident: he could not have run such a vast works as Crewe, probably the largest of any kind in the country, for so long and successfully under Moon if it were not so. Given this responsibility it is unfortunate that Webb is remembered by many only for alleged shortcomings; no better example being than the chain brake and the controversy surrounding his compound locomotives.

It seems that Moon had little input into Webb's 1881 design venture into compounding other than his ready approval for any change that would bring about inceased efficiency and cost savings. The principle was not new, it was applied to marine engines and a French designer, Mallet, had introduced it in France in 1876. Given a steady constant load significant economy in coal and water consumption could be achieved by using the waste steam from a high pressure cylinder to power an additional low pressure one. And by driving their own axles on a locomotive there would be no need for expensive coupling rods. Webb used both reasons for the development although to what extent he considered this was the only way to meet the need for more powerful engines is not clear. With two high pressure cylinders his "Experiment" three cylinder compound was built in 1882 and the modified "Compound" the following year; in all a total of thirty were produced by the summer of 1884. By 1888 forty more of an improved heavier "Dreadnought" class had been built and ten further as the modified "Teutonic" class in 1890, the latter design proving the most successful in both speed and load pulling capacity.

Mention has been made of heavier engines. It should be noted that Webb had eventually convinced Moon that plans for developing a new larger compound, the "Greater Britain" class, should go ahead, although by the time it was introduced Moon had retired. At nearly 15% heavier than the Teutonics this locomotive was then said to be the largest British tender engine built. Ten were built by 1894, three of which were named after Richard Moon, William Cawkwell and George Findlay. As has been previously noted no locomotive was named after Moon during his chairmanship. When these three engines were all scrapped by 1907 their names were carried forward by Webb's successor Whale on his new 4-6-0 "Experiment" class and lasted under the LMS into the 1930s.

Webb had persisted with his compound designs despite recurring technical faults and criticism from contemporary observers. He could not have done so without support from Moon.

And Webb did not neglect the updating with rebuilds of earlier 'simple' designs, in particular his highly successful 2-4-0 "Precedents". However this is not the place to pursue these developments, or the later unsuccessful introduction of the four cylinder compound all driving on the one axle, which needed the re-introduction of the coupling rods. In the summer 1888 race to Edinburgh it was an improved Precedent class, 275 *Vulcan* built in January, that put in one of the finest performances.

Before detailing the racing events it is perhaps relevant to mention the carriages. From his early Stores Committee days and subsequent pursuit of rationalising production at Wolverton, Moon would have remained closely involved in their design and build. He had personally chosen Bore as his Wolverton superintendent. However as was the case in so many areas, L&NW carriage building did not set the pace in innovative design. Bore's standard six wheel carriage chassis remained in effect the basis of all new developments during most of the superintendent's long years in office. That this was yet another cost restraint imposed by Moon would probably have

80. Precedent class locomotive *Charles Dickens*

L&NW 2-4-0 locomotive 955 *Charles Dickens*, last of the original Precedent class
built in 1882 as illustrated in the company's 1903 booklet describing Crewe works.

81. 1888 Race to Edinburgh

Caledonian Railway 4-2-2 locomotive no. 123 hauling West Coast express in
the 'races' of 1888. Painting by Jack Hill commemorating the record Carlisle to
Edinburgh run of 9 August.

been his defence. Competitors were introducing longer carriages with bogies to accommodate the increased lengths demanded by improved amenities and increased capacities; the L&NW only extending theirs so that the extra length could be carried by replacing the centre axle with a radial axle added outside each of the end ones. It was not until well after C.A.Park took over in 1886 and Moon had retired that significant improvements were made including the use of chassis bogies and the first corridor train in 1893.

It was in the summer of 1888 that an outburst of competitive acceleration between the West and East Coast routes for the London to Edinburgh traffic first caught the public's imagination. Denounced by some shareholders as 'insane competition', this episode appears so out of character for Moon that it needs explaining. Neele, who at the time was the company's Passenger Superintendent under Findlay wrote that Moon was 'was constantly impressing on our manager and his subordinate officers the importance, in a dividend point of view, of economy in the expenditure of locomotive and running expenses and of avoiding excessive speed'. He added that 'forty miles an hour was about his standpoint, and he ridiculed the idea of speed prestige being any advantage'.

So how had Moon allowed himself to condone the race to Edinburgh? In a bid for the summer holiday traffic the L&NW had reduced in June their express time from Euston to Edinburgh from ten hours to nine. By July the Great Northern, the lead East Coast company, had responded with 8½ hours from Kings Cross.

Neele had complained that the L&NW had issued their July to September timetable still with the original times, implying that either Moon or Findlay was responsible for not initially responding more aggressively. 'Much dissatisfaction was felt', he wrote, 'both by the Caledonian officers [West Coast partners] and some of the head authorities at Euston, at the "back seat" position thus thrust on the royal mail route'. Clearly action was needed and after a meeting with the Caledonian it was agreed to amend the public timetable, though it was not until 27 July that, according to Neele, a special issue of West Coast time tables for August was published. This showed that the 10 a.m. express would also run to Edinburgh in 8½ hours. The GN 'lost no time in making a further advance; and by the 1st August they had arranged for an 8 hour service'. The following day the L&NW's special committe formed to coordinate the company's response decided to make a similar acceleration.

The situation then appeared to get out of hand. By 13 August the GN had announced a reduction to 7¾ hours and the L&NW had responded by achieving a running time of 7 hours 38 minutes. And the next day the East Coast had run in 7 hours 32 minutes. This was the day of the L&NW's mid August shareholders' meeting. Whether Moon was fully aware of the situation is not clear. In responding that he did 'not know why people should find fault with us' he explained that they had 'borne very patiently' the East Coast running in an hour less time:

> But they began to encroach a bit further, and we could not bear it, and all this row and noise has been made because we are simply doing it in the same time that they have done. ... We were only four miles farther to Edinburgh than they are ... so out of 400 miles it is no hardship to go in the same time that they do. ... Is there any fault in our going in that time? When we went in 9 hours, they said, "We will go in 8½." Then they said, "We are not content; we will go in 8 hours." Very well; "Just the time when people are going to Scotland," we said, "we will run in 8 hours," and we are proposing to run this month in 8 hours; and all we can say is, we are as much entitled to go in 8 hours as they are. The curious part of it to me is this: we do not want to run fast, or throw out any of our side connections, or incur the extra expense.

Connecting services being sacrificed by running non-stop between key points plus the increased fuel consumption, wear on track etc., were clearly more painful than curious to Moon. On the back foot he recalled the competition for the London Manchester traffic, saying that their route was 21 miles longer, but 'what do they do? They go in the same time as we do. But we have not complained. If it is right for the Great Northern to run London to Manchester in the same time that we do, it cannot be wrong in us to run London to Edinburgh in the same time':

But it has never been our policy, you must live and let live, to try and run our neighbours off the road. All I say is, we must have a fair measure of the traffic. When we have that we are content. We could as easily run to Manchester in 3¾ hours as they could to Edinburgh in 8; but we are content to do what they do. We have one or two trains - and so they have - that go in 4¼ hours. The Great Western go to Birmingham the same time as we do; that is, 129 miles against 113. We cannot get it all, and we must be content to have a fair share. That has been our principle, and it is our principle today. And Mr Findlay this afternoon is going to meet the managers of the North Eastern and Great Northern railways [the English East Coast partners], and I do hope they will come to see that which is good for them in Manchester is good for us in Scotland. We should make some amicable settlement of the present difficulty, but take it for granted it is no fault of ours.

Whatever his personal view, this statement can be said to be another example of Moon's public support for his management. What is not known is his private brief to Findlay to settle the matter. Reason finally prevailed, the L&NW's 8 hours and the GN's 7¾ remained for August but thereafter were 8½ and 8¼ hours respectively. These times remained until well after Moon retired. However keen rivalry for the Scottish traffic remained, the emphasis shifting to Aberdeen after the Forth Bridge opened in 1890, which eventually culminated in a new outbreak of racing in 1895. But by then Moon had been retired for over four years.

Moon formally announced his intention to retire at the 15 August 1890 L&NW board meeting. The minute read: 'Acting on the imperative advice of his physician he felt obliged to intimate that he did not propose to offer himself for re-election at the next half-yearly meeting of February 1891, though he hoped that his health would admit of his continuing to hold his present position until that date.'

Although Bickersteth as deputy chairman was present it was the oldest director William Tipping who responded. He was a substantial stock holder from Kent who became a member of the shareholders' Audit Committee in 1863 and been elected to the board the following year. With his interest mainly financial, he was never a member of the board's Special Committee. He had been an MP for Stockport. While recognising that 'under the circumstances ... the chairman's decision was, in the interests of himself and his family, a right one', Tipping expressed their 'deep regret' and 'sense of the devotion and conspicuous ability and success with which Sir Richard Moon had directed the affairs of the company for the long period of thirty one [sic] years as well as their personal regard and esteem'.

In September Moon was seventy-four, his wife seventy. In apparent robust health for most of his life he had at last begun to feel his age. In the February of the previous year he had brushed off national concern over an escape from a nasty accident. The incident had been widely reported. Apparently inspecting the line at Walsall, he claimed he knew what he was doing 'perfectly well' and that he had seen the whole operation, 'whereas the people who reported it were 200 or 300 yards away. ... If there was any danger in crossing the line at Walsall, which I doubt, I can only say that I afterwards crossed the line at Edge Hill, where there is some danger, without the least accident. Be sure that as long as I am here I will take care of myself'.

The *Crewe Chronicle* for 22 November 1890 reported his last visit to Crewe to distribute the prizes to students of the Mechanics' Institute. He told them he did 'not feel equal to that which I did in old days, for without a man is able to devote his whole soul and his whole life to watching over the interests of this company he ought to give place to younger hands'. In sadly confirming that 'this would be the last time he would be amongst them', he said that 'it gave him very great regret to part from them because he had derived great pleasure from meeting with them'.

The details covered by the Board in the last five years of his chairmanship had become quite voluminous as the monthly meetings were combined with those of the alternate fortnightly Special Committee, the sixteen members of which were the effective board of the company. What is remarkable is that so many detailed matters continued to be referred to Moon personally right up to his last meeting. For example despite Cawkwell's long experience and position as one of the two deputy chairman, he still found it necessary, even as late as May 1890, not only to write formally to

Moon requesting signed approval for a 'new connection between the down main line and the carriage shed sidings at Victoria Station Swansea', but to give the detailed reasons justifying the request. That the reason seemed so self-evidently routine is even more remarkable: the siding simply made it 'possible for carriages on trains which have arrived at Swansea to be pushed direct into the carriage shed sidings instead of being propelled for a considerable distance along the main line and then backed into the sidings in question'. And such were the quirks of the directors' deliberations that at the same meeting Moon also reported another decision, not quite so momentous, that as the 'Crewe Park' had facilities to play cricket it was no longer necessary to rent the ground from a Mr Broughton at £12 per annum.

To be fair however an increasing number of decisions were by then being referred to the general manager Findlay. Moon's deputies Cawkwell and Bickersteth were rarely assigned responsibilities for reviewing specific operating matters. Whether this was due to the character of Findlay or reluctance on the part of the two directors to become involved in management detail is difficult to determine. Yet Findlay was also carrying the heavy burden of representing the company in the negotiations over freight rates.

Findlay's chief goods manager, Frederick Harrison, was already taking some of the internal overall management load and also attending directors' committee meetings. In December 1888 Moon had approved the advancement of Harrison's salary to £2,000 and two years later to £2,500 with additional responsibilities to assist Findlay as general manager. The salaries of Findlay and Charles Mason, the company solicitor, were then both dramatically increased to £5,000. Mason had been appointed company solicitor in 1883 at a salary of £2,000, the same as his predecessor Roberts. Although Moon had never hesitated to pay top salaries for key management his approval in December 1890 for Mason's salary to equal Findlay's is remarkable. Not only did it reflect Moon's assessment of Mason, but how critically he must have seen the legal battles ahead.

However Findlay's own position as general manager must at times have been frustrated by the executive role Moon took as managing director. Never a member of the board, Findlay was nevertheless routinely in attendance at all their Special Committee meetings. Whether Moon ever contemplated having Findlay on the board as his eventual successor with the ambitious Harrison groomed for the manager's position is not known.

Including Moon there would have been three director vacancies in February 1891. However the previous board meeting had agreed to aim for a maximum membership of only twenty-four and Moon recommended that the vacancies should not be filled. Incidentally at that same board it is to be wondered what evoked a particularly wordy resolution on purchasing. The principle was reaffirmed that all contracts made by the Stores Committee be ordered through that committee, 'and that purchases of, or contracts for, such stores made otherwise than through the Stores Committee be reported from time to time to that committee by the committee authorising or sanctioning such purchases or contracts'. Shades of Moon's old days in the 1850s; indeed just what were Moon's thoughts as he took his last board on Friday 20 February 1891, one of the few where all the directors were present together with the senior officers, and afterwards when he led the group into the shareholders' room for his last half-yearly meeting?

Less than three weeks before the meeting his wife had died. As Neele was to recall, her death seemed 'a shock which much unnerved him'. It seems that Eleanor may have been ill for some months, which must have put an additional strain on him. The previous summer he had uncharacteristically announced there would be no meetings of L&NW committees in September, and in November was warning colleagues that he was not proposing to hold the meetings scheduled around the year-end.

When Moon rose to speak at his last half-yearly meeting he broke with precedent, clearly aware of speakers waiting to pay him tribute, by first calling the necessary Special meeting to approve new capital. Only after this did he make his usual review of the accounts. He made one last appeal for 'justice and fair play' in the Government rates and charges review, rousing himself to attack again the 'dilettanti gentlemen in Parliament' (notwithstanding that he knew a cabinet minister was present as a shareholder and four of the board were MPs).

After arguing against a motion for the company to indemnify holders of the company's stock against the risk of forgery, incidentally the only issue on which he was recorded as speaking from the floor after he retired, Moon concluded by proposing that his personal remuneration of £2,000 'be continued to the chairman of the company for the time being'. His closed with the simple words: 'that is the end of the business to-day'.

It was of course not the end. The company's published *Half-Yearly Report* of 20 February 1891 contained a full account of what followed. Three speakers had been chosen to mark the occasion, two from shareholders and one from the directors. First to speak was the Rt.Hon.W.H.Smith, the Conservative Leader of the House of Commons and First Lord of the Treasury. Explaining he had been a shareholder for a 'great many years' he reminded those present of the 'very peculiar circumstances' of the chairman. He [Moon] had joined the company as a director some forty years ago, was elected chairman thirty years ago or more and during that time had devoted himself to the company's service as the occupation of his life:

> He has not sought honour in other directions; he has not sought profit in other employment; and what is the result? That single-minded, that absorbing devotion which he has given to the company has resulted in this - that the 34,000 shareholders in this company have, in a manner which is almost unexampled, continued year after year, half-year after half-year, to express their unabated confidence in the direction of the company.

Smith went on to say that although the company's success was due not only to Moon, 'there is one characteristic about a man who is capable of leading - that he is also capable of surrounding himself with men who are as capable almost as he is himself in giving effect to the policy for which he is responsible'. After acknowledging the support Moon had had from the officers and servants of the company, Smith said that progress had been made 'side by side with vigilant competitors, all of them trying to serve the public as well as they can and thus to secure for their own shareholders and their own companies the traffic and advantages which a good service produces. But the North Western Company has held its own'.

One of the "vigilant" competitors was the Great Northern whose chairman, Lord Colville, was present as a shareholder to second Smith. He thanked Moon 'for his devotion to the interests and welfare of the company and its employees' and to 'hope that he may long enjoy peace and rest in his retirement'. In acknowledging the duties and responsibilities of a railway chairman, Colville considered that his own company's capital of £42 million and 800 miles of railway was as much as he wished personally to carry on his shoulders, but Moon 'has had to deal with a capital of no less than, now, £110 million and 1,900 miles of railway to look after'. For thirty years 'Sir Richard Moon has been the guiding spirit of the L&NW. He has moulded it into what it is now, the first, the leading railway company, I believe in the world. He now leaves it not only financially sound, but in every other respect it stands as a monument of solidity and good management'.

The directors chose D.R.Plunket to add their tribute. Elected a director in 1881, Plunket, MP for Dublin University, represented the company's interests in Ireland and had been quickly appointed to the board's Special Committee. In adding his words he told shareholders that Moon had devoted his life to their interest in building up the greatness and reputation of the company:

> We, all of us, have seen the result of his labour but it is we who have had the honour and pleasure of serving with him on the Board who best can know how much of the result has been solely due to his unceasing, self-sacrificing services. Sir Richard Moon, you have made our duty as directors easy and pleasant to us by your great personal kindness to us, though I am afraid some of us have often taxed your patience sorely; but we have always felt that the character of the Board was safe in your hands, and that whatever our individual shortcomings might be - come what might - upon your wisdom and experience, your courage and integrity, we could absolutely rely. Sir Richard, I have no intention on this occasion - I am sure it would be distasteful to yourself - to go over again what has been already spoken of the history of your great career as our chairman. That will ever remain bright in the pages of the history of industry and enterprise of England. All that we desire on this occasion ... is to offer you now -

and you have never allowed us to offer you any more substantial token, while we know that by no man are mere words of praise less sought after than yourself - we ask to be allowed to offer you now our heartfelt tribute of admiration and respect.

Neele who was present thought it was a privilege to listen to Plunket's 'highly eloquent and dignified language'. The company's report of the proceedings referred to Moon's 'evident emotion' when he responded:

We have been told that when we have done our duty we are still to be content with having done our duty. I feel that I do not deserve the kind things that have been said of me here today. I equally regret that the feeling that I am no longer able to do my duty has compelled me to retire from the position I have held here. I also desire to say I feel grateful to you for the confidence you have so long reposed in me. I have always tried to do for you what we did for our own credit - to see that our honour and our integrity were maintained, and that whatever we promised should be fulfilled. You have allowed me to do the same here. You have also allowed me without stint to surround myself with officers whom we have been able to put in positions they should be proud of, and to feel they are gentlemen. We have been able to give them proper salaries, and to treat them like ourselves; and not only so, but we have been able to go to the very bottom of the concern, to try and make everybody in our service loyal to you. I believe, today, there is not any society in this country or in the world as loyal to its employers as your people are to you today, and have been all through these years.

My father impressed upon me that he had never had a bad servant. If you are to have good servants you must treat them well and loyally. You must be one of them. We have tried to be one of them. I saw your officers here this week - most of the chief officers - they have all been appointed in my time. I have always said to them, "Remember, first of all, you are a gentleman; next, you are a North Western officer. Whatever you promise you must perform, and therefore be careful what you promise, but take care you perform it". We have tried to get that principle to go down throughout the service, and I believe it does go down. I have had the means of ascertaining it in different parts of the country, in positions we never dreamt of. That is what we must always try and do. I can say no more to you except to thank you all for your confidence in me and your kindness and forbearance towards me. We have been through crises over and over again. Many of my colleagues and friends who helped me in the early days have gone; but I hope that in future, as your concern is bound up with the prosperity of the country, so with God's blessing, our country and our company, long after all we here present have passed away and been forgotten, may still flourish in peace and prosperity.

Among the many press tributes on Moon's retirement none is more indicative of the position he held, not just in the railway world but amongst the business community generally, than the report published by *The Times* the following day, 21 February 1891. The opening paragraph read:

"The ordinary half-yearly general meeting" is the legal and regular description of the meeting of London and North-Western Railway proprietors held yesterday, but it seems singularly inappropriate in view of the business transacted. A meeting to which was announced the retirement of Sir Richard Moon from the chairmanship and the direction of the company is at once removed from the category of things ordinary, and must figure as memorable in the minds, not only of the shareholders, but of the public. To the present generation Sir Richard Moon is an institution. He has been chairman of the North-Western since 1862 [sic], and has so impressed the management of that great company with his individual character that to name the North-Western is to call up his image in the minds of all who are in any degree conversant with railway business. His unique position has been attained and kept by virtue of business faculties of the very highest order, and of infinite capacity for taking pains which Carlyle identified with genius. To splendid organising ability he added unwearied inspection and supervision of every part of the vast and complicated machinery developed under his care. His extraordinary thorough grasp alike of principles and details was attainable only by severe concentration of his energies. Neither ambition nor desire for gain ever tempted him to travel beyond his sphere as chairman of the North-Western, or draw from that position more than a very modest honorarium. His opportunities for securing ornamental and highly paid directorships must have been unlimited, but he left duplication of functions to others, and allowed no rival company to establish a claim upon his time or ability. To his close attention to its affairs and his continuous efforts on its behalf the North-Western largely owes the commanding position it occupies among the great and soundest of commercial enterprises. The railway world, and even the commercial world in general, owes him a debt of gratitude for the example he has given of unswerving commercial integrity. We have every reason to feel pride in the general record of our English railway system, which contrasts most forcibly with the general laxity, to use no harder word, noticeable elsewhere. But the standard has been upheld by no company more consistently than by the North-Western under Sir Richard Moon's strong and steady guidance.

Of the many other press tributes at the time all praised his single-minded dedication and the resulting strength and soundness of the company. Of course Moon had not been without his critics. *The Times*, in a special feature on him published the day before its report of the meeting, had made reference to these. It commented that some have declared that 'the North-Western policy to be mainly one of negation. A more unfair charge has not often been made'. The article continued:

The North-Western has admittedly seldom led the way in reform. But when once the change has been made and proved a success, the North-Western is prepared to go further and faster than the best of them. It left it to the Midland to try the great third-class experiment. All honour to that company for so doing, but it cannot boast today that it serves third-class passengers any better than its rival. It is the Great Northern which has forced the pace of expresses, but today the west coast Scotch express is, on the whole, the fastest train in the world. The North-Western may have neglected to win the popularity which comes, and rightly comes, to the company which is the first and the readiest to meet a public demand, but in the end it has always met it completely

It seems that few would have quarrelled with the *The Times* when they concluded by thinking that Moon would be 'satisfied to know that he would leave his line as he found it - the premier company, the accepted representative of English railway management at its best'.

CHAPTER 28

CLOSING YEARS

Once he had retired from the L&NW Moon took no further part in the company's affairs, nor had he any other business interest to occupy his time. Unlike many of his contemporaries Moon had stood neither for Parliament nor sat on the boards of unrelated companies. His refusal to join other organisations with the exception of the Railway Companies Association, although even here he never agreed to head that body, is demonstrated by a letter he wrote, admittedly near the end of his career declining an invitation to become a vice president of the International Congress on Inland Navigation: he invoked his 'invariable rule of adhering solely to matters connected with this railway'.

Before leaving the L&NW some comment on the succession to his office is of interest. Throughout his chairmanship, even in the early days of Brown-Westhead, the position of deputy seemed to have carried little weight with Moon and for many years he operated without one. There was no obvious like-minded figure among the directors to replace him. The nearest possibility was the general manager Findlay who had in effect been operating at board level for some time in terms of relationships with Parliament and competitors. *The Times* summed up the position well when it wrote that 'the place of Mr Moon must remain unfilled ... no one again will ever know the system as he knew it, will be able at once to keep in his mind all the threads of its policy, and in his memory all its vast and voluminous details. Mr Moon's own memory and industry would not have sufficed for the task had he not grown up with the North-Western from the day of small things'. The paper went on to comment that it would be difficult for those who believed in the private commercial management of railways, not to feel that perhaps Moon had been taken away from the evil to come:

With the railway revenues compulsorily cut short by the direct action of Parliament, the frugal vigilance of Mr Moon would only be wasted. With the hours of labour prescribed, with the number of horse-boxes on every train fixed, and the position of every signal regulated, not by the company but by a state official, the strong individuality of the late chairman would be out of place.

There was of course intense speculation over who the successor might be. The possibility of Findlay has been mentioned. Another rumoured to have been a contender was Ismay. The *Liverpool Mercury* and the *Shipping Telegraph* on 24 November 1899, in reporting Thomas Ismay's death, both commented that Ismay had been the board's unanimous first choice. Apparently he turned the position down as he wished to concentrate on his shipping business. Twenty years younger than Moon, Ismay, founder of the White Star line, had been an active L&NW director since 1882 when replacing the Liverpool director and colliery owner Sir James Bourne Bt.

Ever anxious to ensure influential representation at board level for the principal interests and geographical areas served by his railway, Moon could well have encouraged the appointment of someone with the standing of Ismay. Although Ismay had quickly joined many of the board's committees and became chairman of the one covering the permanent way, he was not, at the time of Moon's retirement, on the board's ruling Special Committee.

The two most senior directors were of course the joint deputy chairmen Cawkwell and Bickersteth. Both had been closely associated with Moon in directing the affairs of the company, but the former was over seventy and the latter approaching sixty-five. Excluding Moon, who at seventy-six was the oldest by far, the average age of the Special Committee was sixty in 1891. Cawkwell's history of health problems as well as his age would presumably have ruled him out, but Bickersteth must have been considered and it may have been significant that the meetings convened to appoint the successor were chaired by Cawkwell. However no record of lobbying or discussions on candidates has been found.

At what stage the fifty-four year old Lord Stalbridge emerged as the front runner is not clear. With the exception of the Marquis of Stafford (who was to succeed his father as Duke of Sutherland in 1892), Stalbridge was the youngest of the Special Committee. It was at a special board chaired by Cawkwell after the shareholders meeting on 21 February that the minutes simply record that, proposed by Cawkwell and seconded, not by Bickersteth but Ismay, Lord Stalbridge was elected unanimously.

Stalbridge had first joined the L&NW board in 1870 as the thirty-two year old Lord Richard Grosvenor MP, taking the seat vacated by the resignation of Glyn. He had been been a member of Special Committee since 1874. Although a member of several other committees, he had never chaired one. No doubt preoccupied with his political duties (he had been elected a Liberal MP when only twenty-four for a family seat in Flintshire) he had become Chief Whip in Gladstone's 1880 Government. His Liberalism however did not extend to supporting Gladstone's 1886 Irish Home Rule Bill and he resigned. Nevertheless in appreciation of his previous political services he was then given his peerage taking the name Stalbridge from the family's estates in Dorset. In the meantime his elder brother, who had inherited as Earl Grosvenor the family's main estates in Cheshire, had been created Duke of Westminster in 1874, also on the recommendation of Gladstone. Politically and socially well connected Stalbridge was in these respects a similar choice as the young Chandos had been during the difficulties of the 1850s, except of course that Stalbridge already had many years of experience as a politician and railway director.

Although the first tasks that Stalbridge set himelf are not relevant to the continuing story of Moon, some reference is helpful in reflecting on the work of Moon. In reviewing 'the arrangement for the conduct of the business of the company', Stalbridge generally confirmed the principle of Moon's system although he made changes to a number of committees, the most far reaching was to split the Traffic Committee into separate Goods and Passenger responsibilities. With the clamour over rates and charges it was not surprising that 'Goods' merited separating from the previous all embracing single 'Traffic' Committee. What is not evident from the minutes of meetings detailing these changes is the step back taken by Stalbridge from the

82. Lord Stalbridge
Lord Stalbridge (1837-1912), Moon's successor as chairman of the L&NW.
Elected a director in 1870, when Lord Richard Grosvenor, he was created a baron
for services to the Liberal party in 1886. LNWRS

83. J.P.Bickersteth
J.P.Bickersteth (1826-1909), one of the two L&NW deputy chairmen with
W.Cawkwell from 1881, first elected a director in 1867 after an earlier
commercial career in India.

executive chairmanship style of Moon, to one where the board took more collective responsibility. This was most evident under the new Goods and Passenger Committees to whom the functional managers for those responsibilities were directly accountable. As Malcolm Reed has commented, in his company history, this was almost a reversion to Moon's own use of committees before he became chairman.

Unfortunately for Stalbridge he was not able to rely on Findlay for long. He became seriously ill and was in attendance at his last board in January 1893 and died in March. Aged sixty-three Findlay had only the previous May been knighted on Stalbridge's recommendation. Bickersteth, deputising for Stalbridge at the shareholders' meeting, (Stalbridge was also ill at that time) had to admit that he could not make as 'full and clear a statement as I could have wished because I have not had the benefit of conferring and consulting with Sir George Findlay'. Having said that Bickersteth acquitted himself well, giving an extremely detailed and clear explanation of the accounts and of two of the major issues of the day: the Government deadline for publishing new goods rates and the Forged Transfers Act.

Considerable agitation, seemingly out of all proportion to the cost implications, had arisen over the Transfer Bill, which required companies to guarantee their stock register. Moon at his last meeting as chairman had condemned the need for such legal protection saying it was up to buyers of stock to ensure the validity of their purchase and that it was only the stockbrokers looking to protect themselves who wanted it. However the Bill had been enacted and the L&NW had controversially introduced a charge of 1d. per £25 value of stock transferred as a premium to cover the risk. Moon was present as a shareholder at Bickersteth's meeting and chose this issue to speak for the first time since retiring. Following a motion put from the floor to withdraw the charge, Moon insisted the Act was 'a move from the Stock Exchange from the beginning to the end. The broker is the party responsible ... for the indefeasibility of title because he knew his clients. They persuaded you, whether in a weak moment or not I will not say, to adopt the Act'. He thought that it was not a matter of sympathy or popularity but 'a matter of business only, and everyone who pays his 4d. per cent and gets his security assured at the risk of the company is certain that his transfer is indefeasible. My advice to you is to let the thing go on as it is, and as the chairman said, you will be able to see later where you are'.

In their tribute to Moon published the day after his retirement *The Railway Times* had not been able to resist attacking him over this issue. After admitting that his conservative policies had saved the company from striving for popularity for popularity's sake, 'it has sometimes made it wanting in enterprise, and the introduction of useful reforms has too often been left to younger companies'. And no better illustration of this, the article maintained, was his last official act to condemn as dangerous and unnecessary a motion in favour of the company guaranteeing its register. 'The condemnation was a characteristic one. Nevertheless we have no hesitation in predicting that either by statutory requirement or of its own motion every company in the kingdom will guarantee its register before ten years are over.'

Moon was not recorded as speaking again at a company meeting. Retiring to his vast mansion Copsewood Grange, he must have found the change in his life dramatic. For forty years his consuming interest had been his railway, for over fifty he had enjoyed the support of his wife. A couple of family photographs taken in 1893 certainly seem to depict a sad and lonely figure. Given Moon's attitude to personal publicity, he may have only reluctantly agreed in his closing years for his family (probably youngest son Ernest) to use one of these photos (Illustration 84) to have his portrait painted; although any artist of stature would almost certainly have demanded personal sittings.

84. Moon with with youngest grandsons 1893

Moon with grandsons Basil (left) and Arthur, sons of his youngest son Ernest,
taken at his home Copsewood Grange in 1893. Dilly Cloag

85 Moon with daughter and some of his family 1893

Moon in retirement at Copsewood Grange in 1893 with daughter Edith
(standing behind), Frideswide (wife of his brothers's eldest son Edward)
and grandsons Arthur (left) and Basil. Dilly Gloag

86. Carter's first portrait of Moon

William Carter's portrait of Moon completed for the family in 1898. It seems
the artist used a 1893 photo (see Illustration 84) in helping compose this work.

Christine Watson

87. Carter's 1900 portrait of Moon

Portrait of Moon by Carter commissioned by the railway and completed after
Moon's death in 1900. Though it was clearly based on the first portrait, more
severe features further distort the comparison with the photograph. NRM

The artist was William Carter, brother of Howard Carter the archaeologist of Tutankhamun fame. The choice of artist could possibly have resulted from Ernest's legal contacts in the railway or banking world (for instance, the second Lord Wolverton's children were painted by Carter at the time). Carter signed off his portrait for the family in 1898. Later it seems the L&NW also wished to commission a portrait by him. This second, near identical one, but with more severe features, seems a straight copy as it is signed 1900, which was after Moon's death in November 1899. It is the one by which he is generally depicted: the Hamilton Ellis 'face severe to the point of caricature'. Roger Lloyd, in his *Railwaymen's Gallery*, wrote that this company portrait hung in the Directors' Luncheon Room at Euston. It is now in the portrait collection of the National Railway Museum. The family one, having presumably been passed down from Ernest, is currently with Mrs Christine Watson, his granddaughter.

It would have been unusual, despite Moon's known distaste of personal publicity, if shareholders or the board had made no attempt to have a portrait painted before he retired. It was certainly the case with deputy chairman Cawkwell. In June 1889 the L&NW board had resolved that 'having regard to Mr Cawkwell's long connection with the company it was unanimously agreed that his portrait be painted and exhibited at the half-yearly meeting room at Euston, the choice of artist being left to Mr Cawkwell's own decision'. In his *Reminiscences* Neele noted Cawkwell's 'extensive knowledge of painting and art culture'. What seems remarkable is that the artist chosen by Cawkwell agreed to the commission. Professor Hubert von Herkomer, then at the peak of his career (Slade professor at Oxford), had recently exhibited portraits of such worthies as the Speaker of the House of Commons and the Archbishop of Canterbury (admittedly he had two years earlier painted the redoubtable railwayman Watkin, although it was at the time of Watkin's baronetcy for political services).

It seems quite understandable that Neele recorded that the 'old chairman frequently sent communications to the secretary and manager conveying his views on current questions', particularly objecting 'to the extension of Sunday trains, however urgent the demand. One day, calling at my office, he told me if things went wrong they would have to send for "Cincinnatus" again to take up the control'. Cicinnatus, the 5th century BC Roman general, after retiring to his farm was called back twice to save his city state.

Such sentiments may not have been entirely in jest. Moon's closing years could not have been in greater contrast to the decades of toil and travel that had been his life. There is little record of what occupied his time during retirement but what has been uncovered suggests he found relaxation in his garden and the church affairs of his local parish. It seems that in the former he shared an interest with Webb. There are references, for example, in the *Crewe Guardian* (10 August 1878 and 14 August 1886) to Moon and his wife accompanying Webb to the local flower show and Webb being vice-president of the chrysanthemum and horticultural societies. The *Coventy Herald* (22 November 1889) reported Moon winning one of the prizes at the Birmingham Chrysanthemum Show. As will be seen he was a generous supporter of local charities and at least on one occasion, noted by the *Liverpool Mercury* in its obituary of 18 November, he chaired a meeting of the Coventry branch of the Church Missionary Society (in 1893). It is to be wondered if he ever dwelt on his energetic days as churchwarden in Claines, in particular his work for the parish in seeking out 'nuisances'. But now in his advancing years he clearly was content with a lower profile. It was reputed that his local vicar received a cheque each Christmas 'in thankful acknowledgement to Almighty God for sparing me another year'.

Neele had written that Moon was always glad to welcome any of his old officers at his home but it is not known if Stalbridge himself ever did. It requires little imagination to envisage the aging Moon's reaction when reading the 1897 correspondence in *The Times* which culminated in the paper complaining in their 30 October issue, that his old company had entered into 'an appreciable decline from the high excellence attained under his vigorous rule of thirty years'. The paper featured an article in which it commented, 'Sir Richard Moon has retired and Sir George Findlay is dead. It is a signal illustration of the close dependence of even the greatest of corporations on the capacity and devotion of a few individuals that since the withdrawal of these two really great railway magnates the London & North Western Railway has, to all appearances, been going steadily downhill'. After referring to Findlay 'proudly and justly' claiming that the company was the most punctual line, the article continued:

A deplorable abatement of this high ideal is attested in the letters which we have printed during the last few weeks from travellers and dwellers on the line. Ordinary traffic dislocated and passengers gravely inconvenienced and delayed by some local but not unforeseen congestion of special traffic, local trains leaving Euston day after day 30 or 45 minutes after the advertised time, the officials of the line standing helpless and appalled. ... It may not always be possible to find a chairman like Sir Richard Moon or a general manager like Sir George Findlay. But it ought always to be possible to find and employ men who are at least capable of working efficiently a system devised and successfully conducted by better men than themselves.

One of the letters had been critical of Stalbridge. A Liverpool shareholder asked 'is the present chairman and are the directors quite of the right "kidney" for a large commercial undertaking? ... Perhaps the chairman was the best selection available ... but would not a thorough practical business man be more suitable?'. However Stalbridge was to remain chairman of the L&NW for twenty years, his time in the chair being second only to Moon in the history of the company. Malcolm Reed has written that Lord Stalbridge 'despite the distinction of his predecessor ... successfully led the company through the difficulties which faced it in the 1890s and 1900s'.

Harrison had taken over from Findlay and his position as chief goods manager was filled by Frank Ree, who in turn replaced Harrison on retirement, both following in the tradition begun with Findlay of being knighted for holding the position of L&NW general manager.

During the summer and autumn of 1899, in his eighty-sixth year, Moon's failing health led his doctor to confine him to the house. Weakening as the winter approached, he became bedridden and died in the early hours of Friday 17 November. He was buried the following Tuesday.

The weekly *Coventry Times* on the 22 November included a long notice of Moon's death. Under the heading "The Evening of His Life", the notice told of his 'interest in the affairs of the parish', that he had 'laid the foundation stone of the vicarage in November 1892'

88. Lime Street arrivals 1901
Somewhat disorderly arrivals at Liverpool's Lime Street in April 1901. Loco is 66
Experiment, the first compound built in 1882. LNWRS

89. Approach London Road 1904
Approach to Manchester's London Road July 1904. Note destinations
listed including those of joint users Great Central Rly. The MS&L changed
its name to GC in 1897. LNWRS

and 'planted a tree on the site of the well-known "Dick's Tree". Sir Richard consented to perform the ceremony, so that the young tree might still bear its predecessor's name'.

The local paper's article commented how the 'falling years of his life have been greatly cheered by the devoted attention of his daughter, Miss Moon, who outside Copsewood is regarded as the "Lady Bountiful" of the parish. Of Sir Richard the words may be repeated of one who knew him well. "His commercial career was of the highest integrity; his private life unimpeachable; his liberality great; his services to the railway system cannot well be measured"'. The article continued:

> Sir Richard was a large-hearted philanthropist, and contributed frequently and generously to charities in different parts of the country. He had a positive horror of publicity, and his donations were invariably made on condition that nothing should be published about them in the newspapers. It was due to this trait in his character that it is not generally known that he gave the pulpit to Stoke Church and on two other occasions presented £100 to the National School Fund.

From the scrap-book kept by Moon's grandson, Jasper, a press cutting from the *Liverpool Courier* of 18 November 1899 notes that Moon 'had a few peculiarities of physique and temperament. He lacked the sense of colour and of smell. He signed cheques with the single word "Moon". He never fired a gun'.

The funeral was held locally at what the *Coventry Times* recorded as the 'prettily situated churchyard at Binley' where his wife had been buried. The *Coventry Standard* rather more sombrely set the scene thus: 'the morning was a typical November one - dull and damp - and the well wooded country which lies around Copsewood bore few signs of life'. A week after his death the *Coventry Herald*, in describing the funeral, wrote:

> The occasion afforded evidence of the great regard in which the deceased baronet was held by his old colleagues connected with the L&NW company. A special train run

from Euston in the morning brought the chairman and
principal directors and many of the officials as well as
representatives of other railway companies, all gathered
together to pay their last tribute of respect to a man who
was for so long a time the ruling spirit of the L&NW.
They drove direct to Copsewood Grange and thence,
having been joined by the hearse and other mourners the
solemn procession slowly wended its way to Binley Church.
Here a large number of inhabitants of the surrounding
neighbourhood had assembled. Within the church the
Rev L.Richardson (vicar) and the Rev Canon Blyth (vicar
of Stoke) officiated and the service at the graveside was
conducted by the Rev Canon Moore [sic] of Gainsborough.

Canon Charles Moor, as has been noted, was the husband of
Moon's niece Constance, the second of his brother Robert's three
daughters. Over twenty carriages took the official party from the
house to the church. Of the closest family members listed as being
present, in addition to Edith, were her brothers Richard and Ernest
and three of Moon's grandsons, Reginald, Arthur and Hubert. Other
members of the families of both Moon's brother Robert and brother-
in-law Ralph Brocklebank (Robert had died in 1889, his sister Eliza
in 1885 and Brocklebank in 1892) were strongly represented, with
the Rev W.Macgregor and H.T. Wood representing Moon's sisters
Ann and Mary. Lord Stalbridge headed the small party of L&NW
directors and most of the principal officers of the company attended,
including Webb, Mason, Harrison and Stevenson.

The forty-eight year old unmarried daughter Edith, for so long
her father's loyal companion, apparently could not face the graveside
ceremony and remained in the church. Among the many national and
local tributes accorded her father, one that stands out to the author
is a private letter written to Edith by the elderly manager responsible
for the L&NW's declining Lancaster Canal operations (a copy of
which was found in Jasper's Scrap Book). He wrote:

> Will you permit me to express my sympathy in your great
> loss? I think there are few if any now living in the service
> of the company who have more reason than I have to

remember Sir Richard both with awesome respect from a long knowledge of his high character and wonderful powers of Government and with affectionate gratitude for the long and uniform confidence and kindness which he showed towards myself. I attended him to Binley Churchyard on Tuesday and please forgive my not calling to leave a card. Mr Brocklebank with whom I travelled gave you some memoranda part of which I had given to Sir Richard in 1887. You are of course quite at liberty to keep them. I write now to enclose a contribution which I made to a local paper on Friday last on the connection of Sir Richard Moon with Lancaster [notes on being a freeman]. With sincere sympathy believe me

Yours very respectfully, Jonathan Slinger.

Mr Brocklebank (Ralph junior) was Edith's cousin, also unmarried, who had been an L&NW director since 1883.

At the burial cermenony the grave was lined with white chrysanthemums and the coffin inscribed simply, "Richard Moon, baronet, born 1814 died 1899". These words mark the gravestone today with the addition of "Chairman of the London and North Western Railway Co. 1861 to 1891".

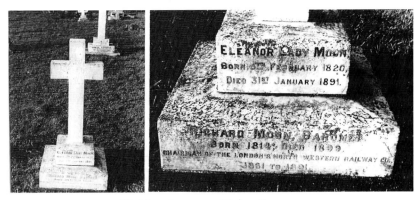

90. Moon's grave at Binley, Coventry
Moon and his wife's modest grave in Binley churchyard, Coventry, with
inscription enlarged. P.J.Sperring

91. Locomotive *Richard Moon*
Greater Britain class compound 528 *Richard Moon.* Built some three years after
Moon's retirement, it was the first locomotive named after him. LNWRS

CHAPTER 29

EPILOGUE

So little remains to remind future generations of the Moons that it seems almost sad to note that, apart from his grave at Coventry, the only other in situ public monuments found to the family are a church window at Llanymynech (dedicated to his second son Richard and wife Sarah) and an inscription on a public hall in Scotland in memory of a grandson. Neele writing in 1904 recalled that there was no memorial of him in the shareholders' meeting room at Euston: 'indeed there are only two chairmen represented in that Valhalla: the one Lord Wolverton, the first chairman, by his portrait in oils, the other Mr Moon's predecessor by his bust - Admiral Moorsom - "executed", so the tablet somewhat awkwardly reads at the wish of some of his friends'. However Moon was eventually commemorated in the meeting room by a bust, the portrait remaining in the dining room.

As for Moon's descendants his sons had given him eleven surviving grandchildren. Grandson Arthur, shown in the 1893 photo, died aged seventy-nine in 1961, but 2nd Lieut Basil was killed in 1915. With a home at Balhomie in Perthshire, Basil's father Ernest, Moon's youngest son, built as a memorial to his son a public hall for the nearby village of Wolfhill. After Winchester and Cambridge, Ernest distinguished himself as a lawyer and was retained by many railway companies needing representation in Parliament and he served frequently as an independent chairman in labour disputes. He sat on various Board of Trade committees dealing with railway legislation, which ironically included Lord Ashfield's that led to the end of his father's company under the 1921 grouping Act. For his committee work he was appointed KCB in 1919. He had also been counsel to the Speaker of the House of Commons for twenty-one years when he retired in 1928.

Moon's eldest son Edward had married Jessie Darbyshire in

1866. He had entered the shipping business. His death in 1893 meant that their eldest son, Cecil Ernest, born in 1867, succeeded to the baronetcy. Cecil was ranching in Colorado at the time of his inheritance. Married twice he did not have children and on his death in 1951 the baronetcy passed, successively, to the grandsons of Moon's second son Richard. Richard, at one time a member of the Institute of Mechanical Engineers, worked for a short time at Crewe before retiring early to Shropshire where descendants of his youngest son Jasper still live.

Reverting to Cecil, who first succeeded to the baronetcy, colourful stories abound of his time in the States after his first marriage when he was only twenty-one. Alleged to be the black sheep of the family, apparently banished to a mining town in Colorado, he had then tried ranching. He met his first wife when she apparently looked after him during an illness. Said to be a former barmaid, an Irish immigrant, Kate Lawder had been married a local miner but divorced him to marry Cecil in 1888. On his inheritance Cecil returned to the UK, but Kate was apparently socially unacceptable to his mother and they returned to the States. Cecil eventually filed for divorce and sued Kate to recover 'substantial monies'. The marriage was dissolved in 1910 and Cecil married again two years later. A legend in Fort Collins for high living, Kate seems to have inspired a long running radio serial in the States. The story of Colorado's 'Lady Moon' is to be found in Fort Collins, Colorado, Public Library. Cecil lived to be eighty-three, dying in a Buxton nursing home in 1951. The *Buxton Advertsiser* for 25 February commented on his many years abroad and that 'during a seven year stay in New Zealand he took an active interest in the cricketing life of that country'.

The baronetcy in 2010 is held by Roger, the ninety-five year old second son of Jasper with the last of the male line being Humphrey, his ninety year old brother. Both live in the Welsh border country near the former home of their father at Llanymynech, Powys, where an unmarried sister still lives. Mary Moon died in 2004.

Under his original will Moon named only his sons Richard and Ernest as executors and trustees of his estate. He added his daughter in a codicil in 1896. The will was proved on 18 February 1900 at a gross value of £394,646.18s.2d.

His first instruction was to 'bequeath the diamond necklace, pendant and bracelet which were presented as a testimonial to me by the London & North Western Railway Company to my said trustees upon trust to permit my daughter Edith May Moon to have the use and enjoyment of such jewels during her life or until she shall marry'. On her death the jewels were to revert to the trustees.

The second instruction was to entrust £30,500 of his company's 4% stock, £14,000 GW stock (mainly 5% rent charge) and £2,000 Birmingham Canal stock for his daughter's income, which incidentally would have given her almost the £2,000 a year the company paid Moon as a salary.

After legacies of £20,000 each to his sons and grandson Hubert Charles (second son of Edward, Moon's eldest son), the balance was to be split into three equal shares. The first two for the absolute use and benefit of his sons Richard and Ernest, which gross would have been just under £90,000 each, and the remaining third for the benefit of his deceased son's descendants. The beneficiaries of the latter were legacies of £20,000 to oldest grandson Cecil Ernest, £5,000 to granddaughter Muriel Eleanor, and an annual income, unless she remarried, of £1,200 to daughter-in-law Jessie; the income from the balance of the share going to Hubert, which would have given him a comparable sum to his mother (see Appendix: Moon Family Tree). What is of interest is the different treatment accorded the two grandsons Cecil and Hubert.

Although the legacy to the oldest grandson Cecil was substantial, no other provision was made for him or his descendants. However in Hubert's case, although his legacy was conditional, his descendants would benefit. Hubert would have been twenty-five at the time of the will. Unmarried he appears to have been borrowing heavily from his grandfather, to what extent and for what purpose is not known, but the £20,000 could have been by way of writing off a debt. Moon had specified that an annual interest rate of 3% should be charged 'from the dates of such advances or payments respectively (and the entries in my private ledger shall be taken as absolute and conclusive evidence of the amounts and dates of all such advances or payments by me)'. However on his mother's death (or remarriage) Hubert was to enjoy the benefit of the whole income from the reversionary third share and on his own death the capital was to pass to his children.

He never married and was killed in 1940 (the capital then reverted to the executors of his uncles Richard and Ernest).

Copsewood Grange was to be sold or let with Moon's older surviving son having first option if he wished to purchase. He did not. The estate did not sell easily. At an auction in 1900 it was withdrawn at £23,000 and not sold until 1903 and then for only £17,000. In 2001 the estate, developed industrially by GEC (subsequently Marconi) with part of the parkland becoming a golf course, was bought by British Land for almost £16million; the house itself became the Copsewood Grange Sports and Social Club.

A final twist: Moon's trustees were free to invest in a wide range of stocks, public companies, property, municipalities, etc., but specifically not in 'mining or banking'. Was this simply an emotional reaction to an unfortunate family experience, an aversion to perceived market volatility or what? As with so much else that possibly motivated the man, it has been frustrating not to know more.

C H A P T E R   3 0

REFLECTIONS

Over a century has passed since the death of Sir Richard Moon. The light that the elegant Plunket thought would remain bright forever was extinguished within a generation, the company too consigned to history. The company, for which Moon prayed would flourish in peace and prosperity long after he and his colleagues had passed away and been forgotten, lost its identity following a war that changed the world. The hundred or so separate companies which had been the basis of Britain's nineteenth century railway structure were swept away under the grouping of the 1921 Railways Act. Moon's company and its rival the Midland were merged to form part of one of four new companies: the London Midland & Scottish Railway. Despite being the largest constituent, the premier company as *The Times* had called it and even its competitors acknowledged, and having already had its merger with the Lancashire & Yorkshire authorised ahead of the grouping Bill, the London & North Western not only lost its distinctive identity but allowed the Midland to dominate the newly created company. And by 1948 the LMS too, after only twenty-five years of existence, lost its identity in the nationalised British Railways. The control by the state that Moon had fought so hard to resist then finally became a reality.

Although acknowledged by his contemporaries as the leader of Britain's largest company and of an industry employing over half a million people, Moon is not a name generally spoken of today in the same breath as the giants that built the early railways such as the Stephensons and Brunel. Looking back it is difficult not to be struck by a feeling of sadness that, unlike the memorials to the engineers, nothing remains to mark forty years of painstaking administrative toil and dedication. What memories do linger are contorted by the caricature lurking in the vaults of the York railway museum.

92. Bust of Moon

Bust of Sir Richard Moon Bart, with years L&NW director (left)
and chairman (right) plus personal motto below *vincit omnia veritas*
(truth overcomes all things). NRM

93. Shareholders' Meeting Room Euston

The Shareholders' Meeting Room at Euston c.1939, showing centrally
placed bust of Moon and portrait of John Ellis (L&NW director 1851-59
and Midland chairman 1849-58). NRM

Most modern commentators have painted an unsympathetic picture of Moon. In this he was probably his own worst enemy. His reserve could be interpreted as aloofness, his analytical approach as coldness, his focus on the most minute costs as penny pinching, and his exacting standards as intolerance. Yet the reports of so many of his regular half-yearly speeches to his shareholders evoke, if not always agreement with his views, some admiration for the uncompromising way he expressed them.

His turn of phrase at times amuses in his depiction of the company's fight against real or perceived adversity, his humour dry and at times wry. A favourite simile was to compare himself to Sisyphus in having to keep rolling the 'dividend stone' up the hill; the company even named locomotives after the legendary character! Opinionated he may have been, but his words have appeal. In likening his shareholders to being physically attacked, he asked should they defend themselves or 'stand still and be hit'? That they were not going to be 'pushed back in a ditch'; that not objecting to small parliamentary Bills was an invitation for competitors to 'come and tread on them'. Many other such examples have been quoted and do not need to be repeated here.

He claimed he was not a politician and did not trust those who were (his amusing speech at the Crewe jubilee celebrations highlighted this). Yet despite insisting his company maintained a neutral position, he was always quick to defend what he considered were his company's rights when railing against the Government, any Government. Over the freight rates and charges issue, he warned his shareholders over trusting the same houses of Parliament who under Gladstone had passed the Irish Land Act, which 'ruthlessly took away the property of the Irish landlords in 1881 and gave it to another class'. Expressing such views privately was one thing, but openly espousing them had to be at times counter-productive.

Though there was always a fair sprinkling of MPs of different persuasions on his board, there is liitle evidence that they ever formally debated public issues other than their negative impact on company profitability. The recognition given to the Midland's James Allport, knighted in 1884, for pioneering third class travel showed what benefits an enlightened policy could bring to the travelling public.

Perhaps the phrase that most typically characterised Moon's approach was one he used when first in the chair: 'there is nothing to be done but by pure and deliberate hard work and a constant watching of the concern'. He never ceased to apply those qualities. It was as if he saw them as his mission in life, his duty. Significantly the reason he gave for retiring was that he was *no longer able to do his duty* [author's italics]. The question, however, which is difficult to avoid is whether all the hours he spent in travel, meetings and consuming minutes were the right duties for a chairman of such a large undertaking. Absorbed by so much detail did he lose sight at times of the wider perspective? In terms of financial results, he certainly kept well in focus his own stated aim: to make the most money for the company. Should this have been his only aim?

As chairman, the principal representative of the shareholders, Moon rightly saw his main responsibility to be to them. However he was more than that. For many years he was not only the managing director but also effectively his own general manager. That he did hold all three positions for so long, maintaining a grip on the detail so impressively in a company the size of the L&NW, is no doubt a remarkable testament to hard work; but clearly hard work alone could not account for the company's continuing success.

There is no question Moon became what Wrigley had said the company lacked at the time: a managing director capable of taking executive control. With his knowledge and dedication, he was able to exert an influence far beyond that of any other member of the board. However was this at the expense of the future strategic direction of the company? Should he have better placed the company, indeed his industry, to avoid the turmoil over freight rates and, for example, the lack of a common braking standard, even anticipating an improved accommodation with the government over wider regulation? Or is expecting such enlightenement unreasonable, he was, after all, a man of the nineteenth century. Nevertheless, the question has be asked as to how much of the company's success was the result of proactive planning, as opposed simply to responding to chance and opportunity. It could be argued that continuing profitability resulted from the innate strength of the company Moon inherited: a leviathan with a force of its own needing only the skills of a watchful pilot to keep it from foundering.

The author is all too conscious that little attempt has been made to answer such questions, other than to reflect on some of the issues raised. For example an interesting comparison can be made by contrasting Moon with Edward Tootal. Tootal was not interested in day to day detail, only the broader picture, as evidenced by his Trent Valley coup and his attempt to contain Watkin's ambitions for the MS&L by absorbing that company jointly with the Great Northern (even if it did unwittingly bring down Chandos). And it would have been in character for such vision to have prevented the Midland's own line to Carlisle. Moon's initial reaction to the Midland threat can be seen in retrospect as narrowly negative; it being difficult to refute the charge he himself once levied against Huish of arrogantly over playing his hand.

On the technical front, Moon's defence of outmoded braking and signalling certainly suggests he let his judgement be coloured by an undue obsession with costs. And, in the final confrontation with Government over freight charges, the criticism levied at him of agitating the public mind instead of endeavouring to cooperate, to be aware of wider community interests, has to be valid even to the extent of accepting he could be accused of deploying resources to delay the inevitable.

That Moon kept all the reins of control in his own hands gives rise to charges of authoritarianism. Dispensing with a deputy and keeping a weakened general manager may have been justified by expediency for a period, but it appears to have taken an independently minded director with the status of the Duke of Sutherland to make him concede the desirability of change. After the failed merger with the Lancashire & Yorkshire, he took no action on filling the general management position until belatedly confirming Findlay in the post. And appointing two, clearly conciliatory, deputy chairmen made little difference to his overall control.

Not to give Moon significant credit for his company's nineteenth century dominanace however is to be as unfair as holding him responsible for the company's unpreparedness in facing the twentieth century. Whatever drove the company's success, he has to be rghtly praised for his ability to not only appoint the right managers to key positions, but also to secure their loyalty. After the Crewe intimidation affair, whatever Moon may have felt about Webb, he never expressed his view publicly. *The Times* comment is worth repeating. It wrote of 'a chief who, while perhaps over-ready to mark what is done amiss, yet trusts wholly and supports loyally his officers when he believes they are acting rightly, deserves, and may look to obtain, loyal and devoted service in return'.

The criticism that he was not an innovator has validity as he moved into old age. He resisted the introduction of modern technology and left it to others to set the pace in spreading third class travel. He believed himself a better judge of the public's needs than both his contemporaries and the travelling public themselves. His attitude to cheap travel, 'contract tickets', is sharply exemplified in a letter he wrote to his old enemy Watkin over the suggestion to offer lower fares on the joint MSJ&A line in 1881. 'It will never do for us to give way to outside clamour otherwise the Public will think we can easily frighten into doing anything they may desire.'

Yet it must not be forgotten that as a young reforming director, Moon was a force for internal change. For example, the brief he gave to the newly appointed horse superintendent Livock was a classic in modern management. His drive to centralise both locomotive manufacturing and dedicated rolling stock facilities had to be fought against entrenched traditionalists. Such work set the scene for much of the administrative efficiency that enabled the company to prosper operationally in later years, as was the effect of consolidating the financial structure in the money markets. Although he may not have led in speed, power of engines, or third class facilities, what was wrong with the perception that what the travelling public wanted was service, reliability and punctuality? The L&NW was inferior to none in any of these aspects.

The accusation that he ruled by fear, rather than persuasion, ought also to be questioned. It is evident that he did not tolerate poor performance or failure lightly. When pleading to Disraeli for the rejection of the Employers Liability Bill, his comment that 'workmen were well able to take care of themselves, they could leave at any time' sounds particularly insensitive to twenty-first century ears. However, he frequently praised his men's endeavours and stressed how reliant the company was on them. And, from the pens of those who knew him well, how significant are comments such as David Stevenson's that he was 'always approachable to those in whom he believed', or Neele saying he was endorsed by laconic but friendly approval, and Slinger writing of awesome respect but also affection? Admittedly, it is doubtful if either Trevithick or McConnell marked their enforced resignations in anything like such generous terms.

That he gave short shift to poor performers cannot be disputed, but the *Railway Herald's* allegation that he was a bitter opponent of the rights of labour needs to be seen in the context of the age. And it may be worth quoting a letter from his early days in the chair in responding to criticism over the local sacking of a stationmaster owing to deafness. 'I should not feel at liberty under these circumstances to question the propriety of the Committee's decision. I will however cause enquiry to be made whether there is any situation open which the poor man would be competent to fill.'

Regarding his personality, what little references have been found all refer to his retiring and reserved nature. Stevenson's description of him as 'a man of grave aspect, with a pleasant smile enhanced by its rarity' seems almost touching. From the letters Moon wrote, before he became chairman, to Chandos, it is clear he was not immune from feelings of wounded pride. His bitterness over his Stores resignation is all too apparent as is his anger in walking out of Moorsom's meeting over the West Midland. And there are a few occasions where even the detached formality of meeting records cannot hide the emotions roused. The most obvious was after the Abergele disaster when he was unable to prolong discussion. At his board meetings he was deeply affected in announcing the deaths of close colleagues Reay and Crosfield. On the brighter side he showed both pride and warmth in reminding shareholders of 'the two beautiful steamers, the *Lily* and the *Violet* - most magnificent models'. His family life too seems to have been one from which he drew contentment, his marriage stable and long lasting.

Finally, perhaps the most enigmatic reflection of all, what motivated such unusual dedication? Power for power's sake, greed, self-interest, personal financial gain, all appear to have played no part in his make-up; however loyalty, both to family and company, integrity, pride and hard work clearly did. But it needs words like faith, an almost religious belief in doing one's duty, in his case to the L&NW, to get anywhere near understanding what became an obsession: that turning down a gas light in Euston could be equated with a decision on how much over £2 million should be dispensed in half-yearly dividends. How should the balance be struck?

The Times called him an institution, by which is presumably meant the established, permanent, as far as any person can be, figurehead of his industry: one of the great railwaymen of the nineteenth century. Is this description justified? The answer to that probably lies in responses to a number of other questions. That he succeeded in maintaining his company for so long in its pre-eminent position is unquestioned; that he gave his ordinary shareholders consistently better yields than most other comparable companies indisputable; yet in the final analysis did he eventually impede progress and leave the railway unprepared for the changes necessary to meet the challenge of a new century? Whether, as the classic Victorian, this criticism can be fairly made, must remain an open question. Undoubtedly he was unique in his single-minded dedication and met Carlyle's criterion for genius in his unlimited capacity for taking pains. He was a leader who commanded loyalty and respect yet he was not a visionary. So was he a great man?

It was Buchan who said that a great man lays upon posterity the duty of understanding him. He was writing about Oliver Cromwell. Whether a Cromwell or not, although perhaps he was the nearest to it among the figures dominating Britain's railway world of the second half of the nineteenth century, Moon was not in the business of caring whether anyone understood him or not. However the question whether he merits posterity caring for him at least deserves further consideration, which has been one of the justifications for having written this book.

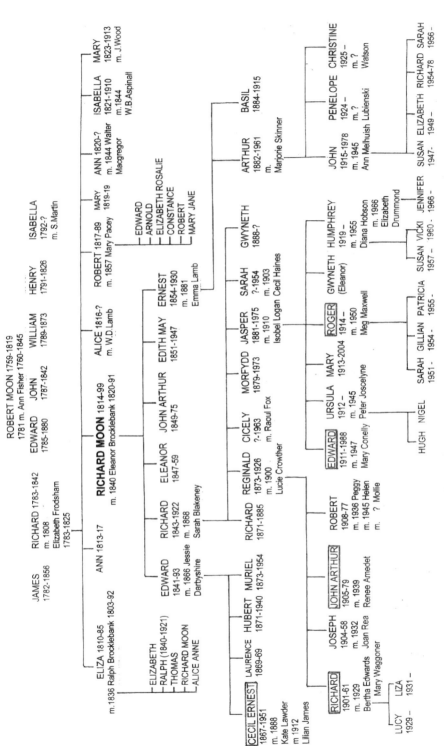

MOON FAMILY TREE

Twentieth century inheritors of the baronetcy shown boxed
(last of direct male line (at 2010) is great-grandson Humphrey, born 1919)

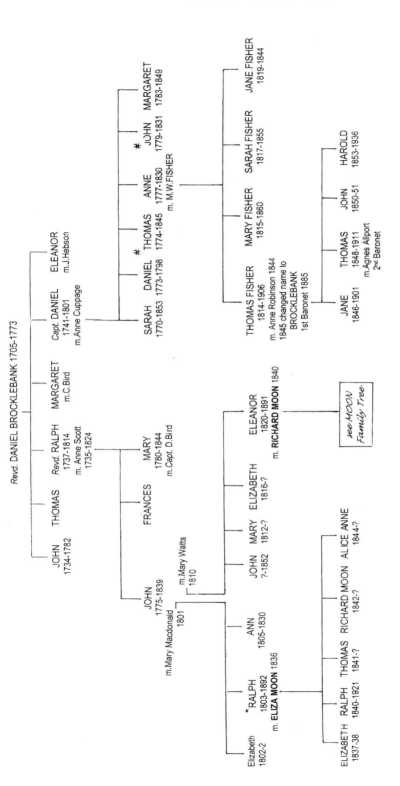

Revd. DANIEL BROCKLEBANK 1705-1773

THE BROCKLEBANK CONNECTION

T&J Brocklebank shipbuilding partnership in Whitehaven formed on founder Daniel's death. By 1865 had concentrated on ship owning in Liverpool, Ralph & Thomas Fisher partners 1843.

Note: Ralph left over £790,000 estate. Agnes Allport was the daughter the Midland Rly. Gen.Man.

SOURCES AND BIBLIOGRAPHY

References are listed in two parts: Part 1 covers Moon's personal
and family details, and Part 2 railways and general background..

PART 1: PERSONAL

1.1. ANCESTRY & EARLY DAYS
Lancashire
Burkes Peerage
C.Moor, *Erminois: A Book of Family Records*, Titus Wilson 1918
H.Fishwick, *The History of the Parish of Garstang*, Chatham Society 1878
G. Jackson, *Woodplumpton and Its Families Religion Houses*, 1971
H.O.Aspinall, *Aspinall and Aspinall Families of Lancashire*, Pollard 1923
'Sir Richard Moon and Lancaster', article by J.Slinger, *Lancaster
Guardian*, 24 Nov.1899
Liverpool
Parish registers (Liverpool Record Office):
   Holy Trinity, St Anne Street,
   baptisms 1813-1830: *283 HOL 2/1182*
   burials 1817-1842: *283 HOL 4/1-2*
   St Mary's Walton-on-the-Hill,
   baptisms 1820-1830: *283 SMW 2/1*
   St Anne's Richmond, marriage 1806-8: *ANN 3/6*
1841 Census
West Derby Electoral Registers 1844-48 (Lancashire Record Office), *EL
1/12S-1/16S*
J.Cooper & D.Power, *A History of West Derby*, Causeway Books 1982
Education
R. Smart, Keeper of the Muniments, St Andrews University Library.
R.G.Cant, *The University of St Andrews*, Scottish Academic Press 1970
D.I.A.Steel, *The Linen Industry of Fife in the Later Eighteenth and
Nineteenth Centuries*, University of St Andrews Phd. thesis 1975
J.H.Gray, *Cambridge University College Histories*, Robinson 1899
W.H.Langhorne, *Queens' College in the Fifties*, 1908
 J.A.Venn, *Alumni Cantabrigienses*, Cambridge University Press 1951
Edinburgh University and Winchester College (1868-78) archives

1.2. LIVERPOOL, TRADE, SHIPPING, BRAZIL

A.R.Allan, *The Building of Abercromby Square*, University of Liverpool

T.Baines, *History of the Commerce and Town of Liverpool and of the Rise of Manufacturing Industry in the Adjoining Counties*, 1852

Buildings of Liverpool. Liverpool City Planning Dept. 1978

Centenary Book of the Liverpool Stock Exchange, 1936

T.Ellison, *The Cotton Trade of Great Britain*, 1886

W.M.Frazer, *Duncan of Liverpool*, Hamish Hamilton 1947

Herdman's Liverpool, Gallery Press reprint 1968

S.Marriner, *Rathbones of Liverpool 1845-73*, Liverpool University Press 1961

B.G.Orchard, 2nd series of Liverpool Exchange portraits, 1884. (*H920. 1 ORC*, Liverpool Record Office)

B.G.Orchard, *Liverpool's Legion of Honour*, 1892

N.Pevsner, *The Buildings of England: Lancashire South*, 1980

Proceedings of the Cotton Brokers Association of Liverpool 1842-1851.

Moon Brothers

Gore's Directory of Liverpool, 1790-1849

Wardle & Pratt and *Pigot Commercial Directory* 1816-20

M.Williams, 'Liverpool Merchants and the Cotton Trade 1820-1850', *Liverpool & Merseyside: Essays in economic and social history of the port and its hinterland*, Frank Cass 1969

Brocklebanks

G.Chandler, *Liverpool Shipping: A Short History*, Phoenix House 1960

J.F.Gibson, *Brocklebanks 1770-1950*, Henry Young 2 Vols. 1953

D.Hollet, *From Cumberland to Cape Horn: the sailing fleets of Thomas & John Brocklebank*, Fairplay 1984

Brazil

A.Draffen, R.Strauss & D.Swaney, *Brazil: A Travel Survival Kit*, Lonely Planet 2nd edn. 1992 (pp.17-24 & 518-30)

Good Relations 1822-1972 with Liverpool, Brazilian Consulate General

A.K.Manchester, *British Pre-eminence in Brazil: Its Rise & Decline*, Univ. of N.Carolina 1933

L&M Project

R.E. Carlson, *The Liverpool & Manchester Railway Project 1821-1831*, D&C 1969

Liverpool & Manchester Rly Proprietors List, National Archives *RAIL 371 13*

T.J. Donaghy, *Liverpool & Manchester Railway Operations 1831-1845*, D&C 1972

1.3. WORCESTER
(BA references Worcester Record Office)
Census, 1851, 1861
Foley Scrap Books Vol.3, *BA 3762/ 8 ref b899 31*
H.W. Gwilliam, *Old Worcester; People and Places,* Vol.2 1977
Lascelles Directory and Gazetteer of Worcester & Neighbourhood, 1851
'Stroller', *Worcestershire Villages Vol.1,* 1927-37
T.C.Tuberville, *Worcestershire in the Nineteenth Century,* 1852

Kempsey
Bank House auction Feb.1846, *Berrows Journal,* 22 Jan. 1846
Bank House auction Jun.1851, *Worcester Herald,* 17 May 1851
Electoral Registers 1844-52, *BA 1015. b153*
Land Tax assessments 1844-52 (& Claines 1850-70), *BA 4609. 260:2091/1*
R.C.Purton, *Collections History of Kempsey,* 1899, Worcester
Cathedral Library
Vestry minutes 1847-50, *BA 2189*

Claines
Census 1851 and 1861
Bevere Manor sale particulars 1896, *BA 5240/l 6 ref. 705:358*
Commutation of tithes Claines 1843, *BA1572. .X760/l 184, F760/184*
Correspondence re Bevere: Mrs D.M.Owen (Claines Vicarage) 1987-92
Correspondence re Bevere Manor: R.Stratton (Worcester Cathedral
Library) 1989
Bevere, *Stroller Worcestershire Villages* Vol.1 p.47

Churchwarden
Claines churchwarden accounts 1851-68, *BA 2863 ref Claines 850*
Claines charities and Church Rate books, *BA 2683*
Martin Curtler Letter books, *BA 2309/ 64, 68, 70 ref. 705:380*
Sir Offley Wakeman Trustee Letter books, *BA 2309/l 66 ref.705:380*
G.F.A.Best, *Temporal Pillars,* Cambridge 1963
O.Chadwick, *The Victorian Church Part 1,* Adam & Charles Black 1966
G.Miller, *The Parishes of the Diocese of Worcester,* Vol 2. Hall &
English 1890

Other
Berrows Journal, 1843-1850
    Progress on constructing OW&W, 6 Apr.1848
    Subscription to building Infirmary chapel, 1 May 1850
    Subscribers to Corn Exchange new organ, 23 May 1850
    Petition against 'Popery', 5 Dec.1850
    Abbots Wood to Worcester railway in 'forward state', 5 Sep.1850

Worcester Herald, 1850-1852
   opening Branch to Abbotts Wood, 5 & 12 Oct.1850
   Mid. Rly. advert. 'Excursion train from Worcester to London and
Back', 26 Oct.1850
   Curtler motion on Popery at public meeting, 21 Dec.1850
   Masonic Ball report, 1 Mar.1851
   Protectionist banquet, 10 May 1851
   Meeting proposed Worcester & Hereford Rly., 19 Jul.1851
   W&H advertisement, 13 Sep.1851
   OW&W remaining link to Stoke Prior, 11 Oct.1851
Applying to join L&NW 1850
Audit Bills 1850, *Railway Times,* 9 Mar., 15 & 22 Jun.1850
Letters, National Archives **RAIL 1008 93**
Local Railway Scene
S.C.Jenkins & H.I.Quale, *The Oxford, Worcester & Wolverhampton
Rly.,* Oakwood 1977
P.J.Long & W.V.Awdry, *Birmingham & Gloucester Railway,* Alan
Sutton 1987
NA&H 1846-59, National Archives **Rail 1110 350** [includes ref. W&H]
W&H Act 15.Aug.1853: *Cap. Clxxxiv. An Act for making a Railway
from Worcester to Hereford, with certain Branches therefrom, and for
other purposes*

1.4. WOLVERHAMPTON WATERWORKS
B.L.McMillan, *History of the Water Supply of Wolverhampton 1847-
1947,* (Wolverhampton Public Library, L628,CMB/WOL/PH/1/20)
S. Staffordshire Waterworks, *Wolverhampton Chronicle,* 27 Oct. and 3
Nov.1858
Wolverhampton New Waterworks Company v Hawkesford:
   English Reports, Vol.141 p.283, 486 1028. Vol.142 p.874
   Holsbury's Laws of England Vol. 7 paras. 1611-1621
   The Digest. Vol.10 companies: Part V1 p.1302
   Wolverhampton Chronicle, 4 & 8 Dec.1858, 4 May 1859

1.5. TAMWORTH, 1872 TESTIMONIAL & HARROW
Tamworth
Census 1871
Correspondence re Wigginton Lodge: E.Ballard, curator Tamworth Castle
Museum 1989 (inc. copy letter 1983 to Mrs Morgan giving 1878 value)
Correspondence re Wigginton Lodge: I.Burley Tamworth Library 1998

Post Office Directory of Staffordshire 1872

Wigginton Lodge auction 1862, *Tamworth Weekly News*, 9Aug.1862

Testimonial 1872

Illustrated London News, 30 Nov.1872, 8 Mar.1873

Harrow

Correspondence re Woodlands: A.W.Ball, Harrow Borough Librarian 1986

W.W.Druett, *The Stanmores and Harrow Weald through the ages*, King & Hutchings 1938

Greater London Record Office:

  Harrow census 1881

  Middlesex Electoral Records 3, *MR/PED (1832-82)*

  Middlesex Deeds Registry, *X/8/51B*

  The Woodlands deeds, *Acc 480*

Kelly's Middlesex Directory 1874

Holy Trinity building fund, *Pinner Parish Magazine*, Nov.1980

Woodlands, 'Not Practical to Employ a Caretaker', *Harrow Observer*, 6 Sep. 1974

1.6. COVENTRY AND JUBILEE

Copsewood Grange

Census 1881

E.B.Bramwell, 'Coventry Cameos' *Loudspeaker,* GEC House Mag.1961

T.A.Blyth, *History of Stoke*, Midland Educational 1897

Land Registry extract, 2006

Lowe Collection, Press cuttings, Coventry Central Library.

Schedule of Deeds, The General Electric Co. Estates Dept. 1998

Jubilee 1887

'The Jubilee Honours', *The Times*, 21 Jun.1887

'The Jubilee of Crewe and the Dedication of the New Queen's Park', 9 Jul.1887 *Crewe Guardian*

Presentation Booklet, Wolverton Officers & Foremen, July 1887, Moon family

PART 2: RAILWAYS AND GENERAL

2.1. BACKGROUND EARLY RAILWAY DEVELOPMENT

E.Cleveland-Stevens, *English Railways Their Development and Their Relationship to the State,* George Routledge & Sons 1915

C.F.Dendy Marshall, *A History of British Railways Down to the Year 1830,* OUP 1938

J.Francis, *History of the English Railway 1820-45*, 2 Vols.1851

H.G.Lewin, *Early British Railways 1801-1844*, Locomotive Publishing 1925

H.G.Lewin, *The Railway Mania and Its Aftermath*, The Railway Gazette 1936.

C.J.A. Robertson, *Origins of the Scottish Railway System 1722-1844*, John Donald 1983

F.Wishaw, *The Railways of Great Britain and Ireland 1842*, D&C reprint 1969

2.2. L&NW MEETING MINUTES AND REPORTS

(*RAIL* references are to the National Archives, Kew, records)

Proprietors 1846-93, *RAIL 410 1-8*

Roll of Directors 1852-1922, *RAIL 410 1267-1268*

Board Meetings Dec.1845-Feb.1892, *RAIL 410 10 to 410 32*

Reports to Board 1852-78, *RAIL 410 54 to 410 63*

(McConnell Ramsbottom re 1859 loco working *Rail 410 730*)

Chairman's 'Special' Committee:

1855-Mar.58, *RAIL 410 148/149* [called 'Executive' for this period]

1858-Nov.61, *RAIL 410 79 to 410 81*

1861-Nov.94, *RAIL 410 82 to 410 120*

Stores Committee (inc. Locomotive Expenditure from Mar.58):

- Jun.1848-May 1861, *RAIL 410 351 350 to 410 351 358*

Other Committees:

Audit 1847-59, *RAIL 410 432/3*

Rates & Taxes 1854-64, *RAIL 410 427*

Church & Schools 1849-65, *RAIL 410 576/7*

NA&H, *RAIL 410 624* (includes W&H 1851-60)

Stour Valley, *RAIL 410 624*

Wolverhampton Station, *RAIL 410 624*

Wolverhampton Joint with GW, *RAIL 759 11*

Companies

Birkenhead Lancashire & Cheshire Junction, *RAIL 35 1-4*

Trent Valley, *RAIL 699 1*

Manchester & Birmingham 1837-45, *RAIL 454 1/2*

Shropshire Union Board and its Committees 1846-95, *RAIL 623 7*

SU Proprietors 1846-1900, *RAIL 623 42/43*

NA&H company 1846-59, *RAIL 1110 350*

Birmingham Canal Navigations 1846- 1920, *RAIL 810 45*

Hotel Committee, Special re Mrs Bisserot 12 Oct.1876, *RAIL 410 458*

   D.Pennington of LNWR Society provided reference to successor]

Railway Companies Association, *RAIL 1098/1099*

2.3. CORRESPONDENCE
Moon personal letters 1852-73, *RAIL 1008 101 R286: 1-41:*
 to Stewart 1852-55, *32-39*
 to Chandos 1857-1860, *1-31*
 to Stewart 1861, *39*
 to Reay 1866-70, *40*
 to Reay 1871-73, *41*
Other letter extracts:
RAIL 1008 111:
 Correspondence MSL GN L&NW competition Jan.1856-Oct.58, *R374*
 Moorsom various, 1838-60, *R211*
 Watkin various, 1846-64, *R372*
 Glyn various, 1837-58, *R306/7*
 McConnell re resignation 1862, *R311*
 Misc. re Huish resignation 1858, *R381-383.*
 Huish resignation letter, *R373*
 Tootal to Glyn re TV staff 1846, *R363*
 Trevithick re resignation 1857, *R379*
RAIL 1008 112: Cawkwell to Chandos/Moon 1836-74
RAIL 1007:
 Webb to Moon/Bickersteth (amongst others), *553*
 Particulars re Cawkwell retirement and director appointment, *556*
L&NW Chairman's 'Out' Letters:
-Mar.1860-Oct.70, *RAIL 410 1621-1629*
-Oct.1870-Jul.91, *RAIL 410 1764-1785*
L&NW Chairman's 'In' letters:
-1864-Feb.91, *RAIL 410 1631-1684*
Other Correspondence
Bright to Watkin, *RAIL 635/11*
Moon to Wilson (L&Y) 1864-69, *Wilson Papers* Manchester
Central Library
Moon to Chandos/Duke of Buckingham 1860-87, *Stowe Papers,*
Huntington Library San Marino California
Moon to Chandos 1856 (8 letters incl. resignation over coke),
LNWR Society
Moon to Glyn Mills, 23 Feb.1891, *Glyn Mills & Co Journal,* Vol.1V, p.96
Duke of Buckingham to Moon, 30 Jun.1871, *LNWR Society*

2.4. PUBLISHED SOURCES FOR L&NW.
Railway Press
Railway Times 1838-1914, National Archives, **Z PER 2**
Herapath Railway Journal 1839-1903, National Archives, **Z PER 3**
Bradshaws Railway Manual, Shareholders' Guide & Directory, 1848-1923
Railway News
Chronologies and L&NW Histories
C.R.Clinker, *Railways of the West Midlands: A Chronology 1808-1954,*
SLS 1954
M.D.Greville, *Chronology of the Railways of Lancashire and Cheshire,*
R&CHS 1981
M.C.Reed, *The London & North Western Railway,* Atlantic Transport
1996.
G.P. Neele, *Railway Reminiscences,* McCorquodale 1904
O.S.Nock, *The London & North Western Railway,* Ian Allan 1960
W.L. Steel, *The History of the London & North Western Railway,*
Railway & Travel Monthly 1914
G.A.Sekon, 'The Inception of the London & North-Western Railway,
Railway Magazine Aug.1906.

2.5. CONSTITUENTS AND AREA HISTORIES
Liverpool & Manchester Rly.
F.Ferneyhough, *Liverpool & Manchester Railway 1830-1980,* Robert
Hale 1980
R.H.G.Thomas, *The Liverpool & Manchester Railway,* Batsford 1980
[see also R.E.Carlson and T.J.Donaghy under Part 1.2. above]
Grand Junction Rly.
N.W.Webster, *Britain's First Trunk Line: The Grand Junction Railway,*
Adams & Dart 1972
London & Birmingham Rly.
D.Jenkinson, *The London & Birmingham; A Railway of Consequence,*
Capital Transport 1988
Special London & Birmingham Railway Edition, *British Railway Journal*
'LMS Centenary of Opening of First Main-Line Railway' *Railway
Gazette,* 19 Sept.1938
A Century of Progress: London-Birmingham 1838-1938, LMS 1938
London Area
R.M.Robbins, *The North London Railway,* Oakwood 1967 (6th edition)
H.V.Borley & R.W.Kidner, *The West London Railway and the
W.L.E.R.* Oakwood 1975

J.B.Atkinson, *The West London Joint Railways,* Ian Allan 1984

LMS, *Old Euston,* Country Life 1938

Midlands Area

R.D.Foster, *Birmingham New Street: The Story of Great Station,* 2 Vols. Wild Swan 1990

D.L.Franks, *The Ashby & Nuneaton Joint Railway,* Turntable 1975

J.T.Leach, *The South Staffordshire Railway 1846-1867,* Staffs. Libraries 1992

J.Gough, *The Northampton & Harborough Line,* R&CHS 1984

South Wales

D.J.Smith, *Shrewsbury to Swansea,* Town & Country Press 1971

W.W.Tasker, *Railways in the Sirhowy Valley,* Oakwood 1978

W.W.Tasker, *The Merthyr Tredegar & Abergavenny Railway and branches,* OPC 1986

G.B.Jones & D.Dunstone, *The Origins of the LMS in South Wales,* Gomer 1999

G.B.Jones & D.Dunstone, *The Vale of Neath Line: Neath to Pontypool Rd.,* Gomer 1996

D.S.M.Barry, *The Rhymney Railway,* Oakwood 1952

D.S.M.Barry, *The Brecon & Merthyr Rly.* (revised R.W.Kidner), Oakwood 1991

North West Area

B.Carman, *Earlestown; Yesterdays of a Railway Town,* Author 1992

G.Biddle, *The Railways Around Preston: An Historical Review,* Foxline & Biddle 1989

P.Norton, *Waterways and Railways to Warrington,* R&CHS 1974

H.J.Hewitt, *The Building of Railways in Cheshire Down to 1860,* Morten 1972

J.Hooper, *Manchester London Road,* Challenger Publications 1995

F.Dixon, *The Manchester South Junction & Altrincham Railway,* Oakwood 1973

M.D.Greville & G.O.Holt, *The Lancaster & Preston Junction Railway,* D&C 1961

J.M.Tolson, *The St Helens Railway,* Oakwood 1983

J.Marshall, 'Lancashire Union Railways' *The Railway Magazine* 1970

T.B.Maund, *The Birkenhead Railway,* RC&TS 2000

A.Rimmer, *The Cromford & High Peak Railway,* Oakwood 1978

J.Marshall, *The Comford & High Peak Railway,* Martin Bairstow 1996

N.Parker, *The Preston & Longridge Railway,* Oakwood 1972

North Wales

P.E.Baughan, *The Chester & Holyhead Railway Vol.1*, D&C 1972

P.E.Baughan, *The North Wales Coast Railway*, Martin Bairstow 1988

V.S.Haram, *Centenary of the Irish Mail 1848-1948*

A.W.H.Pearsall & H.H.Davis, 'The Holyhead Steamers of the LNWR'
Premier Portfolio No.8, LNWR Society

Leeds Lines & the North East

M.Bairstow, *The Leeds Huddersfield & Manchester Railway*, Author 1984

R.Waring, *The Leeds New Line; The Heaton Lodge & Wortley Line*,
Oakwood 1989:

E.Waggot, *Jackson's Town*, Hartlepool Borough Council 1980

Cumbria

W.McG. Gradon, *Furness Railway: Its Rise and Development
1846-1923*,Author 1946

R.W.Rush, *The Furness Railway*, Oakwood 1973

W.McG. Gradon, *A History of the Cockermouth Keswick & Penrith
Railway*, Author 1948

W.McG.Gradon, *The Track of the Ironmasters; A History of the
Cleator & Workington Junction Railway*, Author 1952

Scotland

F.G.MacHaffie, *The Short Sea Route*, T.Stephenson & Sons 1975

H.D.Thorne, *Rails to Portpatrick*, T.Stephenson & Sons 1976

O.S.Nock, *The Caledonian Railway*, Ian Allan 1961

P.F.Marshall, *The Scottish Central Railway, Perth to Stirling*,
Oakwood 1998

Ireland

D.S.M Barrie, *The Dundalk, Newry & Greenore Railway*, Oakwood 1957

K.A. Murray & D.B. McNeill, *The Great Southern & Western Railway*,
Irish Railway Record Society 1976

E.M.Patterson, *The Great Northern Railway of Ireland*, Oakwood 1962

W.E.Shepherd, *The Midland Great Western Railway of Ireland*,
Midland Publishing 1994

W.E. Shepherd, *The Dublin & South Eastern Railway*, D&C 1974

2.6. SPECIFIC ASPECTS OF L&NW
Management, Labour and Regulation

T.R.Gourvish, *Mark Huish and the London & North Western Railway:
a study of management*, Leicester University Press 1972

T.R.Gourvish, 'A British Business Elite: The Chief General Managers of the
Railway Industry 1850-1922' *Business History Review* Vol. XLV11 1973

R.J.Irving, 'The Profitability and Performance of Britain's Railways 1870-1914', *Economic History Review*, 2nd ser. XXX1 (1978), pp.46-66.
N.Crafts, T.Leunig & A.Mulatu, 'Were British railway companies well managed in the early twentieth century?' *Economic History Review,* 61,4 (2008), pp.842-866.
P.S.Bagwell, *The Railwaymen: History of the NUR,* 2 Vols. 1963,1982
G.Alderman, *The Railway Interest,* Leicester University Press 1973
G.Alderman, 'The politics of the railway passenger duty', *Transport History,*Vol.3, 1

Brakes and Safety

R.D.Foster, *A Pictorial Record of L.N.W.R. Signalling,* OPC 1982
L.C.T Rolt, *Red for Danger,* 1955
O.S.Nock, B.K.Cooper, *Historic Railway Disasters,* BCA 1992
R. Weaver, article on brakes, *R&CHS Journal,* Nov.1981
M.Reynolds, *Continuous Railway Brakes,* Crosby Lockwood 1882

Abergele Accident

The Times, 21-22 & 24-29 Aug.1868
'A Full Descriptive Account of the Abergele Railway Accident', Reprint from ILN
The Famous Accident Reports; Five Collisions, reprint of B.of T. reports, Peter Kay.
B.Jones & M.Rawcliffe, *Llandulas: Heritage of a Village,* Gee 1985

Crewe & Wolverton

D.Baxter, *British Locomotive Catalogue 1825-1923, Vols.2A & 2B: London and North Western Railway and its constituent companies,* Moorland 1978, 1979
W.H. Challoner, *The Social & Economic Development of Crewe 1780-1923,* Manchester University Press 1950
C.P.Davis, *The Webb 'Experiment' Compounds,* LNWR Society 1985
D.K.Drummond, *Crewe: Railway Town, Company and People 1840-1914,* Scolar Press
H.Jack, *Locomotives of the LNWR Southern Division,* RC&TS 2001
D.Jenkinson, *Illustrated History of LNWR Coaches,* OPC 1978
H.F.F.Livesey, *The Locomotives of the LNWR,* Railway Publishing Co. 1948
O.S.Nock, *The Premier Line: The story of L&NW Locomotives,* Ian Allan 1952
J.B. Reed, *Crewe Locomotive Works and its Men,* D&C 1982
E.Talbot, *L&NWR Locomotives,* OPC 1985
B.West, *The Trainmakers: History of Wolverton Works,* Barracuda Books 1982

Working the line

G.Findlay, *The Working and Management of an English Railway,* Whittaker 1894

F.B. Head, *Stokers and Pokers,* John Murray 1849 (D&C reprint 1968)

P.& R.P.Hendry, *The North Western at Work,* Patrick Stephens 1990

E.Talbot, *LNWR Miscellany,* 2 vols. OPC 1978 & 1980

E.Talbot, *The LNWR Recalled,* OPC 1987.

E.Talbot, *Railway Heritage: The London & North Western Railway,* Silver Link 1996

Cartage and Pickfords

D.Stevenson, *Fifty Years on the London & North Western Railway,* McCorquodale 1891

F.G.L.Turnbull, *Traffic and Transport: An Economic History of Pickfords,* George Allen & Unwin 1979

Canals

S.R.Broadbridge, *The Birmingham Canal Navigations Vol.1 1768-1846,* D&C 1974

R.Dean, series of historic canal maps, M&M Baldwin, 1993-1997

Replica 1886 Map Shropshire Union, Cartographics 1976

C.Hadfield, *The Canals of South Wales and the Border,* Phoenix House 1960

C.Hadfield, *The Canals of the West Midland,* David & Charles 1966

C.Hadfield & G.Biddle, *The Canals of the North West England,* 2 Vols. D&C 1970

F.C.Mather, *After the Canal Duke,* OUP 1970

R.Shill, *The Industrial Canal: The Coal Trade* and *Railway Interchange Trade,* Heartland Press 1996 & 1998 [Birmingham canals]

E.Wilson, *The Ellesmere and Llangollen Canal,* Phillimore 1975

2.7. COMPETITORS

Great Northern

C.H.Grinling, *The History of the Great Northern Railway 1845-1922,* George Allen & Unwin 1966 edition

O.S.Nock, *The Great Northern Railway,* Ian Allan 1958

J.Wrottlesley, *The Great Northern Railway,* 3 Vols. Batsford 1979-81

Great Western

E.T.Macdermot (revised C.R.Clinker), *History of the Great Western Railway, Vol.1 1833-1863, Vol.2 1863-1921,* Ian Allan 1964

G.A.Sekon, *A History of the Great Western Railway: Being the Story of the Broad Gauge,* Digby Long 1895

Manchester Sheffield & Lincolnshire

G.Dow, *Great Central, Vol.1 1813-63, Vol.2 1864-99*, Ian Allan 1959 &1962

R.P.Griffith, *The Cheshire Lines Railway*, Oakwood 1978

Lancashire & Yorkshire

J.Marshall, *The Lancashire & Yorkshire Railway*, 3 Vols. D&C 1969-72

O.S.Nock, *The Lancashire & Yorkshire Railway*, Ian Allan 1969

J.Wells, *The Eleven Towns Railway: The story of the Manchester and Leeds Main Line*, R&CHS 2000

Midland

E.G.Barnes, *The Rise of the Midland Railway 1844-1874*, George Allen & Unwin 1966

E.G.Barnes, *The Midland Main Line 1875-1922*, George Allen & Unwin 1969

P.E. Baughan, *North of Leeds: The Leeds-Settle-Carlisle Line and its branches*, Roundhouse Books 1966

C.R. Clinker, *The Birmingham and Derby Junction Railway*, Dugdale Society 1956

C.H.Ellis, *The Midland Railway*, Ian Allan 1953

P.S.Stevenson [edit], *The Midland Counties Railway*, R&CHS 1989

C.E.Stretton, *The History of the Midland Railway*, Meuthen 1901

F.S.Williams, *Williams's Midland Railway: Its Rise and Progress*, D&C 1968

North Eastern

C.J.Allen, *The North Eastern Railway*, Ian Allan 1964

R.J.Irving, *The North Eastern Railway Company 1870-1914*, Leicester Univ. Press 1976

W.W.Tomlinson, *The North Eastern Railway*, D&C reprint 1967

Canals

A.H.Faulkner, *The Grand Junction Canal*, W.H.Walker & Brothers 1993

B.T.Leech, *History of the Manchester Ship Canal*, 2 Vols. Sherratt & Hughes 1907

2.8. PERSONALITIES
L&NW:

W.Baker

'Memoirs of Deceased Members', *ICE Minutes of Proceedings* Vol.55 Part 1 1878-9

J.Bancroft

Obituary, *Manchester Guardian*, 3 Mar.1888

Funeral, *Manchester Guardian*, 9 Mar.1888
R.Barrow
S.D.Chapman, *Stanton & Staveley: A Business History*, Woodhead-Faulkner 1981
Obituary, *Derbyshire Times*, 14 Jan.1865
R.Benson
J.Wake, *Kleinwort Benson; The History of Two Families in Banking*, OUP 1997
J.P.Bickersteth
Funeral, *Watford Observer*, 8 May 1909
Will, *The Times*, 29 May 1909
H.Booth
H.Booth, *Henry Booth*, Arthur Stockwell 1980
J.P.Brown-Westhead
Obituary, *Manchester Guardian*, 26 Jul.1877, *Kidderminster Shuttle*, 28 Jul.1877
J.Brook
Obituary, *Huddersfield Examiner* and *Huddersfield Chronicle*, 17 Jul.1858
Funeral, *Hudd. Examiner* and *Hudd. Chronicle*, 24 Jul.1858
"Father of Huddersfield", *Huddersfield Daily Examiner, 30 Nov.1960*
W.Cawkwell
Early career, *Railway Times*, 30 Oct.1858
Marquis of Chandos(1839-61) / **3**[rd] **Duke of Buckingham**(1861-89)
F.B.Heath, 'Richard Grenville: third Duke of Buckingham and Chandos, a case study', PhD dissertation Univ. of Southern California 1959
F.M.L.Thompson, 'The End of a Great Estate', *Economic History Review* Vol. viii
D.& E.Spring, 'The Fall of the Grenvilles', *Huntington Library Quarterly*, Vol.19 1955-56
J.V.Beckett, *The Aristocracy in England 1660-1914*, Basil Blackwell 1986
Obituary, *The Times*, 28 Mar.1889
H.C.E Childers
Obituary, *The Times* and *Doncaster Chronicle*, 31 Jan.1896
Funeral, *The Times*, 3 Feb. and *Doncaster Chronicle, 7 Feb.1896*
H.Crossfield
Inquest, *Daily Albion* and *Daily Post, 31 Jan.1882*
Funeral, *Liverpool Mercury*, 2 Feb.1882
Notice of death, *The Times*, 31 Jan 1982
G.P.Neele, *Atlantic & American Notes*, McCorquodale 1882

H.Earle
B.G. Orchard, *Liverpool's Legion of Honour,* 1897
B.Carman, *Earlestown Yesterdays of a Railway Town,* 1992
G.Findlay
S.M.Phillp, Biographical note in Findlay's *Working & Management of an English Rly.*
G.C.Glyn / 1ˢᵗ Lord Wolverton
R.Fulford, *Glyns 1753-1953: Six Generations in Lombard Street,* Macmillan 1953
Obituary *The Times,* 25 Jul.1873
'George Carr Glyn and the Railways', *Three Banks Review* June 1960
Lord Richard Grosvenor / Lord Stalbridge
L.Clark, 'The Rt.Hon. Lord Richard de Aquila Grosvenor, First Baron Stalbridge', The Society of Dorset Men, *The Dorset Year Book 1993*
M.Huish
T.R.Gourvish, *Mark Huish and the London & North Western Railway,* 1972
Retirement, *The Railway Times,* 18 & 25 Sep. and 4 Dec.1858
T.Knowles
Fergie, 'Memoir of the late Thomas Knowles', reprint *Wigan Examiner,* Dec.1883
M.Lyon
Obituary, *Manchester Guardian,* 16 Jul.1883, *Leamimgton Spa Courier,* 21 Jul.1883
J.E.McConnell
Obituary, *The Engineer,* 15 Jun.1883
C.R.Moorsom
Death announcement, *The Times,* 28 May 1861
Obituary, *The Times,* 30 May 1861
J.Ramsbottom
F.C.Hambleton, *John Ramsbottom, The Father of the Modern Locomotive,* SLS 1937
R.Pennie, *John Ramsbottom:A Victorian Engineering Giant,* L&Y Soc. 2008
[see also Reed's *Crewe Locomotive Works & Its Men*]
J.Slinger
E.Slinger, *In Memorian, J.S.,* 1932 [copy in Lancaster library]
S.Reay
Obituary, *The Times,* 28 Nov.1888 and *Railway Times,* 1 Dec.
Funeral, *Railway News,* 8 Dec.1888

3rd Duke of Sutherland
Obituary and reminiscences, *The Times*, 24 Sep.1892
[for L&NW shares background see Mather's *After the Canal Duke* and E.Richards, *James Loch and the House of Sutherland 1912-1855, 1967*]
E.Tootal
Obituary notice [unattributed], 27 Sep.1873. Manchester Central Library
St Lukes Church, Weaste - History of the Parish during150 years, Salford Library
Bolton (Illustrated) Up to date, 1897 [Tootal Broadhurst Lee section], Bolton Library
Biography of the Lee brothers, *DNB* 1895
F.Trevithick
J.B. Reed, *Crewe ... and its Men*
E.Waterhouse
Jones (edit), *The Memoirs of Edwin Waterhouse*, Batsford 1988
F.W.Webb
J.E.Chacksfield, *F.W.Webb: In the right place at the right time,* Oakwood 2007
J.B. Reed, *Crewe   its Men*
J.E.Spink, Librarianship thesis on sources for study of Webb, 1965, Crewe Library
P.Williams
F.W.Hackworth, *History of Tipton*, 1891 (chap.XLV11)
'Old West Bromwich', *Midland Chronicle & Free Press*, 14 Jul.1944
Other:
T.Ashton
Obituary, *Manchester Evening News*, 21 Jan.1898
Obituary, *Manchester Guardian*, 22 Jan 1898
'New Manchester: Men who helped make it', *Biographical Cuttings*, Vol.8, Manchester Central Library
T.Brassey
C.Walker, *Thomas Brassey Railway Builder*, Frederick Muller 1969
D.Gooch
Diaries of Sir Daniel Gooch Baronet, Kegan Paul, Trench & Trebner 1892
R.B.Wilson(edit), *Sir Daniel Gooch Memoirs and Diary*, D&C 1972
A.Platt, *The Life and Times of Daniel Gooch*, Alan Sutton 1987
J.Locke
N.W.Webster, *Joseph Locke Railway Revolutionary,* George Allen & Unwin 1970

S.M.Peto
J.G.Cox, *Samuel Morton Peto (1809-1899)*, R&CHS 2008
The Stephensons
M.Robbins, *George & Robert Stephenson*, HMSO 1981
E.Watkin
D.Hodgkins, *The Second Railway King: The Life and Times of Sir Edward Watkin 1819-1901*, Merton Priory Press 2002
J.N.Greaves, *Sir Edward Watkin 1819-1901*, Book Guild 2005
T.Wrigley
A.Sparke, 'Memoir of the Late Thomas Wrigley' 1901, Bury Art Gallery

2.9. GENERAL REFERENCE
Railways
Regional History of the Railways of Great Britain, 15 Vols. D&C 1960-89
Regional History of Railways: Vol.16 Ireland, Atlantic 1995.
W.M.Acworth, *The Railways of England*, John Murray 1889
W.M.Acworth, *The Railways of Scotland*, John Murray 1890
O.Carter, *Illustrated History of British Railway Hotels 1838-1983*, Silver Link 1990
H.C. Casserley, *Outline of Irish Railway History*, D&C 1974
C.H.Ellis, *British Railway History*, 2 Vols. George Allen & Unwin 1954, 1959
W.J.Gordon, *Our Home Railways*, 2 Vols. Frederick Warne 1910
O.S.Nock, *Railway Race to the North*, Ian Allan 1958
J.Pendleton, *Our Railways*, 2 vols. Cassell 1896
J.Simmons, *The Railways of Britain*, Macmillan 1986
J.Simmons, *The Railway in Town & Country 1830-1914*, D&C 1986
J.Simmons, *The Victorian Railway*, Thames & Hudson 1991

Politics, Social & Economic
P.Adelman, *Peel and the Conservative party 1830-1850*, Longman 1989
P.Bagwell, *The Railway Clearing House in the British Economy 1842-1922*, George Allen & Unwin 1968
G. Best, *Mid-Victorian Britain 1851-75*, Fontana 1979
A.Briggs, *Victorian People 1851-67*, Pelican Books 1965
J.D.Chambers, *The Workshop of the World: British Economic History 1820-1880*, OUP 1968
R.A.Church, *The Great Victorian Boom 1850-1873*, Macmillan 1975
J.H.Clapham, *An Economic History of Modern Britain: The Early Railway Age 1820-1850*, Cambridge University Press 1939

J.F.C.Harrison, *Early Victorian Britain 1832-51*, Fontana edition 1988

E.J.Hobsbawn, *The Age of Capital 1848-1875*, Weidenfeld & Nicolson 1975

J.R.Kellett, *The Impact of Railways on Victorian Cities*, Routledge & Kegan Paul 1969

H.C.G.Matthew, *Gladstone 1809-1874*, OUP 1988

H.Perkin, *The Age of the Railway*, Panther Books 1970

M.C.Reed, *Investment in Railways in Britain 1820-1844*, OUP 1975

S.B.Saul, *The Myth of the Great Depression 1873-1896*, Macmillan 1969

F.M.L.Thompson, *The Rise of Respectable Society 1830-1900*, Fontana Press 1988

D.Watts, *Tories, Conservatives and Unionists 1815-1914*, Hodder & Stoughton 1994

D.Watts, *Whigs, Radicals and Liberals 1815-1914*, Hodder & Stoughton 1995

INDEX